Six Sigma Best Practices

A Guide to Business Process Excellence for Diverse Industries

Six Sigma Best Practices

A Guide to Business Process Excellence for Diverse Industries

DHIRENDRA KUMAR, PH.D.
Adjunct Professor of Industrial Engineering
University of New Haven
West Haven, Connecticut

J.ROSS PUBLISHING

ISBN 1-932159-58-4

Printed and bound in the U.S.A. Printed on acid-free paper
10 9 8 7 6 5 4 3 2 1

Library of Congress Cataloging-in-Publication Data

Kumar, Dhirendra, 1942-
Six sigma best practices : a guide to business process excellence for diverse industries / by Dhirendra Kumar.
p. cm.
Includes index.
ISBN-10: 1-932159-58-4
ISBN-13: 978-1-932159-58-5 (hardcover : alk. paper)
1. Total quality management. 2. Six sigma (Quality control standard). I. Title.
HD62.15.K855 2006
658.4'013--dc22 2006005535

Direct all inquiries to J. Ross Publishing, Inc., 5765 N. Andrews Way, Fort Lauderdale, FL 33309.

Phone: (954) 727-9333
Fax: (561) 892-0700
Web: www.jrosspub.com

TABLE OF CONTENTS

PREFACE

The Six Sigma process, generally known as DMAIC or Define-Measure-Analyze-Improve-Control, is a continuous improvement process. Continuous improvement covers a spectrum of cost reduction and quality improvement processes, with Kaizen being closer to the lower (left) end of the spectrum and Six Sigma being at the upper (right) end of this spectrum. Process reengineering activity falls somewhere between Kaizen and the Six Sigma process. Although several books are available that present the Six Sigma process, this book links process reengineering with the Six Sigma process. Process reengineering is the initial key activity in the Six Sigma process.

Business leadership not only makes the decision to implement the Six Sigma program, but leadership must also make a strong commitment to support the program. This commitment will be long term. Because of global competition among long-term businesses, business leaders must "do their homework" for business strategic planning, manufacturing strategy, production systems and support services, and supply chain areas before implementing the Six Sigma program. (A review of the topics may be found in the Appendices section.)

ABOUT THE BOOK

Additional topics are presented that are not generally found in other books discussing Six Sigma:

- **The Relationship between Operational Metrics and Financial Metrics (Business Metrics)**—Every business has financial (bottom-line) metrics, but usually the relationship with operational metrics is not established. Employees working on the operational side of a business generally have a difficult time relating operational metrics with financial metrics. Yet, understanding this relationship helps operational area employees to understand the value of their contributions on the operational side and their impact on the financial (business) metrics. Any small improvement on the operational side causes very significant improvement on the financial side.

- **Application of Six Sigma Methodology to a Variety of Businesses as Well as to Different Phases of a Business**—Traditionally, Six Sigma books present process applications in manufacturing-type operations, but the applications in this book have been applied to the sales and marketing area of business, e.g., the IPO (**I**nput-**P**rocess-**O**utput) the SIPOC (**S**upplier-**I**nput-**P**rocess-**O**utput-**C**ustomer) processes.
- **Emphasis on the Measure Phase of the DMAIC Process**—Because data play the most critical role in the Six Sigma quality improvement process, discussion about types of data, data dimension and qualification, and the closed-loop data measurement system is presented in detail with examples.
- **Special Discussion with Examples for:**
  - Defects per Million Opportunities (DPMO)
  - Errors per Million Opportunities (EPMO)
  - Process Capability (C_p and C_pk) and Process Performance (P_p and P_pk) Indices
- **Detailed Instructions for Developing a Project Summary**—Understanding the importance of a project report is critical. These documents serve as a virtual history of projects.

THE IMPORTANCE OF SIX SIGMA

Building Six Sigma quality into critical phases of a business is essential. Businesses can achieve the full benefits of Six Sigma if the program is implemented at every phase of the business and it is carefully managed with a rigorous project management discipline. This book presents step-by-step techniques and flow diagrams for integrating Six Sigma in the "best practices" of business development and management. A Six Sigma program also supports financial and value management issues associated with successful business growth.

Six Sigma is one of the most powerful breakthrough leadership tools ever developed. Six Sigma supports business efforts in gaining market share, reducing costs, and significantly improving the bottom-line profitability for a business of any size. Six Sigma is the most recognized tool in business leadership circles. The Six

Sigma process dramatically assists streamlining operations and improving quality through eliminating defects/mistakes throughout the business process from the marketing/sales area to product design and development, to purchasing, to manufacturing, to installation and support, and to finance.

Most businesses operate at a two- to four-sigma level, a level at which the cost of defects could be as high as 20 to 30% of revenues. The Six Sigma approach can reduce defects to as few as 3.4 per million opportunities. To make a business world-class in its industry, Six Sigma concepts should be at the top of the agenda of every forward-thinking executive/leader in any business.

Through the use of analyzing, improving, and controlling processes, Six Sigma incorporates the concept of ERP (enterprise resources planning) and CRM (customer relationship management) from marketing/sales to product/service design, to purchasing and manufacturing, and to distribution, installation and support services. Six Sigma supports and brings integrated enterprise excellence into the total product/service cycle in all businesses in any industry. The Six Sigma approach (methodology) offers a solution to the common problem of sustainable benefits.

INTEGRATION OF STATISTICAL METHODS

This book will provide seamless integration of statistical methodologies to assist businesses to execute strategic plans and track both short- and long-term strategic progress in many business areas. The book has been written to serve as:

- A textbook for Green Belt certification and Black Belt certification courses in Six Sigma quality improvement processes
- A textbook for business leadership/executive training for planning and leading Six Sigma programs
- A textbook for graduate engineering courses on continuous improvement through Six Sigma processes
- A textbook for graduate business and management courses on continuous improvement through Six Sigma processes
- A reference for instructors, practitioners, and consultants involved in any of the process improvements that make a businesses grow and improve profitability

The Six Sigma steps will be presented in commonly used business communication language as well as with applied statistics using examples and exercises so that benefits of the tool are better understood and users may more easily grasp the five steps of Six Sigma:

- **Define** and set boundaries for issues/problems.
- **Measure** problems, capabilities, opportunities, and industry benchmark to determine the gap(s) that exists.
- **Analyze** causes of the problem through graphical and statistical tools and gauge how processes are working.
- **Improve** processes through reduction of variations found in the processes.
- **Control** implemented improvements, maintain consistency, and track progress financially and otherwise.

ABOUT THE AUTHOR

Dhirendra Kumar has been an adjunct professor at the University of New Haven in the fields of Enterprise Resource Planning, Customer Relationship Management, Supply Chain Management, Operations Research, Inventory and Materials Management, Outsourcing, Continuous Improvement (Lean Production and Six Sigma), and Reliability and Maintainability Engineering since 1989.

He has over thirty-five years of technical, management, teaching, and research experience with major U.S. corporations and universities. He has a Ph.D. in Industrial Engineering and a minor in Reliability Engineering.

Dr. Kumar began his career in the heavy equipment industry with John Deere, working on the reengineering and expansion program of the Tractor Manufacturing Operation. In the mid 1980s he continued his career in the aerospace industry with Pratt and Whitney, working on total reengineering of manufacturing technology and the facility to take the company from World War II technology to twenty-first century technology to introduce production of new jet engines. In 1994, he joined Pitney Bowes, Inc., leading the business optimization and development programs and providing modeling and hardware and software solutions, as well as coaching and leading continuous improvement programs (Kaizen, Lean, and Six Sigma).

My sincere gratitude is expressed:

To Alexis N. Sommers, Professor of Industrial Engineering at the University of New Haven, who assisted me in writing this book

To those who gave me permission to use selected materials

To my wife Pushpa and daughter Roli, who have the patience and humor to survive my work, for their support and encouragement

— Dhirendra Kumar

WAV Web Added Value™

Free value-added materials from the Download Resource Center at www.jross.com

At J. Ross Publishing we are committed to providing today's professional with practical, hands-on tools that enhance the learning experience and give readers an opportunity to apply what they have learned. That is why we offer free ancillary materials available for download on this book and all participating Web Added Value™ publications. These online resources may include interactive versions of material that appears in the book or supplemental templates, worksheets, models, plans, case studies, proposals, spreadsheets and assessment tools, among other things. Whenever you see the WAV™ symbol in any of our publications it means bonus materials accompany the book and are available from the **Web Added Value™ Download Resource Cente**r at www.jrosspub.com.

Downloads for *Six Sigma Best Pracices: A Guide to Business Process Excellence for Diverse Industries* include exercises with solutions, a Six Sigma DMAIC process overview, and a sample project proposal, plus an explanation of event tree and fault tree analysis tools. A popular statistical software package known as Minitab® is used extensively in various areas of this text to present examples, exercises, and detailed instruction related to the statistical methods employed in Six Sigma. Business practitioners may obtain this software package at www.minitab.com.

1

INTRODUCTION

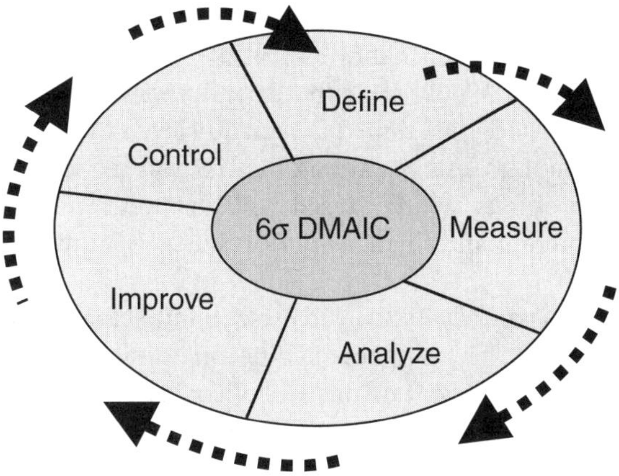

This chapter introduces the Six Sigma concept, philosophy, and approach and includes a beginning discussion of phases of the Six Sigma process. Sections include:

1.1 History
1.2 Business Markets and Expectations
1.3 What Is Sigma?
1.4 The Six Sigma Approach
1.5 Roadmap for the Six Sigma Process
1.6 Six Sigma Implementation Structure
1.7 Project Selection
  1.7.1 Identification of Quality Costs and Losses
  1.7.2 The Project Selection Process
1.8 Project Team Selection

1.1 HISTORY

Following World War II, Japan's economy had almost been destroyed. For world market competition, very few natural resources remained except for Japan's people. Yet, top business leaders in Japan fully supported the concept of quality improvement. They realized that quality improvement would open world markets and that this was critical for their nation's survival.

During the 1950s and 1960s, while the Japanese were improving the quality of their products and services at a rapid pace, quality levels in Western nations had changed very little. Among Western nations, the U.S. was the only source for most types of consumer products, which caused U.S. business leaders to concentrate their efforts on production and financial performance, not quality and customer needs.

By the late 1970s and early 1980s, Japanese manufacturers had significantly improved product quality. The Japanese had become a significant competitor in the world marketplace. As a result of this global competition, the U.S. lost a significant market share to Japan, e.g., in products such as automobiles and electronic goods.

During the 1980s, U.S. businesses realized the value of quality products and services and embarked on quality improvement programs. As a result, over the past 20 years, the U.S. automobile industry has made extraordinary progress, not only slowing but also reversing the 1980s market trend. Started in the 1980s, key national programs are still observed today:

- 1984: U.S. government designated October as National Quality Month.
- 1987: Congress established the Malcolm Baldrige National Quality Award.

Motorola conceptualized Six Sigma as a quality goal in the mid-1980s. Motorola was the first to recognize that modern technology was so complex that old ideas about acceptable quality levels were no longer applicable. Yet, the term Six Sigma and Motorola's innovative Six Sigma program only achieved significant prominence in 1989 when Motorola announced that it would achieve a defect rate of no more than 3.4 parts per million within 5 years. This announcement effectively changed the focus of quality in the U.S. from one in which quality levels were measured in percentages (parts per hundred) to a discussion of parts per million or even parts per billion. In a short time, many U.S. industrial giants such as Xerox, GE, and Kodak were following Motorola's lead.

Quality is a functional relationship of several elements, but eventually it relates to customers (explained in the next section, *Business Markets and Expectations*). Depending on customer expectations, business leaders must set their business goals/objectives and the business process that produces output, and personnel must determine their roles and responsibilities. The entire system can be updated as customer expectations change.

1.2 BUSINESS MARKETS AND EXPECTATIONS

From the 1950s through the 1970s, competition in the U.S. was primarily domestic. As noted earlier, because many European countries and Japan were trying to rebuild their infrastructures following the destruction caused by World War II, the U.S. was the primary source of many products. During the 20th century, U.S. business leaders concentrated their efforts on producing products/services as quickly as possible, with business efforts being primarily linked to productivity. However, by the early 1980s, countries other than the U.S. were producing quality products and were ready to compete in the global market.

During the 20th century, customers defined quality differently. Some thought of quality as product superiority or product excellence, while others viewed quality as minimizing manufacturing or service defects. The current globally competitive marketplace has resulted in continuously increasing customer expectations for quality.

Key components of a manufactured product's quality include performance, reliability, durability, serviceability, features, and *perceived* quality, which are often based on advertising, brand name, and the manufacturer's image. Many of the key components of product quality are also applicable to services. Important components of service quality include customer wait time before service delivery, service completeness, courtesy, consistency, convenience, responsiveness, and accuracy.

Customers judge a supplier's product/service quality. In today's competitive market, customers expect a quality product or service and they expect that it will be delivered on time and have a competitive price. Therefore, a supplier's quality system must produce a product/service that provides value to customers and leads to customer satisfaction and loyalty. Most business leaders agree that quality is now defined as *meeting* or *exceeding* customer expectations.

The traditional definition of *defect* in product manufacturing is that a product does not meet a particular specification. Yet, in today's globally competitive environment, a customer's definition of defect is much broader than the traditional manufacturing definition. For a customer, *defect* can include late delivery, an incomplete shipment, system crashes, a shortage of material, incorrect invoicing, typing errors in documents, and even long waits for calls to customer service to be answered.

An output can be a manufactured product or a service. Any process (manufacturing or service) can be presented as a set of inputs, which when used together generates a corresponding set of outputs. Therefore, "a process is a process," irrespective of the type of organization or the function provided (manufacturing and/or service). All processes have inputs and outputs. All processes have customers and suppliers. All processes have variations. Metrics must be created that are appropriate for the output being measured. It will simply be an excuse for measurement if different output metrics are applied to different outputs. Therefore, acquiring breakthrough knowledge is required about how to improve processes and how to do things ***better***, ***faster***, and ***at lower cost***.

To summarize:

- Business market competition changed from domestic to global.
- Customer expectations in quality have continuously increased.
- Business efforts during the 20th century were directed at productivity.
- Business efforts during the 21st century are directed at achieving higher-quality goods and services.
- The definition of defect changed.

In a production environment, the familiar, well-known definition of *defect* is "when the product manufactured does not meet certain specifications." Yet, today, *anything* that prevents a business from serving its customers as they would like to be served is the definition of ***defect***. Based on today's definition, would the following be recognized as defects?

- Late deliveries
- Incomplete shipments
- System crashes
- Shortage of material
- Incorrect invoicing
- Typing errors in documents
- Long waits for calls to a business to be answered

The answer is "yes."

- Organizations often waste time creating metrics that are not appropriate for the output being measured.
- All processes have inputs and outputs, have customers and suppliers, and show variations.
- Breakthrough knowledge must be acquired to improve processes so that they are done better, faster, and at lower cost.

This breakthrough concept is known as *Six Sigma.* The Six Sigma approach will be presented in several chapters of this book, but first: what is ***sigma***? Before moving on to a discussion of sigma, consider Exercise 1.1:

Exercise 1.1: Product Manager

You are a product manager for a riding lawn mower company. You are responsible for product design, manufacturing, sales/marketing, and service. The lawn mower manufacturing company is well known for its product brand names. List ten quality items you would provide in your product to satisfy customers.

1.3 WHAT IS SIGMA?

Sigma represents the standard deviation in mathematical statistics. It is represented by the Greek letter "σ." The normal distribution (also known as Gaussian) has two parameters: the mean, μ, and the standard deviation sigma, σ. These Greek letters are used to represent the mean and the standard deviation. Their theoretical values are "zero" and "one," respectively. These distribution values can be estimated from the sample data.

The standard deviation is a statistic that represents the amount of variability or nonuniformity existing in a process (manufacturing/service). Generally, process data are collected and the sigma value is calculated. If the sigma value is large, related to the mean, it indicates that there is a considerable variability in the product. If the sigma value is small, then there is less variability in the product and, therefore, the product is very uniform.

The sigma value can be calculated from the sample as follows (the sample sigma is generally represented by "*s*" and the population sigma is represented by "σ"):

$$s = \sqrt{\frac{\sum_{i=1}^{n}\left(X_i - \bar{X}\right)^2}{(n-1)}}$$

where:

s = Sample's standard deviation

X_i = Sample data, for $i = 1, 2, 3, \ldots, n$

$\bar{X}$ = Sample's average (mean)

n = Number of data values in the sample

Note: Information about normal distribution is presented in *Probabilistic Data Distribution* in Chapter 3 (*Measure*). Additional information can be found in any statistics textbook that discusses probabilistic distributions.

1.4 THE SIX SIGMA APPROACH

Before discussing the Six Sigma approach, consider some definitions:

Six Sigma
Because *Six Sigma* has several definitions and is used in various ways, it can sometimes be confusing, but a few explanations should clarify Six Sigma:

Six Sigma, the Goal—In true statistical terms, if Six Sigma ($\pm$ 6σ) is used as a quality goal, Six Sigma means "getting the product very close to zero defects, errors, or mistakes." However, "zero defects" does not indicate *exactly* zero—zero is actually 0.002 parts per million defective, which can be written as:

0.002 defects per million

0.002 errors per million

0.002 mistakes per million

0.002 parts per million (ppm)

However, for all practical purposes, Six Sigma is considered to be *zero* defects. (*Note:* The concept of 3.4 defects per 1 million opportunities is a Motorola concept, i.e., a metric, that will be discussed later.)

Before Motorola's concept, Six Sigma was understood by individuals/institutions (academia, research institutions, and businesses) to be plus and minus three sigma ($\pm$ 3σ) within specification limits. The following discussion explains the $\pm$ 3σ concept:

Assume the process builds a shaft and the important characteristic is shaft diameter. Therefore, the shaft diameter has a design specification. The design specification has an upper specification limit (USL) and a lower specification limit (LSL). In reality, when these limits are exceeded, the product fails its design requirements.

Say that you have manufactured shafts and have measured their diameters (i.e., you have collected data). Now you can compute the sigma and predict the process variability. In this example, process variability is related to only one characteristic: shaft diameter. The area under the normal distribution curve between $\pm$ 3σ is about 99.73% of the distribution. Although 99.73% does not encompass the entire distribution (100%), for all practical purposes, it is close enough to be

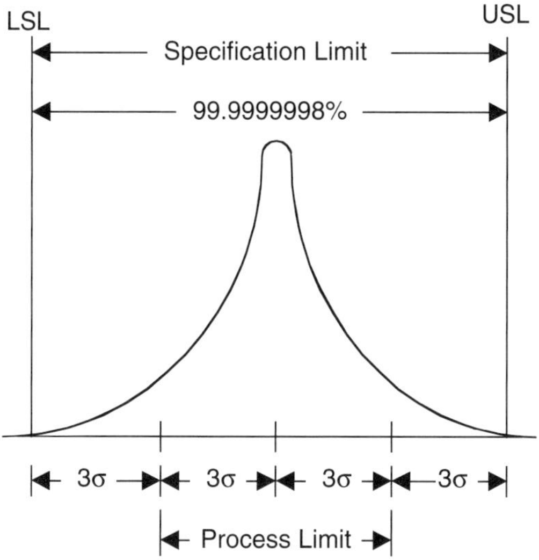

Figure 1.1 Motorola's concept of Six Sigma.

considered "all." Therefore, when the process variability is computed, "almost all" are included, and the result is accepted as if it were "all."

Note: From an academic point of view, C_p (the process potential index) and C_pk (the process capability index) can also be calculated (see Chapter 3, *Measure*, under *Process Capability Index*).

Motorola's definition of Six Sigma (a concept started in 1987) stipulates that the product specification limits should have plus or minus six sigma ($\pm$ 6σ) standard deviations. The product specification limits are known as the product design specification that has an upper specification limit (USL) and a lower specification limit (LSL). These two limits demarcate a design tolerance. The process variation limits are the same as defined earlier (before 1987 or $\pm$ 3σ).

Therefore, in Motorola's new approach in 1987—to take a particular product and measure the characteristic of interest and estimate its sigma—the value of sigma should be such that a 12 sigma specification characteristics should fit within the specification limits. This concept was very different from what had been understood or referred to as Six Sigma up until that time. (Remember that before Motorola's new approach, Six Sigma had always been $\pm$ 3σ and not $\pm$ 6σ within specification.) The Motorola Six Sigma concept is presented in Figure 1.1.

Product specification is nothing more than what the customer needs, and customer needs must be met on time. Another way to present Motorola's concept is shown in Figure 1.2. As variation goes down and customer needs are met on time, customer satisfaction goes up.

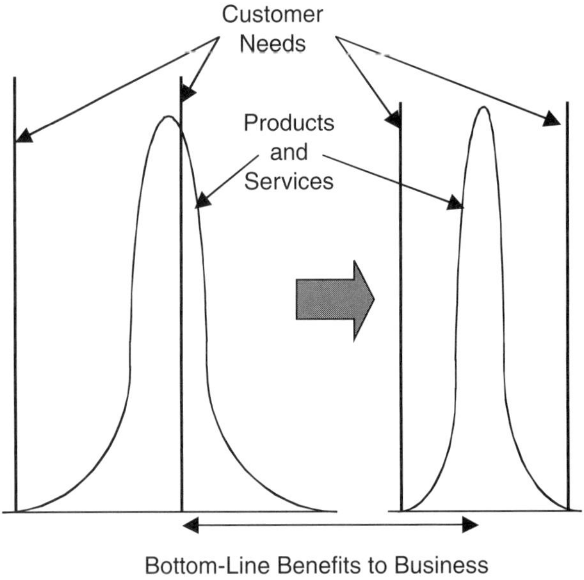

Figure 1.2 The Six Sigma concept: customer needs vs. products and services.

Six Sigma is applicable to technical and nontechnical processes. A manufacturing process is viewed as a technical process. There are numerous input variables that affect the process, and the process produces transformation of inputs to an output. The flow of product is very visible and tangible. There are numerous opportunities to collect data. In many instances, variable data may be collected.

Nontechnical processes are more difficult to visualize. Nontechnical processes are identified as administrative, service, and transactional. Some inputs, outputs, and transactions may not be tangible. Yet, they are certainly processes. Treating them as systems allows them to be better understood and, eventually, to be characterized, optimized, and controlled, thereby eliminating the possibility for mistakes and errors. Examples of nontechnical processes include:

- Administrative: budgeting
- Product/service selling: service
- Applying for school admission: transactional

Six Sigma is a highly disciplined process that helps organizations/businesses to focus on developing near-perfect products and services. It is a statistical term that measures how far a given process deviates from perfection. The central idea behind Six Sigma is that if the number of "defects" in a process can be measured, it is possible to systematically figure out how to eliminate them to get as close to "zero defects" as possible. Key concepts of Six Sigma include:

- Critical to Quality—The attribute most important to meet customer needs
- Process Capability—What the process can deliver
- Defects, Errors, and Mistakes—Failure to deliver what customer wants
- Variation—What the customer perceives related to expectations
- Stable Operation—Maintains a consistent and predictable process to improve throughput that the customer perceives related to expectations
- Design for Six Sigma—A Six Sigma program that allows the organization/business to meet customer needs and process capability

As an example, assume that a business manufactures 2-inch-thick, 3-ring binders. The manufacturing cost of a binder is $3.00, which is inclusive of all costs, including equipment, supplies, and production and supportive labor. Say that if production yields at the 2.5 sigma (2.5 s) level, the business would reject (or produces in relation to defined specifications) 158,000 of 1,000,000 binders produced due to defects. The higher the sigma level, the better the performance. If the business were moved to the Six Sigma level, only 3.4 defective binders would be rejected per 1,000,000 productions. Visualize what that would mean to the profit margin.

Six Sigma, the Metric—The Six Sigma concept is also used as a metric for a particular quality level. As an example, assume that a high sigma level may relate to a three sigma process, implying plus or minus three sigma ($\pm 3\sigma$) within specifications. The quality level might be considered good, compared to a two sigma process ($\pm 2\sigma$), in which there may be a plus or minus two sigma within specifications, and in which the quality level is not so good. Therefore, the higher the number of sigma values within product/service specifications, the better the quality level.

Six Sigma, the Strategy—Six Sigma can also be used in developing a business strategy for a product/service. For example, a product strategy could be based on the interrelationship that exists between product design, manufacturing, delivery, product lead time, inventories, rework/scrap, mistakes in different processes through to delivery, and the level to which they impact customer satisfaction. The value of Six Sigma is written statistically as follows:

$$\pm 6\sigma = 12\sigma$$

Six Sigma, the Management Philosophy—Due to global competition, Six Sigma is also a customer-based approach, realizing that defects/errors/ mistakes are expensive and result in lower revenue and profit margin. Fewer defects mean lower costs and improved customer satisfaction and loyalty. Therefore, the lowest-cost and highest-value producer is the most competitive provider of products and services. Six Sigma is a method to accomplish strategic business results.

With an understanding of Six Sigma, the next question might be "Who needs Six Sigma?" Consider two business situations:

- A business is performing poorly.
- A business is performing very well.

If a business is performing poorly, it might be experiencing some or all of the following issues:

- Poor product quality
- Losing market share
- Competition gaining market share
- Business operating very inefficiently
- Poor service; customers complaining

Using the above-described situation, think how Six Sigma can help.

Six Sigma can be applied to the product design process, making the product more robust, with improved manufacturability, which may result in better quality and reliability to meet customer needs. Six Sigma can help the business to understand the science of its process. It can also help to reveal the variables that significantly affect the process and the variables that do not.

Once identified, variables affecting the process can be manipulated in a controlled fashion to improve the process. When variables that *truly influence* the process are known with a high level of confidence, it is possible to optimize the process by knowing what inputs to control to maintain the process at optimum output performance.

If the business is performing very well, it may be selling more products/services than before and therefore needs more employees and a greater capacity to deliver more products/services in the same time frame to meet growing customer demand. Six Sigma is more important for this business than for the business doing poorly. The successful business has more to lose than the one doing poorly. If the business is doing well, it must strive to excel through improvements and innovations to become the standard by which others benchmark themselves.

Table 1.1. Six Sigma Interpretation of Product/Service Quality

Product/Service Acceptable Range Sigma	Yield (%)	DPMO[a]
1σ	31.0	690,000
2σ	69.2	308,000
3σ	93.3	66,800
4σ	99.4	6,210
5σ	99.97	230
6σ	99.99966	3.4

[a]DPMO, defective per 1 million opportunities.

So far, "What is Six Sigma?" and "Who needs Six Sigma?" have been answered. The next logical question could be "What are the indications that Six Sigma is needed?"

If a business is experiencing some of the following, then it needs to implement the Six Sigma program:

- Customers complaining about product/service quality or reliability
- Losing market share
- High warranty cost
- Unpaid invoices due to customer complaints
- Wrong parts from suppliers
- Unreliable forecasts
- Actual cost frequently over budget
- Recurring problems, with the same fixes made repeatedly
- Design products very difficult to manufacture
- Frequency of scrap/rework too high and uncontrollable

Once any business leadership decides to implement the Six Sigma concept, leadership must understand the relationship between the sigma value and defects in products/services. The numerical concept of Six Sigma is now introduced.

Numerical Concept of Six Sigma—Any process operating at ± 6 sigma is almost defect-free and therefore is considered to be "best in class." In pure statistical terms, ± 6 sigma means 0.002 defect per million parts, or 2 defects per billion, or a yield of 99.9999998%. Motorola modified the pure statistical concept (known as Motorola's Six Sigma values). Some of these values are presented in Table 1.1. The bottom-line impact of Six Sigma is to reduce defects, errors, and mistakes to *zero defects*. The process will yield customer satisfaction, and happy customers usually tell their friends about how pleased they are with a product or service.

Because Six Sigma philosophy strives to produce a significant change in the process/product, a major barrier to Six Sigma quality is *behavioral* issues, not *technical* issues. Fundamental rules for any significant change include:

- Always include affected individuals in both planning and implementing improvements.
- Provide sufficient time for employees to change.
- Confine improvements to only those changes essential to remove the identified root cause(s).
- Respect an individual's perceptions by listening and responding to his/her concerns.
- Ensure leadership participation in the program.
- Provide timely feedback to affected individuals.

Therefore, Six Sigma is a quality improvement process with emphasis on:

- Reducing defects to less than 4 per 1 million
- Having aggressive goals of reducing cycle time (e.g., 40 to 70%)
- Producing dramatic cost reduction

According to Michael Hammer[1] of Hammer & Co., Six Sigma is a powerful tool for solving certain kinds of business problems, yet it has severe limitations. For example, Six Sigma assumes that an existing process design is fundamentally sound and only needs minor adjustments. To be fully effective, Six Sigma should be paired with other techniques that create a new process design that dramatically boosts performance. Process reengineering knowledge should show the user how Six Sigma should be positioned relative to other performance improvement techniques.

There may be situations in which a process reengineering[2] application may be required before implementing the Six Sigma concept. The concept of process reengineering will now be briefly introduced. Details of this concept are presented in Chapter 5 (*Improve*).

Process activities are classified into three groups:

- Value Added—The customer supports the activity and is willing to pay for it.

- Non-Value Added—The customer is not interested and is not willing to pay, but the manufacturer/supplier needs the activity to support the business.
- Waste—The activity does not support either the customer or the manufacturer/supplier and nobody wants to pay for it.

The best ways to improve the process are to:

Eliminate—Waste
Minimize—Non-value added
Reprocess—Value added

The next section briefly introduces the steps of the Six Sigma process.

1.5 ROAD MAP FOR THE SIX SIGMA PROCESS

This discussion will start with a simple product life cycle, in which a customer identifies the need; the supplier designs, manufactures, and delivers the product; and the service organization supports the product. The process to produce the product to meet customer needs is a set of structural and logical activities that focuses on the customer, cultivates innovation, ensures product robustness and reliability, reduces product cost, and ultimately increases value for the end customer and business owner (shareholders). Product quality must meet or exceed customer expectations. The quality concept in Six Sigma can be divided into two phases:

- A Product Design Quality Level Program
- A Product Manufacturing, Sales, and Service Quality Level Program

Product Design Quality

In the Six Sigma concept, product design quality is identified as a DMADV process (also Design for Six Sigma, DFSS methodology), where:

Define—Define the project goals and customer (internal or external) deliverables.

Measure—Measure and determine customer needs and specifications.

Analyze—Analyze the process options to meet customer needs.

Design—Design (detailed) the process to meet customer needs.

Verify—Verify the design performance and ability to meet customer needs.

Table 1.2. Differences between DMADV and DMAIC

DMADV	DMAIC
Focuses on the design of the product and processes	Looks at the existing processes and fixes problem(s)
Proactive process	More reactive process
Dollar benefits more difficult to quantify and tend to be much more long term; may take 6 months to a year after launch of the new product before business will obtain adequate accounting data on the impact	Dollar benefits quantified rather quickly

The DMADV process (DFSS methodology) should be used when:

- A product or process is not in existence at a business and one needs to be developed.
- The existing product or process has been optimized using either DMAIC (to be discussed later) or some other process and it still does not meet the expected level of customer needs or Six Sigma level metrics.

A documented, well-understood, and useful new product development process is a prerequisite to a successful DMADV process. DMADV is an enhancement to new product development process, not a replacement. DMADV is a business process concentrating on improving profitability. If properly applied, it generates the correct product at the right time and at the right cost. DMADV is a powerful program management technique.

Six Sigma initiatives at the product design quality level are tremendously different from initiatives at the product manufacturing, sales, and service quality levels. However, the DMADV process is beyond the scope of this book, and its process details will not be presented here. The fundamental differences between DMADV and DMAIC are presented in Table 1.2.

Product Manufacturing, Sales, and Service Quality Level Program

Any process beyond the scope of DMADV is a part of a program called DMAIC, pronounced (Duh-May-Ick), where:

Define—Define the project goals and customer (internal and external) deliverables. **D**efine is the first step in any Six Sigma process of DMAIC and identifies important factors, such as the selected project's scope, expectations, resources, schedule, and project approval. This Six Sigma process definition step specifically identifies what is part of the project and what is not and explains the scope of the project. Many times the first passes at process documentation are at a general level. Generally, additional work is required to adequately understand and correctly document the processes.

Measure—Measure the process and determine current performance. The Six Sigma process requires quantifying and benchmarking the process using actual data. Yet, a Six Sigma process is not simply collecting two data points and extrapolating some extreme data values. At a minimum, consider the mean or average performance and some estimate of the dispersion or variation (calculating the standard deviation is beneficial). Trends and cycles can also be very informative. Process capabilities can also be calculated once performance data are collected.

Analyze—Analyze the data and determine the root cause(s) of the defects. Once the project is understood and baseline performance is documented, establishing the existence of an actual opportunity to improve performance, the Six Sigma process can be utilized to perform a process analysis. In this step, the Six Sigma process utilizes statistical tools to validate root causes of problems (issues). Any number of tools and tests can be used. The objective is to understand the process at a level that is sufficient to facilitate formulation of options (development of alternative processes) for improvement. A team should be able to compare the various options to determine the most promising alternative(s). It is also critical to estimate financial and/or customer impact on potential improvement(s). Superficial analysis and understanding will lead to unproductive options being selected, forcing a recycle through the process to make improvements.

Improve—Improve the process by eliminating defects. During the Improve step of the Six Sigma process, ideas and solutions are implemented. The Six Sigma team should discover and validate all known root causes for the existing opportunity. The team should also identify solutions. It is rare to come up with ideas or opportunities that are so good that all of them are instant successes. As part of the Six Sigma process, checks must ensure that the desired results are being achieved. Sometimes, experiments and trials are required to find the best solution. When conducting trials and experiments, it is important that all team members understand that these are not simply trials, but that they are actually part of the Six Sigma process.

Control—Control the implemented process for future performance. As a part of the Six Sigma process, performance-tracking mechanisms and measurements must be in place to ensure that the gains made in the project are not lost over a period of time. As a part of the control step, telling others in the business about the process and the gains is encouraged. By using this approach, the Six Sigma process starts to create potentially phenomenal returns: ideas and projects in one part of the business are translated to implementation in another part of the business in a very rapid fashion.

The DMAIC process can also be presented as:

Define ➠ Measure ➠ Analyze ➠ Improve ➠ Control

These are the five key steps in the Six Sigma process. Every process goes through these five steps. The steps are then repeated as the process is refined.

Key *guiding elements* that team members should strive to avoid or minimize as they go through the Six Sigma process include:

- Leadership resistance
- Unclear mission
- Limited dedicated time for the project
- Prematurely jumping to a solution
- Untrained team members
- Unsatisfactory implementation plan

To implement the Six Sigma program, business/organization members must be assigned defined responsibilities. These members must take their responsibilities seriously.

As a high-level organization structure is defined, the management group should also begin identifying Six Sigma projects. The implementation structure and project selection are parallel processes. The next two sections will discuss the Six Sigma implementation structure (identifies program participants and their responsibilities) and program selection (selecting a project that qualifies as a Six Sigma project).

1.6 SIX SIGMA IMPLEMENTATION STRUCTURE

Implementation of the Six Sigma program is very demanding. Simply explaining the implementation of Six Sigma to employees and expecting them to implement the program is an approach that is clearly not enough for a program such as Six Sigma that has a demanding level of excellence. This type of approach would create numerous unanswered questions and have undefined directions for almost all employees. Specifically, inexperienced employees would struggle, developing their own version of what the Six Sigma program is or ought to be and how it should be carried out. Generally, this type of approach would yield a very poor success rate and probably lower program acceptance and expectations. It could also shorten the program's life. A practical strategy is required. It must include all necessary elements for a successful implementation of the Six Sigma program.

Organization structure is one of the challenges in implementing the Six Sigma program. In the last 10 to 15 years, major corporations such as Motorola, GE, and Xerox have implemented the program very successfully. Their organizational structures had a critical role.

The Six Sigma Challenge

Once executive leaders of a business have decided to implement the Six Sigma program, they must challenge each employee in the business. Six Sigma involves all employees.

Because the process is physical and tangible, and metrics are commonly utilized to judge the output quality in a manufacturing environment, it is easy (and obvious) for manufacturing employees to implement the program. (*Remember*: Administrative and service activities do not have similar metrics.)

Each employee in the business provides some kind of service. Therefore, employees must assess their job functions and/or responsibilities in relationship to how the Six Sigma program will improve the business. Employees should define what would be their ideal service goals in support of customer (internal and external) needs and wants. Once their goals are established, employees should quantify where they currently are in relationship to these goals. Then they must work to minimize any gaps to achieve Six Sigma goals in accordance with target dates.

Prerequisites for the implementation structure and the functional concept of the organization as presented in Figure 1.3 include:

- Businesses with profitable Six Sigma strategies are successful.
- Profitable businesses must maintain effective infrastructures.
- Profitable businesses are continually improving and revising through executive planning.
- Businesses must be creative and customer-focused.
- Implementation of Six Sigma is a team process.
- Executive leadership and senior management must be part of the process.
- Six Sigma is not a quick-fix process. It requires a months-long to multi-year commitment.
- Key participating leaders must be supported by an organizational infrastructure with key roles:
  - Executive Leadership
  - Steering Committee
  - Champion
  - Master/Expert/Project Team(s)

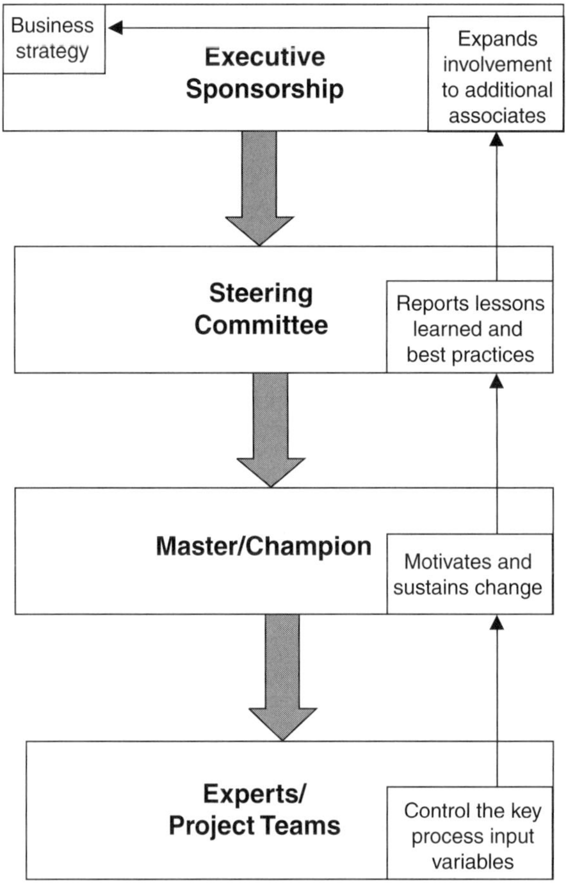

Figure 1.3 The Six Sigma implementation structure.

Chief Executive's Commitment

Once the business leader (Chief Executive) expresses his/her commitment to converting the business into a Six Sigma organization, he/she establishes the challenges, vision, and goals to meet customer needs and wants. The new metrics and new way of operating the business are also established. Old vs. new ways of doing business are compared. New ways of working toward excellence and establishing a common goal for all employees in the business reduce variability in every process they perform.

Employees' Role

Each employee in the business is involved in the Six Sigma program and has a significant role in bringing the business to a world-class level of performance organization. Commonly used roles and responsibilities include (see Figure 1.3):

- Executive Leadership
- Steering Committee
- Champion
- Big Group: Master, Expert, Team Leader, and Team Members

Executive Leadership

Along with already-identified responsibilities, leadership must link the Six Sigma program to an overall business strategy (see *Appendix A1* for additional information). Business strategy depends on the state of the business. Commonly defined states of business include:

- Matured Business—Typically there is no growth in a matured business, e.g., in an e-mail communication and electronic on-line bill payment environment, a hard copy mail-generating business would be considered to be a matured business.
- Growing and/or Changing Business—To meet customer needs and wants, these businesses are either growing and/or changing, e.g., the automobile industry is changing in the U.S. and Europe, but it is growing in countries such as China and India.
- Infant Business—These are new businesses that are growing very rapidly, e.g., biomedical research in equipment, genetic research, etc.

Executive leadership must allocate sufficient resources to support the Six Sigma program. A business must grow in terms of revenue, profit, and cash flow. Leadership must direct the financial group to validate all Six Sigma programs with return-on-investment (ROI) status.

Business leadership must also have total commitment to the implementation of Six Sigma program. Their responsibilities can be summarized as follows:

- Establish a Six Sigma Leadership Team.
- Tie Six Sigma to overall business strategy.
- Identify key business issues.
- Create customer feedback processes.
- Allocate time for experts to make breakthrough improvements.
- Set aggressive Six Sigma goals.

- Allocate sufficient resources.
- Incorporate Six Sigma performance into the reward system.
- Direct finance to validate ROI for all Six Sigma projects.
- Evaluate the corporate culture to determine if intellectual capital is being infused into the company.
- Expand involvement to additional associates.

Steering Committee

The Steering Committee is a high-level group of managers (executives) who reports program status and achievements to the business CEO in relationship to overall business strategy. The Steering Committee must continuously evaluate the Six Sigma implementation and development process and make necessary change, as well as:

- Define a set of cross-functional strategic metrics to drive projects.
- Create an overall training plan.
- Define project selection process and criteria.
- Supply project report-out templates and structured report-out dates.
- Evaluate diversity issues and facilitate change.
- Provide the appropriate universal communication tools whereby individuals must feel that there is something for everyone.
- Collect lessons learned and share best practices.

Champions

Champions are managers at different levels in the business. They define the studies and/or projects. Projects are either improvement or characterization studies. Project savings could vary from several thousand dollars (U.S.) to as much as a million dollars. Savings depend on business size, project scope and duration, and project activities. A Champion's function is to inform the steering committee and keep track of the project team's progress. Champions also provide high management visibility, commitment, and support to empower team members for success. They provide strategic directions for the projects and ensure that changes, improvements, or solutions are implemented. They must motivate experts and sustain change. Champions officially announce the project team and the project completion after all project objectives are met and the documentation is completed. They also organize the team's presentation to senior management. Champions are also responsible for:

- Selecting at least one project in each standard business unit that will have the most benefits.
- Selecting the experts from the cross-functional team members.
- Identifying the appropriate project leaders among the experts.
- Monitoring team progress and help remove barriers.
- Converting gains into dollars.

Big Group: Master, Expert, Team Leader and Team Members
Responsibilities of this large group can be divided into subgroups: Master and Expert, Team Leader, and Team Members

Master—A Master (also Master Black Belt) is generally a program-site technical expert in Six Sigma methodology and is responsible for providing technical guidance to team leaders and members. Often a Master is dedicated to support the program full time. A Master is considered to be an expert resource for the teams: for coaching, statistical analysis, and Just-In-Time (JIT) training. A Master, along with team leaders, determines team charter, goals, and team members; formalizes studies and projects; and provides management leadership. A Master can support up to ten projects.

Expert, Team Leader, and Team Members—These resources are a critical part of studies and projects:

Expert. Generally, an Expert is not a full-time member of the team. An Expert is invited to participate when there is a need for explanation, advice, technical input, etc. An Expert trains and coaches team members on tools and analysis. An Expert also helps the team if there is any misunderstanding or incomplete understanding of the process.

Team Leader. A Team Leader (at the least a Black/Green Belt-trained person) is responsible for implementing the team's recommended solution to achieve the defined goals of the Six Sigma project. He/she is an active member of the team and also is in charge of the overall coordination of team activities and progress. A Team Leader is responsible for assigning responsibilities to all team members, tracking the project goals and plans, managing the team's schedule, and handling administrative responsibilities. Improvement projects must demonstrate substantial dollar savings and significant reduction in variation, defects, errors, and mistakes. The Team Leader position is not necessarily a full-time team assignment unless the project requires a full-time Team Leader or if the Team Leader is leading two or three projects.

Team Members. Team Members are employees who maintain their regular jobs, but are assigned to one or more teams based on their knowledge and experience in selected Six Sigma projects. They have full responsibility as Team Members in the project. Team Members are expected to carry out all assignments between meetings, devote time and efforts toward the team success, conduct research as needed, and investigate alternatives as necessary.

Common responsibilities of Master, Expert, Team Leader, and Team Members include:

- Measure the process.
- Analyze/determine key process input variables.
- Improve the process as they recognize and make changes as necessary.
- Control the key process input variables.
- Develop the Expert's network to enhance communication.
- Convert gains into dollars.
- Use the Six Sigma DMAIC process to solve problems and/or improve process.

If Master, Expert, and Team Members were compared, a few distinctive qualities would be found (see Table 1.3). A conceptual flow chart is presented in Figure 1.3.

As indicated earlier, the Six Sigma Implementation Structure and the Project Selection are almost parallel processes.

1.7 PROJECT SELECTION

All businesses face problems that are solved on a daily basis by employees as a part of their normal jobs. Routine, daily problems should not become Six Sigma projects. If a business is functioning well, there is probably no need for a Six Sigma project, but if employees are trapped in a constant cycle of reacting to problems instead of fixing the root causes, then ways that Six Sigma could help might need to be explored. A list of issues that indicate signs of existing problem may be found in an earlier section (*The Six Sigma Approach*). If any of these issues are found in the following situations, then the issue or problem has become a candidate for a Six Sigma project:

- The business has tried to fix the process several times (three to four) with no success.
- The business has tried to fix the process, and the problem stopped occurring, but it has recurred.

Table 1.3. Profile Comparison of Master, Expert, and Team Member

Master	Expert	Team Member
Manager, experienced employee, respected leader and mentor of business issues	Technically oriented, respected by peers and management	Highly visible in company and trained in Six Sigma
Strong proponent of Six Sigma; asks the right questions	Master of basics and advanced tools	Respected leaders and mentors for experts

Considerations include:

- Project Choice—Management should be careful to choose projects that are large enough to be significant, but not so large as to be unwieldy.
- Business Case—What are the compelling business reasons for selecting this project? Is the project linked to key business goals and objectives? What key business process output measure(s) will the project leverage and how? What are the estimated cost savings/opportunities on this project?

Six Sigma program is highly mathematical. Its basis is the application of statistics in engineering for the reduction of variability and for meeting customer needs. Therefore, to understand project selection for a Six Sigma project, the explanation must be a bit technical.

Generally any product selected as a Six Sigma project will have numerous characteristics. Consider a very simple product such as a lid for a glass bottle. A lid has at least five characteristics: diameter, depth, threads, material, and paint. A more complex product such as power chain saw could have as many as 300 characteristics. An even more technically complex product such as riding lawn mower could have several thousand characteristics. Finding a product with a single characteristic is impossible.

Yet, a product with only one characteristic will be used for our purposes of discussion. Assume that the quality level or performance in producing this characteristic follows the "old concept" of specification limits of $\pm$ 3 sigma ($\pm 3\sigma$). It can be inferred that about 99.73% of the product would be good and about 0.27% would be defective by failing for that characteristic. The product yield of such a process would be 99.73%. This result is referred to as a three sigma product ($\pm 3\sigma$).

Historically, a process that was capable of producing 99.73% product within specifications was considered to be very efficient. In such a process, only 0.27% product would nonconform to specifications and might be rejected. If 10,000 units of that product were produced, 9,973 units would be good and 27 units would be defective. Now, if 1 million units of that product were produced, 997,300 units would be good and 2,700 units would be defective and most likely would be reworked.

These situations do not seem to be too bad, but, unfortunately, not even the simplest of products has only one characteristic. Now consider a product that has more than 1 characteristic, e.g., a power chain saw for which 300 characteristics have been identified. Imagine that product quality is defined based on performance of only four characteristics at a plus or minus three sigma levels ($\pm 3\sigma$). This implies that each of the four characteristics has a fraction nondefective of 0.9973 and a fraction defective of 0.0027. If these characteristics were independent, then the yield would be 98.92% ($0.9973 \times 0.9973 \times 0.9973 \times 0.9973 = 0.9892$).

This result also does not appear to be of great concern, but if all 300 characteristics were performing at a three sigma ($\pm 3\sigma$) level, each with a quality of 0.9973 fraction nondefective, then the yield for the power chain saw would be 44.437%, i.e., yield $= 100 \times (0.9973)^{300} = 44.43\%$. Therefore, for every 100 power chain saws, only 44 would go through the entire production process without a single defect and about 56 of them would have at least 1 defect. If this manufacturer has received an order for 1 million power chain saws, and 1 million power chain saws were produced, then only 444,371 would be defect-free and the other 555,629 would have at least 1 defect per power chain saw.

The example clearly demonstrates that to be competitive in the marketplace and to build a product with zero defects, the first time, with no scrap, the quality at the characteristic level has to be much better than 99.73% or three sigma ($\pm 3\sigma$).

To produce power chain saws with zero defects, no scrap, and no rework the first time around, the manufacturer has to increase the performance capability at the characteristic level to Six Sigma—or 99.9999998% nondefective. If every characteristic in the power chain saw was performing at Six Sigma, then the first-pass yield would be 99.99994% or $100 \times (0.999999998)^{300}$.

In the power chain saw example, if all 300 characteristics are at Six Sigma, and the manufacturer has produced 10,000 power chain saws, all would be defect-free. If the manufacturer were to produce 1 million power chain saws, only 1 might have defects or be defective and the other 999,999 would be defect-free. Under these conditions:

- There would be no need to have a rework line.
- There would be no cost for rework, personnel, and equipment.

- There would be minimal to no scrap.
- There would be a significant reduction in product cycle time.
- Predictability of on-time delivery would be realized.

Clearly, achieving all the product/service characteristics at a Six Sigma level makes the process defect-free, cost-effective, and potentially very profitable. The power chain saw example provides a prospective for project selection. It is a two-step process:

- Identification of Quality Costs and Losses
- The Project Selection Process

1.7.1 Identification of Quality Costs and Losses

When choosing Six Sigma projects, not overlooking the cost-savings potential of solving less-obvious problem issues is important. Traditionally, costs related to poor quality are identified by:

- Rejects
- Scrap
- Rework
- Warranty

Other issues that impact quality and increase product/service costs must not be excluded from Six Sigma projects:

- Engineering change orders
- Long cycle time (order booking and manufacturing)
- Time value of money
- More setups
- Expediting costs
- Allocations of working capital
- Excessive material orders/planning
- Excess inventory
- Late delivery
- Lost customer loyalty
- Lost sales

1.7.2 The Project Selection Process

One of the most difficult activities in Six Sigma deployment is the project selection process. Projects can be divided into two types based on project savings: hard (bottom-line) savings and soft savings. *Hard savings* data can be obtained from a financial analysis of year-to-year spending, budget variance, and improvements in revenue. *Hard savings* could be a result of cost reduction, revenue enhancement, or a combination of both. Examples are presented in Table 1.4. *Soft savings*, on the other hand, are difficult to quantify, but soft savings may result in lowering capital and/or budget requirements. Examples are presented in Table 1.4. Additional examples are on-time delivery, customer satisfaction, improvement of the system's process potential index (C_p), and improvement of the system's process capability index (C_pk). C_p and C_pk are discussed in Chapter 3, *Measure*.

Additional elements impact selection of the right project:

- Correct selection of a right project can have a tremendous effect on the business. Once the project is implemented, processes will function more efficiently, employees will feel satisfied, and ultimately, shareholders will see the benefits.
- If a right project selection is made incorrectly and the selected project does not have full business buy-in, project roadblocks may not be removed due to other business priorities, the project team may feel ineffective, and the end result may be less than ideal. No one wins under these situations. Select a right project that is in line with business priorities.
- Ask business leaders, "What are the three greatest issues facing the business?" Ensure that the project chosen addresses one of these issues or is directly related to one of them. Including an important issue will increase the probability that the management team provides the proper attention and quickly removes hurdles to ensure successful completion of the project.
- Ask a similar question to customers. "As a customer, what are the three greatest issues at our company that are of concern to you?" To support customer issues, investigate data from sources such as customer complaints. Specifically call customers who have cancelled services from the business.
- A selected project should be completed within 6 months. If the selected project is of longer duration, the team leader may lose team members as they take on other projects or other jobs.

Information presented so far provides a broad view of project selection, savings, and sources. The following are more formalized steps for the project selection process that will lead to the project's mission statement:

1. Identify potential problems.
2. Obtain information/data.
3. Prioritize problems.
4. Characterize problems.
5. Evaluate and select project.
6. Prepare mission statement.

Discussing the six steps is facilitated by using an example. The setting is a jet engine manufacturing company. Assume that the company has a Six Sigma team leader. He is an employee in the jet engine manufacturing company. He has asked the company's business leaders a question: "What are the three greatest issues facing the business?" Responses from the business leaders would likely include:

- Losing revenue
- High inventory
- High resources cost

The following discussion will utilize the six steps to identify potential problem(s) for the jet engine manufacturing company.

Step 1: Identify Potential Problems

The Six Sigma team leader wants to identify the potential problem(s) that result in loss of revenue. Revenue is derived from customers when they purchase jet engines. The Sales group sells the engines and the Service group provides service for the engines after they are sold. Generally, the Sales and Service groups are the last groups that maintain contact with customers.

As previously discussed, sales and services are processes just like any other process such as product designing and manufacturing. A process can be presented as a set of inputs, which, when used together, generates a corresponding set of outputs. Therefore, "a process is a process," regardless of the type of organization and the function of the process. All processes have inputs and outputs. All processes have customers and suppliers. All processes may exhibit some level of variation. The Six Sigma team has to understand the root cause(s) of the variation, find alternative solutions, and select and implement the best possible alternative to minimize/eliminate the variance. To identify a potential problem(s), the team leader needs to analyze the inputs, the process, and the outputs with the key elements as listed below. This process is known as **IPO** (**I**nput-**P**rocess-**O**utput):

Inputs:

- Cost of unacceptable quality
- Unsatisfied customer
- Business strategy and plans
- Reviews and analysis of input data
- Management and other employees

Process:

- List potential problems as identified by each source and their impact on:
  - Maintaining existing customers
  - Attracting new customers
  - Return on investment
  - Reducing the cost of unacceptable quality
  - Improving employee satisfaction
- Investigate key information sources in the organization.

Outputs:

- Evaluate process inputs.
- Develop a detailed list of potential Six Sigma projects.
- Input information into project evaluation.

Note: *Output* from an IPO process becomes *input* for a project evaluation process, in which it is compared with customer needs. IPO output must meet customer needs.

It is critical to understand the IPO process and relate how inputs are linked to outputs. The IPO process is used to develop a list of potential Six Sigma projects. (*Remember*: Six Sigma applies to manufacturing and nonmanufacturing processes.) Because revenue lost is a sales process, an IPO diagram for a sales process has been developed (Figure 1.4). The next step is to investigate and obtain prime sources of information managed by the manufacturer (the jet engine company) and by customers.

Step 2: Obtain Information/Data

Several sources of information can help uncover issues affecting revenue:

- Customers—Customer opinions are important. Customer complaints can provide clues to problems that need to be addressed.

Table 1.4. Examples of Hard and Soft Savings

Savings Type: Revenue improvement

Savings Category: Hard savings

Definition: Increased throughput over the planned level to meet market demand without any major capital expenditure. Additional savings will be a product of an increase in throughput and the product's profit margin.

Example: A Six Sigma project was implemented in the inserter manufacturing area. The project improved throughput by 16% above the planned baseline.

Savings Type: Cost reduction

Savings Category: Hard savings

Definition: Decrease in spending from prior year's baseline budget. These savings can be normalized for changes in production.

Example: The Six Sigma project improved the efficiency of the heating system in the customer service building, resulting in a 15% savings in heating gas year after year.

Savings Type: Cash flow improvement

Savings Category: Soft savings

Definition: Reduction of capital tied up in inventory/components, WIP, and finished products.

Example: A Six Sigma supply chain project was implemented, resulting in 25–50% reduction in suppliers' lead time. Therefore, inventory was reduced.

Savings Type: Capital avoidance

Savings Category: Soft savings

Definition: Eliminated or deferred future capital. This was an approved capital funding either for the current year or for a future year.

Example: The Six Sigma project improved the grinding process, resulting in eliminating the need for an additional set of grinders.

Savings Type: Cost avoidance

Savings Category: Soft savings

Definition: Eliminated or deferred future expenses. These expenses have not occurred and they were not budgeted.

Example: A test machine was consuming more-than-normal material to perform a test. A Six Sigma project was implemented to reduce material consumption at the test machine. The Six Sigma project brought material requirements to normal levels.

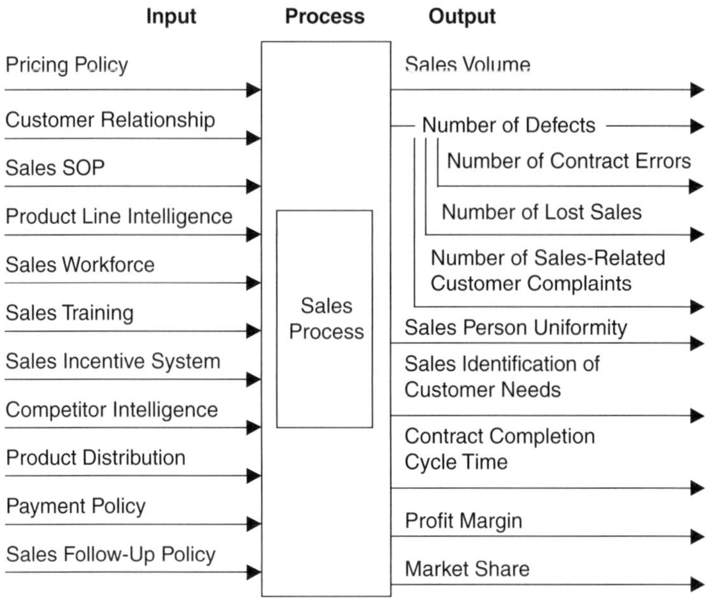

Figure 1.4 Input-Process-Output (IPO) diagram for sales process.

- Product Reviews/Audits—Many manufacturers maintain data on the cost of poor quality in the areas of Quality Assurance, Internal Audit, and Management Engineering.
- Business Plans—Businesses develop strategic plans with goals and other business objectives. Some of these plans may call for significant quality improvement projects.
- Managers/Other Company Employees—Managers and other associates are often the first to recognize opportunities to improve the product and customer service.

As information is obtained from the sources helps to identify problems, collect specific objective data on each problem or process that has been identified as a potential project. Collected/available data should answer some of the following questions:

- What complaints and dissatisfaction issues are most likely to drive away existing or new customers? *Example*: Commercial jet engine customers are typically airlines. Airlines cannot afford to keep a jet plane on the ground because a few jet engine parts are needed from the jet engine manufacturer.

- What are our most costly deficiencies? *Example*: The jet engine manufacturer's difference (deficiency) in original cost estimation for overhaul of a jet engine vs. the final billing. Generally, original estimates are too low compared to the final cost of overhauling a jet engine.
- What level of performance does the competition deliver and how does it compare with our level of performance?
- Which deficiencies in our internal processes have the most adverse affect on employees?

Brainstorming. Sometimes brainstorming can be used to develop a list of potential problems. Brainstorming is an excellent approach to generate a list of ideas, but it must not be a substitute for information or data collection. There must be no judgment or analysis of ideas during a brainstorming session. One or a few individuals should not dominate the presentation of ideas.

In brainstorming, it is critical to recognize that the differences between creativity and logical thought do not imply that there are differences in the *truth* or *usefulness* of ideas produced. It is the *method* by which an idea is produced that is the difference. Logical thought follows rules and can be reproduced by anyone using the same rules. Creative thought is not determined by rules and usually cannot be duplicated by others. Key steps in a brainstorming process include:

1. Preparation for the Session—The purpose statement must focus on the issue. The statement must be broad enough to allow creativity, but have no leading emphasis. Communicating the purpose of the session ahead of time is very helpful for participants. An ideal number of participants would be six to ten.
2. Introducing the Session—Describe and review basic brainstorming rules:
   - Ideas will be listed on a flip chart or a visible screen.
   - No criticism or evaluation of any type will be permitted.
   - Use unconventional thinking.
   - Aim for many quality ideas in a short time.
   - Using another person's idea as a basis for one's own idea will be allowed and acceptable.
   - Make contributions in turn.
   - Contribute only one idea per turn.
   - A participant may pass.
   - Do not provide an explanation of ideas.

3. Warming Up—Sometimes it is helpful to conduct a warm-up session with a neutral topic for 5 to 10 minutes.
4. The Session—Explain the issue. Write the issue so that it will be visible to all participants. End the session before participants show fatigue. A session can last for 20 to 40 minutes.
5. Processing Ideas—Once the brainstorming session is over, continue working with the team to:
   - Clarify each idea
   - Combine and group similar ideas
   - Collect data on ideas wherever available
   - Proceed with a cause-and-effect diagram for the ideas that have no data

By this time, the problems that have been identified must be in list form. Working on all problems on the list may not be possible. Therefore, the problems must be prioritized.

Step 3: Prioritize the Problems

Once a list of problems is developed, the next step is to select a problem from the developed list. Key elements must be kept in mind when evaluating problems for selection:

- What are the costs and paybacks?
- How much time is needed to find a solution and implement the solution?
- Probability of success in developing and implementing a solution both technologically and organizationally?
- What processes are you responsible for?
- Who is the owner of these processes?
- Who are the team members?
- How well does the team work together?
- Which processes have the highest priority for improvement?
- How was this conclusion reached? Do data support this conclusion?

The nominal group technique (NGT) is a structured process that *identifies* and *ranks* major problems or issues that need addressing. The NGT is used for:

- Identifying the major strengths of an institution/unit/department and making decisions by consensus when selecting the problem solution

- Providing each participant with an equal voice (e.g., defusing a dominating sales team member or influential employee who tends to control the discussion and dominate the process)

Steps to follow when conducting the NGT include:

1. Request that all participants (usually five to ten people) write or state the problem/issue that they perceive is most important.
2. Develop a master list of the problems/issues (e.g., losing revenue in a jet engine business).
3. Generate and distribute to each participant a form that numbers in no particular order the problems/issues. Request that each participant rank the top five problems/issues by assigning five points to the problem they perceive to be most important and one point to the least important of their top five.
4. Tally the results by adding the points assigned to each problem/issue. The problem/issue with the highest score will be the most important problem for the total team.
5. Discuss the results and generate a final ranked list for action planning.

The NGT application is presented in Example 1.1. This process will be repeated for each issue. Finally, there will be a proposed solution for each issue. The business may not have enough resources to solve all of the issues at the same time. Therefore, the issues with their proposed solutions must be prioritized again. As problem solutions are selected through NGT, these problems should be characterized according to customer needs and business strategy before going on to the next round to prioritize the selected solutions for the issues.

Note: The goal of every business is to completely satisfy customers and also to improve profit margin. Customer satisfaction is derived by meeting customer needs; the profit margin is linked to business strategy.

Example 1.1: An NGT Application

Five possible solutions to a problem have been identified. There are six team members who must decide which solution should be attempted first. The solutions are identified as I, II, III, IV, and V. The team members are identified as A, B, C, D, E, and F.

Each member of the six-person team orders the potential solutions, producing the following matrix:

Solution	A	B	C	D	E	F	Total
I	1	2	1	4	3	5	16
II	5	5	2	5	5	4	26
III	4	3	3	3	1	2	16
IV	2	1	4	1	2	1	11
V	3	4	5	2	4	3	21

Based on the matrix, solution II should get the highest priority followed by solution V.

Step 4: Characterize the Problems

Although each of the following questions might not apply to the solution of every issue, the following questions are commonly asked. They help to identify the needed information as well as to sort the information:

- How is the process performed?
- What are the process performance measures and why?
- How accurate and precise is the measurement system?
- What are the customer-driven specifications for all of the performance measures?
- How good or bad is the current performance?
- What are the improvement goals for the process?
- What are all the sources of variability in the process?
- Which sources of variability do you control? How do you control them and how is it documented?
- Are there any sources of variability that are supplier-dependent? If so, what are they, which supplier(s) is responsible, and what is being done about it?
- What are the sensitive (key) variables that affect the average and the variation of the measures of performance? Support the characteristics with data.
- What are the relationships between the measures of performance and the key variables? Do any variables interact? Support/validate the characteristic with data.

Once the listed questions have been answered, enough identified and sorted information exists to move on to Step 5, which is to evaluate and select a solution for the issue. This becomes the Six Sigma project for the team.

Note: Because data from the jet engine manufacturing company are confidential, information about the issue of "losing revenue" is not presented here.

Step 5: Evaluate and Select

The elements of this step are summarized in the IPO process with the nominal group technique (NGT), where:

Input is a list of top-priority projects (with decision-making data).

Process is to evaluate the top-priority projects utilizing NGT, with the following as some of the key criteria:

- Continuing problem
- Significant improvement in product/service
- Measurable improvement
- Support the business strategy
- High probability of success
- Customer satisfaction
- Support resistance
- Project risk

Output is to select a Six Sigma project. Once the project is selected, preparing the mission statement is next.

Step 6: Prepare Mission Statement

Management should review the mission statement following Step 6 of the project selection process. The defined mission statement should *describe the problem* that the project team has to *resolve*. The IPO process can be used to prepare the mission statement, where:

Input identifies the problem/issue (e.g., losing revenue)

Process describes the problem/issue and identifies the project team's objectives to resolve the problem.

Output develops a mission statement to resolve or minimize the problem.

The following criteria apply to the problem description and the mission statement. An effective problem description and a mission statement must be:

- *Specific*—Explain exactly what is incorrect; do not include other business problems. Similarly, state what is to be accomplished in the mission statement.

- *Measurable*—The scope of the problem must be quantifiable. Be prepared to answer questions such as "How many?" "How often?" "How much?" (Also be prepared to state the case for the mission statement.)
- *Observable*—Project team members and/or others should be able to actually observe the problem (also the case for the mission statement once the proposed solution is implemented).
- *Manageable*—The problem can be resolved in a clearly defined time.

A mission statement:

- Must consider business objectives and strive to understand what the business wants to accomplish.
- Must indicate the objective of the project, i.e., what the project team must do to solve the problem.

An effective problem description and a mission statement must exclude:

- *Blame*—Assigning blame. Do not assign blame to any individual and/or group. Assigning blame may create defensive behavior and interfere with the team's ability to collect and analyze data objectively.
- *Cause*—Identifying a cause. Identifying a cause(s) in the mission statement may prevent discovery of the true cause(s) of the problem.
- *Remedy*—Suggesting a solution. Do not suggest/propose a solution. A suggested solution might be incorrect. Product/service quality may become worse than expected.

Therefore, problem statement for the jet engine manufacturing company might be: "The Company is losing revenue of $200 million a year, which is 1% of the world's commercial market."

A flow chart of the process described in this section is presented in Figure 1.5 and Examples 1.2 and 1.3. Analyze the team's mission statement from the perspective of what must be included and what must be excluded from a mission statement. Different views of the objective are presented in Example 1.4. Once the project's problem description and mission statement are prepared, the next step is to select the project team.

Example 1.2: Write an Effective Problem Statement

"Our construction company's house foundation construction project takes 8 days longer on average than our major competitors take."

The problem statement must have four key characteristics: specific, measurable, sbservable, and manageable. These four key characteristics are also appropriate for the mission statement. The following is the statement analysis:

- *Specific*—The statement names a specific process and identifies the problem.
- *Measurable*—House foundation construction time is measured in days.
- *Observable*—Evidence of the problem can be obtained from internal reports and customer feedback. The process can be physically observed.
- *Manageable*—The problem is limited to one type of construction procedure, which can easily be managed.

Example 1.3: Analyze Ineffective Issues in the Problem Statement

Avoid suggesting who is to blame, the cause, and a remedy in the mission statement and the problem statement, e.g.:

- *Assigning Blame:* "Our construction company's house foundation construction project takes 8 days longer on average than our major competitors take. The foundation design department needs to improve their work procedures to reduce the time needed to construct the house foundation."

  Comment: This problem statement implies that the foundation design department is to blame for the problem. If any project team member is from the foundation design group, he/she would manifest a defensive behavior, which could hurt the team's ability to collect and analyze data objectively.
- *Implying a Cause:* "Our construction company's house foundation construction project takes 8 days longer on average than our major competitors take. We should improve the communication process between the foundation designers and the concrete company."

  Comment: Implies that the communication process between the foundation designers and the concrete company needs to be improved. After collecting and analyzing data, communication between the foundation designers and the concrete company might not be the main cause of the problem.
- *Suggesting a Remedy:* "Our construction company's house foundation construction project takes 8 days longer on average than our major

Step 1: Identify Potential Problem(s) ➔
Sample Business – Jet Engine Manufacturing Company
Potential Problems
- Losing Revenue
- High Inventory
- High Resources Cost

Selected Problem – Losing Revenue
Process IPO – Applied to Sales Process
Analyzed – Inputs, Process, and Outputs

Step 2: Obtain Information/Data ➔ Obtained information directly or through the following sources:
- Customer
- Product Review/Audit
- Business Plans
- Managers and/or other employees
- Another source could be used

Brainstorming session – Follow the procedure; will provide a list of problems that might be creating the selected issue (losing revenue)

Step 3: Prioritize the Problem ➔ Utilize Nominal Group Technique to prioritize the identified problems.

Step 4: Characterize the Problem ➔ A list of problem characteristics is provided. Answer as many characteristic questions as applicable.

Step 5: Evaluate and Select ➔ Even though the problems have been prioritized using NGT, at this step, evaluate the prioritized problems in relation to problem characteristics and select one that could be used to write the mission statement.

Step 6: Prepare Mission Statement

Figure 1.5 Process flow chart of project selection.

competitors take. Install a designers' log on the company web page to speed up the communication process."

Comment: Without knowing the cause of the problem, finding an effective solution to the problem is impossible.

Exercise 1.2: Evaluate Problem Descriptions

Read each problem statement. Decide if a statement is effective or ineffective. Rewrite any ineffective statement.

1. Our on-time delivery of systems is low.
2. Our service department on an average receives 20 complaint telephone calls per week about unsatisfactory service.
3. Communication between our departments at this facility is poor.
4. More than 40% of our customers responded in a mid-year survey that they were very or somewhat dissatisfied with our service response time.

Example 1.4: Presenting Different Objective Views from a Problem Statement

Problem: Too many software programs must be modified to support the installation of a message printing and packaging system. On average, 30% of all programs must be modified at least once, which causes missed project completion (due) dates and expenditures that are above the budgeted amount.

Objective 1: Reduce the number of program modifications.
Comment: There is a high probability that Objective 1 could be met by increasing the allocated program design time, but that would not guarantee that programs would not require modification by the program team and that project due dates would not be missed.

Objective 2: Reduce the number of project run-over days from defined due date.
Comment: Objective 2 might focus on scheduling an additional programming resource or overtime hours to complete the installation by due date.

Objective 3: Reduce the installation margin so that the actual cost of installation will not exceed budget.
Comment: Objective 3 focuses on completing the installation project within budget estimates.

Choosing between the three objectives will be determined by the concern that is of most importance to the business: customers complain about installation due dates being missed; the cost incurred is high, and the installation due date is being missed; or program modification is required when the installation design is defective.

Exercise 1.3: Evaluate Mission Statements

Mission statements include problem and objective descriptions. Read these mission statements and provide an opinion about whether the statements are effective or ineffective. If a statement is ineffective, indicate how it could be improved.

1. Reception (guest checkout desk) at Hotel X does not inform the Housekeeping group quickly when a guest checks out of the hotel.
   Objective: Improve communications between Reception and Housekeeping to reduce the time needed for room cleaning/preparation.
2. Shipping Department takes too long to ship spare parts to dealers.
   Objective: Reduce the time it takes for parts to reach dealers.
3. We need a project scheduling and tracking website to plan a project's activities, to target milestone dates, and to track the actual completion of planning activities.
   Objective: Procure and install e-project management system by the end of the fiscal year.
4. Credit Corporation C experienced interest loss of $1 million last year due to billing errors and the resulting late credit card payments.
   Objective: Minimize the interest loss resulting from card billing errors.

1.8 PROJECT TEAM SELECTION

Team members chosen to work on solving a problem should be the most qualified individuals in the company. Showing appreciation of differences in team members is the key to acknowledging the value of each team member. Differences are the "raw material" for healthy discussions among the team members. The team selection process should follow these steps:

- Business areas that are the most closely connected to the problem should be identified. Ask:
  - Problem ***location***—Where is the problem observed?
  - Problem ***source***—Where could sources or causes of the problem be found?

- Problem ***root cause and solution***—Who has knowledge, understanding of the problem, or capabilities to uncover the root cause(s) of the problem?
- Group ***to implement problem solution***—What group in the business organization would be helpful in implementing a solution?

- Team members should represent the required business areas.
- Each team member should have direct and detailed personal knowledge of some part of the problem.
- Time required for meetings and time required for team-related work between meetings should not be during the team members' spare time.
- Team members should be able to accurately describe the processes associated with the problem and the interconnecting links associated to the problem elements.

Members selected for the project team should have as many of the following qualities as possible:

- Participates based on agreed upon goals/objectives
- Listens and analyzes all brainstorming ideas
- Has clear objectives
- Accepts differences
- Engages in healthy conflict
- Not dominating
- Trusts others in group
- Supports team decision process
- Shares information with team members
- Clearly perceives roles and work assignments (Expectations about the role of each team member should be clearly defined. When action is taken, assignments are clearly made and are accepted and carried out. Work should be fairly distributed among the team members.)

Once the project team has been identified, the team leader must develop the project plan and start thinking about how to manage the project from implementation to final documentation.

1.9 PROJECT PLANNING AND MANAGEMENT

Project planning starts once the project has been identified. The first step in the process is project justification and approval. Generally, the assigned project leader develops a document known as the *Project Proposal* for project justification and approval. Once the project is approved, the project leader's responsibility is to achieve the project objectives within budget and on time. This process is known as *Project Management.*

1.9.1 Project Proposal

A business determines how the project proposal form is developed. A sample format is presented in Figure 1.6. A project proposal generally begins with identification of the project:

Project: ______________________________
Project #: ______________________________

Key sections in the proposal should include:

Problem Statement: Describe the problem/opportunity that is forcing the business to develop the proposal. Answer important questions such as:

- What is the problem?
- Under what conditions does the problem occur?
- What are the extent and the impact of the problem?

Example: "In the past 2 years, 150 cases of customer complaints have occurred in the U.S. market: 65 of 100 printing through message packaging systems were installed that were more than 10 days after customers' requested dates. Customer complaints and ad hoc attempts to resolve installation issues caused loss of productivity (i.e., wasted time and productivity), internal conflict among staff, and loss of potential revenues and repeated business."

Objective Statement: State what is expected to be accomplished in specific, measurable, observable, and manageable terms once the project is completed, based on a given budget and time duration.

Example: "To reduce from 65 to 25 of 100 installations of printing through message packaging systems taking more than 10 days from the customer-requested date by improving the process capability from 1.1 sigma to 2.2 sigma in the next 6 months. This will provide a 2.7 times improvement in the process."

Project: ____________________ **Project #:** ______________

Problem Statement:
Objective Statement:
Expected Benefits:

Project Scope:
Project Criteria:
Project Plan:
Project Team and Expertise:

General Information:
Business Strategy:
Critical Quality Issue:
Current Process Capability:
Comments (Remarks):

Project Review Dates (Dates to Complete Each Phase)

Start Date:	______________	**Define Date:**	____________
Measure Date:	______________	**Analyze Date:**	____________
Improve Date:	______________	**Control Date:**	____________
Closure Date:	______________		

Approval Signatures:

Functional Manager		**Champion**	
______________	______ **Date**	______________	______ **Date**
Experts		**Team Leader**	
______________	______ **Date**	______________	______ **Date**
Other		**Other**	
______________	______ **Date**	______________	______ **Date**

Figure 1.6 Sample project approval form.

Expected Benefits: Identify the importance of the project and its relationship to the company's business strategy. State the financial benefits that are expected and how these benefits will be achieved.

Example: "Targeted savings: DPMO reduction (defects per million opportunities):

- Reduction of system installation delays (from 65 to 25 of 100 system installations that are completed beyond 10 days of the customer-requested date).

The team would expect total financial benefits of $100,000 before taxes in the next 12 months and an additional cost savings of $20,000. The qualitative benefits would be reduction in staff conflicts, reduced customer complaints, and improved customer satisfaction."

Project Scope: Specifically identify what is included and what is excluded in the scope of this project.

Example: "The project team will focus on the process from order booking through system installation: starts once the customer signs the contract and ends when the system installation is complete. Customer credit check and payment days are excluded from the process."

Project Criteria: State the relationship of this project to other projects as applicable. If this project is a part of a program (a program is made up of several projects), identify and link to the program. Specify if ROI is required or if any specific person/group is to approve the activity/output.

Example: "Message printing through packaging system's pricing policy will be updated based on the results (output) of this project."

Project Plan: Identify key activities that would lead to the project objectives.

- Develop material and process flow charts.
- Collect routing and volume data.
- Collect material lead time.
- Develop area layout with assumed constraints.
- Develop hardware and software integration milestone activities.

Project Team and Expertise: State the responsibilities of individuals/groups.

- Management team
- Project leader and his/her team—Core team members who have the strongest interest in the process improvement (These individuals are involved in day-to-day work on the project and devote a significant amount of their time to the project.)
- Core team members—Subject matter experts who will be called upon from time to time if specialized knowledge is required for the project

Note: Team leaders must define their responsibilities and provide a realistic expectation of the time commitment required.

General Information: Any general information about the business strategy, critical quality issues, current process capability, and comments (remarks). Review dates and approval signatures are also key areas in a project proposal.

Financial Benefits: Give special attention to financial benefits. Financial benefits should be estimated based on the business case language, which should come directly from the owner. If the business owners are not identified, the team will need to draft its own rationale. Financial benefits may change as the project progresses from one stage to the next. Therefore, the following are critical to estimate financial benefits:

- Financial benefits should be estimated at the beginning of the project. They should be linked to business strategy.
- Financial benefits should be based on the project definition, best available data, assumptions, and auditable benefits. They should be adjusted as the project progresses through the different phases of the DMAIC process and reaches implementation stage.
- As process performance is measured against the baseline, any incremental improvement will be measured and recognized.
- As the project goes through the Analyze phase, the team determines the root causes of the problem and assesses the assumptions used in estimating the benefits. Financial estimates should be revised to incorporate the new data.
- As the best solution is selected to improve the process, a complete cost/benefit analysis should be done to incorporate the cost of implementing the selected solution and should be adjusted the bottom-line benefits of the improvement (projected benefits).
- As the project is implemented, measure and report the actual benefits.

Note: It is important to list all the assumptions made at the different stages of the project.

1.9.2 Project Management

Project management can be described in simple terms:

- Project management is the business of securing the end objectives in the face of all risks and problems that are encountered from beginning to end of the project.
- Project success depends largely on carrying out the constituent tasks in a sensible sequence and deploying resources to best advantage.

Project Leader: As a minimum, the project charter must provide that the Project Leader will:

- Be accountable for accomplishing the project objective with the available or anticipated resources and within the constraints of time, cost, and performance/technology.
- Clearly define the "deliverables" to be given to the sponsor (champion) at the end of the project.
- Maintain prime customer liaison and contact.
- Be responsible for establishing the project organization and provide an effective orientation for the project staff at the beginning of the project.
- Provide for a well-balanced workload for the project team.
- Ensure that the best performers are assigned to work on the "critical path" activities of the project.
- Develop and maintain project plans (who does what, for how much, and when).
- Negotiate and contract with all functional disciplines to accomplish the necessary work packages within time, cost, and performance/technology.
- Provide technical, financial, and schedule requirements direction.
- Analyze and report project performance.
- Define and communicate security and safety requirements for the project as appropriate.
- Serve as an effective conductor in coordinating all-important aspects of the project.
- Get problems "out in the open" with all persons involved so that problems can be resolved.
- Make a special effort to give recognition to each staff member for his/her individual accomplishments.
- Maintain a current milestone chart that displays planned milestones and actual achievement of milestones.
- Review the technical performance of the project on a continual basis.
- Prepare a formal agreement if there is any scope change agreed to with the sponsor (champion).

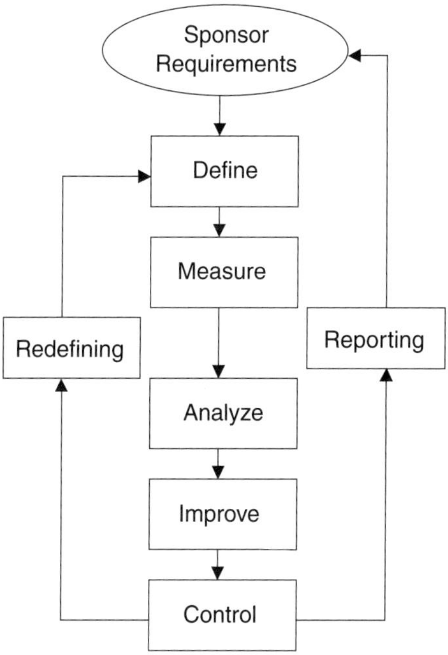

Figure 1.7 Project activities flow chart.

Project Activities: A project activities flow chart is presented in Figure 1.7.

Project Success: Potential challenges to the project's success include:

- Sponsor (Champion) is not actively involved.
- Project objectives are not clearly and precisely defined.
- Results metrics is not clearly defined.
- Project team is large (ideal size is 8 ± 2).
- Team members do not have enough time to support the project.
- Project does not support the business strategy.
- Very difficult to obtain the required data.
- Team members do not have proper training.

Exercise 1.4: Project Activity

Develop project approval information to cover the first three sections of the sample form presented in Figure 1.6.

1.10 PROJECT CHARTER

Generally, a project charter is a one-page report, presenting business information about the project. A project charter is the easiest way to communicate information about the project to others in the company. It includes the following, but it is not limited to only to these items:

- Business Case—Briefly states how the project is related to the business (organization)
- Goal Statement—Primarily contains the mission statement with expected benefits
- Project Plan/Time Line—Provides the project schedule with some key milestone activities and sigma metrics (if possible) (The project schedule should include at least the time line for the different phases of the DMAIC process.)
- Opportunity Statement—Presents statements about the project that will provide qualitative and quantitative benefits to the business
- Scope—Identifies the key issue areas
- Team Members—Identifies full-time and part-time participating team members

A sample project charter is presented in Figure 1.8.

1.11 SUMMARY

Overview information presented in this chapter includes:

- Recent past history of quality leading to the birth of the Six Sigma concept
- Discussion of how the business market has changed and its expectations
- Statistical meaning of sigma
- Qualitative and quantitative meaning of Six Sigma
- Organizational commitments and responsibilities in a Six Sigma program
- Quality and business loss relationship
- Road map for Six Sigma process (a brief definition of each step in the process)
- Impact of Six Sigma program on organizational structure
- IPO analysis approach
- Problem ranking procedure
- Problem characteristics

Project Charter
Manufacturing Cycle Time Reduction for Product XYZ

Business Case: Because the customer is expecting a quality product with on-time delivery at a competitive price, the company must produce the product with increased quality and reduced cycle time and business cost. This project will reduce manufacturing cycle time.

Goal Statement: Reduce the manufacturing cycle time

- For product XYZ1 from 45 calendar days to 30 calendar days, 33% cycle time reduction by **Month Year**
- For product XYZ2 from 95 calendar days to 70 calendar days, 26% cycle time reduction by **Month Year**

- Improve the inventory turns from 4 to 4.5 per year by **Month Year**
- Reduce inventory (Raw, WIP, and Finished) from **$XX millions to $YY millions by Month Year to provide $(XX – YY)** freed-up capital

Project Plan/Timeline: Based on **Year XXXX** objectives, Six Sigma goal metrics projections:

	Six Sigma Metric		
Product	Jul XX	Oct XX	Dec XX
XYZ1	1.4	1.6	1.8
XYZ2	1.7	1.9	2.1

Opportunity Statement: Reducing the manufacturing cycle time will:

- Speed product delivery
- Reduce inventory
- Reduce manufacturing cost
- Improve customer satisfaction

Scope: Reduce the manufacturing cycle time of products XYZ1 and XYZ2 by resolving/minimizing the following issues:

- Product stability
- Engineering support on the manufacturing floor
- On-time delivery of quality material on the manufacturing floor
- Process reengineering the manufacturing activities

Team Members: John Smith – Black Belt (Team Leader);
Dave Moore – Champion; Thomas Murphy – Master Black Belt;
Robert Lynch – Green Belt: Ram Dosi – Green Belt;
Carol Perez – Financial Support; Brad Potter – Expert

Figure 1.8 Sample of project charter (names of team members are hypothetical).

- Description of problem and development of mission statement
- Project team selection process
- Project proposal development
- Project leader's responsibilities
- Potential challenges to project success
- Project charter

The program implementation structure has been defined, the project mission has been stated, the project team has been selected, and the team has defined how to plan and manage the project. Think about answers to the following questions before moving on to the discussion in Chapter 2 (*Define*):

- Has the project team charter been defined clearly, including business case, problem and mission statement, project scope, milestones, roles and responsibilities, and communication plan?
- Who are the improvement project team members, including Project Leader/Black Belts, Master Black Belts/Coaches, Team Members, and Experts?
- Has each member of the team, including the Team Leader, been properly trained in DMAIC?
- Will the team meet regularly?
- Do the team members regularly have 100% attendance at team meetings? If any team member is absent and appoints a substitute to attend the meeting, does the substitute preserve cross-functionality and full representation?
- Has the project work been fairly and/or equitably divided and delegated among team members who are qualified and capable of performing work? Is each member of the team contributing?
- Are there any known constraints that would limit the project work? How is the team addressing them?
- How is the team tracking and documenting their work?
- Has the team been adequately staffed with the required cross-functionality? If not, what additional resources are available to the team to minimize the gap?

REFERENCES

1. http:/www.hammerandco.com/PowerOfProcessFrames/PowerOfFrames9.html.

2. Hammer, M. 1996. *Beyond Reengineering*, Harper Collins Publishers, New York, 1996, Part I (Work) and Part II (Management).

ADDITIONAL READING

Dean, J.W., Jr. and J.R. Evans. 1994. *Total Quality*, West Publishing, St. Paul, MN, Chapter 1.

2

DEFINE

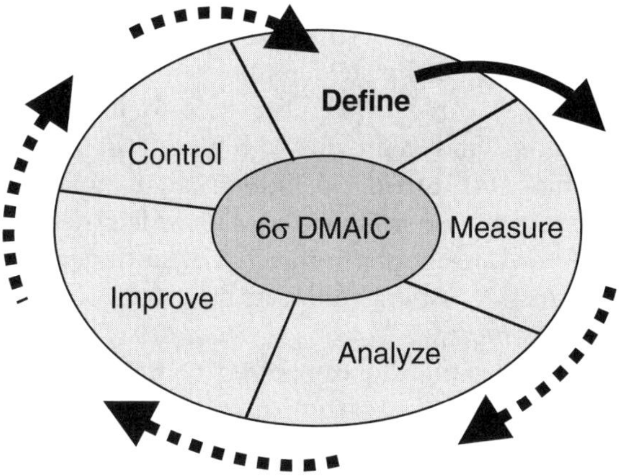

Define means to establish the cause of a problem and to set the boundaries of the problem. The **D**efine phase helps the team to picture the process over time and provides insight for the team about where the focus of improvement efforts should be (e.g., on improving the door seal on a frost-free refrigerator). *Define* also applies to customers, customer needs, and customer requirements (known as critical to quality characteristics or CTQs) and to the core business processes involved.

CTQs are the key measurable performance characteristics of any product, process, or service that satisfy external (ultimate) customers. CTQs must be met.

In the **D**efine phase, it is critical *define* who the customers are, what their requirements for products and services are, and what their expectations are. It is also important to *define* the project's boundaries—where to start and where to stop the process. Additionally, there must be definitions of the process and what the team must improve. Process understanding can be obtained by mapping process flow. Sections include:

2.1 THE CUSTOMER

The traditional definition of a customer is "someone who buys what the supplier (company) sells," but in today's global competitive market, the traditional definition is neither a precise nor a complete definition. A better definition is "a customer is a person who a company/supplier tries to understand (e.g., their reactions and expectations) and to provide with products/services that meet the customer's needs." This much broader definition is far more useful in today's increasingly complex business environment with its wide variety of customers. A customer does not see or care about a company's organizational structure or its management philosophies. A customer only sees the products and experiences the services offered by that company.

A company/customer relationship can be very complex. In the following list, who is a customer of a pharmaceutical company?

- The patient, who uses the medicine
- The pharmacist, who dispenses the medicine
- The physician, who prescribes the medicine
- The wholesaler/distributor, who is an intermediary between the manufacturer and the pharmacy
- The Food and Drug Administration scientists and officials, who approve the use of medicine
- An insurance company that pays indirectly for the medicine

The answer is *all* in the list are customers. Therefore, a pharmaceutical company must understand the requirements (needs) of all of these individuals and institutions.

Another type of company is one that produces consumer goods. This company has at least two types of customers: individuals who purchase and use the company's products and retailers. A customer goods company can influence these customers in two ways:

- The company wants retailers to carry its products, to allocate substantial shelf space to them, and to promote the products in advertising pieces.
- The company wants to influence customers to select and use in its products.

This presents a very complex company/customer relationship. The fundamental relationship between a company and its customers is not based on the exchange of products or services for money. It is actually based on providing valued products/services that meet customer needs in a timely manner and at competitive prices.

"What is a business?" If contemporary managers, executives, and economists were asked this question, most likely they would answer, "The mission of a business is to create shareholder value." This answer is neither irrational nor unreasonable, but nonetheless it is "wrong." Why?

Because shareholders provide capital that produces an income stream, shareholder concern must be central to an enterprise. Yet, exclusive focus on capital and those who provide it can be a distraction in a company from what really counts. Fundamentally, every company is in the same business—the business of "identifying and meeting customer needs." Customers *define* product/service needs that a manufacturer/supplier delivers. Customers can be divided into three groups: internal, external, and stakeholders.

Note: Unfortunately, shareholder concern was not a primary concern during the 1960s and the 1970s. Many executives ran their companies as if the companies were their personal businesses. These executives followed business strategies that mainly boosted their egos and personal incomes. Many received a nasty surprise in the takeover wave of the 1980s.

Internal Customers. Internal customers are a part of the total process if they receive internal/external output and utilize it as an input in their process to support their customers. These customers may be another internal customer or the external ultimate customer (the ultimate user of a product/service).

External Customers. External customers are not only product/service users, but also governmental agencies (e.g., regulators and law enforcement agencies) and the public (or community). An external customer could be domestic or foreign. Most business revenue is generated from external customers, making them the most important customers.

Stakeholders. Stakeholders sponsor the project. Periodically, the project team reports project status to stakeholders. Stakeholders impact the process or the process impacts them.

Customers and Critical to Quality Characteristics

If a company is working on something that is aligned to its strategic business priorities, then any improvements made for an internal customer will ultimately lead to a quantitative improvement for external customers. The product/service performance characteristics must also satisfy customers. Additionally, a supplier must understand the needs of customers. Customer-needs information can be collected by surveys, e-surveys, focus groups, etc. Information collected must be translated into comments, issues, and specifications. These comments, issues, and specifications then become customer CTQs. A CTQ is a product or a service characteristic that must be met to satisfy a specification or a requirement(s) of a customer (i.e., the recipient of a final or an end product/service, generally an external customer). A CTQ may also be referred to as project Y [as in $Y = f(X)$]. The following example relates CTQs to customers.

Suppose that your company produces software packages for sale to customers (external). To define design specifications and develop the software, you must understand the CTQs of the customers. You also must understand time-to-market, total software development cost, and on-time delivery of quality software (in terms of defects) to meet customers' needs. Customers (internal and external) can be identified as:

- Purchasers/users of the software
- Stakeholders imposing requirements on the software:
  - Shareholders
  - Regulators
  - Government agencies
- Users of internal software
  - Business partners

Once identified, customers can have different requirements that must be considered in determining CTQs. Therefore, to ensure that the "proper" requirements have been considered when collecting customer data, all possible customer and stakeholder groups must be identified. Internal stakeholders often speak for external stakeholders (customers); their process requirements must be met if the business is to be successful. Key internal stakeholder groups and their requirements could include:

- Financial—Internal Revenue Service (IRS), Securities and Exchange Commission (SEC)

Identify → **Research** → **Translate**

Figure 2.1 Steps of a CTQ Defining Process

- Legal—Regulatory agencies
- Compliance—Government agencies
- Human Resources—Occupational Safety and Health Administration (OSHA), Equal Employment Opportunity (EEO)

Therefore, the term "needs" (requirements) must consider stakeholder groups and customer segments to accurately determine CTQs.

CTQs Defining Process

Defining customer CTQs is a three-step process:[1] identify, research, and translate (Figure 2.1). The process delivers:

- Prioritized list of internal and external customers and stakeholders
- Prioritized customer needs
- CTQs to support needs

Identify: Customer—As presented in Figure 2.1, and with the types of customers identified with examples in the previous section, the next step in the process is to prioritize the customers. The highest priority goes to the external (ultimate) customer, prioritized as:

1. External customer (ultimate customer)
2. Individual/groups that have direct or indirect responsibility for the product, service, or process:
   - Business shareholders
   - Internal/external regulators
   - Government agencies
3. Internal/external service groups and material suppliers:
   - Business partners

Listening to customers and collecting pertinent data that reflect their input are important. Internal customers often develop solutions for the ultimate customer and their requirements. Internal customer departments could include:

- Business development
- Financial

- Personnel
- Legal
- Safety and security

Example 2.1: A CTQ Process—House Construction Proposal

The process is a house construction proposal from a general contractor to an external customer (ultimate customer). An architect will develop a house design package for a general contractor (internal customer). The package will include a house design, drawings, and construction cost estimates. The general contractor will prepare the final document for an external (ultimate) customer.

Identify Internal and External Customers:

Internal Customer(s)

-
-
-
-

External Customer(s)

-
-
-
-

Identify CTQs:

Sample CTQs: House Design Quotation

- House design to meet customer requirements
- House layout to meet space requirements
- House construction to meet budget and schedule requirements
-
-
-
-

Once customers have been identified, the next step is to research the customers.

Research Customer—Before beginning this step, first determine how well you understand and listen to your customers. Do you have little or no information or do you have detailed information? Are you confident about the quality of your customer information? If data are historical, answer the following:

- What do you know about the data?
- What is your level of certainty that your customer data represent the opinions/needs of the majority of your specified customers and/or groups?
- Are your data reliable and representative of all your customers?

A natural progression of this step is that you might start with no information, but conclude with quantified, prioritized customer needs and expectations, as well as information about your competitor.

The three elements of a Research Customer process (Figure 2.2) include:

- Collect data.
- Analyze data.
- Prioritize data.

A basic guideline for Research Customer is presented in Table 2.1.

Note: A detailed discussion of data collection may be found in the *Data Collection Plan* and *Data Presentation Plan* sections of Chapter 3 (*Measure*).

Collect data. Based on the available information, determine if additional information is needed, e.g., to fill "data gaps." Then develop a data collection plan to close the gap(s) between "where you are" and "where you need to be." Data can be collected in several ways, e.g., sampling methods include:

- Listen to sales representative, service representative, and customer complaints and to customer compliments.
- Analyze product returns.
- Perform a direct contact survey.
- Analyze contract cancellations.
- Survey, e.g., with direct mail questionnaires and e-questionnaires (website).
- Analyze customer defections.
- Interview new customers.
- Interview focus groups.

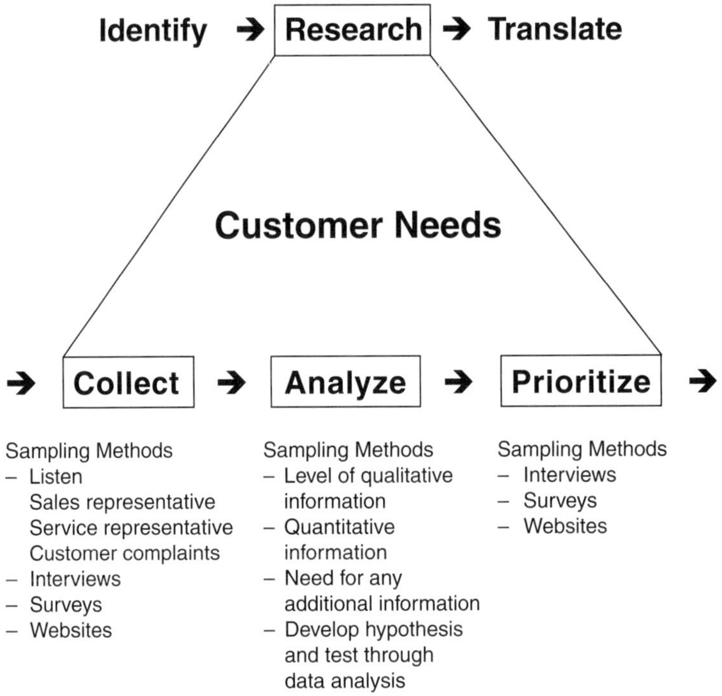

Figure 2.2. Research Customer Analysis

Analyze data. As data are collected, a *high level* of data analysis will indicate:

- If any additional information is needed
- If complaint data indicates the cause of dissatisfaction (which could facilitate collecting the additional needed data)

Sometimes the initial analysis reveals that additional information still is needed.

This high-level data analysis will identify customer requirements and help the team to develop a detailed plan to validate and translate "the voice" of the customer. As data are collected and analyzed, understanding the following is critical:

- What percent of the customer base is covered by data collection?
- What level of customer needs will be satisfied by the selected priorities?
- How reliable are the data?
- How is information collected, analyzed, and prioritized?

Table 2.1. Selecting the Appropriate Research Methods

Input:	No information (data)
Research Method:	Analyze information requirements. Interview individual/focus groups. Listen to customer complaints.
Output: What you get:	Customer needs and wants providing general ideas; combination of qualitative and quantitative information; unprioritized
Input:	If preliminary customer needs and wants are known
Research Method:	Interview individual/focus groups. Analyze underlying needs and develop specific questions.
Output: What you get:	Customer needs and wants — Clarified; more specific; prioritized Customer input to list — Best in class; may be a competitor
Input:	Qualitative; prioritized customer needs and wants
Research Method:	Survey — Face to face; regular mail; electronic mail; telephone Questions based on most important requirements
Output: What you get:	Quantified and prioritized customer needs and wants May get competitor's comparative information

- What competitor information has been collected?
- What level of "gap" analysis is performed prior to collecting any data?

Collected data may be either *qualitative* or *quantitative* or a *combination* of both. Collected data could also be defined as independent or dependent variables. To establish a relationship between dependent and independent data, the project team may have to develop a hypothesis and then test it. The hypothesis concept is discussed in Chapter 4 (*Analyze*).

Prioritize data. Customer needs should be translated into product/service functionalities, which can be classified into five categories:

- Expected—Satisfaction derived from expected functionalities is directly proportional to the availability of these functionalities in the product/service, i.e., when they are fully functional.
- Required—Some customers have a specific requirement of functionalities. If required functionalities are not up to the required level, customers become dissatisfied. Yet, if the required functionalities were above the customer's required level, customer satisfaction would not increase, e.g., a mainframe computer's required up-time is 99%; during the last 5 days, up-time was 99.5%, but the customer/user satisfaction level did not increase.
- Optional—The customer is more satisfied if optional functionalities are added to the product/service, but the customer is not less satisfied in the absence of them, e.g., a five-speed standard transmission in an automobile instead of a four-speed standard transmission.
- Indifferent—If advanced functionalities were provided in a product/service, only a small fraction of customers would be interested in using these functionalities. These functionalities generally do not change customer satisfaction values, e.g., Microsoft® Office with a special feature such as Excel Solver.
- Reserve—Sometimes reserve functionalities cause dissatisfaction, particularly if they negatively impact the customer's plans or activities. Customer satisfaction then decreases, e.g., some vacation resorts provide computer games, but the parents prefer that their children engage in personal interaction.

Once the customer's information is prioritized, going back to the customer to validate the assigned priorities is critical. Communication with a customer might include interviews, surveys, and a website.

The Research Customer process is presented in Figure 2.2. In summary, at a minimum, Research Customer is a three-step process. If time permits, use additional steps to achieve a better understanding of customer "needs and wants:"

- Selecting the right tool to collect customer information is very important. If no customer "needs and wants" information is available, talk to or interview focus groups and evaluate: "What is important?" and "What are customer needs and wants?"
- After obtaining the preliminary customer "needs and wants" information, interview additional customers from different geographic locations to help develop specific requirements. Then prioritize the "needs and wants" requirements.

- Survey customers. Commonly used methods include:
  - Face to face
  - e-mail
  - Electronic
  - Mail
  - Telephone

Quantify the survey results and then try to analyze the competitor's information.

The conceptual relationship between customer satisfaction and product/service is presented in Figure 2.3. This concept is based on Kano's theory. The line passing through the origin at 45 degrees represents the situation in which customer satisfaction is directly proportional to the functionality of the product/service, meaning the product/service functionality is meeting customer needs. The customer is more satisfied with a more fully functional product/service (per customer needs) and is less satisfied with a lesser functioning product/service. According to Kano's definition, such requirements are known as "one-dimensional" requirements.

In Figure 2.3, if the customer satisfaction and product/service relationship resides in the first quadrant, the product/service will be unacceptable to customers and the business will not survive. If the product/service is functional and a good percentage of customer needs are being met, then the product/service and customer satisfaction relationship will fall in the second quadrant. However, to produce a fully functional product/service, a business must implement a continuous improvement program. A continuous improvement program will move the product/service and customer satisfaction meeting point into the third quadrant as shown by the dashed arrow. Yet, if the product/service is functional, but customer satisfaction is low, then the product/service and customer satisfaction relationship will fall in the fourth quadrant. This situation indicates the business is on a critical path for survival: the combination of customer satisfaction and product/service would need to follow the dashed-line arrow in the fourth quadrant.

Using an automobile as an example, priorities in a competitive market include:

- Automobile reliability and safety
- Driver and passenger comfort

If the automobile (the product) meets these requirements, it would be in the third quadrant. If the automobile is reliable and safe, but the driver and passengers are uncomfortable, the automobile will fall into the second quadrant. It is now on a critical path. For the business to survive, significant effort will be required by the business to make the automobile fully functional and to fully satisfy customers.

In a scenario in which the driver and passengers in the automobile are comfortable, but the automobile has reliability and safety ratings that are low, the rela-

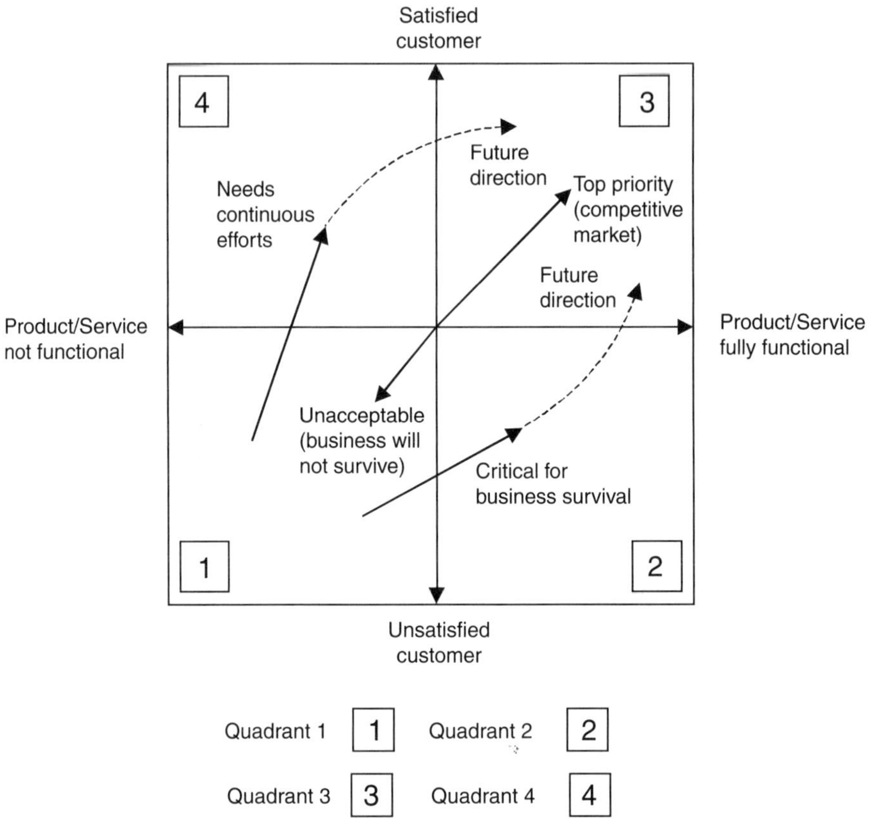

Figure 2.3. Product/Service Provider's Research Quadrants

tionship of product and customer satisfaction will reside in the fourth quadrant. In this case, improvement in reliability and safety of the automobile will need a continuous improvement effort for survival of the business.

Translate Customer Information—The third step to obtain customer CTQs is to translate the customer research data. The relationship of this step to previous steps is presented in Figure 2.4.

Ensure that all information (e.g., from team members and customers) is in the "same language," i.e., the information is presented consistently. Now compare research output with customers' suggested "needs and wants" and prepare a gap analysis. This gap analysis will lead to customer CTQs.

Note: "Same language" mainly refers to applicable *measuring units*, *environment*, and *constraints*. As an example, for an automobile in the U.S., gas mileage is

Identify ➔ Research ➔ Translate

Figure 2.4. Steps to Obtain CTQs

measured in miles per gallon, but in most other countries, gas mileage is measured in kilometers per liter. In some countries, automobile traffic is disciplined, i.e., it follows specific rules, while in other countries, it does not. Gasoline used in one country may be more environmentally friendly than the gasoline used in other countries.

If the customer information needs translation into "your language," follow these steps:

- Identify key issues—Take these issues and group them into categories or themes. Do not try to force customer comments into the categories you have created. List customer comments separately if they do not fit into a category.
- Write CTQs from the key issues—Document customer needs that represent issues. Sometimes a customer need may become part of a structural tree that represents an issue, which will lead to a CTQ. Ensure that the customer need is identified as a specific and measurable requirement and that it is understood by the customer and the project team. The team must have an unbiased approach in translating the customer needs.

Sample translations of customer data are presented in Table 2.2. As analyzed data are translated into CTQs, it is critical to have feedback from customers. Customer feedback can be obtained from numerous sources:

- Surveys
- Regular mail
- e-mail
- A website

Customer inputs have now been identified and segmented into their needs/requirements and wants and have also been translated and understood as customer CTQs. Next in the process is for the project team to understand the high-level process, but first consider Exercise 2.1.

Exercise 2.1: A Class Project

Build a house according to customer needs and wants. The customer negotiates a contract with the general contractor. The architect works for the general contactor. The architect designs the house and develops drawings and material and cost

Table 2.2. Translate—Sample Survey Analysis

Customer Comment	Key Issue	Customer Need	CTQ
"Difficult-to-understand professional language"	Communication not clear	Easy to read, understandable language	Give simple instructions to complete the survey in less than 10 minutes
"Too many questions to answer"	Takes a long time to finish survey	Consolidate questions	Use less than 20 questions that are pertinent to geographic location
"Takes too long to set up the equipment and bring it into production"	Simplify equipment set up	Shorter set-up time	Complete set up in less than 5 minutes
"Equipment breaks down all the time"	Equipment capability and down time	Equipment availability	Equipment availability better than 98%

estimates. The general contractor obtains a loan from a bank to build the house. The bank is a separate institution. Provide information for the following:

1. List internal and external customers.
2. Determine customer "needs and wants."
3. Recommend a method of data collection.
4. Assuming that the data collection method is a survey, brainstorm a list of questions to ask the external (final) customer.
5. Request that the customer fill out the survey.
6. Translate customer responses and issues into customer needs and wants and verify them with the customer.

2.2 THE HIGH-LEVEL PROCESS

The objective of creating a high-level process map is to achieve the same level of understanding among members of the project team concerning the process that the team will be using to improve the process and accomplish the project goal(s). So what is the process?

Process—The supplier(s) provides the input(s) and the business/organization performs one or more operations on the input and changes it into an output to meet customer demand (see Figure 2.5).

Guidelines—Two guidelines are important for constructing a high-level process map:

- Construct the process map to reflect the current process ("As Is").
- Keep the process map at a "high level," e.g., divide the process into approximately four to six key steps.

Once the high-level process is completed and validated, it will provide a common, base understanding for all team members. Eventually the team will need a *detailed* process map when working with the **M**easure and the **A**nalyze phases of the DMAIC process (**D**efine, **M**easure, **A**nalyze, **I**mprove, **C**ontrol). If team members find it necessary to develop a detailed process map immediately after completing the high-level process map, they should go ahead and complete it now.

Everyone takes inputs from suppliers, adds value through their processes, and provides an output(s) to meet or exceed the customer need(s) and related CTQs. It is not necessary for every operation to add value for the customer. This will become clear when the team works on the **A**nalyze phase of DMAIC process. Critical to remember is that the process map developed at this stage of the project must reflect the activities "As Is" (or just as they are) to correctly represent the way things are being done now. A sample high-level process map is presented in Figure 2.5.

Next is to analyze the business process mapping, which is also known as SIPOC: the **S**upplier(s) (S) for the process, the **I**nputs (I) to the process and the inputs coming from suppliers, the **P**rocess (P) your team is planning to improve, the **O**utputs (O) of the process, and the **C**ustomers (C) receiving the processed

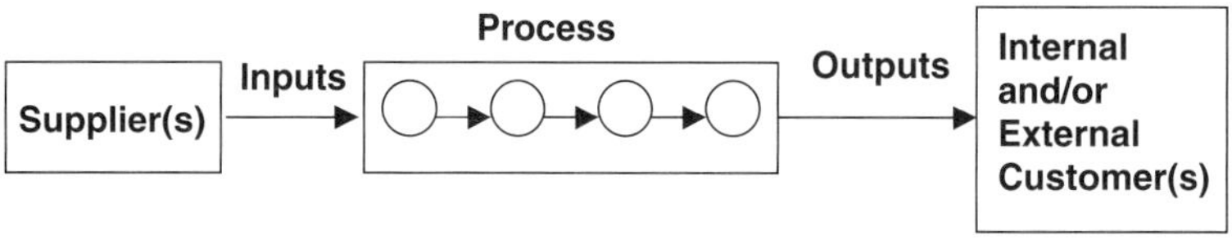

Figure 2.5. A Typical High-Level Process Map

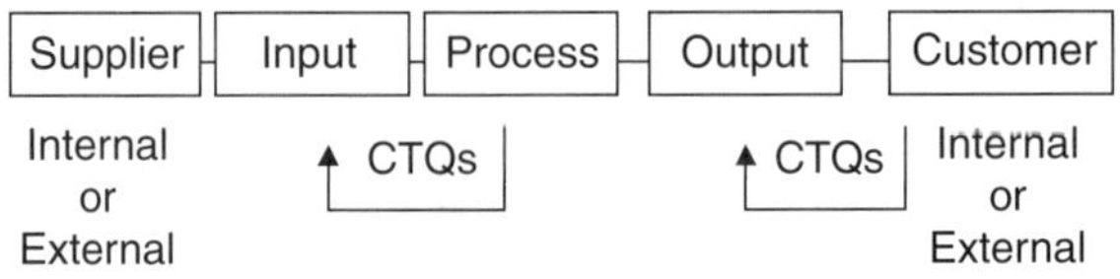

Figure 2.6. SIPOC Chart

outputs. A SIPOC diagram is presented in Figure 2.6. The terms in SIPOC can be defined as:

- Supplier—A source or a group of sources that provides the inputs to process
- Input—Resources (e.g., equipment, facility, material, people, technology, and utilities) and information (i.e., data) required to execute the process/operation(s).
- Process—A collection (series) of operations (activities) that is performed over one or more inputs that produces the output to meet customer demand (*Note*: The limits of a particular process or the Process Boundary are usually identified by the inputs and the outputs as outside the process boundary.)
- Output—The tangible product or service that results from the process to meet customer demand
- Customer (internal and/or external)—An individual and/or organization receiving the processed output (Remember: CTQs are the performance standards of critical measurable characteristics of a process or product that must be met to satisfy the customer.)

The SIPOC tool is especially useful when certain information is unclear:

- Who supplies inputs to the process?
- What specifications (CTQs) are placed on the inputs?
- Who are the true owners of the process?
- Who are the true customers of the outputs?
- What are the requirements (CTQs) of the customers?

Following these steps allows completion of the SIPOC diagram:

1. Begin with the process and map it in four to five high-level activities.
2. Identify the outputs of this process.
3. Identify the customers who will receive the outputs of this process.

4. Identify the inputs required for the process to function properly.
5. Identify the suppliers of the inputs.
6. Discuss with project sponsor, champion, and other involved stakeholders for verification.

Not required, but useful, is identifying the preliminary requirements (CTQs) of the customers. This will be verified during the **M**easure phase of the DMAIC process.

As an example, consider Tractor Dealer XYZ, in which manufacturers supply the product (tractors and accessories) and other suppliers provide the elements required to operate the dealership and support customers (e.g., diesel fuel, repair tools, cleaning supplies, etc.). Farmers purchase tractors and support products from the tractor dealership. The dealer makes financial arrangements for farmers (buyers) with financial institutions (banks). Farmers define tractor specifications to meet their needs. There is one exception: farmers have no color option for tractors. Each tractor manufacturer has its own defined color; all tractors from a specific manufacturer are painted the same color. The SIPOC diagram for Tractor Dealer XYZ is presented in Figure 2.7.

2.3 DETAILED PROCESS MAPPING

The process mapping concept is applicable to both product and service organizations. Advantages of process mapping include:

- Easy visualization of the total process
- Easy analysis of the total process
- Easy identification of non-value added and waste activities
- Easy communication of the impact of process improvement
- Easy identification of the process cycle time for each operation and for the total process

Next is developing the business process map. The concept is similar to the high-level process map, but each process section is mapped in more detail. Key steps in mapping and analyzing the business process flow chart include:

1. Define and name the process to be mapped. Establishing the start and stop points of a process is a critical first step in process mapping. Typically, the start point of a process is the first step that receives inputs from suppliers and the end point is delivery of the product or service to the customer.

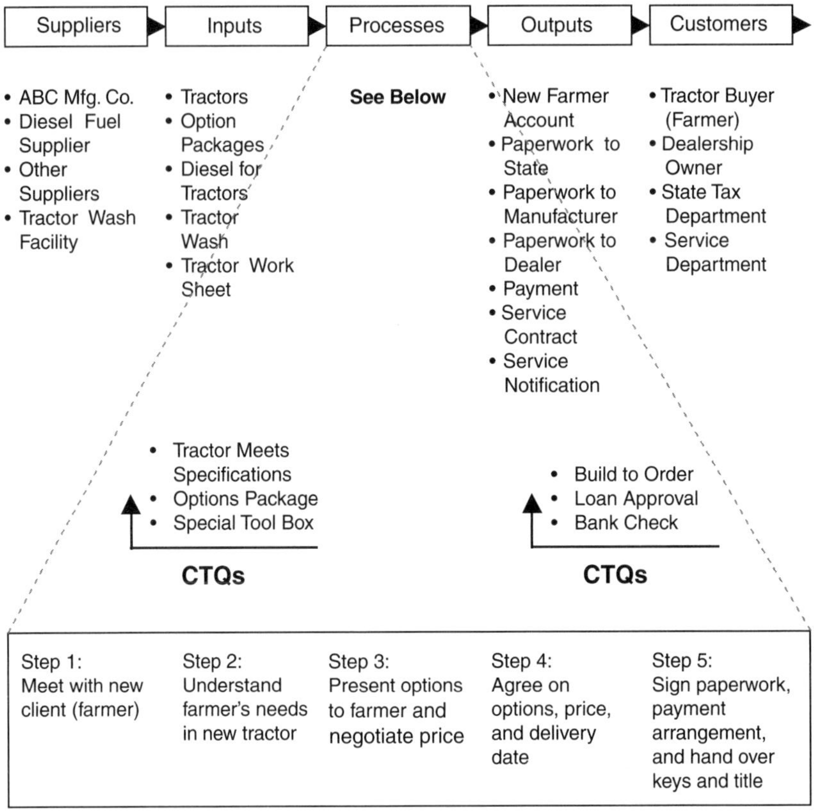

Figure 2.7. SIPOC Diagram for Tractor Dealer XYZ

2. Familiarize the team (participants) with the flow chart symbols.
3. Identify customer needs (CTQs) and outputs. Survey and convert customer needs into customer CTQs. Output must satisfy those CTQs on demand (on time).
4. Identify the process steps. Identify the sequence of process activities. Draw the process and diagram the flow consistently from top to bottom or from left to right.
5. Identify a decision point or branch point. Choose one branch and continue flow diagramming.
6. Identify the process that is unclear or unfamiliar to team members. Make a note and continue flow diagramming.

7. Brainstorm the major steps (tasks) in the work process. Do not be concerned about the sequence at this point. Ask questions such as "What really happens next in the process?" and "Does a decision need to be made before the next step?" and "What approvals are required before moving on to the next task?"
8. Repeat Steps 4 through 7 until the team reaches the last (or first) step in the process.
9. Go back and flow diagram the other branches.
10. Put the steps in the proper sequence. As this is done, the team may begin to add minor points as necessary. At this point, all the steps have been identified and sequenced. Now assign the appropriate symbols to each step (see the discussion in the *Flow Charting* section of Chapter 3) and connect the steps with arrows to show the flow of the process.
11. Identify critical inputs. Some inputs may be required at the beginning of the process, while others may be required during the process.
12. Identify each supplier from which the process owner receives each input.
13. Validate process map. To validate the map, make sure that the process is represented "As Is." Now work on process validation with key stakeholders and/or with functions that perform the process steps. A process has three possible versions:
    - ***What you think it is***—One that is based on the individuals who touch the process.
    - ***What it really is***—One that is based on reconciling what the process map really is. The consolidation of the first two versions of the process map constitutes what is referred to as the "As Is" process map. The effectiveness of the next two phases, **M**easure and **A**nalyze, will depend on the accuracy and detail of the process map.
    - ***What it should be***—As the team moves forward and conducts process analysis and problem solving, the third version of the process map—the "should be" map—is developed. Critical at this point is to check if the output from this process is meeting or exceeding the customer needs/requirements or if it is not.

As the team analyzes the process activities, the team should also try to determine answers for the following:

- Each decision point:
  - Is this a checking activity?
  - Is this a redundant check?

- Each rework loop:
  - Does this rework loop prevent the problem from recurring?
  - How long is this rework loop? (Analyze the loop in terms of number of activities/operations, time consumed, and resources required.)
  - Can this rework be prevented?
- Each regular activity:
  - What is the value added through the activity in relation to cost?
  - How can the team make the activity error-proof?
  - What is the time per event and can the cycle time be reduced?
- Each activity's supportive documentation and data:
  - Is this necessary?
  - How is the update?
  - Is there a single source or multiple sources?
  - Are tasks identified as value added, non-value added, and waste.

Commonly used terminology in a processing map includes:

- Cycle Time—Types of cycle times may be defined as:
  - Order to cash (revenue) cycle—Cycle time starts once the customer signs the purchasing contract and ends once the supplier delivers the product/service to the customer and the customer makes payment.
  - Product/Service delivery cycle—Cycle time starts once customer signs the purchasing contract and ends once the supplier delivers the product/service to customer.
  - Manufacturing cycle time—Cycle time starts once the product manufacturing starts and ends once the last activity/operation is complete.

- Process Time—Process time is the total time consumed on one unit of product/service, excluding any time due to delay and/or waiting, but including the time required for job set-up/preparation, inspection, processing, internal/external failure test, and moving to the next process.

- Delay Time—Total time lost due to waiting for anything is delay time (e.g., material and/or people to complete the process).

Delays are often "disconnect" processes. Sometimes delays create defects. Commonly observed elements can result in delays:

- Bottlenecks—Any location where assigned load is equal to or greater than available capacity.
- Conflicting objectives—The goals of one group can create problems or errors for another group, e.g., when one group is focusing on process speed while another group is concentrating on error reduction. One result may be that neither group accomplishes its objectives.

As the team continues to analyze the process map, other issues the team may encounter include:

- Common Problem Areas—This situation can occur when operations/activities are repeated at several locations in a process, e.g., a rotational part for a jet engine may go through two to four turning machines as part of the rough turning operation before it moves on to the finishing operation. These locations can provide insight into potential solutions. The team should encode these "disconnects" and highlight them directly on the process map.
- Gaps—The process seems to go off track or the defined process for a given activity is unclear or wrongly interpreted.
- Redundancies—If more than one group is responsible for the process, redundancies can occur when different groups take action, but are unaware that actions are being taken elsewhere in the process by another group.

Process mapping is a special situation of flow charting. The flow-charting concept will be discussed further in the *Measuring Tools* section of Chapter 3 (*Measure*). If the team leader was not in a position to develop the project charter at the end of Chapter 1, he/she must be in a position to develop one now.

Before moving on, consider Exercise 2.2.

Exercise 2.2: Develop a High-Level Process Map

As a class project, develop a high-level process map that includes:

- What is the name of the process?
- What are the outputs?
- Who are the customer(s) of those outputs?
- What are the inputs and their suppliers?
- Process:
  - Start point
  - End (completion) point

- First operation (activity)
- Last operation (activity)

2.4 SUMMARY

This chapter has been a continuation of the discussion of the Define phase of the DMAIC process. Key topics discussed in this chapter include:

- Customer definition—internal, external, and stakeholders
- Critical to quality characteristics (CTQ)
- Research customer
- Customer research methods
- Customer feedback
- Key steps of a total process from supplier through customer (SIPOC)
- Key definitions of the total process elements
- Process mapping

The project team must check *customers and CTQs* and *business process mapping* before proceeding to Chapter 3:

Customers and CTQs:

- Has the customer(s) been identified?
- Has the improvement team collected the "voice of the customer" (obtained feedback qualitatively and quantitatively)?
- What customer feedback methods were used to solicit customer input?
- Have the customer needs and requirements been translated into specific, measurable requirements?

Business Process Mapping:

- Have high-level and "As Is" process maps been completed, verified, and validated?
- Has a SIPOC diagram been developed describing the suppliers, inputs, process, outputs, and customers?
- Is the project team aware of the different versions of process maps, e.g., what the team thinks the process is vs. what the process actually is?

- Is the current "As Is" process being followed? If not, what are the discrepancies?
- What procedure was used to develop, review, verify, and validate the "As Is" process map?
- What tools and methodology did the team use to get through the **D**efine phase?

REFERENCES

1. Juran, J.M. 2002. Juran Institute's Transactional Breakthrough Strategy. Southbury, CT: Juran Institute. Chapters 1 and 2 from notes given to students in a Black Belt certification training class.

ADDITIONAL READING

Juran, J.M. and A.B. Godfrey. 1999. *Juran's Quality Handbook, Fifth Edition* New York: McGraw-Hill.

The Juran Institute. 2002. *The Six Sigma Basic Training Kit.* New York: McGraw-Hill.

3

MEASURE

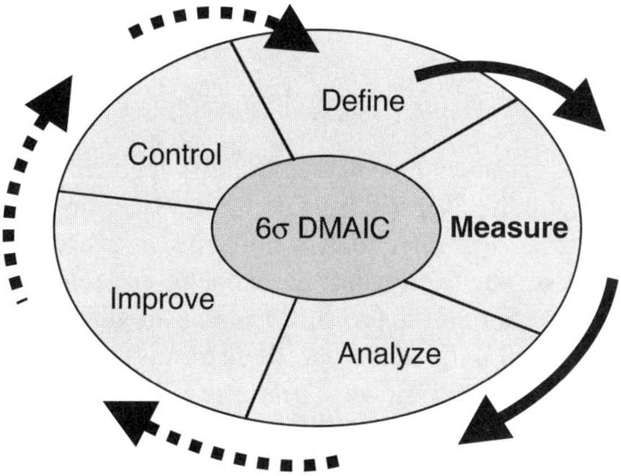

Process definition and data collection plans build validity and consistency into data. Data reflect process performance and provide insight and knowledge about a process. If a team wants to evaluate variation in a process, it will need to collect data. A data collection system is a type of measurement system.

Any business or organization must know "where it stands" currently if it is attempting to achieve a defined goal(s). Six Sigma uses a measurement system to establish a baseline, which will identify where a product/service is in relationship to defined goals. To establish a baseline, current measurements are needed. Once a business knows where it is and where it wants to go, existing gaps can be determined and the business can also assess the efforts and resources needed to reduce the gap(s) in product/service quality and thereby achieve the goal(s).

Think about the SIPOC process (**S**upplier-**I**nput-**P**rocess-**O**utput-**C**ustomer), in which measurement occurs at three different stages of the process—inputs, process, and outputs.

Input measures represent measures of the key CTQs (critical to quality characteristics) placed on suppliers. Input measures indicate supplier performance and also correlate to output measures. Input measures are defined as independent variables and are represented by the letter *X*. *Process measures* are internal to the process and include key control elements for improving the output measures. *Output measures* are defined as dependent variables and are represented by the letter Y. Meaningful process measures will correlate with output measures. The letter Y also represents process measures.

Output measures are used to determine how well customers' CTQs are being satisfied. Independent variables are represented by *X*s; dependent variables are represented by *Y*s. When appropriate independent variables are measured and tracked, they can be used to predict the dependent (*Y*) variable. The relationship is presented as:

$$Y = f(X_1, X_2, X_3, \ldots, X_n)$$

where one dependent variable (*Y*) is a function of (dependent on) *n* independent variables ($X_1, X_2, X_3, \ldots, X_n$). Once the project has a clear definition with a clear measurable *Y*, the process is studied to determine the key process steps and the key inputs for each process. The team will analyze the potential impact of each input with respect to the variation of the project *Y*. Inputs are then prioritized to establish a short list to study in more detail how these inputs can "go wrong." Once the cause for input failure is determined, a preventive action plan can be put into place. Discussion in this chapter will be limited to current data collection, data collecting tools, how to present data, some basic probabilistic distributions representing the data and their application, and a discussion of process capability.

Chapter topics include:

- 3.1 The Foundation of Measure
  - 3.1.1 Definition of Measure
  - 3.1.2 Types of Data
  - 3.1.3 Data Dimension and Qualification
  - 3.1.4 Closed-Loop Data Measurement System
- 3.2 Measuring Tools
  - 3.2.1 Flow Charting
  - 3.2.2 Business Metrics
  - 3.2.3 Cause-and-Effect Diagram
  - 3.2.4 Failure Mode and Effects Analysis (FMEA) and Failure Mode, Effects, and Criticality Analysis (FMECA)
    - 3.2.4.1 FMECA

3.1 THE FOUNDATION OF MEASURE

Every product/service goes through three stages of the SIPOC process—input, process, and output—as presented in Figure 3.1. These three stages are also critical stages for measurement. As identified earlier, output is dependent on input and process. There may be a variety of inputs that may go through the process to produce an output to meet customer needs on time. Inputs could be people, material, a machine, a procedure, an environment, etc. An example of *inputs*, *in process*, and *outputs* is presented in Example 3.1.

Example 3.1: Stages of an Architect's House Design Services

Identify stages for an architect's house design services and classify the variables into independent and dependent categories.

The architect's services can be divided into three stages—input, in process, and output. Variables for each stage are classified as:

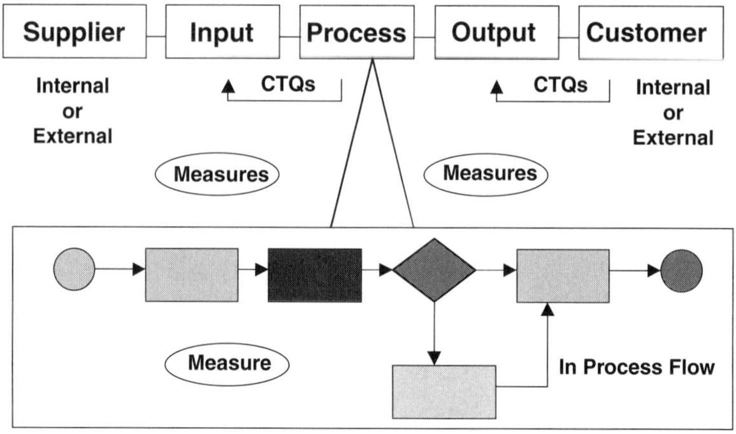

Figure 3.1. Measures in SIPOC Chart

- Input—Customer needs and wants are *independent* variables:
  - X_1—Master bedroom
  - X_2—Daughter's bedroom
  - X_3—Son's bedroom
  - X_4—Guest bedroom
  - X_5—Master bedroom bathroom
  - X_6—Main bathroom
  - X_7—Guest bedroom bathroom
  - X_8—Living room space
  - X_9—Kitchen and dining space
  - X_{10}—Extra storage space in kitchen
  - X_{11}—Sunlight windows in the ceiling

- In Process—Output is *dependent* on input and in process variables:
  - X_{20}—Total bedroom space
  - X_{21}—Total bathroom space
  - X_{22}—Total hallway space
  - X_{23}—House entrance space
  - X_{24}—Utilities space

- Output—The architect's service output must meet the customer's CTQs:
  - Y_1—House layout
  - Y_2—House material requirements
  - Y_3—House construction cost

All outputs may not be the same, i.e., there may be some variation in outputs. The next step is to investigate the sources of variation. There are two sources of variation—common cause and special cause.

Common cause is due to inherent interaction among input resources. Common cause is predictable, random, and normal. ***Analyze*** the key possible variations and ***improve*** solutions based on these variations. Key to minimizing common cause is focusing on fundamental process change.

Special cause is due to especially large influence by one of the input resources. Special cause is generally unpredictable and abnormal. ***Investigate*** specific measurements (data points) related to the special cause. ***Develop*** solution(s) for the special cause, implement the most appropriate solution, and ***measure*** again. Key to minimizing special cause is focusing on investigating special causes.

To develop a sound strategy for process control and improvement, and customer satisfaction, it is important to understand the sources of variation. Appropriately responding to the source of variation in a process provides the correct economic balance, as opposed to overreacting or underreacting to variation from a process.

If the process shows common cause variation, investigate all the data points. It is difficult to relate common cause variation to a few causal input factors (*X*s). If there is a common cause variation, then focus on fundamental process change. (A detailed analysis will be presented in the Analyze phase of the DMAIC process in Chapter 4, *Analyze.*)

If the process shows special cause variation, the appropriate action is to investigate those specific data points related to the special cause signals. In most cases, the analysis will show the relationship. The results should be integrated into an action plan as quickly as possible to address the special cause.

To build a strong foundation for measure, understanding Sections 3.1.1, 3.1.2, 3.1.3, and 3.1.4 is important.

3.1.1 Definition of Measure

Measurement is a *procedure* that provides the most general approach to any physical problem. *Measure* is a *reference standard* used for the quantitative comparison of properties. For a process or population of a product/service, measure describes:

- Dimension

- Surface
- Capacity
- Performance
- Quality
- Characteristics

Sample units of measure include:

- Product dimension—Inches, feet, and centimeters
- Product manufacturing cycle time—Hours, days, and weeks
- Product heat-treating surface—Square inches
- Product holding capacity—Gallons
- Product characteristics—Tight tolerances, surface hardness
- Product performance—Miles per gallon

Effectiveness and efficiency are two types of measures:

- Effectiveness of measures—Any process/system is meeting and exceeding the customer needs and requirements, e.g., service response time, percent product defective, and product functionality.
- Efficiency of measures—Any process/system is meeting and exceeding the customer requirements based on the amount of the resources allocated, e.g., product rework time, product cost, and activity time.

Measure can be qualitative or quantitative:

- Qualitative measure—A variable that normally is *not* expressed numerically is measured qualitatively. These variables differ in type, e.g., qualitative variables are sex, race, job title, etc. Qualitative variables can be subdivided into two categories—dichotomous qualitative variables and multiqualitative variables.
  - Dichotomous qualitative variables—These variables can be in only two categories, e.g., male or female, employed or unemployed, correct or incorrect, defective or satisfactory, elected or defeated, absent or present, etc.
  - Multiqualitative variables—These variables can be in more than two categories, e.g., job titles, colors, languages, religions, type of businesses, etc.
- Quantitative measure—A variable that is normally expressed numerically is measured quantitatively. These variables differ in degree, e.g.,

years of service, annual salary, etc. (Most of the discussion in this book will be related to quantitative measure.) Quantitative variables can be subdivided into two categories—discrete variables and continuous variables:

- Discrete variables—A discrete variable is based on counts. Some of the measurement observations fall in this category with a finite number of possible values, but the values cannot be subdivided meaningfully, e.g., the number of unacceptable parts in the received shipment.
- Continuous variables—A continuous variable has a large number of values with no special category label attached to any particular data value. Data can conceptually take on any value inside some interval. Continuous data are the actual measurement values, e.g., the amount of time to complete a task, the distance between two points, etc.

3.1.2 Types of Data

The assignment of numbers to characteristics that are being observed (i.e., collected), which is also a measurement, can yield four types of data of increasing complexity:

- Nominal data
- Ordinal data
- Interval data
- Ratio data

Nominal Data

The weakest level of measurement produces nominal data. These numbers are merely names or labels for different things and thus can serve the purpose of classifying observations about qualitative variables into mutually exclusive groups, e.g., "night" might be numbered as 0 and "day" as 1, but alternative labels of "night" = 10 and "day" = 3 would serve as well. Other examples of creating nominal data would be classifying defective units of a product as "0," good (nondefective) units as "1," or labeling houses on a street with 10, 21, 30, 41, etc. These examples confirm that it never makes sense to add, subtract, multiply, or divide nominal data, but these numbers can be counted. If there are five 0s based on the above-defined defective code, then there are five defective units.

Ordinal Data

These numbers are by their size order or they rank observations on the basis of importance, while intervals between the numbers or the ratio of such numbers are meaningless, e.g., assessments of a product as *great, good, average,* and *poor* might be recorded as 4, 3, 2, 1 or 10, 8, 6, 5. The important point is that larger numbers denote a more favorable assessment or a higher ranking, while smaller ones denote the opposite. Ordinal data make no statement about how much *more* or *less* favorable one assessment is compared to another. A 4 is deemed better than a 1, but not necessarily 4 times as good; a 100 is deemed better than a 10, but not necessarily 10 times as good; a 3 is deemed worse than 9, but not necessarily a third as good. Teaching staff titles at any university of professor, associate professor, and assistant professor, with an ordinal coding as 3, 2, and 1, is simply a coding and does not imply that, in some sense, professors are viewed as more important than assistant professors. Similarly, a nominal coding of male = 10, female = 3 does not imply the superiority of males over females any more than a coding of male = 1, female = 4 denotes the opposite. There are no arithmetic operations with the data.

Interval Data

Interval data are somewhat more sophisticated. These data allow at least addition and subtraction. Interval data are numbers that *by their size* rank observations in order of importance and the distance or interval between the points is comparable, but their ratios are meaningless. Because these data do not possess an intrinsically meaningful origin, their measurement starts from an arbitrarily located zero point and utilizes an equally arbitrary unit distance for expressing intervals between numbers. Commonly used examples of interval data are temperature scales. The Celsius scale places 0 at the water-freezing point and places 100 at the water-boiling point. The Fahrenheit scale places 0 far below the water-freezing point in Celsius and the water-boiling point is far above the Celsius water-boiling point. Within the context of either scale, the unit distance (degree of temperature) has a consistent meaning. Each degree Celsius equals 1/100 of the distance between water's freezing and boiling points; similarly, each degree Fahrenheit equals 1/180 of that distance. An interesting point is that zero, being arbitrarily located, does not denote the absence of the characteristic being measured. Also note that any ratio of the corresponding Celsius figures (for 45°F and 10°F) does not equal to 3:1, but for Fahrenheit, the ratio is well over 4:1.

Ratio Data

Ratio data (numbers) are the most sophisticated data. Ratio data are the most useful type of data and can be ranked by:

- Size—Size ranks data observations in order of importance and between which intervals. All types of arithmetic operations can be performed with each datum because these numbers have a natural or true zero point that denotes the complete absence of the characteristic they measure and makes the ratio of any two such numbers independent of the unit of measurement.
- Importance—Ratio data are meaningful data, e.g., the measurement of distance, height, area, volume, or weight produces ratio data. As an example, it is meaningful to rank height data and to say that a 20-foot pole is taller than one of 10 feet, which is taller than one of 5 feet. Pole data give the kind of ordinal data information. It is also meaningful to compare intervals between pole height data: it is easy to say that the distance between 20-foot and 10-foot poles is two times the distance between 10-foot and 5-foot poles. Furthermore, these data are ratio data because it can safely be stated that a 15-foot pole is three times taller than a 5-foot pole. Even if the unit of measurement is changed, e.g., from feet to inches or from feet to yards, this conclusion does not change.

3.1.3 Data Dimension and Qualification

Next in data measurement is identifying data dimension and qualification. Identifying data dimensions (or units) is important. Data dimensions support activities such as data collection and analysis, process validation, quality improvements, etc. Remember from Section 3.1.1 that the *qualitatively* measured variables differ in type, e.g., sex, race, job title, etc. and that there are no established units of measurement (a unit). The *quantitatively* measured variables involve both a number and a standard of comparison, e.g., 3 feet, 5 pounds, and 25 minutes are the numbers and the standard of comparison (i.e., feet, pound, or minute) is arbitrarily established and is called a unit.

Abstract data must be broken down into identifiable and measurable data. For example, *appearance* of the entrance lobby of an office building is certainly a quality feature, but it also looks like an abstraction. The features need to be divided into observable parts and identified into those specifics that collectively constitute appearance, e.g., the quality and condition of the carpet, the quality and style of furniture, the size of windows, etc. Once data dimensions have been established for each piece or item, the team should summarize the data into an index, e.g., number of damaged or soiled carpets to total number of office rooms, number of rooms with old and damaged furniture, etc.

Data are also qualified/classified based on local environment, applications, and decision-making. Classifications include:

- Broadly applicable—Some data dimensions that are broadly applicable can help to answer such questions as:
  - Is the product/service quality getting better or worse?
  - Which one of the products/services provides the best quality?
  - How can all of the business operations be brought up to the best level?
- Common basis of decision making—Measurement units should be such that the data will provide assistance for a decision-making group made up of diverse people.
- Compatibility—Sometimes data are measured in simple units to apply to a wide variety of situations.
- Economical to apply—There must be balance between the cost of collecting data and the benefits of having the data. Sometimes data precision also relates to marginal benefits.
- Measurable in abstraction—Some quality features stand apart from physical things (are subjective), e.g., taste, feel, sound, aroma, and beauty.
- Understandable—Technological data generally have highly standardized dimensions. However, the dimensions of managerial level data are not standardized. Local dialects may be understood by local business people, but not by outsiders, e.g., world-class quality, on-time arrival, etc. These types of measurement qualifications are vague and/or create confusion that can divide the team.

3.1.4 Closed-Loop Data Measurement System

Many measurement systems follow the closed-loop system concept due to lower computing costs and great technological growth. As an example, consider the thermostat control in a heating and/or cooling system. The quality of this device needs to be evaluated. One of the key elements in making the evaluation is the sensor. A sensor is a specialized detecting device or measurement tool. It is designed to recognize the presence and intensity of certain phenomena and to convert this sensed knowledge into information. In turn, the resulting information becomes an input to decision-making, enabling the team to evaluate the actual performance. (Similarly to technological instruments, which obviously have sensors, humans and animals use their senses the same way.) A closed-loop system generally follows four key steps:

- Data recording—As a system is functioning, defined data are measured.
- Data processing—Measured data are processed. This processing may happen within same system or outside the measuring system.

- Comparing data—The processed performance data are compared with goals and standards.
- Actuating—The control system adjusts the processes to bring performance into conformance with standards.

The project team will handle two types of data to measure and appreciate the size of performance problem(s) (as defined in Section 1.10, *Project Charter*, in Chapter 1):

- Dependent data—Also known as "*Y*s"
- Independent data—Also known as "*X*s"

Several techniques are available to identify the *Y*s data—brainstorming, business metrics, a data selection matrix, and a performance measure matrix. The selected Ys data must satisfy certain requirements. They must be:

- Consistent with project charter
- Consistent with customer expectations
- Supportive of business strategy, i.e., business goals, competitors, benchmarking, existing specifications, and regulations (national/ international)

Once the selected list is developed, apply the following criteria to select the highest-ranking *Y*s:

- *Y* is measurable.
- *Y* must be linked to customer CTQs.
- *Y* is a direct measure of the process.
- *Y* addresses the process defect problem.
- Volume of the product or process is large enough to support the improvement project.
- Data on *Y* are easy to collect.
- Cost of product failure is high.
- Continuous data (generally) are preferable over discrete data.

A ranking matrix can be developed utilizing the concept of assigned numbers that can range from 1 through 10, with 10 meeting the criteria perfectly and 1 not meeting the criteria at all.

Similarly, there are several techniques available to identify the *X*s data, e.g., brainstorming, process mapping, and cause-and-effect diagrams. Key considerations in selecting *X*s are the *elimination/minimization of variation* and that the selected *X*s must be *measurable*. Measurement occurs at three stages of the SIPOC process—inputs, process, and outputs—therefore, identify potential project *X*s that will be measured in the data collection plan. The selected *X*s should be prioritized utilizing commonly available tools such as:

- Prioritization matrix
- Failure mode effect analysis (FMEA)

Next is creating a matrix relating the *X*s and the *Y*s variables:

- List the selected project *Y*s along the top section of the matrix.
- Assign weight to each project *Y* (generally using 0 through 5), with the most important output receiving the highest number.
- List all potential causes (inputs) from this process and cause-and-effect analysis that can impact the various project *Y*s along the left-hand side of the matrix.
- Quantify the effect of each input on each project *Y* in the body of the matrix.
- Use the results to analyze and prioritize the team's focus and data collection.

Numerous tools are available to measure data, but only a few will be discussed in Section 3.2, *Measuring Tools*. Before moving on, consider Exercise 3.1.

Exercise 3.1: A Class Project

What is the registration process for entering freshmen students at the University of New Haven (or any selected university)?

- Develop a process flow chart.
- Brainstorm opportunities.
- Review CTQs for the project.
- Develop project information based on applicable elements:
    - Possible process activities
    - Measurable?
        - Unit of measure
        - Frequency of measurement
    - Opportunity defined?
    - Linked to CTQs?
    - High-priority issue?
    - Cost of failure?
    - Easy to collect data?
    - Data type?
- Appoint a spokesperson to report to class.

3.2 MEASURING TOOLS

Several applicable tools are available in the literature to eliminate obvious causes of variation in the performance of the selected project, therefore only flow charting, business metrics, the cause-and-effect diagram, and FMEA and FMECA (failure mode, effects, and criticality analysis) will be discussed in this section.

3.2.1 Flow Charting

Flow charting is a quality improvement tool specifically used for process analysis, understanding, presentation, and improvement. Flow charts tend to provide users with a common language or reference point for a project or process. A flow chart has several definitions:

- A flow chart is a *pictorial representation* of a process in which all the steps of the process are presented.
- A flow chart is a *planning and analysis tool.* It is a graphic of the steps in a work process.
- A flow chart is a *formalized graphic representation* of a work or process, programming logic sequence, or similar formalized procedure.

Uses of process mapping (a special-case flow chart described in Chapter 2, *Define*) may be summarized. Uses include:

- To visualize how an entire process works
- To define and analyze processes, e.g., "What is the registration process for entering freshmen students at the University of New Haven?" or "How can an invoice be created?"
- To build a step-by-step picture of the process for analysis, to identify the critical points, bottlenecks, and problem areas in a process or for communication purposes, e.g., "Is it possible to shorten the length of time it takes for a student to complete the program?"
- To see how the different steps in the process are related and then to define, standardize, or find areas for improvement in the process
- To identify the "ideal" flow of a process from start to finish
- To design a new work process

Although there are various types of flow charts, three types are commonly used in process analysis:

- Top-down flow chart—This chart starts with the major steps drawn horizontally. The detail is provided in numbered subtasks under each major task. The top-down flow chart does not show decision points and reworks. Therefore, it is not as detailed as a process or deployment flow chart.
- Detailed process flow chart—This chart is also known as process mapping. It has been discussed previously (see Chapter 2) and it is most useful when analyzing a specific function, activity, or process.
- Deployment flow chart—This chart is useful when analyzing a process that involves more than one group or several individuals. When a process calls for a deployment flow chart, it may first be helpful to construct a process flow chart with only the major steps and then modify it by assigning the appropriate groups or individuals to each step.

Process flow charts should divide the process into two stages:

- The product's manufacturing process—Typically incorporates all types of manufacturing, assembly, and test operations
- The finished product process—Incorporates other activities associated with the product, e.g., transporting the product

These two stages of the process should be considered using separate flow charts.

The Manufacturing Process Flow Chart

Generally ANSI (the American National Standards Institute) standard symbols are used. The most commonly used symbols are presented in Figure 3.2A. Examples of terms within the symbols include:

- Operation—Material turning, grinding, pouring cement, building house structure, and typing e-mail
- Transportation—Moving material using a transport vehicle (truck, fork truck, etc.), conveyor belt, and manually
- Storage—Storing material (raw, work-in-process, and finished) in containers, pallets, etc. or storing filed documents
- Delay—Material is waiting at the processing machine (turning, grinding) for documentation, inspection, etc. or material is waiting to use an elevator
- Inspection/Measurement—First-piece checking on a manufacturing machine to meet specifications and product quality, reading documents for the accuracy of stored information, and reading gauges
- Combined Activities—Two combined activities such as the joint process of operation and inspection

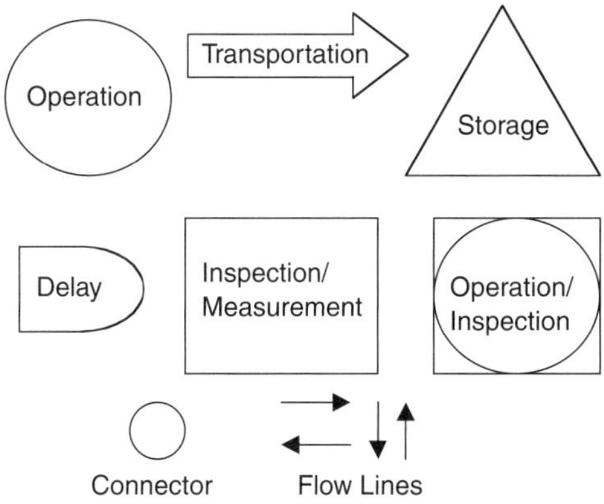

Figure 3.2A. ANSI Standard Symbols

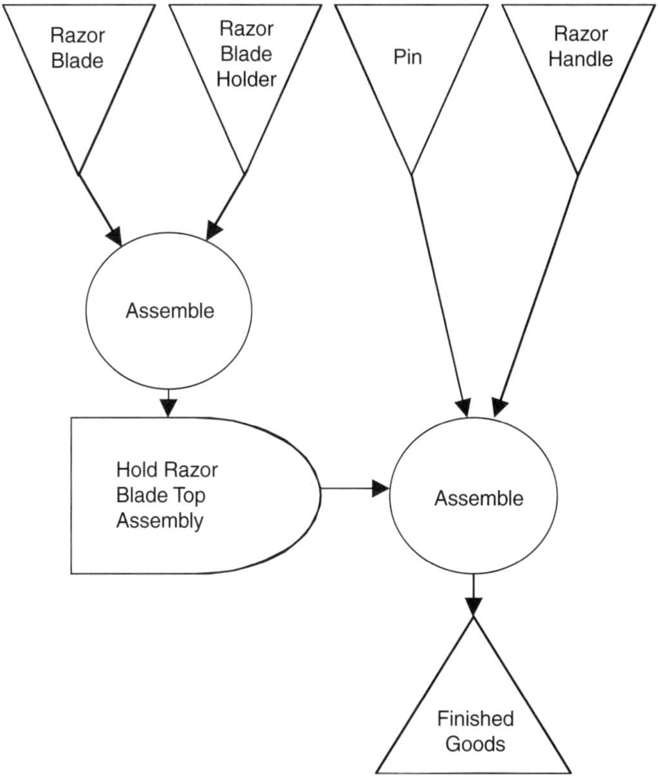

Figure 3.2B. Razor Blade Assembly Process Flow Chart

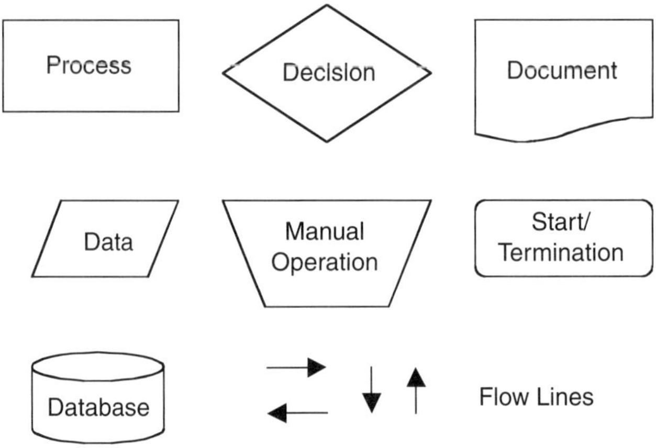

Figure 3.3. Finished Product—Process Flow Chart Symbols

As an example, think about a razor blade assembly process that shows the application of these process symbols. Assume that there are four components in the assembly—a razor blade, a razor blade holder, a razor handle, and a pin—and that these components are assembled as presented in the flow chart shown in Figure 3.2B.

The Finished Product Process

Commonly used process flow chart symbols are also presented in Figure 3.3. Assume that the manufactured razor blade assemblies (*Finished Goods*) are stored in cardboard boxes. These assemblies are packaged for market, but the packaging building is 5 miles away. Therefore, razor blade assemblies have to be transported to the packaging building. The transportation flow chart is presented in Figure 3.4.

3.2.2 Business Metrics

Measurement systems are utilized to evaluate a product (goods and/or services) at different stages of product life. Selection of a measurement system depends upon the product and the life state of the product. Some products may require a very precise and sophisticated measurement tool, while other products may need a very simple measurement tool, e.g., a carpenter's steel hammer will have very simple specifications compared to an orthopedic surgeon's steel hammer. Key product measurements include:

- Cost
- Material

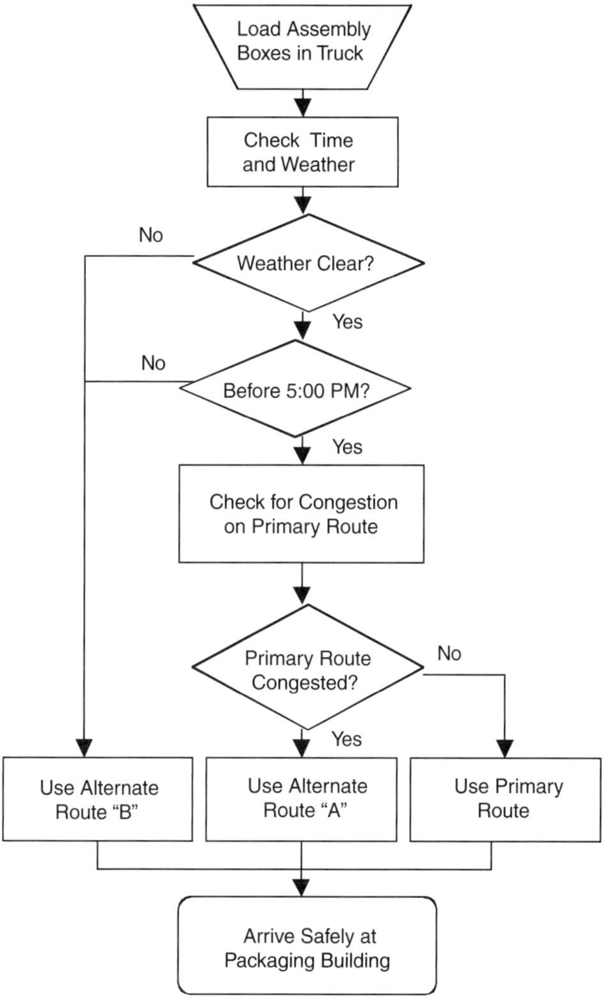

Figure 3.4. Transportation Flow Chart—Blade Assemblies

- Safety and security
- Satisfaction
- Service
- Specifications
- Quantity
- Time

The effect of operational measures on financial measures (the bottom line) is the same for all the products. Therefore, the following measurement system analysis applies to all products. Three factors account for the power of the operational measures [throughput (T), operating expense (OE), and inventory (I)].[1]

- *First*, all three measures are intrinsic to every production process.
- *Second*, the measures are straightforward, easy to understand, and easy to apply.
- *Third*, once the impact of any action on these measures is calculated, the impact on the bottom-line measures can also be determined.

Example 3.2 demonstrates exactly how the operational measures relate to the bottom-line measures of net profit (NP), return on assets (ROA), and cash flow (CF).

Example 3.2: Business Metrics

XYZ is an outsourced messaging center. It packages outgoing messages for customers. The center has one printer and two inserters. Customer jobs are printed and inserted at the XYZ center. Data for a typical job are as follows:

Average material cost:	8.6 cents per message
Average operating expense:	6.3 cents per message
Average message revenue:	15.8 cents per message

The XYZ messaging center had throughput of 13,900,000 messages last year, with the following year-end financial status:

Net sales	$2,196,200
Cost of messages produced	$2,071,100
Total assets (including inventory)	$ 925,000
Inventory (book value)	$ 53,700
Inventory (material value)	$ 40,000
Annual inventory carrying cost	16% per year

Based on this financial status, the following values are known:

Throughput (T) = (Dollars generated through sales) – (Material cost of goods)
= $2,196,200 – $(8.6/100)(13,900,000)
= $2,196,200 – $1,195,400
= $1,000,800

Operating expense (OE) = (Total cost of goods) – (Material cost of goods)
= $2,071,100 – $1,195,400
= $875,700

Inventory (I) = Money invested in materials that the business intends to sell
= $40,000

Net profit (NP) = Throughput – Operating expense
= $1,000,800 – $875,700
= $125,100

Return on assets (ROA) = (Net profit)/(Total assets)
= ($125,100)/($925,000)
= 13.52%

Cash flow (CF) = Available cash
= $125,100

Assume that business XYZ is going through some continuous improvement processes. These process improvements will impact the operations measures positively. The following analysis will show that their impact on financial measures will be very significant. The following data are a continuation of the above example with four process improvement scenarios.

The four process improvement scenarios are:

- **Case 1:** Assume that throughput increases by 5%, while operating expense and inventory remain unchanged.
- **Case 2:** Assume that operating expense is decreased by 5%, while throughput and inventory remain unchanged.
- **Case 3:** Assume that inventory is decreased by 10%, while throughput and operating expense remain unchanged.
- **Case 4:** Assume an outstanding continuous improvement process, in which throughput is increased by 5%, operating expense is decreased by 5%, and inventory is decreased by 10%.

Case 1 assumes that throughput increases by 5%, while operating expense and inventory remain unchanged. Because operating expense is unchanged, both throughput and net profit increase by 5% of throughput dollars ($1,000,800):

A throughput increase by 5% = $1,000,800 × 5% = $50,040.

New throughput = $1,000,800 + $50,040
= $1,050,840

New net profit = $125,100 + $50,040
= $175,140

Percent increase in net profit = ($175,140)/($125,100)
= **40%** ⇧

New return on assets = (New net profit)/(Total assets)
= ($175,140)/($925,000)
= 18.93%

Percent increase in return on assets = (18.93%)/(13.52%)
= **40%** ⇧

New cash flow = $125,100 + $50,040
= $175,140

Percent increase in cash flow = $175,140/$125,100
= **40%** ⇧

Case 2 assumes that operating expense is decreased by 5%, while throughput and inventory remain unchanged.

A 5% reduction in operating expense translates to a dollar saving of 5% × $875,700 = $43,785.

New operating expense = $875,700 – $43,785
= $831,915.

New net profit = Throughput – New operating expense
= $1,000,800 – $831,915
= $168,885

Percent increase in net profit = ($168,885)/($125,100)
= **35%** ⇧

New return on assets = (New net profit)/(Total assets)
= ($168,885)/($925,000)
= 18.26%

Percent increase in return on assets = (18.26%)/(13.52%)
= **35%** ⇧

New cash flow = $125,100 + $43,785
= $168,885

Percent increase in cash flow = 168,885/125,10
= **35%** ⇧

Case 3 assumes that inventory is decreased by 10%, while throughput and operating expenses remain unchanged. If inventory is cut by 10%, then the asset base is reduced by 10% of the inventory book value:

Reduction in inventory book value $= 0.10 \times \$53,700$
$= \$5,370$

New total asset $= \$925,000 - \$5,370$
$= \$919,630$

Operating expense will also be reduced because the cost of carrying inventory will be reduced. Because the inventory carrying cost is 16% per year,

Reduction in operating expense $= 0.16 \times \$5,370$
$= \$859$

Net profit will increase by the amount of the reduction in operating expense:

New net profit $= \$125,100 + \$859$
$= \$125,959$

Therefore, there is a one time inventory reduction of \$5,370 and an annual operating expense reduction of \$859.

New return on assets $=$ (New net profit)/(New total assets)
$= (\$125,959)/(\$919,630)$
$= 13.7\%$

There represent two types of cash flow improvements:

One-time cash flow $=$ 10% of inventory material value
$= 0.10 \times \$40,000$
$= \$4,000$

New annual cash flow $= \$125,100 + \$859$
$= \$125,859$

Case 4 is an outstanding continuous improvement process, where assumptions are that throughput is increased by 5%, operating expense is decreased by 5%, and inventory is decreased by 10%. If all the three changes take place, then:

Increase in net profit $= \$50,040 + \$43,785 + \$859$
$= \$94,684$

New total net profit (excludes one-time inventory reduction) $= \$125,100 + \$94,684$
$= \$219,784$

New return on assets $= (\$219,784)/(\$919,630)$
$= 23.9\%$

First year cash flow increase $= \$50,040 + \$43,785 + \$859 + \$4,000$
$= \$98,684$

Table 3.1. The Absolute Impact of Selected Changes in the Operational Measure on the Bottom-Line Financial Measures

Change in Operational Measure	Net Profit ($)	Return on Assets (%)	Cash Flow ($)
With no change/ original status	125,100	13.52	125,100
5% Increase in T	175,140	18.93	175,140
5% Decrease in OE	168,885	18.26	168,885
10% Decrease in I	125,959	13.7	129,959
All of above changes	219,784	23.9	223,784

The absolute impact of variable changes in the operational measures on the financial measures is presented in Table 3.1. The percentage impact of the selected changes on the financial measures is presented in Table 3.2.

The operational measures of throughput (T), operating expense (OE), and inventory (I) will not replace the bottom-line financial measures, but they are a very effective link to measure the impact of production actions on the financial measures.

Productivity must be measured from the perspective of the entire production operation. Therefore, the productivity of any production action can be measured as well as linked to financial measures at the business level.

3.2.3 Cause-and-Effect Diagram

Dr. Kaoru Ishikawa, a Japanese quality control statistician, invented the fishbone diagram. The design of this diagram looks like the skeleton of a fish. The fishbone diagram is also referred to as a cause-and-effect diagram. A cause-and-effect diagram is an analysis tool that provides a systematic way of looking at the effects and at the causes that create or contribute to those effects. These diagrams are useful in several situations, including:

- Summarizing knowledge about a process
- Searching root causes
- Identifying areas where problems may exist and comparing the relative importance of the different causes

A cause-and-effect diagram is designed to assist teams in categorizing the many potential causes of problems or issues in an orderly way and to identify root

Table 3.2. The Percentage Impact of Selected Changes in the Operational Measures on the Bottom-Line Financial Measures

Change in Operational Measure	Percentage Increase of the Bottom-Line Financial Measures		
	Net Profit	Return on Assets	Cash Flow
5% Increase in T	40.0	40.0	40.0
5% Decrease in OE	35.0	35.0	35.0
10% Decrease in I	6.9	1.3	3.9
All of above changes	75.7	76.8	78.9

causes. The diagram provides a single outcome or trunk. Extending from the trunk are branches that represent major categories of inputs or causes that create a single outcome. These large branches then lead to smaller and smaller branches, which indicate smaller and smaller causes. The diagram provides a *qualitative* answer to a question, not a *quantitative* answer as some other tools do. Therefore, the main value of this tool is to identify the theories that the project team will be testing. These tests should result in root causes (Xs). A cause-and-effect diagram is a tool that provides a highly focused way to produce a list of all known or suspected causes that potentially contribute to the dependent variable (Y). Therefore, the diagram should be used when one:

- Needs to study a problem/issue to determine the root cause, e.g., "Why is enrollment in the school of engineering dropping?" or "Why are production defects per system suddenly increasing?"
- Wants to study all possible reasons why a process is beginning to have difficulties, problems, or breakdowns
- Needs to identify areas for data collection
- Wants to study why a process is not performing properly or not producing the desired results

It is critical that all team members agree on the problem statement before starting a cause-and-effect diagram. Construction steps of a cause-and-effect diagram include:

1. Draw a large arrow horizontally across the page pointing to the name of an effect or a problem statement.

2. Draw four to six branches off the large arrow to represent the main categories of potential causes. For example, in a manufacturing problem, the main categories could be Method, Material, Machinery, Manpower (people), and Measurement (also known as 5Ms). Similarly, the 5Ps could be Place, Procedure, People, Policies, and Patrons (customers).

Note: Any combination(s) of issue categories can be used. Although combinations of issues are not limited to five major issues, do not use more than seven to eight issues.

3. Draw horizontal lines against each branch and list the causes for each category on these branches.
4. Use an idea-generating technique (e.g., brainstorming) to identify the factors within each category that may be affecting the problem/issue and/or the effect being studied. For example, the team should ask, "What are the *Machine* issues affecting/causing …?"
5. Repeat this procedure with each factor under each category to produce subfactors. Continue asking, "Why is this happening?" Put additional segments on each factor and subsequently under each subfactor.
6. Until no useful information is obtained, continue asking, "Why is that happening?"
7. After team members agree that an adequate amount of detail has been provided under each major category, analyze the results of the cause-and-effect diagram. Do this by looking for items that appear in more than one category. These items become the *most likely causes.*
8. The team should prioritize the *most likely causes*, with the first item being the *most probable cause.* For example, each team member can be given a specified number of votes. Each team member votes for the top five ideas. An X is added next to each idea for each vote that the idea receives.

Now, consider Example 3.3.

Example 3.3: Cause-and-Effect Analysis

To improve the flow solder process, a team consisting of the flow solder operator, the shop supervisor, the manufacturing engineer responsible for the process, and a quality engineer will meet to study potential causes of solder defects. The team conducts a brainstorming session and produces the cause-and-effect diagram in Figure 3.5.

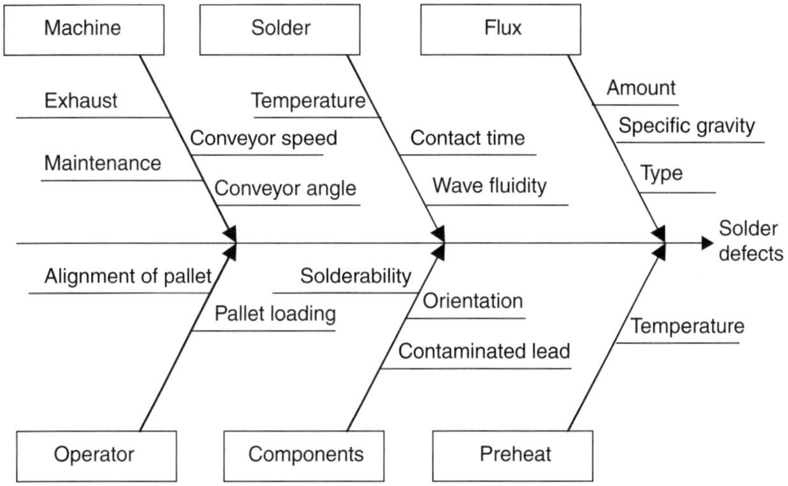

Figure 3.5. Cause-and-Effect Diagram—Printed Circuit Board Flow Solder Process

From Figure 3.5, the phenomenon to be explained is *Solder Defects*. Possible key factors contributing to the solder defects are *Machine, Solder, Flux, Operator, Components*, and *Preheat*. Each of these major cause categories may in turn have multiple causes. For example, *Machine* issue may be due to the machine's exhaust, maintenance, conveyor speed, and conveyor angle. The relationship can be traced back even more steps in the process if necessary or appropriate.

Once the diagram is completed, one should be able to start at any end point and read the diagram as follows: using *Solder Defects* as the main effect, the conveyor's high speed forced the *Machine* to move the product faster, producing a defective solder. It can also be said that the *Machine* was moving the product faster because the conveyor speed was so high that the conveyor speed resulted in a defective solder.

As a result of the brainstorming session, the team tentatively identifies the following variables as potentially influential in creating solder defects:

1. Flux specific gravity
2. Solder temperature
3. Conveyor speed
4. Conveyor angle
5. Preheat temperature
6. Pallet loading method

A *statistically designed* experiment could be used to investigate the effect of these six variables on solder defects. A defect concentration diagram of the product could also be sketched with most frequently occurring defects shown for the part.

The diagram in Figure 3.5 reveals that this tool has three good features:

- It is a visual representation of the factors that might contribute to an observed effect or phenomenon that is being analyzed.
- The interrelationship among the possible causal factors is clearly shown. One causal factor may appear in several places in the diagram, e.g., if temperature affects both solder and preheat, then temperature would appear in both places.
- The interrelationships are generally qualitative and hypothetical. A cause-and-effect diagram is usually prepared with a preconclusion that data development would be needed to establish the cause effect empirically.

A cause-and-effect diagram presents and organizes theories. When the theories are tested with data, only then can the team prove causes of the observed phenomena.

Some shortcomings of the tool include:

- In some circumstances, the orderly arrangement of theories developed in a cause-and-effect diagram with the real data obtained through empirical testing represents a misuse of time and information.
- If the team does not test each causal relationship in the cause-and-effect diagram for logical consistency, usefulness of the tool is reduced and valuable time can be wasted.
- Limiting the theories that are proposed and considered may unintentionally block out or eliminate the ultimate root cause(s).
- Developing the cause-and-effect diagram before the symptoms have been analyzed, as thoroughly as existing information will permit, can lead to a large, complex diagram that can be difficult to use.

Once the initial relationship between the Ys and the Xs has been identified utilizing the cause-and-effect tool, the next step is to prioritize the Ys, possibly utilizing 0 to 5 weighting methodology. List all the potential causes (inputs) along the top of the matrix from the process and the cause-and-effect analysis that can impact the project Ys along the left hand side of the matrix. The next step is to quantify the effect of each input on each project Y in the body of the matrix and use the results to analyze and prioritize the team's focus and data collection.

3.2.4 Failure Mode and Effects Analysis (FMEA) and Failure Mode, Effects, and Criticality Analysis (FMECA)

The next tool is FMEA. The methodology of FMEA is systematic in identifying the possible failures that pose the greatest overall risk for the product. Product risk depends on:

- The cause of product failure mode is one of the ways in which the product can fail and the cause could be one of its possible deficiencies or defects.
- The cause of failure is one of the possible causes of an observed mode of failure.
- The effect of failure is the consequences of a particular mode of failure.

Once the above elements have been identified, then the analysis quantifies three factors:

- The frequency with which each cause of failure occurs
- The severity of the effect of the failure
- The chance that the failure will be detected before it affects the customer

The combined impact of these factors is called the risk priority and is presented in the next section.

The Society of Automotive Engineers[2] defines FMEA as a structured, qualitative analysis of a system or function to identify potential system failure modes, their causes, and the effects on the system operation associated with the failure mode's occurrence. FMEA is one of the most powerful and practical reliability tools in manufacturing today. Industries (e.g., aerospace, automotive, defense, and electronics), along with several consumer goods industries, have used FMEA to successfully improve product performance and reliability. The tool can help in:

- Improving product reliability and reducing design lead-time
- Developing trouble-free manufacturing processes and avoiding expensive engineering changes
- Predicting potential and unavoidable problems and identifying possible causes in order to assess effects and plan corrective actions before these problems occur

3.2.4.1 FMECA

FMEA can be extended to include an assessment of the severity of the failure effect and its probability of occurrence. This analysis is called a FMECA (failure mode, effects, and criticality analysis). FMECA is a method of looking into the future and determining where potential failures might be located. This method sounds wonderful in theory, but a tremendous amount of time and energy is required to do this.

If a team has limited time and resources in its product design and manufacturing organizations, then the team must find a way to make the process less burdensome. A modified approach makes one simple change to the process. Instead of looking into the future, the team will look at past failures. This modification to the process reduces analysis time significantly and makes the process more practical in its organizations.

FMECA, criticality assessment, FMEA, and modified FMEA will be discussed. Brief historical FMECA information includes:

- 1960s: Because of increased customer demand for higher product reliability, component failure studies were broadened to include the effects of component failures on the system of which the component(s) failures were a part.
- 1970s: A formal approach to the analysis was developed and documented in U.S. Military Standard 1629: Procedures for Performing a Failure Mode, Effects and Criticality Analysis.[3]
- 1984: U.S. Military Standard 1629, most recently updated as MIL-STD-1629A/Notice 2, defines the basic approach for analyzing a system.[3]

FMECA is an iterative process. It is used for system design, manufacturing, maintenance, and failure detection. Key functions include:

- To identify unacceptable effects that prevent achieving design requirements
- To assess the safety of system components
- To identify design modifications and corrective action needed to mitigate the effects of a failure on the system

FMECA users include:

- Product designers
- A Reliability and Maintainability group
- A Manufacturing and Testing Engineering group
- Quality Assurance engineers
- A System Safety group
- A customer

Methodology. FMECA provides a basis for early recognition of the effects of component failures and their resolution or mitigation through design changes, maintenance procedures, or operational procedures. The FMECA methodology is based on a hierarchical, inductive approach to analysis. An analyst must determine how every possible failure mode of every system component affects the system's operation. Bowles and Bonnell[4] describe the procedure using several steps:

1. Define the ground rules and assumptions (such as the system operational phases, operating environment, and mission requirements).
2. Identify the hierarchical (indenture) level at which the analysis is to be done.
3. Define each item (subsystem, module, function, or component) to be analyzed.
4. Identify all item failure modes.
5. Determine the consequences of each item failure for each failure mode.
6. Classify failures by their effects on the system's operation and mission.
7. Identify how the failure mode can be detected (especially important for fault-tolerant configurations).
8. Identify any compensating provisions or design changes to mitigate the failure effects.

Steps 1, 2, and 3 are done prior to starting the detailed FMECA analysis. Steps 4 through 8 are repeated for each item identified in Step 2. The results of Steps 5 through 8 may vary depending on the operational phase being analyzed.

Guidance. General information about the process includes:

- The analysis proceeds in a bottom-up fashion.
- Failure modes are postulated for the lowest-level components in the hierarchical system structure.
- These failure modes may be functional, if only functional modules have been defined, or physical, if piece part components have been identified.
- The local effect of the failure at the lowest level propagates to the next higher level as the failure mode for the module at that level. The failure effects at that level then propagate up to the next level, continuing in this manner until the system level is reached.

As Bowles and Bonnell's procedure[4] and the general guidelines are followed, design information is also needed to perform a FMECA study for a component or equipment.

Design information. Design information includes:

- Components and equipment drawings, original design descriptions and design-change history, functional block diagrams with their descriptions, and system schematics
- Relevant industry, company and customer-provided specifications and guidelines
- Reliability data (e.g., historical failure data, cause-and-effect analysis of previous failures, component failure rate, customer site service data) and the effects of environmental factors (e.g., temperature, relative humidity, dust, vibration, radiation, etc.) on the component and equipment
- Operating specifications and their limits, interface specifications, and configuration management data

The role of FMECA in the design process is critical. During the product life cycle, most systems progress through several phases such as the phases presented in Figure 3.6. Product development starts based on research advances and customer needs, and the product follows its life cycle.

As the product goes through its life cycle, FMECA helps to keep each responsible group focused on its responsibilities. In FMECA, the system is treated as a "black box," with only its inputs, the corresponding outputs specified, and the system's failure data. The assigned project team would not be able to perform FMECA on every subsystem due to time and money constraints. Therefore, the team has to prioritize the failure projects based on failure criticality.

3.2.4.2 Criticality Assessment

Criticality assessment is an attempt to prioritize the failure modes identified in an analysis of the system based on their effects and likelihood of occurrence. Several methods are available, but two are most commonly used:

- Criticality number (C_r)—The criticality number calculation is described in MIL-STD-1629A.[5] C_r is commonly used in nuclear and aerospace industries.

$$C_r = \sum_{n=1}^{j} (\alpha \beta \lambda_p t)_n$$

where:

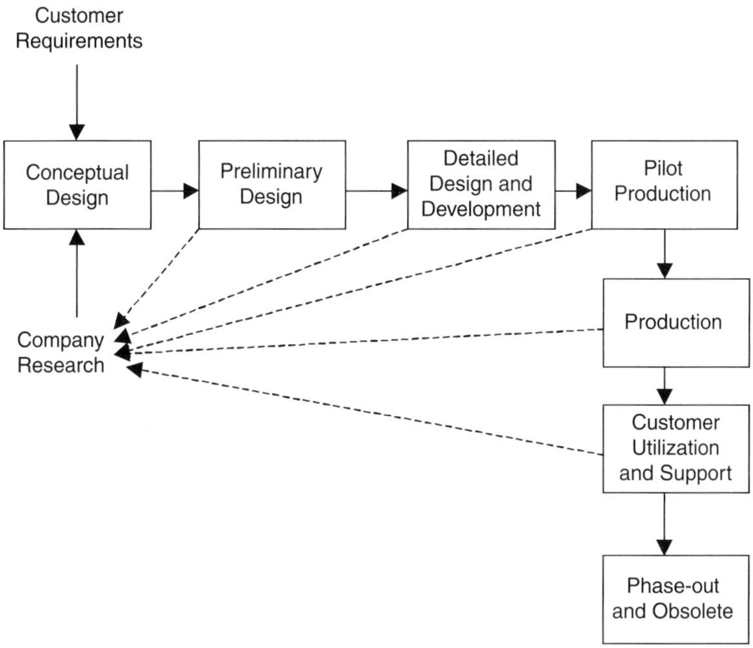

Figure 3.6. Typical Product Life Cycle

$n = 1, \ldots, j$ are the item failure modes with the severity classification of interest

C_r = The criticality number (assuming a constant failure rate)

α = The failure mode ratio

β = The failure effect probability

λ_p = The past failure rate

t = The operating time

- Risk priority number (RPN)[6]—RPN is most commonly used in the automotive industry. The RPN is calculated as the product of the ranking assigned to each factor:

  RPN = Severity ranking × occurrence ranking × detection ranking

Severity ranking tables are presented in Tables 3.3, 3.4, and 3.5. Failure modes having a high RPN are assumed to be more important and are given a higher

Table 3.3. Ten-Level Automobile Industry Severity Ranking Criteria

Effect	Ranking	Criteria: Severity of Effect
Hazardous (without warning)	10	Very high severity: a potential failure mode affects safe vehicle operation and/or involves noncompliance with government regulations
Hazardous (with warning)	9	Very high severity: a potential failure mode affects safe vehicle operation and/or involves noncompliance with government regulations
Very high	8	Vehicle/item inoperable, with loss of a primary function
High	7	Vehicle/item operable, but at reduced level of performance; customer dissatisfied
Moderate	6	Vehicle/item operable, but comfort/convenience item(s) inoperable; customer experiences discomfort level
Low	5	Vehicle/item operable, but comfort/convenience item(s) operable at reduced level of performance; customer experiences some dissatisfaction
Very low	4	Cosmetic defect in finish, fit, and finish or squeak/rattle item that does not conform to specifications; defect noticed by most customers
Minor	3	Cosmetic defect in finish, fit, and finish or squeak/rattle item that does not conform to specifications; defect noticed by average customer
Very minor	2	Cosmetic defect in finish, fit, and finish or squeak/rattle item that does not conform to specifications; defect noticed by discriminating customer
None	1	No effect

Source: Adapted from the Society of Automotive Engineers. 1994 July. Potential Failure Mode and Effects Analysis in Design (Design FMEA) and for Manufacturing and Assembly Process (Process FMEA). Instruction Manual.

Table 3.4. Four-Level Military/Government Severity Ranking Criteria

Category	Explanation
I	Catastrophic: a failure which can cause death or system loss (e.g., aircraft, tank, missile, ship)
II	Critical: a failure which can cause severe injury, major property damage, or major system damage which will result in mission loss
III	Marginal: a failure which may cause minor injury, minor property damage, or minor system damage which will result in delay or loss of availability or mission degradation
IV	Minor: a failure not serious enough to cause injury, property damage, or system damage, but which will result in unscheduled maintenance or repair

Source: Society of Automotive Engineers. 1993. Failure Mode, Effects and Criticality Analysis. Aerospace Recommended Practice, unpublished paper. Available at http://www.sae.org/technical/standards/AIR4845.

priority than those having a lower RPN.[6] The product of degree of severity (S), chances of occurrence, and detection ability (D) calculates the value of RPN as presented in Table 3.5.

3.2.4.3 FMEA

FMEA is not as complicated as FMECA. The RPN is most commonly used for FMEA. The RPN is a product of three elements—severity ranking, occurrence ranking, and detection ranking. These elements are presented in Table 3.5. The RPN value can range between 1 and 1000. The higher the RPN value, the higher the risk of product/service failure. Commonly used steps in conducting FMEA include:

1. Develop a simple matrix spreadsheet with basic information columns. (Table size will grow with product hierarchy.)
   - Failure mode
   - Cause of failure
   - Effect of failure
   - Severity ranking
   - Occurrence ranking
   - Detection ranking
   - Risk priority
   - Suggested improvement

Table 3.5. Guidelines for Risk Priority Number (RPN)

Ranking	Degree of Severity	Chances of Occurrence	Detection Ability
10	If safe system fails without warning that creates danger and hostile effect on customer; government regulations violation	Failure assured (from warranty data)	Current controls positively will not detect the potential failure
9	If safe system fails without warning that creates danger and hostile effect on customer; government regulations violation	Failure almost certain (from warranty data or significant testing)	Current controls most probably will not detect the potential failure
8	Very high level of dissatisfaction due to loss of function, but without negative impact on safety or government regulations	High failure rate (without any supporting documentation)	Very highly possible that the potential failure will not be detected or prevented before reaching the next customer
7	High degree of customer dissatisfaction due to component failure without complete loss of function, but productivity impacted by high scrap or rework levels	Relatively high failure rate (with supporting documentation)	Highly possible that the potential failure will not be detected or prevented before reaching the next customer
6	Significant complaints about manufacturing, assembly, or warranty	Moderate failure rate (without supporting documentation)	Likely that potential failure will not be detected or prevented before reaching next customer

5	Customer productivity reduced by continued degradation of effect or customer made uncomfortable	Relatively moderate failure rate (without supporting documentation)	Moderate likelihood that the potential failure will reach next customer
4	Customer dissatisfied by reduced performance	Occasional failures	Controls may detect or prevent potential failure from reaching next customer
3	Customer experiences annoyance due to slight degradation of performance	Low failure rate (without supporting documentation)	Low likelihood that potential failure will reach next customer undetected
2	Customer experiences slight annoyance	Low failure rate (without supporting documentation)	Almost certain that potential failure will be found or prevented before reaching next customer
1	Customer will not notice effect or effect not significant	Remote likelihood of occurrence	Certain that potential adverse failure will be found or prevented before reaching next customer

Source: Juran, J.M. 2002. Juran Institute's Transactional Breakthrough Strategy. Southbury, CT: Juran Institute. Chapter 3 (student material from Black Belt certification training class).

2. Obtain ranking data from Table 3.5. It is important to note that the failure occurrence ranking will depend upon who is using the product, e.g., a hammer being used by a carpenter vs. the hammer being used by an orthopedic surgeon. The team should choose values based on product history, similar models, actual occurrence data (generally from customers), process capability studies, simulation/mathematical modeling, and testing.
3. Identify the cause of failure based on past experience, cause-and-effect analysis, or from some other source. If there is more than one potential cause for failure for each mode, list all of these causes directly under each other on a separate line. Analyze how each failure will affect customers, the overall product, or the system.
4. From Table 3.5, evaluate the degree of severity for each failure and choose an appropriate ranking from the table.
5. Analyze and choose the detection ranking value from Table 3.5. Take advantage of historical data if available.
6. Calculate the RPN factor by multiplying all three of these factors. The cause that receives the highest score is the one that requires the most attention from the team so that a method(s) to correct the failures can be identified.
7. The best time to apply the FMEA tool is when the product/service is in design stage. Generally, design actions are not performed for each mode that might fail, but only for the "critical" modes. Take advantage of Pareto Analysis to rank the "risk priority." Once the team selects the modes which require further attention, design actions will reduce the level of failure rate that is acceptable to the team.
8. Validation of each solution is important. Validation will ensure that the design action will reduce potential failure to an acceptable level. It is important to design a plan to validate the effectiveness of each action and revise the design as needed.

The FMEA process is explained in Example 3.4. See Section 3.2.4.4 for a discussion of the modified FMEA process.

Example 3.4: The FMEA Process

The product is *New Employee Business Card*. Business cards are sent to each new employee after he/she joins the company. The component being evaluated is *Business Cards*. The failure mode is *Business Cards Are Printed Incorrectly*, with the following elements:

- Employee's name is incorrectly spelled.

Table 3.6A. Historical Error Statistics

Ranking	10	9	8	7	6	5	4	3	2	1
	Error Frequency per 10,000 Data Entries									
Office and printing industry	45	40	35	30	27	22	17	10	6	<2
Banking industry	45	38	32	27	22	18	14	10	6	<2

- The office telephone number is incorrect.
- Employee's e-mail address is incorrect.

Possible causes of failure are numerous, e.g.,

- Request form—Employee's name on request form is in cursive writing.
- Data entry error—Historical data show approximately 27 errors per 10,000 telephone number data entries.
- Employee's e-mail address—Employee's *first name dot last name@ company name dot com* is in cursive writing.

Historical data entry error statistics for some industries is ranked and presented in Table 3.6A. The FMEA information is presented in Table 3.6B.

The combined highest RPN factor is 216 for *Data entry error.* Such an error is likely to cause a complaint; yet it has some chance of detection before the error affects the customer. Therefore, to minimize this risk, a special review step is required in the software.

3.2.4.4 Modified FMEA

The modified FMEA process will be discussed utilizing an example from a manufacturing area. Modified FMEA is used to determine failures that are occurring in a manufacturing facility and to determine their impact and frequencies. Discuss a hydraulic pump in a tractor with the following data:

- Failure event—Failure of pump
- Failure mode—Bearing failures
- Frequency—9 failures per year
- Impact—$3,000 per failure
- Total loss—$27,000 per year

Table 3.6B. FMEA Information for Employees' Business Cards

Mode of Failure 1	Cause of Failure 2	Effect of Failure 3	Degree of Severity 4	Chances of Occurrence 5	Detection Ability 6	RPN (1–1000) 4×5×6	Proposed Improvement
Business cards printed incorrectly	Employee name written in cursive	Must reprint cards	6	4	8	192	Write name in capital letters
	Data entry error		6	6	6	216	Have review step in software
	e-mail address written in cursive		6	4	8	192	Write e-mail address in capital letters

If a similar type of calculation were performed on every failure, the results would be astounding, but they would not be cost-effective. Working on every failure event is not practical. Therefore, determine the most significant failure events utilizing the concept of Vilfredo Pareto, the well-known Italian economist. The concept of the 80/20 rule is that 80% of failure losses may be coming from only 20% of the parts/assembly. This means a root cause failure analysis (RCFA) does not have to be done for every failure event, only for the ones that are the *most* important. The analysis process can be divided into steps:

1. Complete preparatory work.
2. Collect failure and related data.
3. Summarize information.
4. Analyze information for losses.
5. Determine significant elements.
6. Validate results.
7. Develop a report with recommendations.

Step 1. Complete Preparatory Work

It is important to do some preliminary preparatory work before starting any analysis. A Six Sigma mission statement has already defined the issue for this analysis, i.e., a hydraulic pump. Cover the following elements in Step 1:

- Develop a failure definition.
- Draw a contact flow chart.
- Calculate the gap analysis.
- Develop a preliminary interview schedule.

Developing a *failure definition* seems trivial, but it is an essential step in the analysis. If a large group of people (say 50) were asked to define *failure*, there would probably be 50 different definitions, which would make the analysis far too broad and difficult to complete. Focus on the things that are most important to satisfy customers and the business. For instance, if the tractor stays operational, this situation is *good* for the customer, but it is *critical* for the business; therefore, center the failure definition on keeping the tractor operational. Commonly used failure definitions include:

- Failure is a loss of equipment availability.
- Failure is a deviation from the status quo.
- Failure is any loss that interrupts the continuity of operation/production.
- Failure is not meeting expectations.

There are no perfect failure definitions. Because the product is analyzed based on the *defined* definition of failure, a precise failure definition is not important. Consider some simple rules when developing a failure definition:

- It must be concise and easily understandable; otherwise the failure definition will leave excessive opportunities for interpretation.
- It should not have to be interpreted.
- It must address only one topic.
- It should be approved and signed (if possible) by someone with authority.

Next, draw a *contact flow chart*. Developing a contact flow diagram will allow the system to be broken down into smaller, more manageable subsystems. The rule for a contact flow chart is to map all the process units that come into contact with the product.

Then calculate the *gap analysis*, which helps uncover the disparity between what the company is producing now and what its potential production is. Apply gap analysis to the hydraulic pump to get some indication of the potential opportunity in the manufacturing facility. For instance, the company is producing 15,000 hydraulic pumps per year; however, the potential is 25,000 per year. The company has a gap of 10,000 hydraulic pumps per year.

Developing a *preliminary interview schedule* is the final step in the preparation stage. Design a preliminary interview sheet and a schedule for interviewing people. This will lead to data collection.

Step 2. Collect Failure and Related Data

There are two ways to collect failure and related data for this analysis:

- From a data file maintained in the system
- By interviewing people who are closest to the work

Although each data source has its advantages, interviewing people is probably better than obtaining information from the data file because information from an interview is "straight from the source." If there is enough confidence in the company data files, they can be used to validate the interviews.

It is best to interview the people who are closest to the work, e.g., machine operators, mechanics, assembly employees, and test employees. Talk to supervisors and managers, but certainly not to the same extent as with mechanics, operators, and assembly employees.

Explain the process to the interviewees, ask the questions, and note the information on a log sheet. The interviewing task can be quite an experience.

Interviewing tends to be more of an art than a science. Tips for conducting an interview include:

- Take care to ask exactly the same question to each of the interviewees. This helps eliminate the possibility of having different answers depending on interpretation of the question.
- Expand on the questions if further clarification is required.
- Ensure that participants know what is being worked on and the purpose of the interview. If the purpose and process are not clearly understood, the interview process might appear to the interviewees to be more like an interrogation than an interview.
- Allow the interviewees to see that their answers are written on the interview form. Never use tape/video recording equipment in an interview session because it tends to make people uncomfortable and less likely to provide information.
- Never argue with an interviewee. If an interviewer does not agree with the person, it is best to accept what he/she is saying at face value and check it against the information from other interviews.
- Always be aware of interviewees' names. People love to hear their own names. Write interviewees' names in a prominent place for easy reference.
- Develop a strategy to draw out quiet participants. Many quiet people in the workforce have a wealth of data, but are not comfortable with providing it to others.
- Be aware of body language. Although books have been written on this science, being an expert in reading body language is not required. Yet, it is important to recognize that significant human communication is provided through body language.
- Note extraordinary contributors. In any set of interviews, some people are able to contribute more information to the process than others. Make a list of extraordinary contributors so that they can provide assistance later in the analysis.
- Use the failure (defect) definition and flow chart to keep interviewees on track if they begin to wander from the subject.

Step 3. Summarize Information

Once the information is collected, the next activity is to analyze the data for the possibility of redundant entries. Convert frequencies from the interviewees' measurement units into occurrences per year (e.g., 1 per week translates to 52 times per year).

Input this information into an electronic spreadsheet. Once the information is input, sort the raw data first by subsystem and then by failure event. This will provide a closer look at the events that are redundant.

The hydraulic pump example data are summarized in Table 3.7. The data suggest that the first three items are the same because all impact the bearings and have fairly consistent frequencies and impacts. The last three items are also related to bearings, but they go one step beyond the others. The hydraulic pump not only lost a bearing, but it also has a failed seal, a clogged filter, and a cracked shaft, which indicates three separate modes of failure. A summary of the information is presented in Table 3.8.

Step 4. Analyze Information for Losses

Once the product and time losses have been identified, a simple calculation determines total loss for each event in the analysis:

$$\text{Total loss per year} = \text{Frequency} \times \text{loss per occurrence (impact)}$$

The example data are presented in Table 3.9.

It is important to ensure that loss is communicated in the most appropriate units. In Table 3.9, losses are shown in hours of downtime, which might not mean much to some people. It might be more advantageous to convert the number from hours per year to dollars per year because everyone can relate to dollars.

Step 5. Determine Significant Elements

As indicated earlier, utilize the 80/20 rule, in which 80% of the losses are representative of 20% of the issues (failures). The concept is visible in the Table 3.9 data as well. The total loss is 442 hours. Bearing failure accounts for 360 loss hours, which is equal to 81% of the total loss hours. Therefore, bearing failure is a significant element. Now, instead of doing RCFA (root cause failure analysis) on everything, RCFA is only done on bearing failure.

Step 6. Validate Results

Validation of collected data at this point is important. Gap analysis (compare interview data with the system failure data file) can be used to ensure that all of these events add up to ±10% of the gap. If collected data end up being less, some important failure events have probably been omitted from the listing. If there is more than the gap, then results have probably not been summarized well enough. There may be some redundancies on the list. Sometimes many small events (e.g., a few minutes of repair) are never even recorded in the system failure data file.

Table 3.7. Summary of the Interview Data—Hydraulic Pump Failure

Subsystem	Failure Event	Failure Mode	Frequency	Impact (Lost Time)
Load lift	Recirculation pump	Bearing pails	1 per month	1 shift
Load lift	Recirculation pump	Oil contamination	1 per month	10 hours
Load lift	Recirculation pump	Bearing freeze	1 per month	10 hours
Load lift	Recirculation pump	Seal fails	1 per 2 months	1 shift
Load lift	Recirculation pump	Shaft cracked	1 per year	10 hours
Load lift	Recirculation pump	Filter clogged	1 per month	2 hours

Table 3.8. Analyzed and Summarized Data

Subsystem	Failure Event	Failure Mode	Frequency	Impact (Lost Time)
Load lift	Recirculation pump	Bearing problem	36 per year	10 hours
Load lift	Recirculation pump	Seal fails	6 per year	8 hours
Load lift	Recirculation pump	Filter clogged	12 per year	2 hours
Load lift	Recirculation pump	Shaft cracked	1 per year	10 hours

Table 3.9. Yearly Product Loss Data

Subsystem	Failure Event	Failure Mode	Frequency	Impact	Total Lost Production (Hours/Year)
Load lift	Recirculation pump	Bearing fails	12 per year	10 hours	360 hours
Load lift	Recirculation pump	Seal fails	6 per year	8 hours	48 hours
Load lift	Recirculation pump	Filter clogged	12 per year	2 hours	24 hours
Load lift	Recirculation pump	Shaft cracked	1 per year	10 hours	10 hours

Total Time Loss = 442 production hours

A second validation method is to have a group of experienced people from the manufacturing facility to review the findings. This will help ensure that the findings are not too far off base.

Step 7. Develop a Report with Recommendations

Communicating the findings to all interested parties is important. The report should include:

- An explanation of the analysis technique
- The failure definition that was utilized
- The contact flow diagram that was utilized
- Graphically displayed results, as well as the supporting spreadsheet lists
- Recommendations of failures that are candidates for RCFA
- A listing of everyone involved in the analysis, including all of interviewees

Communicate results of the analysis to the interviewees, so that all participants will have a sense of accomplishment and ownership. Most organizations collect significant amounts of data, but the question is, "Will this data provide the information that will be needed for the project?" If the collected data does not provide the necessary information, develop a data collection plan. Section 3.3 will discuss the data collection plan, but before proceeding to Section 3.3, consider Exercises 3.2 and 3.3.

Exercise 3.2: Process Improvement

Using information in Example 3.1 as a basis:

- Develop a detailed process map.
- Develop a list of potential improvements. The architect has designed a fancy house. The estimated cost for the house is very high. The customer's main complaint is the expensive house design. Use process map analysis and the cause-and-effect diagram to develop a list of potential improvements.
- Prioritize the improvement list.

Exercise 3.3: A FMEA Analysis

The product to be considered is new checks for a new joint money market account. The component being evaluated is *New Checks*. The new checks will be mailed to the customer, a married couple. This new account is a joint account in which both spouses have check-writing privileges and both authorizing signatures are required when a check is issued from the joint money market account. The new checks are printed incorrectly:

- Incorrectly spelled customer names
- Only one line for authorizing signatures
- Incorrect account number

Possible causes of the errors are numerous. One cause could be a data entry error. Historical data show approximately 27 errors in 10,000 account number data entries. Such an error is likely to cause a complaint, yet the chance of detection before this error affects a customer is low. Ranking of historical data entry error statistics for sample industries is presented in Table 3.6A.

Perform a FMEA analysis and make recommendations.

3.3 DATA COLLECTION PLAN

In the measurement phase, Six Sigma project leaders should develop a sound data collection plan. Data are nothing but facts. Generally, most organizations have vast stores of information about their operation, but when a Six Sigma team begins working on a project, they often find that the information they need does not exist. Sometimes the project team's collected data does not contain the information that the project leaders are looking for. Therefore, project leaders should think about:

- What information is wanted and how will it be obtained?
- What information collection tool should be used and where can the information be found?
- How will the information be utilized to achieve conclusions?

There is no need to utilize a sophisticated statistical sampling plan if the collected information does not answer a question or if users do not care about the benefit.

Like any planning process, some iteration may be required to complete the design of a good data-collection system. Data collection is very similar to a production process and, like any process, critical is first understanding the process and then improving the process.

Note: Significant work has been done on the data collection process. Information is available in the literature.

Several crucial steps need addressing to ensure that the data collection process and measurement systems are stable and reliable. Once these steps have been incorporated into the data collection plan, the probability that the collected data and the measurement system will meet project requirements will increase. A data collection plan can be divided into six data collection steps:

1. Define goals and objective.
2. Develop good questions.
3. Define operational definitions and methodology.
4. Ensure repeatability, reproducibility, accuracy, and stability.
5. Define the data collection process.
6. Review data collection.

Step 1. Define Goals and Objectives

Identify the purpose of data collection and how it will support the project objectives. A good data collection plan should include:

- A precise and focused project description
- The specific data needed to support the project
- The supporting reasons for collecting the data
- Insight information that the data might provide about the project and how it would help the project team
- How data will be utilized once it has been collected

Understanding these elements will facilitate accurate and efficient data collection by the team. For example, a project's goal is to reduce printer assembly and test time. As the project team develops a process flow chart and identifies the activities as value added, non-value added, and waste, the next step will be to either find the historical data or, if historical data are not available, to collect the data. Analysis of the collected data will provide team members with a better understanding of the distribution of assembly and test cycle time into value-added, non-value added, and waste. To reduce cycle time, the team would try to minimize non-value added activities and eliminate waste activities. Some commonly utilized non-value added activities are material movement, material storage, and data entry; waste activities are waiting for parts, assembling wrong parts, etc. Therefore, defining goals and objectives in a data collection plan is a critical step. Next is developing good questions about the type of information that should be collected.

Step 2. Develop Good Questions

Asking the right questions is important in any successful data collection process. Questions should be prioritized based on the expected information as it relates to project requirements. Higher-priority questions should provide pertinent information for the project.

Higher-priority questions clearly indicate the data that need to be collected. The initial effort invested in formulating specific, well-focused questions is more likely to provide a better return and also reduce the efforts required to design, implement, and analyze the information from the data collection system. Particularly beneficial to the project is input from a person(s) who understands an area and the project requirements very well. For example, the answers from questions 1b and 2b are more informative than the answers from questions 1a and 2a:

1a. Are Customer Support groups handling Customer Issue Reports in a timely manner?

or

1b. When the Field Service Organization receives a Customer Issue Report from the Customer Support group, how much time is left for the repair technician to resolve the problem relative to the service time that Customer Support representative promised the customer?

2a. Are branch offices making errors in the new account applications that waste resources in the main office operation?

or

2b. What percent of new-account applications from branch offices are received at the main office that require follow-up with a branch office representative or a new-account customer because information is missing, conflicting, or incorrect on the application form?

Also advisable is thinking about data analysis and presentation before beginning any data collection. Sometimes, a team has to repeat a data collection study or, even worse, make a decision based on an incomplete analysis because the team's data are not complete enough to support the level of analysis the team wants to perform.

Step 3. Define Operational Definitions and Methodology
To facilitate measurement, a Six Sigma team should clearly define and decide:

- What and how data will be collected
- What will be evaluated and how a numerical value will be assigned

The team should consult customers to see if they are already collecting the same or similar data. If so, comparisons should be made and the best practices should be shared. The team should also define the additional scope:

- How many observations will be needed?
- What will be the time interval for subsequent data collection?
- Will past, present, and future data be collected?
- What methodologies will be employed to record all the data?

Note: If the team wishes to include historical data as part of the study, pay careful attention to how reliable the data and its source have been and if continuing to use such data is advisable. Suspect data should be discarded.

When all the data on a population are collected, this data are often referred to as a *census*. A portion or subset of the total data collection process is known as *sampling*. There are three key sampling advantages:

- The objective is to predict or draw conclusions about the population using the sample.
- Often collecting all the data is impractical or too costly.
- Sometimes data collection is a destructive process.

Sampling data must have qualities that meet certain criteria:

- Unbiased
- Random
- Representative of population

Unbiased

The project team must inspect the data before using in the project. If a sample appears to be different from the population or the process due to the presence or influence of any factor, the sample is known as a biased sample. As data are collected, biases may occur:

- Estimation bias—If repeated random samples from a given population produce a statistic with a mean or expected value that differs from the target to be estimated, it is defined as estimation bias (illustrated in Figure 3.7). Conversely, a sample statistic on the average and across many samples that takes on a value equal to the population parameter that is to be estimated is called an unbiased estimator. For example,

Let:
T = True value of population parameter or the target value
E = Sample estimator
μ_E = Mean of sampling distribution

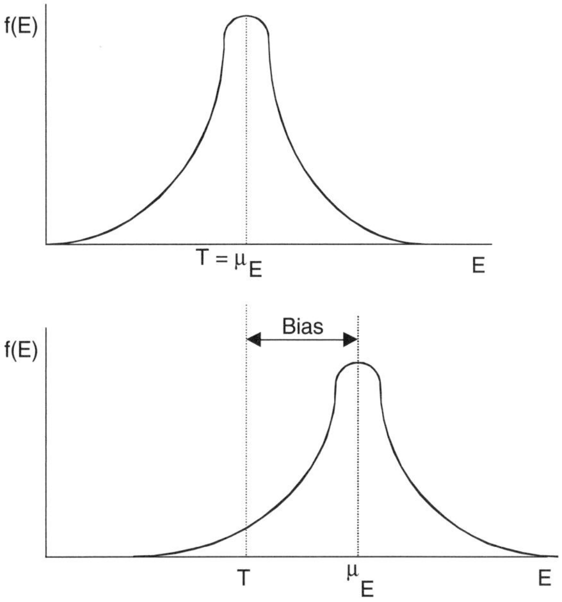

Figure 3.7. Unbiased vs. Biased Estimator

Then:

$\mu_E - T$ = Sample bias

Bias was introduced when the data were collected without regard to key elements that could influence the population or process. A sample is considered to be representative of the population only when it is bias-free.

- Exclusion bias—Service call response time is defined as "the clock starts once the message is read/listened to and the clock stops when the service person reaches the customer site." If any portion of this service call response time is excluded from the analysis, the analysis is defined as exclusion-biased.
- Inclusion bias—The service time clock starts when the service technician reaches the customer site and the clock stops when the service technician completes the job and leaves the customer site. If the service technician's travel time from the office to the customer site is included in the data, the data is inclusion-biased.

Accuracy and precision. Collect several measurements on a single unit of product and then compute the mean. The accuracy of the collected data would depend on the difference between the *sample mean* and the *true mean*. The spread of values around the mean is called the precision, or repeatability, of the system. Usually accuracy and precision are thought of in reference to meters and gauges, but it is important to note that these concepts also apply to human sensing. For example, if four product-checking inspectors work on a manufacturing floor and examine the same product separately, a high probability exists that each inspector may find a different number of errors—a result known as *lack of precision*. Furthermore, all of the inspectors may fail to identify a specific error—a result identified as *lack of accuracy*. Training classes for product checkers and inspectors and ongoing audits are the techniques for ensuring accurate and precise data.

Another way of looking at sample data accuracy is with a scenario. For example, a team wants to establish the accuracy of its process to measure defects in purchase orders. First, the team collects a "standard group" of purchase orders. Then this team has an "expert group" establish the type and number of defects in the collected group of purchase orders. Next, a "normal group" (regular employees working in the purchasing department) checks the standard group of purchase orders. Differences between what is found in the standard group of purchase orders by the normal group and what the known defect level is as established by the expert group represent the inaccuracy or bias of the measurement process.

- Missing data bias—Missing data can bias conclusions.
- Professional bias—Failure to follow an established data collection process is the most common professional bias.

Random

Randomness in the collected data helps to avoid biases. Data should be collected in no predetermined order, and each element should have an equal probability of being selected for measurement:

- Time specific
- Order of data collection
- Data collector

Representative of Population

Collected sample data should accurately reflect the population or process. Representative sampling would help the project team to avoid biases, specifically in the proposed process or the population under investigation. If the population is small, there is always the option of not taking samples, but instead to use the option of collecting data from the entire population. This option might provide the most accurate measure of the average (mean) value, but for logistic and/or cost reasons, it might not be practical.

A commonly used approach is to obtain a representative sample and estimate the parameters based on the sample. This approach costs less, but does not provide as much accuracy as would be obtained from the population.

If the team knows the degree of accuracy about the sample mean in relation to population mean, then the team assigns the usefulness value to the sample data in the decision-making process—known as the *confidence interval*. For example, when estimating the average service time from samples, the team may obtain a 95% confidence interval for the average of 2.5 to 3.5 hours, which means that if the team takes repeated samples from the population, 95 out of 100 times the team would expect the sample average to be between 2.5 and 3.5 hours. The statistical theory that supports the confidence interval is known as the Central Limit Theorem. (See the discussion in Section 3.7, *Probabilistic Data Distribution.*)

Sample size and sampling frequency are important issues in data collection. A rule of thumb in sample size is that between 25 to 45 data points are considered a good sample. (See Section 3.6, *Determining Sample Size.*) Sampling frequency depends on the data collection objective. For example, if the data collection objective is to understand hour-to-hour variation, samples would need to be taken at least every hour, preferably more than one data point every hour.

Step 4. Ensure Repeatability, Reproducibility, Accuracy, and Stability

The project team must recognize that over any length of time, and if data are not conforming to the *repeatability*, *reproducibility*, *accuracy*, and *stability* factors, unreliable data may be collected. A good practice is testing, perhaps on a small scale, how data collection and measurement should proceed. Upon simulation, the possible factors and what could be done to mitigate the effects of these factors or to eliminate the factors altogether should become apparent. Next is a short description of each factor.

Repeatability

The data being collected (measured) should be repeatable. In the same setting, an operator/collector should be able to reach essentially the same outcome multiple times for a defined process/product when using the same equipment. For example, an operator is producing a rough-turned steel shaft on a turning machine. Production time takes 5 minutes. If the same setting is used to produce a second shaft, the production time should be very close to 5 minutes.

Reproducibility

All data collectors who are measuring the same items with the same equipment should reach essentially the same outcomes. For example, consider a packaging operation. A packaging operator is wrapping each book individually, then packing five books in a box, and then sealing and labeling the box. A member of the data collection team timing the packaging cycle time recorded the time as 6 minutes. If another person from the data collection team collects the packaging cycle time data, then he/she should measure almost the same time.

Accuracy

The degree to which the measurement system is accurate would generally be the difference between an observed average measurement and the associated known standard value. For example, if the inches on a ruler were divided into eight (8) parts, the smallest measurement on the ruler would be an eighth (1/8) of an inch. If this ruler were used to measure the length of a bar, then the smallest fraction value that could represent the difference between the observed and the standard value measured would be an eighth of an inch (1/8 inch).

Stability

The degree to which the measurement system is stable is generally expressed by the variation resulting from the same data collector measuring the same item with the same equipment over an extended period. For example, in the heat-treating process of a shaft, if *smaller* were the variation in the processing time and heat-treated shaft quality, then *higher* would be the system stability.

Step 5. Define Data Collection Process

Data collection steps 1 through 4 assist a team in defining/identifying their data specifications and requirements. The data specifications and requirements will lead to defining the data collection process. Once the data collection process has been defined and developed, follow-through from start to finish of the process will ensure that the plan is being executed consistently and accurately.

The project leader has the responsibility of communicating what is to be collected and the rationale behind it to all data collectors and participants. Additionally, the team leader should review all applicable definitions, procedures, and guidelines and confirm with each team member that there is universal agreement among the team members. Follow-up could be some form of training or a demonstration of the data collection process as defined in the plan.

Oversight by the team leader during the data collection process is preferred. Oversight allows participants to know if the plan is being followed properly or improperly. Failure to oversee the data collection process at the early stages might mean that a later-course correction will be required. Much of the data collection and/or measurement efforts would be wasted.

It is important to realize that data are being collected for a Six Sigma project—the project has already been recognized as having a serious problem. Therefore, there is a high probability that the process has numerous rework loops and complex flow patterns that have been added over the years in an effort to keep the process working despite its problems. This type of process complexity makes data collection difficult. For example, an inserter manufacturing company discovered that their customer order booking process could follow as many as six different paths due to changes in system configuration, customer job requirements, and poor communication between customers and manufacturer's technical group. Data collectors must identify the exact process as they collect data in this type of process.

Six Sigma team leaders should think carefully about the possibility of bias before asking a person in the process area to collect data. If bias is a possibility, the team leader should select an *independent observer* to collect information (data). Specific examples include:

- If a Six Sigma team member is collecting data, a probability of process alteration exists. This alteration is nothing more than a minor inconvenience to the process team, but this team member may introduce new conditions into the process, which fundamentally change the process performance and can result in biased data or a misrepresentation of the actual process.
- Although it may be tempting and convenient to use supervisors or managers as data collectors, resist this temptation. Sometimes, members of management cannot resist the temptation to draw their own conclusions and begin tampering with the process during the data collection effort. Additionally, if employees learn that their manager is collecting data, they might alter the process during the study period.

In either case, the result can be biased data.

- Commonly project team members serve as data collectors, a practice which can also produce biased data. For example, if a team member has some advanced theory or hypothesis about the cause of the problem, and this team member has been assigned to collect data, he/she may unintentionally disregard observations that are not consistent with his/her theory or hypothesis or he/she may inadvertently tamper with the process by discussing suggestions for changes with the process resource while collecting data. Assignment of the persons who will perform the data collection task is critical.

An "independent observer" can also be a technological tool rather than a person. Automated data collection, using self-recording test equipment, video cameras, or computers with verifications and crosschecking, can be a very effective way to collect accurate, unbiased information without disrupting the natural process. Also important is ensuring that the automated data collection device is observing the complete picture.

Another way to avoid bias is to compile existing data for another project (process) and use that data for the selected project. For example, if the team is interested in service response time, it might analyze a service request message for date and time, and then compare that information with the service technician's log-in date and time at the customer site. There would definitely be less potential for bias in this data than there would be in a special study request to the Service Group to collect data.

Once the team has defined the questions, the type of data needed, the data collection points in the process, and the data collectors, the Six Sigma team is now ready to design the data collection form. If data are to be collected on a computer, the team must design the data-reporting screen so that all pertinent data are collected. For example, suppose a team wants to collect start and end times on a machine for an operation. If two machines are available and the operator has the option of selecting either machine, then the data reporting screen must display both machines on the screen so the operator can provide the start and end times for the actual machine used for the operation. Basic requirements in a data collection form include:

- Utilize the concept of KISS (Keep It Simple, Stupid). When people are struggling or are simply too busy trying to deal with a problem, the last thing on their mind is collecting data for a team's project. If the team designs the form and keeps the data collector's needs in mind, people involved in recording the data will be more willing to accept the task.
- Design the form to reduce the possibility of errors in recording or interpreting the data. Provide options when possible, e.g., a checklist.
- Provide pictures, sketches, and examples. "Clues" can help ensure more consistent and reliable data.
- Design the form to also collect additional information for future analysis, reference, and traceability, e.g., reference information such as date, time, shift, place (location), equipment, operator, material, etc.
- Design the form to be as self-explanatory as possible, with minimum instructions.
- Provide a professional looking data collection form or data collection computer screen, e.g., a handmade form with handwritten information is difficult to read and understand.

Once the information collection process has started, next is to audit/monitor the process.

Step 6. Review Data Collection

Referring to the questions of "Are the data collection and measurement systems reproducible, repeatable, accurate, and stable?" and "Are the results (data and measurement) reasonable?" and "Do the results meet the criteria?" is important. For example, the project team should audit the data-collection effort at random by reviewing the data collection process and reviewing the data collected forms. There is no reason to wait until all data have been collected. The nature, degree, and the formality of such audits will vary according to the complexity of the project.

If the results do not meet the criteria, then the team leader should determine where breakdowns exist and what to do with data and/or measurements that are suspect. Review the operational definitions and methodology with the participants (team members) and try to clear up any misunderstandings or misinterpretations that might have caused the breakdowns.

Once the data have been collected, they must be presented. Section 3.4 will discuss the Data Presentation Plan. Before moving on, consider Exercise 3.4.

Exercise 3.4: A Data Collection Plan

Using information in Example 3.1 as a basis:

1. Develop a data collection plan for an architect's house design project.
2. Identify questions to be answered from the collected data.
3. Justify the sampling data plan.
4. Identify data collection points.
5. Develop a data collection form(s).
6. Develop a data audit and validation plan.

Important considerations:

- Ensure that the data collectors are unbiased.
- Provide appropriate instructions with the data collection form(s).
- Provide basic training in data collection if necessary.
- Provide oversight during the data collection process.

3.4 DATA PRESENTATION PLAN

Data present information about a product or process. The data may be qualitative or quantitative. In any project/process, effective presentation of the data is as important as the collection of the data. Weeding out irrelevant information and conveying all relevant information accurately and unambiguously are also important. Because data may support or reject project objectives, data become a very critical part of any project or process.

Numerous data presentation techniques are available to describe data. Some commonly used techniques will be described:

- Tables, histograms, and box plots describe both the central tendency and the distribution of data.
- Bar graphs and stacked bar graphs compare information from different sources.
- Pie charts proportionate the distribution relationship in the data (information).
- Line graphs, control charts, and run charts describe data (information) changes over time.
- Mean, median, and mode describe the central tendency of data.
- Range, variance, and standard deviation describe data distribution.

As a project team analyzes the data, the team must determine which data properties that support project issues/problems are dominant in the collected/historical data:

- If the team is looking for "What is the central tendency of the data?" and/or "Where do the values tend to occur?" then the team should analyze the data for mean, median, and mode.
- If data distribution (dispersion) is the team's interest, then the team should analyze the data for range, variance, and standard deviation and try to summarize the information in tables, histograms, and box plots.
- If the team is interested in knowing the data variation over time and if there is any trend over time, the team should summarize the data in line graphs, control charts, and run charts.
- If the team is interested in the proportionate distribution of data, the team should to summarize data in a pie chart.
- If the team is interested in comparing data from different sources, the team should develop bar graphs and stacked bar graphs.

These data presentation techniques will now be described with examples.

Note: Several software tools such as the MINITAB software package are also available for data presentation and statistical analysis. The application of MINITAB will be briefly discussed in Section 3.5.

3.4.1 Tables, Histograms, and Box Plots

Tables

Constructing a good statistical table is an art that requires a great deal more understanding and participation than simply presenting data in rows and columns. Specific table attributes are necessary to develop tables and to obtain the most useful information to support the project/process (see Tables 3.10 and 3.11 for examples):

Ordered array. Listing data in a table in ascending or descending magnitude is a major improvement. Most users are not interested in the detail contained in the table or they prefer considerable condensation of the data.

Classes. To best serve the goal of clarity, personal judgment is used to determine how many collectively exhaustive and mutually exclusive groupings (classes) of data should be made. An example will explain the concept of grouping:

- Grouping type: *Qualitative*, e.g., the type of business (partnership, proprietorship, or corporation), which is then subdivided into small, medium, and large
- Grouping type: *Quantitative*, e.g., the number of personal computers (PCs) owned by households (households own 0 PC, 1 PCs, 2 PCs, etc.)
- Grouping type: *Continuous quantitative*, e.g., gallons of gasoline produced in the oil refinery industry

In the case of quantitative data, determining class is also considered desirable: approximate class width = (large value – smallest value in data set)/desired number of classes.

Absolute class frequency. The absolute number of observations that falls into a given category is defined as the absolute class frequency.

Absolute frequency distribution. The tabular summary of a data set showing the absolute class frequencies in each of the classes is known as the data set's absolute frequency distribution.

Relative class frequency. Relative class frequency is a fraction or proportion of all observations that fall into various classes, i.e., the ratio of the number of observations in a particular class to the total number of observations collected.

Relative frequency distribution. The tabular summary of a data set presenting the relative class frequencies in each of the classes is known as the data set's relative frequency distribution.

Cumulative class frequency. A *cumulative class frequency* is the sum of the (absolute or relative) class frequencies for all classes in question (project study) for the given quantitative data. Accordingly, a *cumulative frequency distribution* is a tabular summary of a data set showing for each of several classes the absolute

Table 3.10. Cumulative Frequency Distribution of Sales of the Top 100 U.S.-Based Corporations

Class[a]	Absolute Class Frequency[b]	Cumulative Absolute Class Frequency[c] Starting Point	Relative Class Frequency[d]	Cumulative Relative Class Frequency[e] Starting Point
0 – under 500	3	3	0.03	0.03
500 – under 1,000	40	3 + 40 = 43	0.40	0.03 + 0.40 = 0.43
1,000 – under 5,000	33	43 + 33 = 76	0.33	0.43 + 0.33 = 0.76
5,000 – under 20,000	12	76 + 12 = 88	0.12	0.76 + 0.12 = 0.88
20,000 – under 50,000	5	88 + 5 = 93	0.05	0.88 + 0.05 = 0.93
50,000 – under 75,000	5	93 + 5 = 98	0.05	0.93 + 0.05 = 0.98
75,000 – under 120,000	2	98 + 2 = 100	0.02	0.98 + 0.02 = 1.00

Note: Hypothetical data.
[a]Sales in millions of dollars; [b]number of customers in class; [c]number of customers in class or in lower classes; [d]proportion of all customers in class; [e]proportion of all customers in class or in lower classes.

Table 3.11. Sales of Personal Computers in Hartford and Connecticut, 1993–2002

	Thousands of PC Units Sold	
Year	Hartford	Connecticut
1993	20	450
1994	25	550
1995	28	610
1996	32	700
1997	35	750
1998	35	770
1999	40	850
2000	40	870
2001	35	800
2002	30	775

Note: Hypothetical data.

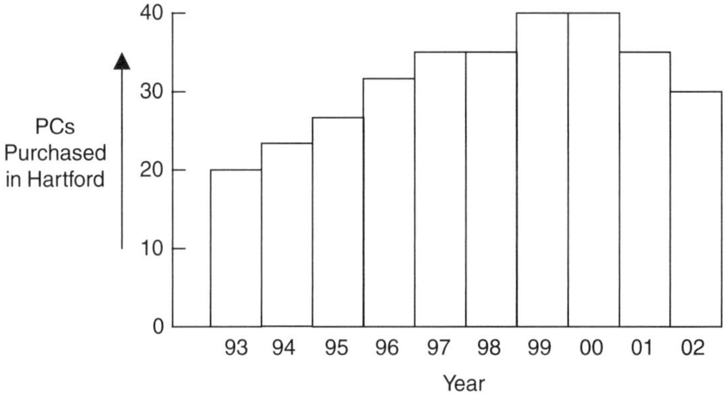

Figure 3.8A. Histogram of PCs Purchased in Hartford

number or proportion of observations that are less than or equal to the upper limits of the classes in question (project study).

Histograms

A histogram presents frequency distribution of a set of data in graphical form. It is a simple and powerful tool for a user that facilitates understanding the product/process and developing a feasible and fact-based solution concept about the root causes of problem(s). The pattern of variation in the data often leads to breaking up of the data in various ways to find additional patterns, a process known as *stratification*, which will be discussed in more detail in Chapter 4 (*Analyze*). If the information can be condensed into any type of table, the same information can also be presented in a histogram. The PCs purchased data for Hartford are presented in table form in Table 3.11. They are presented in histogram form in Figure 3.8A.

Common knowledge is that during the 1990s the economy was growing, the employment level was high, and people were making good salaries. If *PC sales* are any indication of economic prosperity, then PC sale data are plotted in the form of a histogram (Figure 3.8A). This histogram shows a definite growth, with a peak in the years 1999 and 2000. If a team were to plot a histogram for the Connecticut *PC sales* data in Table 3.11, a similar conclusion would be drawn.

Information is easily visible in histogram, e.g.:

- Value variation, if it exists
- Visible pattern or trend, which is sometimes difficult to see in a table

Because interpretation of the collected information is important, the objectives of a histogram analysis include:

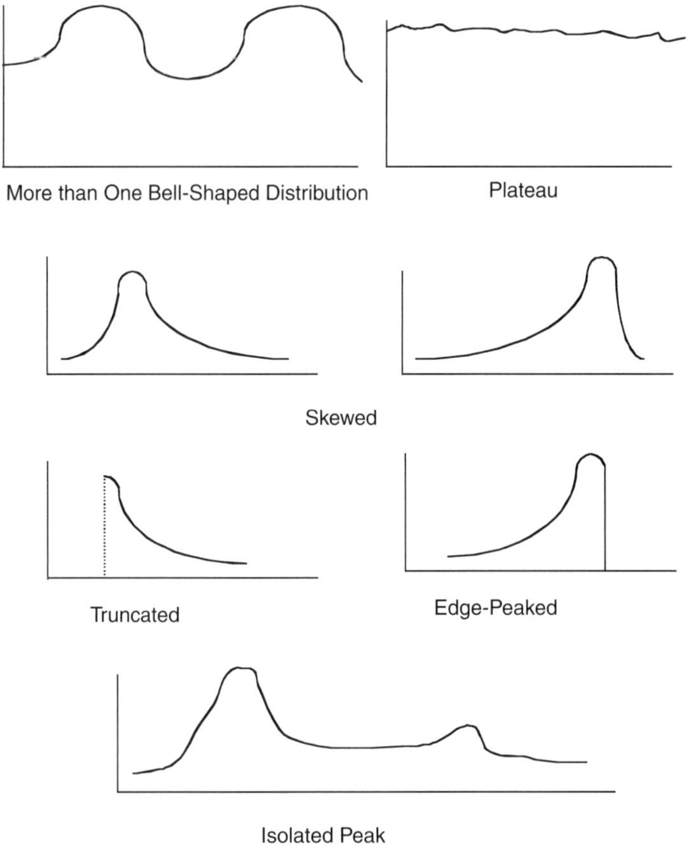

Figure 3.8B. Various Histogram Patterns

- To identify and classify the pattern of variation
- To develop a reasonable and relevant explanation for the developed pattern

Generally, data are collected in tabular form and then transferred to a histogram. The variation pattern in the data often provides leads for the solution or indicates a need for collection of additional data. Project teams may not use a histogram because they assume that the team members already know all they need to know, or the team may assume that the average or range provides an adequate summary of the data. Once the data are plotted in a histogram, the bars that develop can create various patterns (Figure 3.8B):

Bell-shaped distribution. The most typical and natural type of data distribution from a process is a bell-shaped distribution. A non bell-shaped distribution may also be obtained.

More than one-bell-shaped distribution (multimodal frequency distribution). This pattern can be the result of a combination of two or more bell-shaped distributions, suggesting that the data are from two or more processes.

Plateau distribution. This pattern is most likely the result of several different bell-shaped distributions evenly spread throughout the range of the data.

Skewed distribution. A skewed pattern may be skewed either to the left or to the right. This pattern generally occurs when there is a practical limit or a specification limit on one side which is relatively close to the nominal value. These distributions are not considered to be undesirable, but the team should question the impact of these values in the long "tail" data.

Truncated distribution. This type of distribution has generally smooth, bell-shaped distributions, with a part of the distribution removed through external decisions, e.g., a 100% inspection or a review process. These data removal efforts are additional costs and therefore should be good candidates for removal.

Edge-peaked distribution. This distribution occurs when the extended "tail" data of the distribution have been removed and lumped into a single category at the edge of the range of the data. For example, the male population of the U.S. is presented in a histogram, in which each bar represents a certain height group: <5 feet, ≥5 feet, but <5 feet, 1 inch, ≥5 feet, 1 inch, but <5 feet, 2 inches, …, >5 feet, 11 inches. The last bar represents everyone 5 feet, 11 inches and taller. Therefore, all males of height 6 feet, 6 feet, 1 inch, 6 feet, 2 inches, etc. are lumped into a single category at the edge of the range of the data. Most of the time, this shape indicates inaccurate recording of the data.

Isolated peak distribution. This pattern indicates a high probability that two separate processes are at work. The small size of the second peak indicates the presence of unusual conditions.

Box Plot

Box plots[8] are similar to histograms. They provide a graphic summary of the variation in a given set of data. The box plot is useful when working with small sets of data or when comparing several different sets of data.

A box plot displays: the three quartiles — first, d(Q_1), median, d(M), and third, d(Q_3); the minimum (lowest value); and the maximum (highest value) of the data set on a rectangular box. The data are aligned either horizontally or vertically. Horizontally laid-out data goes from left to right, and vertically laid-out data goes from bottom up. The logic for the five values is as follows:

- Arrange data in ascending order (from smallest to largest) and let the number of observations in the data set be n.

- First quartile value, $d(Q_1)$ = Depth of the first quartile, where depth is the number of observations (data points) to count from the beginning of the ordered data set.

  $d(Q_1) = (n + 2)/4$

  If the value of $d(Q_1)$ includes a fraction/decimal, the quartile value is interpolated.
- Median value, $d(M)$ = Depth of median

  $d(M) = (n + 1)/2$

  Same rule applies as above.
- Third quartile value, $d(Q_3)$ = Depth of third quartile

  $d(Q_3) = ((3)n + 2)/4$

  Same rule applies as above.
- Lowest and highest values are self-explanatory.

Example 3.5: Develop a Box Plot

Utilize the PC sales data from Hartford (see data in Table 3.11) and develop a box plot. There are ten observations (n = 10). Arrange these observations in an ascending order: 20, 25, 28, 30, 32, 35, 35, 35, 40, 40.

Lowest value = 20

Highest value = 40

$d(Q_1) = (10 + 2)/4 = 3$

$d(M) = (10 + 1)/2 = 5.5$

$d(Q_3) = ((3)(10) + 2)/4 = 8$

Therefore,

First quartile value, $Q_1 = 28$

Median value = 33.5

Third quartile value, $Q_3 = 35$

The generated box plot is presented in Figure 3.9. The box plot indicates that the distribution of PC sales is not fairly symmetric around the central value because the lowest and the highest values and the length of the left and the right boxes around the median are not the same.

A schematic box plot is similar to box plot; it is created in MINITAB. A schematic box plot follows rules:

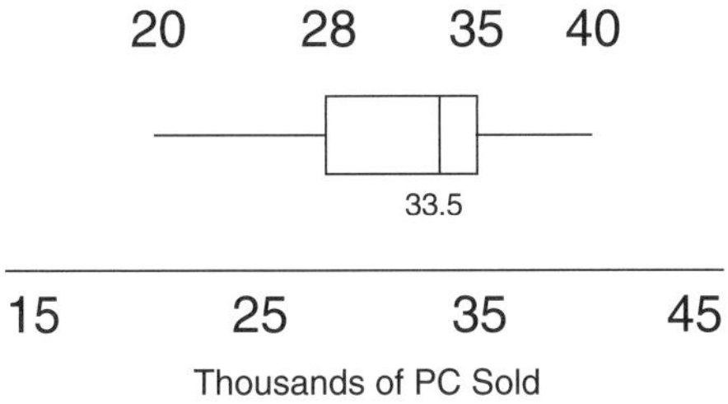

Figure 3.9. Box Plot for Hartford PC Sales Data

- There are five values, similar to a box plot.
- The *whiskers* are now limited and are called the lower *adjacent* value and the upper *adjacent* value instead of the lowest and the highest values. (*Note:* Whiskers are the connecting lines between the lower adjacent value and the Q_1 box and between the upper adjacent value and the Q_3 box.)
- Observation values beyond the adjacent values are called *outliers* and are generally identified with an asterisk (*).
- A new value needs to be calculated, the inter quartile range (IQR). The IQR is the difference between Q_3 and Q_1.
- Determine the lower adjacent value, which is defined as the smallest observation (collected data) = $Q_1 - (1.5)$ (IQR).
- Determine the upper adjacent value, which is defined as the largest observation (collected data) = $Q_3 + (1.5)$ (IQR).
- Plotting follows the same rules as for the box plot.

3.4.2 Bar Graphs and Stacked Bar Graphs

Bar graphs and stacked bar graphs are an extension of histograms. These graphs are particularly effective in presenting data about qualitative or discrete quantitative variables. *Bar graphs* are often used to show a comparison between groups. Examples are presented in Figures 3.10A, 3.10B, and 3.10C. *Stacked bar graphs* place the bars for each group on top of each other. A sample graph is presented in Figure 3.10D. These graphs present the data by a series of noncontiguous horizontal bars or vertical columns, the length of which are proportional to the values that are to be depicted. A large amount of information can be summarized in a small area, communicating complex situations concisely and clearly.

Bar graphs are useful when comparing individual bars within a group as well as the same subgroup across several groups. Stacked bar graphs are useful in

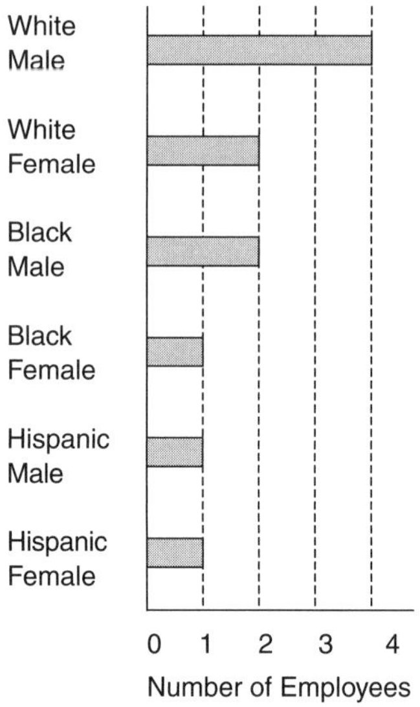

Figure 3.10A. Horizontal Bar Graph of Connecticut Swimming Club's Employee Composition (Hypothetical Data)

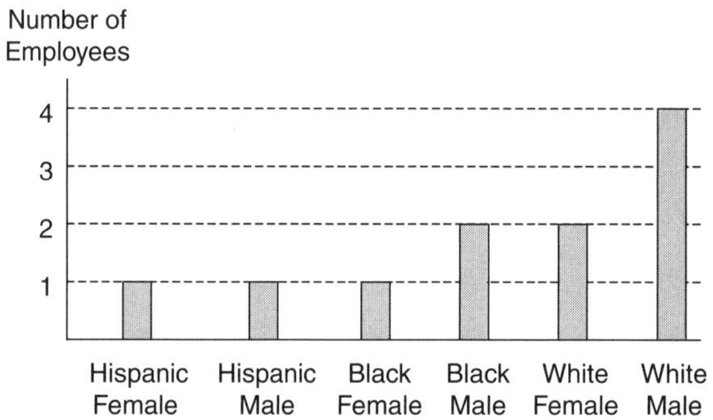

Figure 3.10B. Vertical Bar Graph of Connecticut Swimming Club's Employee Composition (Hypothetical Data)

emphasizing the total of all the parts and the contribution of the individual pieces to the total. Stacking should be done only when the sum of the independent variables is meaningful. For example, in the example of the Connecticut Swimming Club, employee composition is divided into two groups—female and male. A stacked bar graph displays the results. Use a stacked bar graph if higher impor-

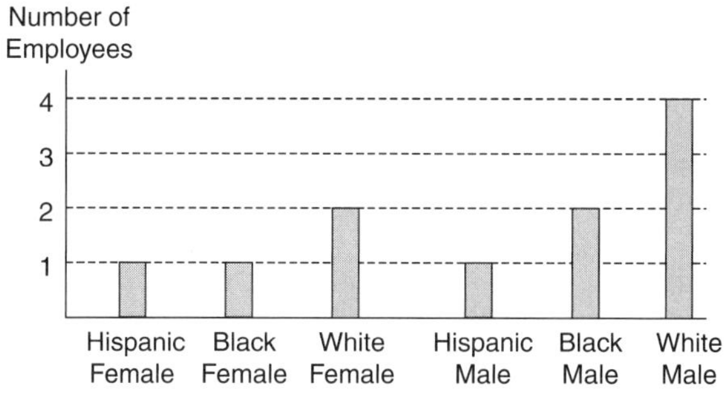

Figure 3.10C. Grouped Bar Graph of Connecticut Swimming Club's Employee Composition (Hypothetical Data)

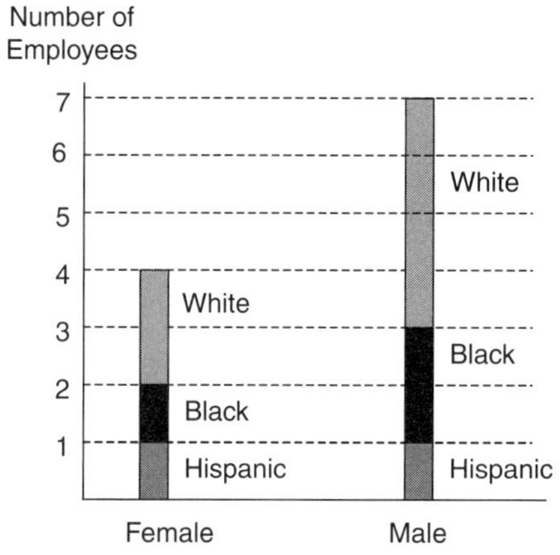

Figure 3.10D. Stacked Bar Graph of Connecticut Swimming Club's Employee Composition (Hypothetical Data)

tance is given on the total of the components and the contribution of the each component to that total.

A grouped bar graph places more than one bar at each value for the independent variables, e.g., a bar graph that is developed to compare the number of customers served by a service company for 3 years by major cities in the Midwestern part of the U.S. (Chicago, Kansas City, Detroit, and Milwaukee). Use a grouped bar graph if the individual variable data do not add up to a meaningful simple total or to facilitate the comparison of not only the individual bars within a group, but also the bars of the same subgroup across several groups. In the above example, the graph not only compares the 3 years of service data within each major city in the Midwestern states, but it also compares service data across the cities.

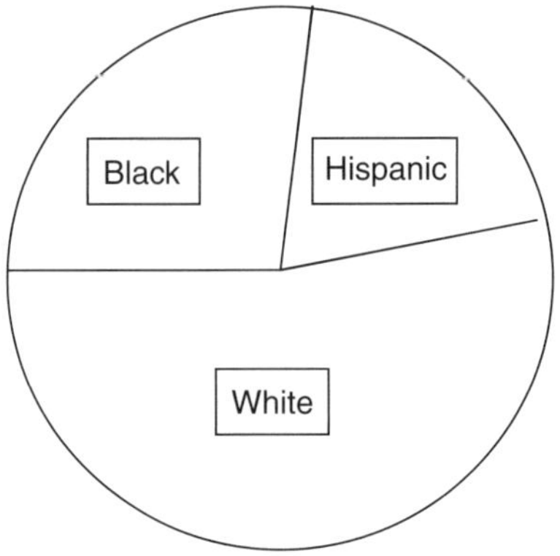

Figure 3.11. Resources Distribution Pie Chart (Hypothetical Data)

3.4.3 Pie Charts

Typically, a pie chart is a segmented circle that is able to portray divisions (proportionate distribution) of some aggregate provided the number of divisions is not excessive. Pie charts are generally utilized to show relative contribution/composition of a whole (also achieved with stacked bar graphs). A sample pie chart is presented in Figure 3.11.

In Figure 3.11, resource employment by race (e.g., black, Hispanic, and white) at the Connecticut Swimming Club clearly stands out: white personnel substantially outnumber other races. To draw a pie chart:

- Determine the percentage for each category.
- Convert the percentage values into degrees of angles by taking the calculated percentage of 360 degrees.
- Draw a circle and mark the segments of the pie chart.
- Label the segments and entitle the chart.

Pie charts can also be used to compare two or more groups and their distribution within each group, e.g., comparing the employment distribution by race among two or more swimming clubs.

3.4.4 Line Graphs (Charts), Control Charts, and Run Charts

Several types of charts are utilized to describe information changes over time. Three types of charts (line, control, and run) will now be described.

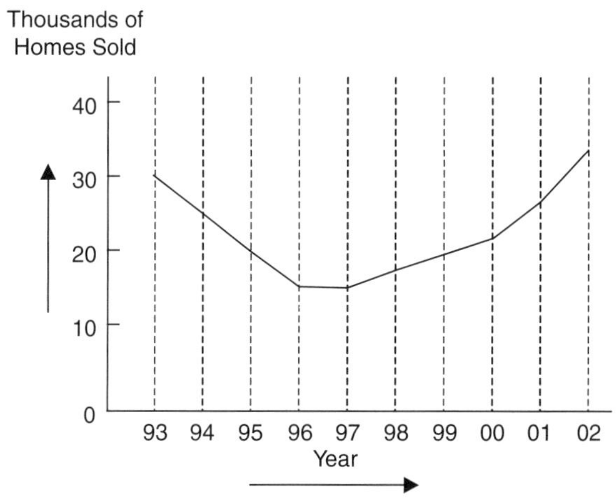

Figure 3.12. Line Chart—Home Sales in Connecticut (Hypothetical Data)

Line Graphs (Charts)

Line charts are useful for presenting the evolution of given variables over time. The time increments can be large or small. A line chart can be utilized when both variables being compared are continuous (or almost continuous), e.g., temperature, quantities, time, length, etc. Line charts are also useful for looking at trends. Line charts are drawn on a regular arithmetic scale as well as on a semilogarithmic scale. An example is presented in Figure 3.12. The chart in Figure 3.12 shows the trend in the number of houses sold in the state of Connecticut.

A line graph can be developed by following these instructions:

- Determine the range of the Y-axis (ordinate) and the size of each increment. Label the ordinate, including the unit of measure.
- Determine the range on the X-axis (abscissa) and the size of each increment. Label the abscissa, including the unit of measure.
- Draw X- and Y-axes (and a grid if needed).
- Plot data points.
- Connect the points with a line
- Label and entitle the graph.

Control Charts

Business leaders know that there is an inherent variability in any data series, whether the series describes the size of inventories, customer service time, labor costs, or even the loss of regular customers. Control charts are graphical devices that highlight the average performance of data series and the dispersion around the average. Control charts are important tools in statistical process control. The average performance of the past is viewed as the standard to which to current performance is compared. Typical dispersion of the past is used to set allowable limits for current performance. When plotting new data, immediately obvious is whether the data fall within the range of the expected or whether there are undesirable trends that need immediate management attention.

Control charts are also utilized to detect assignable causes. The user (the person using the control chart) is responsible for identifying the underlying root cause for an out-of-control condition, for developing and implementing an appropriate corrective action, and then following up to ensure that the assignable cause has been eliminated from the process. Remember these key points:

1. A state of statistical control is not a natural state for most processes.
2. The proper use of control charts will result in the elimination of assignable causes, yielding the process in-control and reduced process variability.
3. A control chart is ineffective without a system to develop and implement corrective actions that attack the root cause of problems. Business leadership and the participating group's involvement are usually necessary to accomplish this.

The user acquires an ability to interpret control charts accurately through experience. Critical and necessary are that the user has a thorough familiarity with both the statistical foundation of control charts and the nature of the process itself. Control charts are time-ordered graphical presentations of data that plot process variation over time. The centerline for the population represents the process average or middle point, while the centerline for the sample is the plotted measure. The sample centerline is expected to vary randomly in relation to the population centerline. Upper and lower control limits define the area—three standard deviations on either side of the centerline. These control limits reflect the expected range of variation for that process. A sample chart is presented in Figure 3.13. Terminology and symbols used are defined as:

μ = Centerline for population (population mean)

$\bar{X}$= Centerline for sample (sample mean)

σ = Population's standard deviation

s = Sample's standard deviation

n = Number of times standard deviation from the mean

UCL (upper control limit) $= \mu + n\,\sigma$ for population

$= \bar{X} + n\,s$ for sample

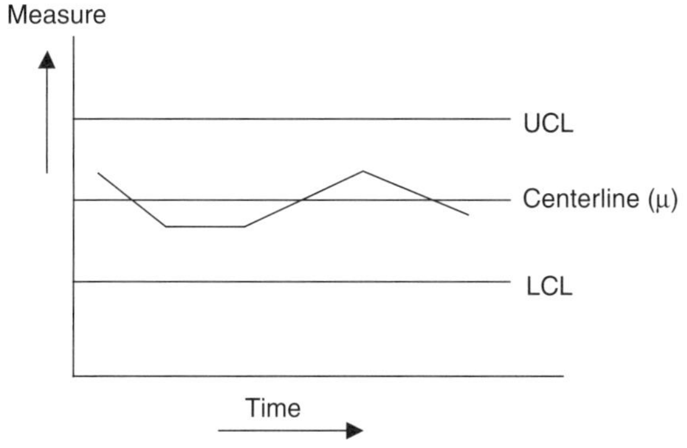

Figure 3.13. Control Chart and Its Components

LCL (lower control limit) = $\mu - n\,\sigma$ for population
= $\bar{X} - n$ s for sample

It is important that the data originally measured can be converted into "standard scores" defined by their own means and standard deviations (to be discussed in more detail in Section 6.4, *Statistical Process Control (SPC) Techniques*, of Chapter 6, *Control.*)

Run Charts

Run charts are simple graphical devices with time-ordered plots that do not identify any limits. These charts can be used to test the presence of special causes. A sample chart is presented in Figure 3.14.

3.4.5 Mean, Median, and Mode

The most important summary measures of central tendency are the mean, the median, and the mode. Keeping their meanings distinct is important so that each summary measure of central tendency can be used appropriately.

Mean

Among measures of central tendency, the most widely known measure is the mean. The correct terminology is the *arithmetic mean*, but this measure is also referred as the *average*. Adding all the data and dividing by the number of observations calculates the average. The average is *strongly affected* by extreme values (see Example 3.6). The following are symbolic expressions of the mean:

X_i = Observed value

where:

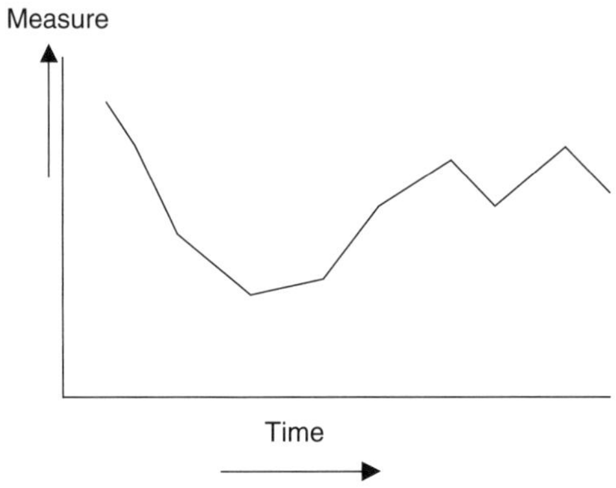

Figure 3.14. Run Chart and Its Components

$i = 1, 2, 3, \ldots, n$ (n = Number of values in a sample)

$i = 1, 2, \ldots, N$ (N = Number of values in a population)

μ = Population mean

$\bar{X}$ = Sample mean

$$\mu = \frac{X_1 + X_2 + \ldots + X_N}{N} = \frac{\sum_{i=1}^{N} X_i}{N}$$

$$\bar{X} = \frac{X_1 + X_2 + \ldots + X_n}{n} = \frac{\sum_{i=1}^{n} X_i}{n}$$

Median

Another important measure of central tendency, but quite different in nature from the mean, is the median. If the values are arranged in an ordered array of data, then the number of observations above and below the median will be equal. The median value is not affected by the extreme values (see Example 3.6):

- If the number of observations is even, the median is the average of the two observations nearest the middle.
- If the number of observations is odd, the median is the middle data observation.

Mode

The mode is defined as the most frequently occurring value in a data set (see Example 3.6).

Example 3.6: A Survey of Process Engineer Experience

A survey of the experience of process engineers in a company was conducted, providing the following data:

Process engineer	1	2	3	4	5	6	7	8
Experience (years)	2	2	4	5	6	6	6	9

Calculate the mean, median, and mode for the process engineers' experience.

Solution:

$$Mean,\ \overline{X} = \frac{2+2+4+5+6+6+6+9}{8} = \frac{40}{8} = 5\ years$$

$$Median = \frac{5+6}{2} = 5.5\ years$$

$$Mode = 6 \text{ years}$$

3.4.6 Range, Variance, and Standard Deviation

Knowledge of the variability or the distribution of data around their center of location is critical in many situations. Consider a person making a decision about which one of two businesses he/she should enter. Both businesses may promise the same median income, yet the incomes expected in one type of business may be scattered widely about the mean, while the expected incomes in the other business fall within a relatively narrow range of the median. Depending on their attitudes about risk, different people will evaluate these two business prospects differently.

Range

The difference between the largest and the smallest observations in a set of ungrouped data is the range.

Variance

The variance is a much more important measure of distribution, which is calculated by averaging the squares of the individual deviations from the mean.

Standard Deviation

The standard deviation is the most important measure of dispersion. The square root of the variance is known as the standard deviation:

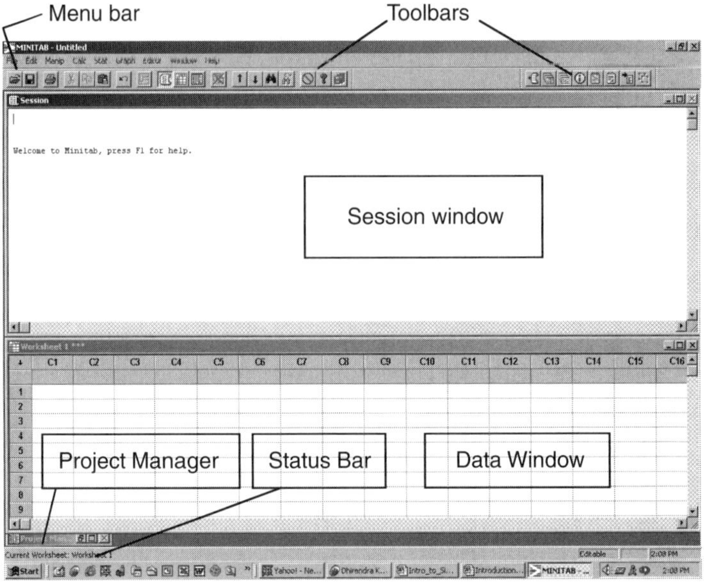

Figure 3.15. First Screen—Login MINITAB

The variance, for population $\sigma^2 = \dfrac{\sum(X - \bar{X})^2}{N}$

The variance, for sample $s^2 = \dfrac{\sum(X - \bar{X})^2}{n - 1}$

3.5 INTRODUCTION TO MINITAB®

This section introduces the MINITAB tool used in this book. MINITAB is one of several statistical software-type packages that are available in the marketplace. Because MINITAB is utilized in this book for statistical analysis, only introductory information is provided. Advanced information is available in books on MINITAB. Once the MINITAB tool is opened, an initial screen opens with the initial windows of MINITAB (Figure 3.15).

Initial Windows

- The *Session* window displays text output such as tables of statistics.
- The *Data* window is where column data for each work sheet are entered, edited, and viewed. This is not a spreadsheet. Columns define

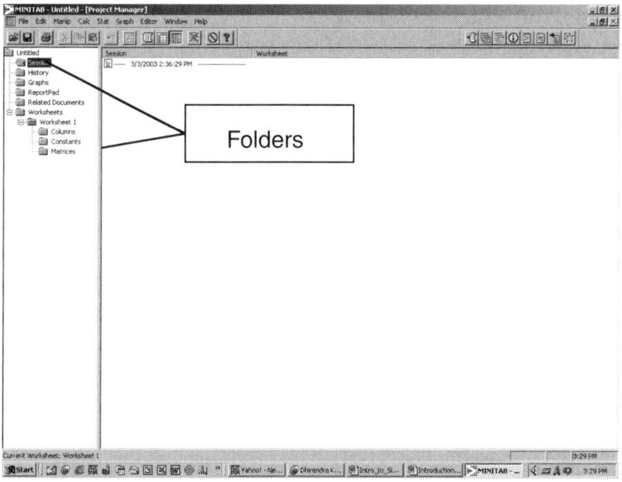

Figure 3.16. Project Manager Screen

variables. Variable names can be listed above the first row. There can be more than one data window.

- *Graph* windows are not displayed in Figure 3.15. These windows display graphs also. Up to 100 graph windows can be open at a time.

Menus and Tools

- The *Menu Bar* is where commands are chosen.
- The *Standard Toolbar* displays buttons for commonly used functions. The buttons change depending on which MINITAB window is active.
- The *Project Manager Toolbar* provides shortcuts to Project Manager folders.
- The *Status Bar* displays explanatory text whenever the cursor points to a menu item or Toolbar button.
- *Shortcut Menus* appear when right-clicking on any window in MINITAB or on any folder in Project Manager. The menu displays the most commonly used functions for that window or folder.

After clicking on Project Manager (PM) tool bar, the PM screen opens (see Figure 3.16). The left-hand column of the screen is a folder that allows navigating, viewing, and manipulating various parts of the project. By right-clicking on either the folders or the folder contents, a variety of menus can be accessed. Folder contents and their uses are listed in Table 3.12.

Table 3.12. Folders in Project Manager

Folder	Contents	Folder Use
Session	List of: - All session window output by command - All graphs	Manage session window output: - Jump to session window output - Copy, delete, rename, or print session window output or graphs - Append session window output or graphs to ReportPad
History	All commands used	- Repeat complex command sequence - Use commands to create macros
Graph	List of all graphs	Manage graphs: - Arrange, rename, or remove graphs - Append graphs to the ReportPad
ReportPad	ReportPad (a basic word-processing tool)	- Create, arrange, or edit reports of project work - Move ReportPad contents to a more-powerful word-processing program for further editing and layout
Reported documents	List of program files, documents, or Internet URLs that are related to MINITAB project	Quickly access project-related, non-MINITAB files for easy reference
Worksheet	Columns, constants, matrices, and design folders for each open worksheet	View summaries of worksheet information: - Column counts, missing values, and column descriptions - Constants, matrices, and design summary

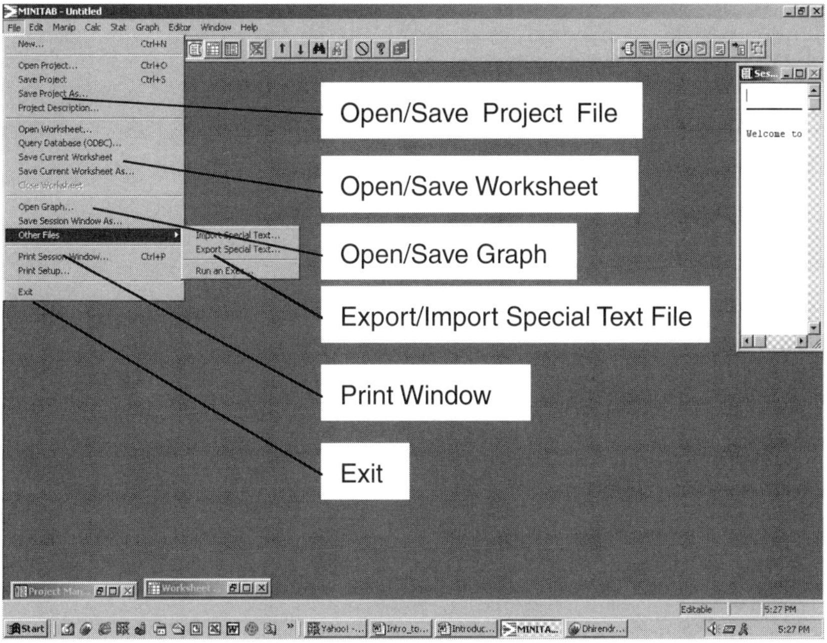

Figure 3.17. File Command from the Menu Bar

Menu Bar—File Command

The file menu is very similar to that of other Windows packages. Only active windows can be saved. Window information is presented in Figure 3.17.

Other Frequently Used Commands

- **Edit**
- **Manip**
- **Calc**
- **Stat**
- **Graph**
- **Editor**
- **Window**
- **Help**

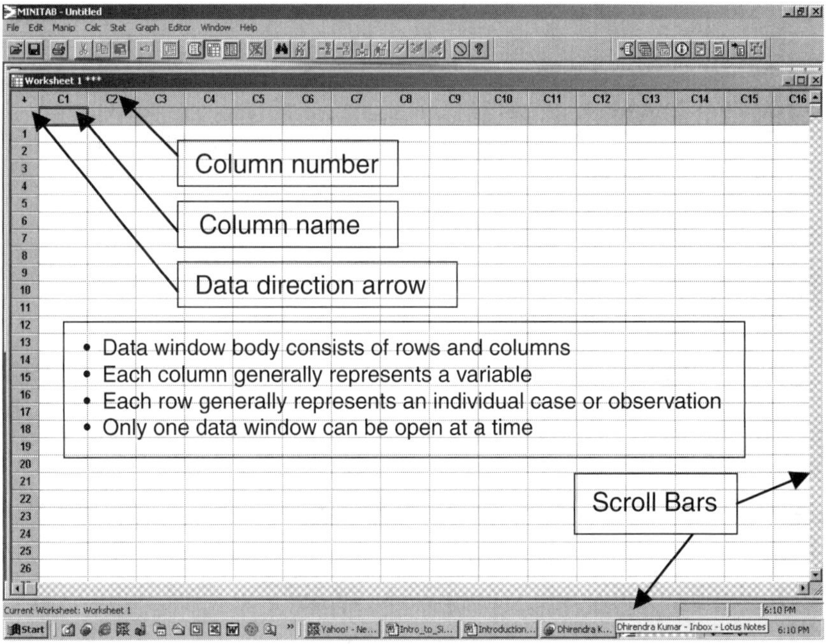

Figure 3.18. Data Window in MINITAB

Data Window

The Data window is a most critical window. Three types of data entered in the Data window:

- Numeric
- Date
- Text

Each column is identified as C1, C2, C3, and .... If the first row cell of any column carries a date, the column number is extended with "-D." If the first row cell of any column carries text, the column number is extended with "-T." A sample data window is presented in Figure 3.18.

Typing Data in the Data Window

To enter a value in a Data window cell, click on the cell, type a value, and press **Enter**. Multiple values can be entered in any order: row by row, column by column, or in blocks. Cells contain *values* only, not *formulas* as in Excel. To perform mathematical functions, use:

Calc > Calculator

Data can also be entered by:

- Copy/Paste from MINITAB and other sources such as Windows software (e.g., Excel)
- Generated from a set patterned data, random data, and storage
- Imported from many commonly used software packages (e.g., Excel, ASCII files)

If a column defined as "text" needs to be converted to "numeric," simply follow the command:

Manip > Change Data Type > Text to numeric

Dialog boxes will appear. Fill in the dialog boxes to indicate the column to be changed and where it is to be stored.

To move between all three data types (Text, Date, and Numeric), follow the command:

Manip > Change Data Type

Entering Data in Columns, Rows, or Blocks

To enter data from one column to the next column:

- Click the data direction arrow so it points down.
- Enter data, pressing **Tab** or **Enter** to move the active cell. Press **Ctrl+Enter** to move the active cell to the top of the next column.

To enter data from one row to the next row:

- Click the data direction arrow so it points to the right.
- Enter data in the cells of a row. Press **Ctrl+Enter** to move the active cell to the beginning of the next row.

To enter data within a block:

- Highlight the selected blocked area.
- Enter data. The active cell moves only within the selected area.
- To unselect the area, press an arrow key or click anywhere in the Data window.

Inserting Empty Cells, Rows, and Columns

- Select one or more cells.
- Choose **Editor > Insert Cells/Insert Rows/Insert Columns.**

Table 3.13. Descriptive Statistics—PC Sales in Hartford, Thousands

Variable	N	Mean	Median	
PC Sales	10	32.00	33.50	
Variable	**Tr Mean**	**SD**	**SE Mean**	
PC Sales	32.50	6.39	2.02	
Variable	**Minimum**	**Maximum**	**Q1**	**Q3**
PC Sales	20.00	40.00	27.25	36.25

Cells and rows are inserted above the selection; columns are inserted to the left of the selection.

MINITAB inserts the number of items that are selected, e.g., if cells in two rows are selected when **Editor** > **Insert Rows** is chosen, two rows are inserted.

Deleting Rows or Columns or Erasing the Contents of Rows or Columns

- To delete rows (or columns), highlight them and select, **Edit** > **Delete Cells**. The remaining rows (or columns) will be moved up (or over).
- To erase the contents of rows (or columns), highlight them and select, **Edit** > **Clear cells**. The other rows (or columns) will not be moved.

Exercise 3.5: Using MINITAB

PC sales statistics for Hartford are found in Table 3.11.

- Construct a histogram.
- Construct a box plot.
- Calculate the mean and standard deviation.

Use the MINITAB command:

Stat > **Basic Statistics** >**Display Descriptive Statistics**

Then select graph options of Histogram, Box Plot, and Graphical Summary. The descriptive statistics are found in Table 3.13. PC sales statistics are presented graphically in Figures 3.19A, 3.19B, and 3.19C.

Trimean. The trimean is computed by adding the 25th percentile plus twice the 50th percentile plus the 75th percentile and dividing by 4. The trimean is almost as resistant to extreme scores as the median. It is also less subject to sampling fluctuations than the arithmetic mean in extremely skewed distributions. The trimean is less efficient than the mean for normal distributions. The trimean is a good measure of central tendency and is probably not used as much as it should be.

Standard error of the mean (SE mean). The standard deviation of the distribution of sample means is commonly called the *standard error* of the mean. Standard deviation of the distribution of sample means = $(1/\sqrt{n})$ standard deviation of the universe of individual values.

3.6 DETERMINING SAMPLE SIZE

Before beginning to collect data, a team must know the sample size. This section will discuss determining the sample size.

To prove that a process has been improved, the team must measure the process capability before and after improvements have been implemented. This measurement allows the team to quantify the process improvement (e.g., defect reduction or productivity improvement) and translate the effects into estimated financial results. Improved financial results are something that business leaders understand and appreciate. If data are not readily available for the process, the team must answer:

- How many members of the population should be selected to ensure that the population is properly represented?
- If the data have been collected, how would the team determine if it has enough data?

Determining sample size is an important issue because samples that are too large can waste time, resources, and money, while samples that are too small can lead to inaccurate results. In many situations, the minimum sample size is needed to estimate a process parameter, such as the population mean μ.

Let, $\overline{X}$ = Sample mean based on the collected data. This sample mean is generally different from the population mean μ. The difference between the sample and population means can be considered to be an error. If E = margin of error, i.e., the maximum difference between the observed sample mean $\overline{X}$ and the true value of the population mean μ, then:

$$E = Z_{\alpha/2}\,(\sigma/\sqrt{n})$$

where:

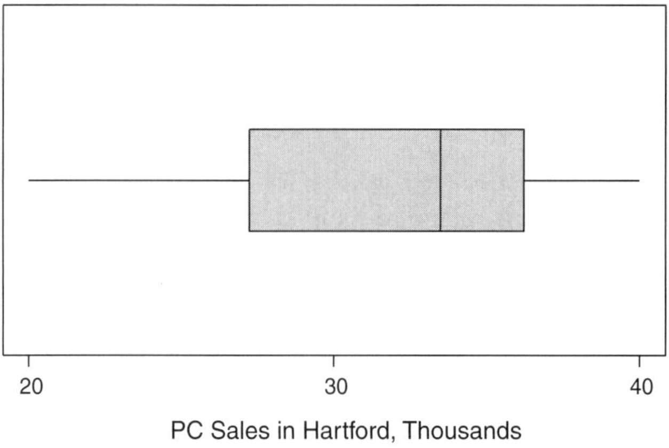

Figure 3.19A. Box Plot—PC Sales Statistics

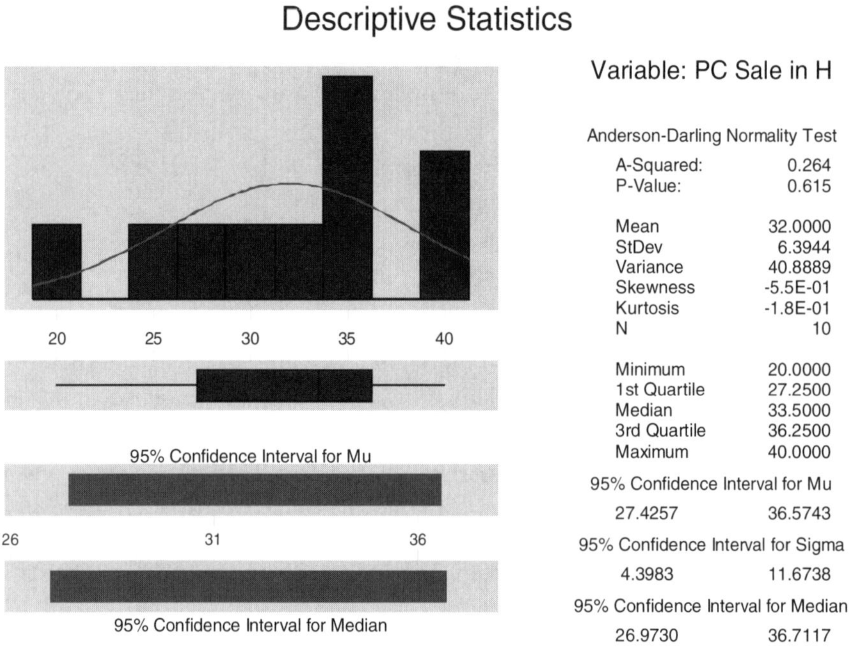

Figure 3.19B. Descriptive Statistics—PC Sales

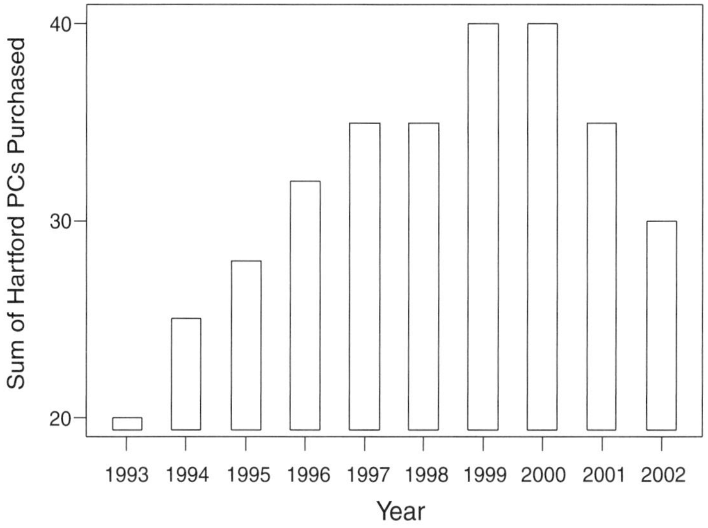

Figure 3.19C. Histogram—PC Sales

$Z_{\alpha/2}$ = Critical value, the positive Z value that is at the vertical boundary for the area of $\alpha/2$ in the right tail of the standard normal distribution (Figure 3.20)

σ = Population standard deviation

n = Sample size

Reorganize the above formula, and solve for the sample size necessary to produce results accurate to a specified confidence and margin of error:

$$n = [(Z_{\alpha/2}\ \sigma)/E]^2$$

This formula can be used when the user knows the process σ and wants to determine the sample size necessary to establish, with a confidence of $1 - \alpha$, the mean value μ to within $\pm$ E. The user can still use this formula if the population's standard deviation σ is not known and the sample size is small (even though it is unlikely that the user knows σ when the population mean is not known). The user may be able to determine σ from a similar process or from a pilot test/simulation. Consider Example 3.7.

Example 3.7: Sample Size Determination

A Quality Group in The Connecticut Precision Manufacturing Company needs to estimate the manufactured blade length. How many blades must be randomly

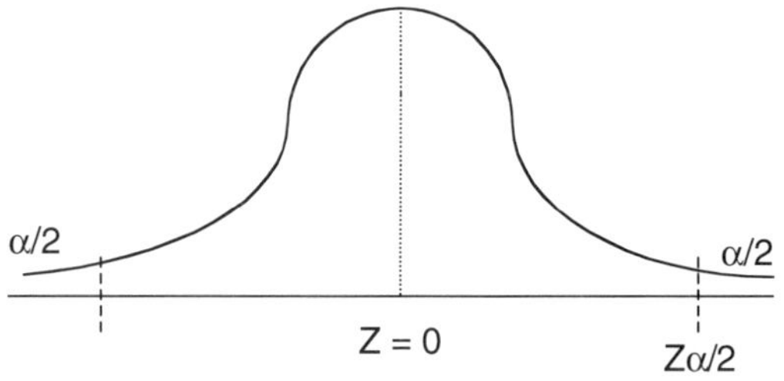

Figure 3.20. Critical Value Location

selected for measuring the blade length to be 99% sure that the sample mean is within 0.0005 mm from the population mean $\mu = 5.00$ mm? Assume that a previous measurement test has shown that $\sigma = 0.002$ mm.

Solving for the sample size, n:

A 99% degree of confidence corresponds to $\alpha = 0.01$.

Each of the tails in the normal distribution has an area of $\alpha/2 = 0.005$.

Therefore, at $Z_{\alpha/2\,=\,0.005} = 2.575$

$$\begin{aligned}\text{Now, } n &= [(Z_{\alpha/2}\, s)/E]^2 \\ &= [(2.575 \times 0.002)/(0.0005)]^2 \\ &= 106.09\end{aligned}$$

Therefore, the sample size should be at least (rounded up) 107 blades randomly selected. With this sample, the Quality Group will be 99% confident that the *sample mean* will be within 0.0005 mm of the true population mean (blade length $\mu = 5$ mm).

Exercise 3.6: Estimating Internet Use

To start an Internet service provider (ISP) business, estimating the average Internet usage by households in 1 week is required for a business plan and model. How many households must be randomly selected to be 95% sure that the sample mean is within 2 minutes of the population mean $\mu = 200$ minutes? Assume that a previous survey of household usage revealed $\sigma = 10.75$ minutes.

3.7 PROBABILISTIC DATA DISTRIBUTION

A great appreciation for probability theory comes from observing the outcome of a real experiment. These experiments are called random experiments. Common characteristics of a random experiment include:

Table 3.14. Possible Outcomes When Tossing a Pair of Fair Dice

(1,1), (1,2), (1,3), (1,4), (1,5), (1,6),
(2,1), (2,2), (2,3), (2,4), (2,5), (2,6),
(3,1), (3,2), (3,3), (3,4), (3,5), (3,6),
(4,1), (4,2), (4,3), (4,4), (4,5), (4,6),
(5,1), (5,2), (5,3), (5,4), (5,5), (5,6),
(6,1), (6,2), (6,3), (6,4), (6,5), (6,6)

- The outcome of the experiment cannot be predicted with certainty.
- Under unchanged conditions, the experiment could be repeated with the outcomes appearing in a haphazard manner. As the experiment-repeating process increases, a certain pattern in the frequency of outcome emerges.

To illustrate random experiments with an associated sample space, consider the following example:

Toss a pair of dice and observe the "up" faces. The total sample space is shown in Table 3.14. Suppose a random variable X is defined as the sum of the "up" faces as events in X that are defined as R_X. Then $R_X = (2, 3, 4, 5, 6, 7, 8, 9, 10, 11, 12)$ and the probabilities are (1/36, 2/36, 3/36, 4/36, 5/36, 6/36, 5/36, 4/36, 3/36, 2/36, 1/36), respectively. Assuming the dice are true and are equally likely, there will be 36 outcomes as listed above. The same output is presented in the equivalent events in Table 3.15.

Product/process data may be deterministic or probabilistic. If the data are probabilistic, data may follow the shape of one or more probabilistic distributions. The remainder of this section will discuss commonly found probability distributions as the product/process data are analyzed: normal, Poisson, exponential, binomial, gamma, and Weibull.

3.7.1 Normal Distribution

The most important of all distribution formulas for continuous variables is that for the normal distribution. The distribution is defined by two parameters: mean (μ) and standard deviation (σ)/variance (σ^2). A random variable X is said to have a normal distribution, with mean $\mu(-\infty < \mu < \infty)$ and variance (square of standard deviation) $\sigma^2 > 0$. The density function in general form is:

$$f(X)=\left(\frac{1}{\sigma\sqrt{2\Pi}}\right)e^{-\frac{1}{2}\left(\frac{X-\mu}{\sigma}\right)^2} \quad \text{where } -\infty < \mu < \infty$$

Table 3.15. Equivalent Events to Toss a Pair of Dice and Observe the "Up" Faces

Events in R_X	Total Set Space	Probability
X = 2	{(1,1)}	1/36
X = 3	{(1,2), (2,1)}	2/36
X = 4	{(1,3), (2,2), (3,1)}	3/36
X = 5	{(1,4), (2,3), (3,2), (4,1)}	4/36
X = 6	{(1,5), (2,4), (3,3), (4,2), (5,1)}	5/36
X = 7	{(1,6), (2,5), (3,4), (4,3), (5,2), (6,1)}	6/36
X = 8	{(2,6), (3,5), (4,4), (5,3), (6,2)}	5/36
X = 9	{(3,6), (4,5), (5,4), (6,3)}	4/36
X = 10	{(4,6), (5,5), (6,4)}	3/36
X = 11	{(5,6), (6,5)}	2/36
X = 12	{(6,6)}	1/36

The distribution is graphically presented in Figure 3.21A. The normal distribution has several important features:

- The total area under the curve represents total probability and is equal to 1.
- The curve is bell shaped, i.e., symmetrical about the mean μ.
- The maximum value of f occurs at $X = \mu$.
- The points of inflection of f are at $X = \mu \pm \sigma$.
- Standard normal distribution is represented by mean (μ) = 0, and standard deviation (σ) = 1, $N \sim (\mu, \sigma)$, and also as $N \sim (\mu, \sigma^2)$.
- Variance controls the shape of the curve. Two situations are shown in Figures 3.21B and 3.21C: first, when distributions have different means, but the same variance (Figure 3.21B); and second, when distributions have the same mean, but different variance (Figure 3.21C).
- The variable Z measures the departure of X from the mean μ in standard deviation (σ) units as expressed below (and shown graphically in Figure 3.22):

$$Z = (X - \mu)/\sigma$$

Consider some simple applications of normal distribution in Examples 3.8 and 3.9.

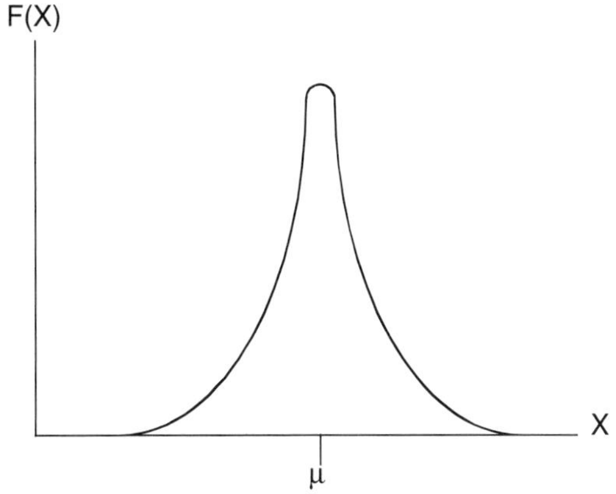

Figure 3.21A. Normal Distribution

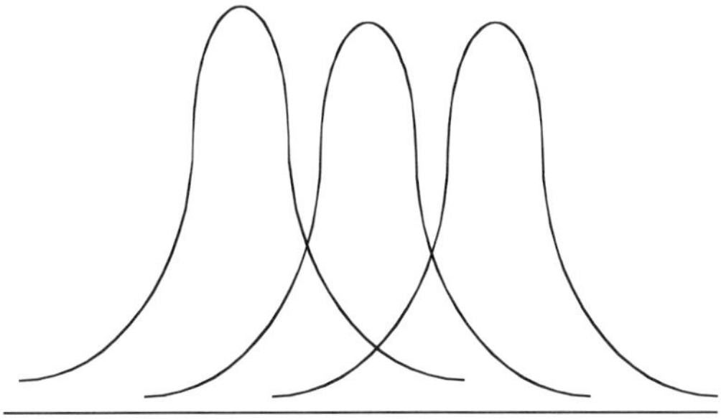

Figure 3.21B. Normal Distribution with Different Means

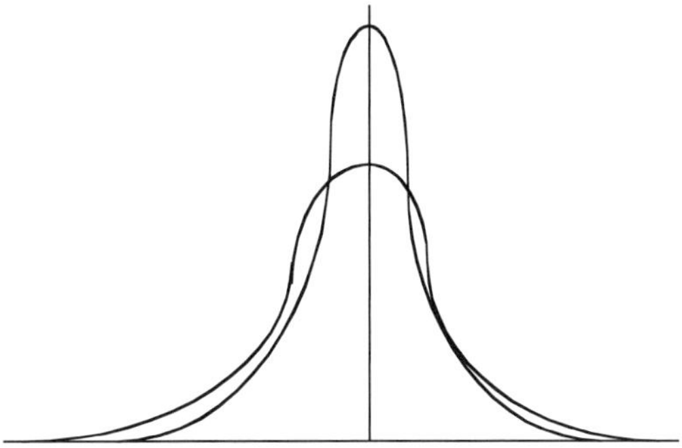

Figure 3.21C. Normal Distribution with Different Variances

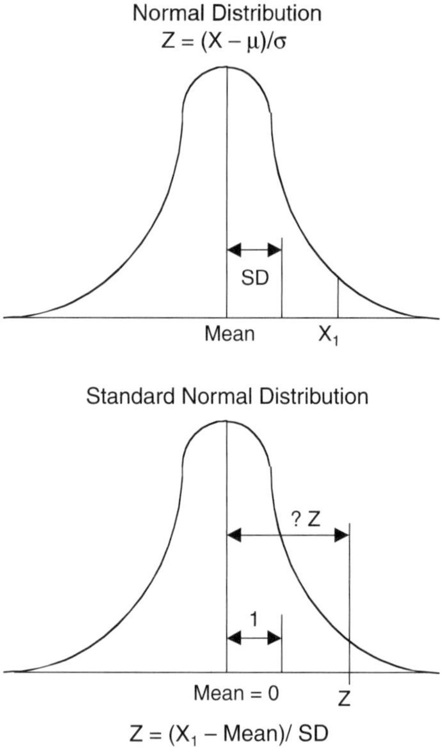

Figure 3.22. Calculation of Z Value

Example 3.8: Repair of Turning Machine

Suppose that a turning machine has broken down and a repairperson is available to repair the machine for 58 minutes. Assume that the repair process is normally distributed with a mean repair time of 50 minutes and a standard deviation of 8 minutes. What is the probability that the repairperson will repair the machine in 58 minutes?

Solution:
Repair time is normally distributed with:

Mean (μ) = 50 minutes

Standard deviation (σ) = 8 minutes

Repair time "X" = 58 minutes

Now, calculate the value of Z, where $Z = (X - \mu)/\sigma$:

$$Z = (58 - 50)/8 = 1$$

Probability $(Z \leq 1) = 0.8413$

Therefore, there are 84.13% chances that the machine will be repaired in 58 minutes.

Example 3.9: Weight of Components

The quantity of 300 small components is packed in a box. The weight of these components is an independent random variable with a mean weight of 5 grams and a standard deviation of 1 gram. Twenty-five boxes of these small components are loaded on the platform of a material-handling device. Suppose the probability that the components on the platform will exceed 37.7 kilograms in weight is needed (neglect both boxes and crate weight).

Solution:
Let,

$Y = X_1 + X_2 + \ldots + X_{7500}$ represent the total weight of the components and

$$\mu_Y = 7500\ (5) = 37{,}500 \text{ grams} = 37.5 \text{ kilograms}$$

$$\sigma_Y = \sigma \sqrt{n} = (1)\sqrt{7500}$$

$$\sigma_Y = 86.603$$

Then,

$$P(Y > 37{,}700) = P\left(Z > \frac{37{,}700 - 37{,}500}{86.603}\right)$$

$$1 - \Phi(2.309) = 1 - 0.98953 = 0.01047$$

Therefore, the probability to exceed the weight of the small components (37.7 kilograms) = 0.01047.

Distribution of Means of Samples from Any Universe

All distributions of sample means ($\mu_{X\text{-}bar}$) have certain properties in common with those of the parent population. Assuming random sampling, these properties include:

- When selection of sample elements are statistically independent events, typically referred to as "the large-population case," where $n < 0.05\,N$.
- The mean of the distribution of sample means ($\mu_{X\text{-}bar}$) is the mean of the universe of individual values (μ) from which the samples are taken, $\mu_{X\text{-}bar} = \mu$.
- The variance of the distribution of sample means ($\sigma^2_{X\text{-}bar}$) equals the variance of the universe of individual values (σ^2) divided by n, the size of the sample, $\sigma^2_{X\text{-}bar} = \sigma^2/n$. (This can also be written as: the standard deviation of the distribution of *sample means* equals $1/\sqrt{n}$ times the *standard deviation* of the universe of individual values, $\sigma_{X\text{-}bar} = \sigma/n^{0.5}$.)
- The form of the distribution of sample means approaches the form of a normal probability distribution as the size of the sample is increased.

and where:

$\mu_{X\text{-}bar}$ = Sample mean

$\sigma^2_{X\text{-}bar}$ = Sample variance

$\sigma_{X\text{-}bar}$ = Sample standard deviation

$\bar{X}$ = Sample mean

while:

μ, σ^2, and σ = population mean, variance, and standard deviation, respectively

n = Sample size

N = Population

Example 3.10 has been developed to validate this relationship.

Example 3.10: Estimating Parameters

Suppose that census-type information is not available and cannot be easily obtained. (In reality, thousands of engineers may be graduating with an engineering degree from universities and colleges and starting their professional career. Collecting information about their starting annual salary would be very expensive and time-consuming.) Therefore, a decision is made to estimate the three population parameters (mean, variance, and standard deviation) by taking a random sample of five engineers with their starting salaries in year 2004. The data are as follows:

Engineer	Annual Starting Salary ($K)
A	39
B	41
C	25
D	55
E	40

Because this is a small population, $N = 5$ and the summary statistics are

$$\mu = \Sigma X/N = 200/5 = 40$$

$$\sigma^2 = \frac{\sum (X-\mu)^2}{N} = 452/5 = 90.4$$

$$\sigma = 9.508$$

Now take a sample of 3 ($n = 3$) without replacement from the above population ($N = 5$) and calculate the sample statistics (X, s^2, and s) as presented in Table 3.16. The possible number of samples of $n = 3$ out of the population of $N = 5$ equals $C_3^5 = 10$ samples.

Now, if the statistics of data $\overline{X}$ (see Table 3.16) is calculated, then:

$$\mu_{X\text{-}bar} = \Sigma\overline{X}/10 = 400/10 = 40$$

$$\sigma^2_{X\text{-}bar} = 15.1$$

$$\sigma_{X\text{-}bar} = 3.886$$

Now apply the logic presented above for a small population, where $N = 5$, and $n = 3$, then:

$$\mu_{X\text{-}bar} = \mu = 40 \text{ and}$$

$$\sigma^2_{X\text{-}bar} = \left(\frac{\sigma^2}{n}\right)\left(\frac{N-n}{N-1}\right)$$

$$\sigma^2_{X\text{-}bar} = \left(\frac{90.4}{3}\right)\left(\frac{5-3}{5-1}\right)$$

$$= 15.07$$

This validates the above concept.

The Central Limit Theorem

Next is a discussion of the Central Limit Theorem with a large population. If the sum of n independent random variables is represented by a random variable Y that satisfies certain general conditions, then for a very large n, Y is approximately normally distributed.

If n independent variables are $X_1, X_2, \ldots, X_n$ and these variables are identically distributed random variables with:

Mean $E(X_i) = \mu$

Variance $V(X_i) = \sigma^2$

$Y = X_1 + X_2 + \ldots + X_n$

then:

$$Z_n = \frac{Y - n\mu}{\sigma\sqrt{n}}$$

has an approximate $N(0,1)$ distribution.

An immediate question that comes to mind is "How large must n be to get reasonable results using the normal distribution to approximate the distribution of Y?" This is not an easy question to answer due to:

- The characteristics of the distribution of the X_i terms
- The meaning of the term "reasonable results"

However, Hines and Montgomery[8] have an answer. From a practical standpoint, some crude rules of thumb can be given where the distribution of the X_i terms falls into one of three arbitrarily selected groups:

1. Well-behaved—The distribution of X_i does not radically depart from the normal distribution. There is a bell-shaped density that is nearly symmetric. In this case, practitioners in quality control and other areas of application find that n should be at least 4 ($n \geq 4$).
2. Fairly well-behaved—The distribution of X_i has no prominent mode. It appears much like a uniform density. In this case, $n \geq 12$ is a commonly used rule.
3. Ill-behaved—The distribution has most of its measure in the "tails." In this case, determining a rule is most difficult; however, in many practical applications, $n \geq 100$ should be satisfactory.

Table 3.16. Possible Sample of n = 3 Taken without Replacement from the Population of N = 5 and Its Statistics

Sample Number	Engineers in Sample	Summary Statistics for Salary $\bar{X}$	s^2	s
1	ABC	35.00	76.00	8.718
2	ABD	45.00	76.00	8.718
3	ABE	40.00	1.00	1.00
4	ACD	39.67	225.33	15.01
5	ACE	34.67	70.33	8.386
6	ADE	44.67	80.33	8.963
7	BCD	40.33	25.33	15.01
8	BCE	35.33	80.33	8.963
9	BDE	45.33	0.33	8.386
10	CDE	40.00	225.00	15.00

Example 3.11: The Central Limit Theorem with a Large Population

Test the theory: "If the sum of n independent random variables is represented by a random variable *Y* that satisfies certain general conditions, then for a very large *n*, *Y* is approximately normally distributed" (a large population).

Utilizing the MINITAB software tool:

- Start the MINITAB software tool.
- Create some simulated data to test this theory.
- Use the following MINITAB commands to create 10 columns of data utilizing a normal distribution with a mean = 35 and a standard deviation = 4:

MINITAB > Calc > Random Data > Normal
Generate 300 Rows
Store in C1 – C10
Mean = 35
Standard Deviation = 4
MINITAB > Calc > Row Statistics >
Mean C1 – C10
Store results into C11
MINITAB > Stat > Basic Stats > Display Descriptive Stat > C1 – C11

The expected standard deviation of mean = $\sigma/\sqrt{n}$:

Let, $n = 9$

Then, standard deviation of mean $= 4/\sqrt{9}$

$= 1.333$

What is the value of the standard deviation of mean in row C11?

The process was repeated 10 times, with the results presented in row C11: the sample mean is very close to the population mean ($\mu = 35$, $\mu_{X\text{-}bar} = 34.99$) and the relationship about the standard deviation is as follows:

$\sigma = 3.99$

$\sigma_{X\text{-}bar} = 1.243$ (which is close to 1.333)

This validates the concept of large population. The summary output from MINITAB is shown in Table 3.17 and in Figures 3.23A and 3.23B. The plotted graphs are C1: the distribution of individual observations (Figure 3.23A); and C11: the distribution of sample mean (Figure 3.23B). The MINITAB instructions are:

- **MINITAB > Graph > Character Graph > Dotplot**
- **Variables:** Select **C1,** Select **C11,** Check box **Same scale for all variables, OK**

3.7.2 Poisson Distribution

The Poisson distribution is utilized when the user is interested in the occurrence of a number of events of the same type. Therefore, the Poisson probability distribution associates probabilities with number of occurrences of some event within specified intervals of time or space as shown in Figure 3.24A by an asterisk (*). This exponential distribution instead associates probabilities with the various gaps, shown by the values of X_1 to X_7 between the Poisson events.

The occurrence of each event is represented as a point on the time scale. The density function is represented by $f(n)$:

$$f(n) = \frac{(\lambda t)^n e^{-\lambda t}}{n!}, \quad n = 0, 1, 2, \ldots$$

$$= 0 \qquad \text{otherwise}$$

where:

t = Time

λ = Constant factor

n = Number of occurrences

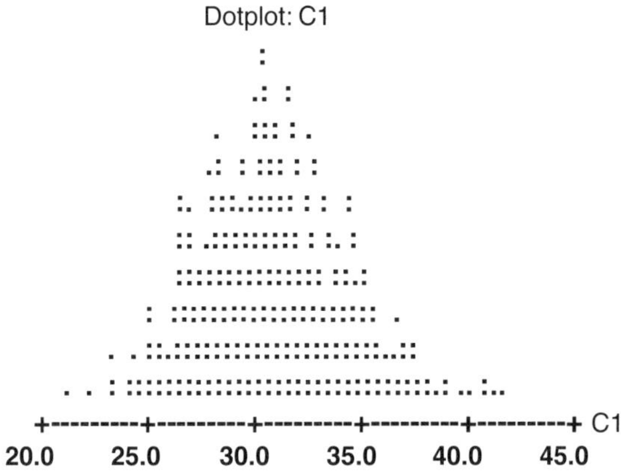

Figure 3.23A. Distribution of Individual Observations (with Each Dot Representing Up to Four Points)

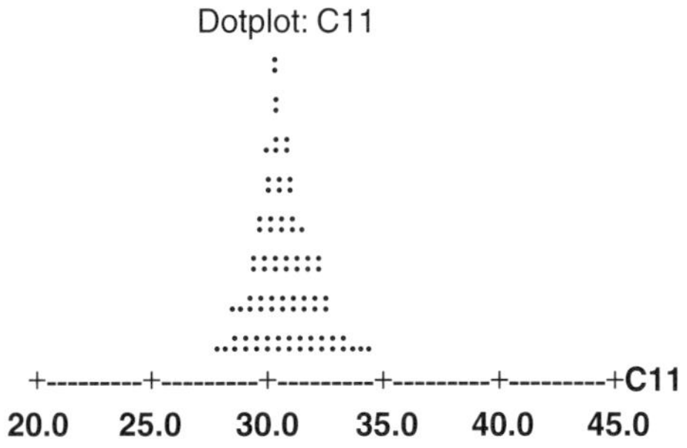

Figure 3.23B. Distribution of Sample Mean

The parameter, mean, and variance of the Poisson distribution are the expressions:

Parameter = λ

Mean (μ) = λt

Variance (σ^2) = λt

A probability density function graph is presented in Figure 3.24B. The parameter λ represents the expected occurrence of the event's rate, e.g., customer arrival rate at a bank, plane landing rate at an airport's runway, engine failure rate at a water pumping station, etc. Example 3.12 will make the concept even clearer.

Table 3.17. Descriptive Statistics Output from MINITAB

Variable	N	Mean	Median	Tr Mean	SD	SE Mean
C1	300	34.595	34.794	34.585	3.991	0.230
C2	300	35.095	35.182	35.087	3.987	0.230
C3	300	34.896	34.786	34.907	3.804	0.220
C4	300	34.923	34.824	34.914	4.171	0.241
C5	300	34.870	34.682	34.865	3.915	0.226
C6	300	35.147	35.113	35.108	3.856	0.223
C7	300	34.909	35.013	34.951	3.875	0.224
C8	300	35.664	35.885	35.598	4.152	0.240
C9	300	34.798	34.861	34.714	3.995	0.231
C10	300	35.000	35.050	35.036	4.066	0.235
C11	300	34.990	35.041	34.998	1.243	0.072

Example 3.12: Plane Arrival Rates

Suppose planes have been arriving at an airport at the rate of two per minute during a Friday evening. The airport manager wants to know the probabilities of 6, 9, and 20 planes arriving between 8:00 and 8:10 p.m.

Assuming that plane arrivals are following the Poisson distribution in the example:

$\lambda = 2$ planes per minute

$t =$ 10 minutes (time between 8:00 and 8:10 p.m.)

$n =$ 6, 9, and 20 (number of plane arrivals during the specified time of 10 minutes)

Since,

$$f(n) = \frac{(\lambda t)^n e^{-\lambda t}}{n!}, \qquad n = 0, 1, 2, \ldots$$

therefore, $\lambda t = 2 \times 10 = 20$:

$$f(n = 6) = \frac{(20)^6 e^{-20}}{6!} = 0.002 \text{ (probability of 6 planes landing in defined period)}$$

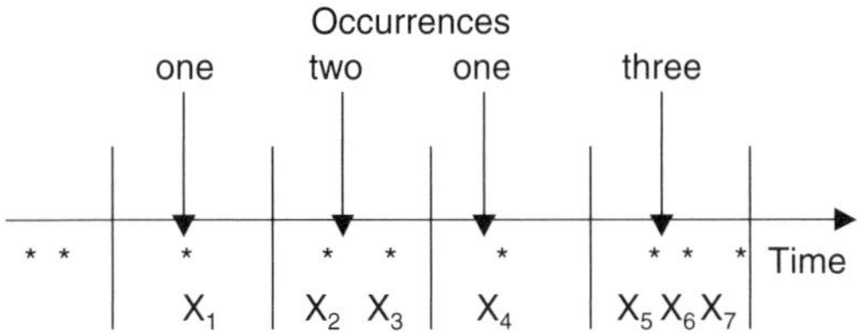

Figure 3.24A. Poisson Events and Exponential Gaps

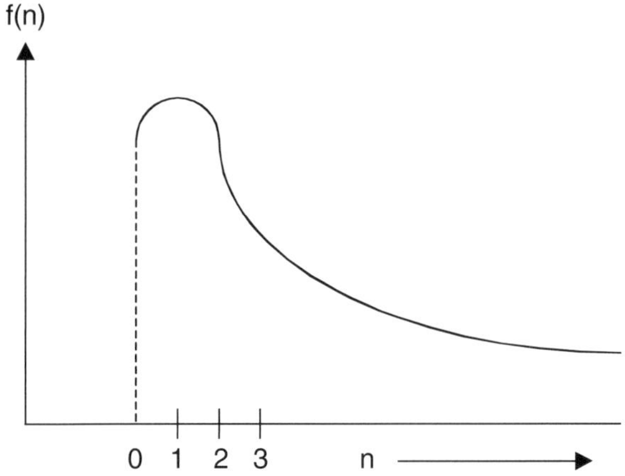

Figure 3.24B. Poisson Density Function

$$f(n = 9) = \frac{(20)^9 e^{-20}}{9!} = 0.0029 \text{ (probability of 9 planes landing in defined period)}$$

$$f(n = 20) = \frac{(20)^{20} e^{-20}}{20!} = 0.0888 \text{ (probability of 20 planes landing in defined period)}$$

3.7.3 Exponential Distribution

The exponential distribution is closely related to the Poisson distribution. For example, if customer arrival at a bank has a Poisson distribution, then customer service time at the bank would have an exponential distribution or the time between customer arrivals in the bank would also have an exponential distribution. Some other examples of exponential distribution are an airline's check-in counter, filling a gas tank in an automobile at the gas station, getting checked out a supermarket's checkout counter, etc. These examples are often assumed to have an exponential distribution.

The exponential distribution has density function:

$$f(X) = \lambda e^{-\lambda X} \qquad X \geq 0$$
$$= 0 \qquad \text{otherwise}$$

where the parameter λ is real and positive constant. The expected value (mean) is $1/\lambda$ and the variance is $1/\lambda^2$. A probability density function graph is presented in Figure 3.25A.

Suppose a small bank has only one person to serve arriving customers and on average it takes 2 minutes to serve a customer. Therefore, the customer arrival rate per minute λ has to be less than 1/2; otherwise a customer would have to wait in a queue at the bank before being served.

The cumulative density function (CDF) of an exponentially distributed random variable $F_X(a)$ is given by:

$$F_X(a) = \int_{-\infty}^{a} f(X)dX$$

$$F_X(a) = \int_{0}^{a} \lambda e^{-\lambda X} dX = 1 - e^{-\lambda a} \quad \text{for a} \geq 0$$
$$= 0 \qquad \text{for a} < 0$$

The function is presented in Figure 3.25B

For example, suppose that the life of a light bulb is assumed to have an exponential distribution. If the bulb lasted 500 hours, the probability of it lasting an additional 40 hours is the same as the probability of it lasting an additional 40 hours if the bulb has lasted 1000 hours. Therefore, the concept is that a brand new bulb is no "better" than one that has lasted 500 hours. The concept of exponential distribution is very important and one that is quite often overlooked in practical life.

Now consider $R(X)$, which is the probability of occurrence (failure) or reliability on $[0, X]$. Because X represents time, this is expressed as $R(t) = e^{-\lambda t}$, where t is the mission time. This concept is explained in Example 3.13.

Example 3.13: Engine Life

Three engines are subjected to a nonreplacement life test, which is to be terminated at 10 hours. Assume failure times to be exponentially distributed with a mean life of 200 hours. As a test engineer for this test, estimate the probability

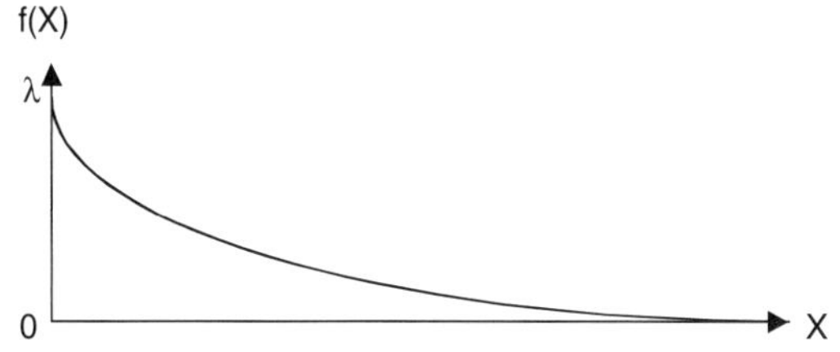

Figure 3.25A. Exponential Density Function

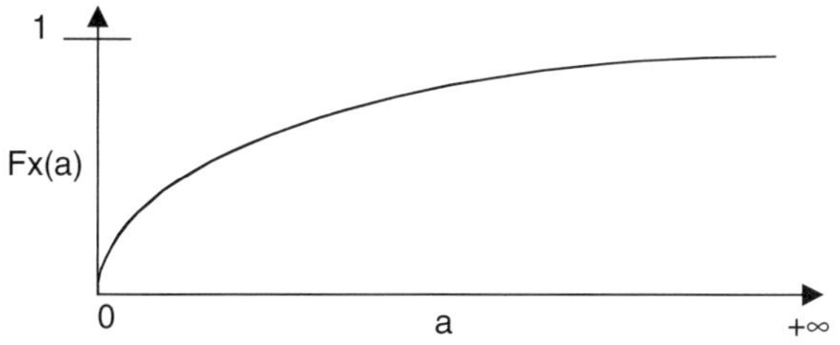

Figure 3.25B. CDF of the Exponential Distribution

that *no failure* will occur and the probability that *one failure* will occur. Utilize the concept of exponential distribution.

Since mean time to failure = 200 hours, therefore, $\lambda = 1/200 =$ a 0.005 engine failure rate per hour.

The mission time is 10 hours, and the mission time reliability of the engine:

$$R(t = 10) = e^{-\lambda t}$$

$$R(t = 10) = e^{-0.005\,(10)} = 0.95123$$

Assume these three engines (i.e., *A*, *B*, and *C*) are identical.

Their probability of success:

$$P(A) = P(B) = P(C) = 0.95123$$

Their probability of failure (complementary probability):

$$P(\bar{A}) = P(\bar{B}) = P(\bar{C}) = 1 - 0.95123 = 0.04877$$

The probability of *no engine failure* during a mission time of 10 hours:

$= P(A \cap B \cap C)$

$= (0.95123)\ (0.95123)\ (0.95123)$

$= 0.86$

The probability of *one engine failure* during the mission time of 10 hours:

$= P[(\bar{A} \cap B \cap C) + P(A \cap \bar{B} \cap C) + P(A \cap B \cap \bar{C})]$

$= 3[(0.04877)\ (0.95123)\ (0.95123)]$

$= 0.1324$

3.7.4 Binomial Distribution

Binomial distribution is used if the possibility of one of the two possible outcomes exists in every trial (e.g., accept or reject, success or failure) and the probability for each trial remains constant. This distribution is also known as Bernoulli's distribution. The density is known as $f(X)$,

$$f(X) = \frac{n!}{X!(n-X)!} p^X q^{n-X}, \quad X = 0, 1, 2, \ldots, n$$
$$= 0 \quad \text{otherwise}$$

where:

X = The number of occurrences (success, accept) in n trials

p = The single trial probability of occurrence

$q = (1 - p)$ = The single trial probability of no occurrence and always

$p + q = 1$

The parameters of the distribution are n and p. The distribution mean (μ) is np and the variance (σ^2) is npq. A probability density function graph is presented in Figure 3.26. Example 3.14 presents an application of binomial distribution.

Example 3.14: An Assembly and Packaging Operation

An assembly and packaging operation consists of assembly operations (X and $X + 1$) on the first two stations and the packaging operation ($X + 2$) on the third station. Material flows on a conveyor belt from the first station through the third station as shown in Figure 3.27.

The quality inspector takes a random sample of 200 units between operations X and $X + 1$ every 2 hours. Past experience indicates that if the unit is not properly assembled at operation X, the next assembly operation $X + 1$ will not be

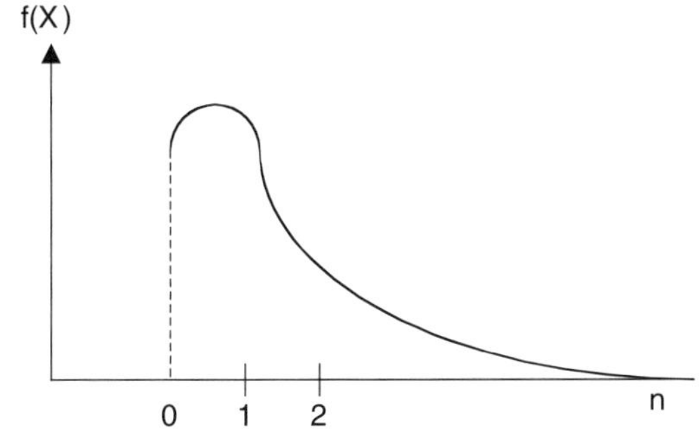

Figure 3.26. Binomial Density Function

successful. On average, 1% of the units are not properly assembled in operation *X*. New employees are working at operation *X*; therefore, the percentage of improperly assembled assembly may go up to 2%. The production manager is willing to accept this quality change during the training period, but more than 2% is totally unacceptable. Therefore, he requests that the quality control department determine the chances of $P(p > 0.02 \mid p = 0.01)$.

The quality control department utilizes the binomial distribution concept as follows:

$$
\begin{aligned}
P(p>0.02 \mid p=0.01) &= 1-P(p \le 0.02 \mid p=0.01) \\
&= 1-P(X \le 200(0.02) \mid p=0.01) \\
&= 1-\sum_{k=0}^{4} C_k^{200}(0.01)^k(0.99)^{200-k} \\
&= 1-0.94826 \\
&= 0.05174
\end{aligned}
$$

Therefore, the probability of having more than 2% unacceptable assemblies from operation *X* is slightly more than 5%.

3.7.5 Gamma Distribution

The gamma distribution is commonly utilized in life-testing situations. The gamma function is defined as:

$$\Gamma(n) = (n-1)\,\Gamma(n-1)$$

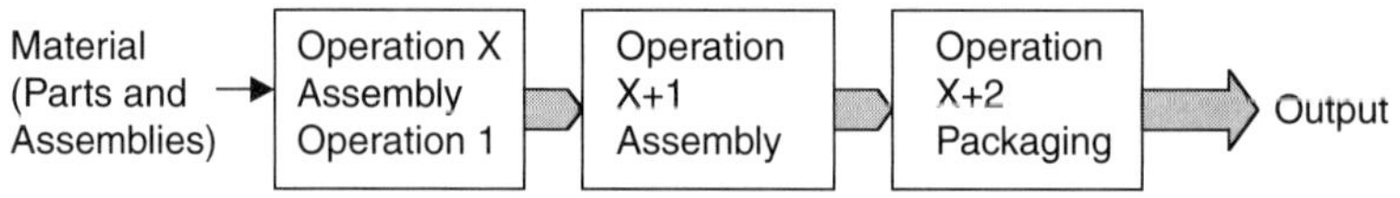

Figure 3.27. Sequential Assembly and Packaging Operations

If n is a positive integer, then:

$$\Gamma(n) = (n - 1)!$$

The gamma probability density function is presented as follows:

$$f(X) = \frac{\lambda}{\Gamma(r)}(\lambda X)^{r-1} e^{-\lambda X} \qquad \text{where } X > 0$$

$$= 0 \qquad \text{otherwise}$$

where:

r = Shape parameter and

λ = Scale parameter

and these parameters are greater than zero, i.e., $r > 0$ and $\lambda > 0$.

r/λ = The distribution mean and

$(r/\lambda)^2$ = The distribution variance

The gamma distribution is an extension of the exponential distribution. When $r = 1$, the gamma distribution reduces to the exponential distribution. Various shapes of the gamma distribution for $\lambda = 1$ and several values of r are presented in Figure 3.28.

The cumulative distribution is represented by $F(X)$,

where:

$$F(X) = \int_0^X f(X)dX$$

$$= \int_0^X \frac{\lambda^r X^{r-1} e^{-\lambda X}}{\Gamma r} dX$$

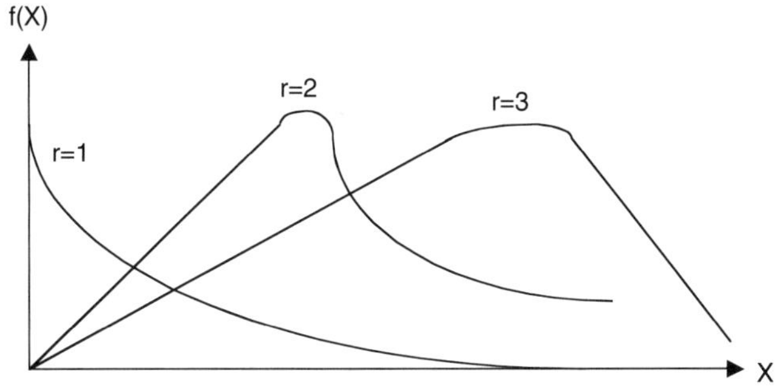

Figure 3.28. Gamma Distribution for λ=1

When $r = 1$, this distribution reduces to exponential form.

$$F(X)=\sum_{i=r}^{\infty}\frac{e^{-\lambda X}(\lambda X)^{i}}{i!} \quad \text{where, } X \geq 0 \text{ and } \lambda > 0, r > 0$$

$$F(X)=1-\sum_{i=0}^{r-1}\frac{e^{-\lambda X}(\lambda X)^{i}}{i!}$$

If r is an integer, and it is known that $R(X) = 1 - F(X)$, where $R(X)$ = Reliability for the mission time X, therefore,

$$R(X)=\sum_{i=0}^{r-1}\frac{e^{-\lambda X}(\lambda X)^{i}}{i!}$$

The application of the gamma distribution concept is presented in Example 3.15.

Example 3.15: Reliability Time

A given item has failure times which are distributed in accordance with the gamma distribution, with $\lambda = 0.5$ and $r = 2$. Find the reliability for a mission time of 10 hours.

Since the reliability for the mission time $X = 10$ hours is presented by,

$$R(X=10)=\sum_{i=0}^{r-1}\frac{e^{-\lambda X}(\lambda X)^{i}}{i!}$$

where:
$X = 10$, $\lambda = 0.5$, and $r = 2$

$$\begin{aligned} R(10) &= e^{-5}(5)^0 + (e^{-5}(5)^1)/1! \\ &= e^{-5}(1+5) \\ &= 0.0402 \end{aligned}$$

Therefore, the reliability for the 10-hour mission time is 4.02%.

A few non-normal distributions have been reviewed. Now, think again about the concept of Central Limit Theorem. The concept says that the distribution of the same means converges to this normal distribution—$N(\mu, \sigma^2/n)$—as n increases, even if the underlying distribution is not normal.

Example 3.16 uses a non-normal distribution (employing binomial distribution) to validate the above-stated point. There are two data distribution plots:

- Distribution of individual data points
- Distribution of sample means (a condensed distribution and close to bell shape)

Example 3.16: Non-Normal Distribution (Binomial Distribution)

Example 3.16 is for a non-normal distribution (employing binomial distribution). Utilizing the MINITAB software tool:

- Start the MINITAB software tool.
- Create some simulated data to test the Central Limit Theory.
- Use MINITAB commands to create 10 columns of data utilizing a binomial distribution with the number of trials = 1000 and the probability of success = 0.65.
- The MINITAB commands:

  MINITAB > Calc > Random Data > Binomial
  - **Generate 300 Rows**
  - **Store in column(s) C1—C10**
  - **Number of trials: 1000**
  - **Probability of success = 0.65**

  MINITAB > Calc > Row Statistics >
  - **Mean**
  - **Input variables C1—C10**
  - **Store results in: C11**

  MINITAB > Stat > Basic Stats > Display Descriptive Stat >
  - **Variables: C1—C11**

  MINITAB > Graph > Character Graph > Dotplot >

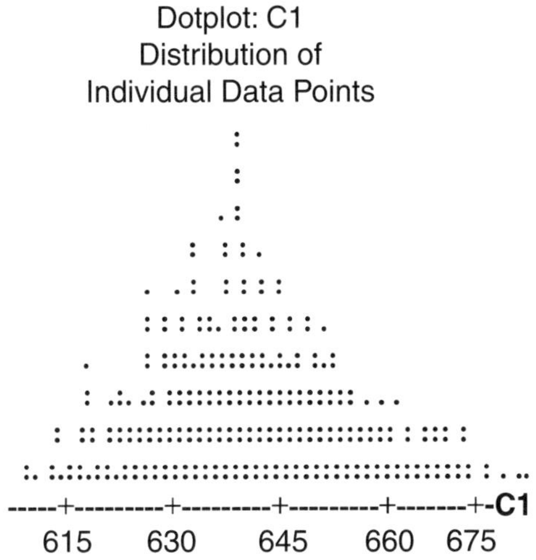

Figure 3.29A. Population Data Plot for a Non-Normal (Binomial) Distribution (with Each Dot Representing Up to Three Points)

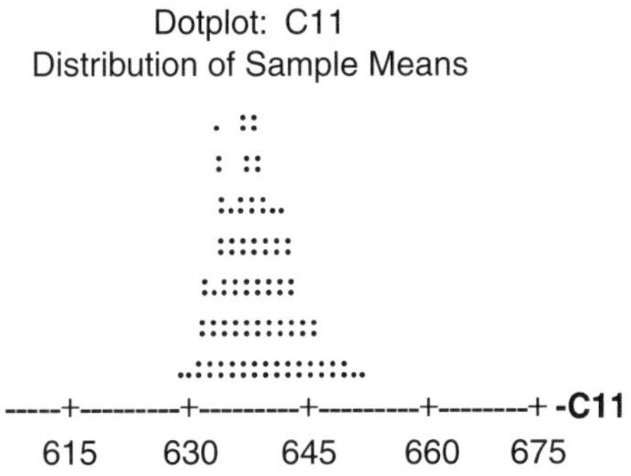

Figure 3.29B. Sample Data Plot for a Non-Normal (Binomial) Distribution

Click C1 > Select > Click C11 > Select >Same scale for all variables

The MINITAB plotted charts are presented in Figures 3.29A and B.

3.7.6 Weibull Distribution

Various applications of the Weibull distribution are used to represent physical phenomena, e.g., the Weibull distribution provides an excellent approximation for time-to-fail in electrical and mechanical components and systems. Product life can be divided into three phases—burn-in period (break-in period), useful life, and wear-out life. The Weibull distribution can represent all three phases of a product life. The probability density function is as follows:

$$f(X) = \frac{b}{n}\left(\frac{X-\alpha}{n}\right)^{b-1} e^{-\left(\frac{X-\alpha}{n}\right)^{b}} \qquad X \geq \alpha \text{ and}$$

$$= 0 \qquad \text{otherwise}$$

where:

$b > 0$

$n > 0$

$\alpha > 0$

and

b is shape parameter

n is scale parameter

α is location parameter

The probability density function for the different values of b is presented in Figure 3.30.

The Weibull distribution is not easy to use. Most of the time the location parameter is zero ($\alpha = 0$), implying that the product will not fail until it has functioned for $1/\lambda$ units of time. Therefore,

when:

$\alpha = 0$,

$$f(X) = \frac{b}{n}\left(\frac{X}{n}\right)^{b-1} e^{-\left(\frac{X}{n}\right)^{b}} \qquad \text{for } X \geq 0 \text{ and}$$

$$= 0 \qquad \text{for X} < 0$$

and

$$F(X) = 1 - e^{-\left(\frac{X}{n}\right)^{b}}$$

and

System reliability = $R(X)$

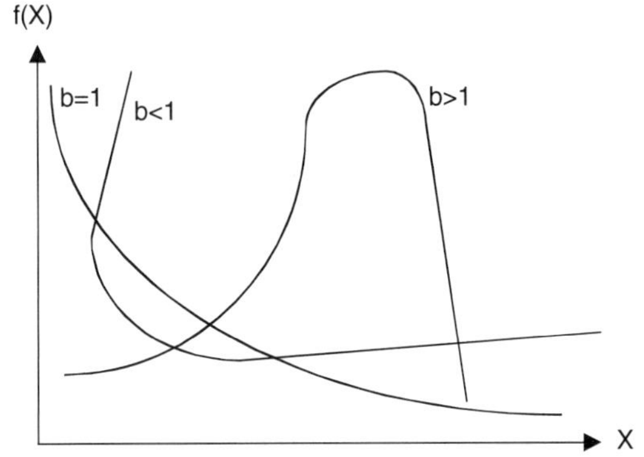

Figure 3.30. Weibull Density Function for Various Values of b

where:

$$R(X) = 1 - F(X) = e^{-\left(\frac{X}{n}\right)^b}$$

This concept is utilized in the sample problem in Example 3.17.

Example 3.17: Reliability for a 1-Hour Mission Time

Failure times for a given product are distributed in accordance with the Weibull distribution with shape parameter of $b = 2$ and scale parameter of $n = 10$. Find the reliability for a 1-hour mission time.

Given: $b = 2$ and $n = 10$

Assume: A location parameter of $\alpha = 0$

Then:

$$R(X) = e^{-\left(\frac{X}{n}\right)^b}$$

$$= exp[-(1/10)^2]$$

$$R(X = 1) = 0.99005$$

Therefore, the reliability for a 1-hour mission time is 99.005%.

The examples in this section have shown how product/process data are represented by some of these probabilistic distributions. Similarly, the project team can utilize these distributions as they fit in their data analysis and presentation.

3.8 CALCULATING SIGMA

Once the historical/collected information becomes available, the next step is to calculate the Sigma metrics to identify the quality level of the current product/process. This section will discuss how to calculate the Sigma metrics value.

The Defects Are Randomly Distributed

If a sample were taken, say that 2.0 defects per unit were found. Now, if another sample were collected in the near future without changing any process, input material, and equipment, exactly same defect rate should not be expected. If the defect rate is different, this result does not necessarily mean that the process has become worse or better.

Based on the given factors (input material, process, and equipment), think about the likelihood of producing a unit (product/service) with no (zero) defects. This would be true only when there is no rework or repair. Therefore, yield and defect counts are related measures, and defect metrics are calculated separately depending on the database. There are two types of process databases:

- Discrete process databases
- Continuous process databases

Discrete Process Database Metrics

Metrics calculations can be divided into two steps:

- Calculate the defect rate (the defect rate could be defects per hundred/thousand/ten thousand/hundred thousand/million).
- Find the Sigma value in Table 3.18.

Calculating the defect rate. Defects are identified in two ways:

- Defects per million opportunities (DPMO)
- Errors per million opportunities (EPMO)

DPMO

This metric is generally applied to products. This metric is for quantifying the total number of defects should a million units be produced and dividing the total defects by the total number of opportunities for defects (TOFD or total opportunities for defects). Assume that,

dpo = Defect per opportunity

dpo = dpu/TOFD

where:

dpu = Defects per unit

and

$$\begin{aligned} \text{DPMO} &= \text{dpo} \times 1{,}000{,}000 \\ &= (\text{dpu/TOFD}) \times 1{,}000{,}000 \\ &= (\text{dpu} \times 1{,}000{,}000)/\text{TOFD} \\ &= \text{dpm/TOFD} \end{aligned}$$

where:

dpm = Defects per million

Consider Examples 3.18 and 3.19. Example 3.18 compares the quality of two different products, and Example 3.19 calculates the likelihood that a product would have zero defects.

Example 3.18: Comparison of Quality for Two Different Products

Discrete Data

There are two production operations. Both operations produce defects. One operation is significantly more complex than the other process:

Production Operation (PO) #1—The process assembles 2 simple components.

Production Operation (PO) #2—The assembly process follows these steps:

- Assembles 5 components to make a subassembly
- Assembles 2 other subassemblies to this created subassembly with 6 screws
- Attaches a bar code label and a product label to the final assembly

Product quality data are as follows:

Production Operation	Sample Size	Defects
PO #1 (simple)	2000	85
PO #2 (complex)	3500	140

Give an opinion of these processes.

Table 3.18. Discrete Process Sigma Conversion Table

Long-Term Yield (%)	Process Sigma (ST)	Defects per 1,000,000	Defects per 100,000	Defects per 10,000	Defects per 1,000	Defects per 100
99.99966	**6.0**	**3.4**	**0.34**	**0.034**	**0.0034**	**0.00034**
99.9995	5.9	5	1	0.05	0.005	0.0005
99.9992	5.8	8	1	0.08	0.008	0.0008
99.9985	5.7	15	1	0.15	0.015	0.0015
99.998	5.6	20	2	0.2	0.02	0.002
99.997	5.5	30	3	0.3	0.03	0.003
99.996	5.4	40	4	0.4	0.04	0.004
99.993	5.3	70	7	0.7	0.07	0.007
99.99	5.2	100	10	1	0.1	0.01
99.985	5.1	150	15	1.5	0.15	0.015
99.977	**5.0**	**230**	**23**	**2.3**	**0.23**	**0.023**
99.967	4.9	330	33	3.3	0.33	0.033
99.952	4.8	480	48	4.8	0.48	0.048
99.932	4.7	680	68	6.8	0.68	0.068
99.904	4.6	960	96	9.6	0.96	0.096
99.865	4.5	1,350	135	13.5	1.35	0.135
99.814	4.4	1,860	186	18.6	1.86	0.186
99.745	4.3	2,550	255	25.5	2.55	0.255
99.654	4.2	3,460	346	34.6	3.46	0.346
99.534	4.1	4,660	466	46.6	4.66	0.466
99.379	**4.0**	**6,210**	**621**	**62.1**	**6.21**	**0.621**
99.181	3.9	8,190	819	81.9	8.19	0.819
98.93	3.8	10,700	1,070	107	10.7	1.07
98.61	3.7	13,900	1,390	139	13.9	1.39
98.22	3.6	17,800	1,780	178	17.8	1.78
97.73	3.5	22,700	2,270	227	22.7	2.27
97.13	3.4	28,700	2,870	287	28.7	2.87
96.41	3.3	35,900	3,590	359	35.9	3.59
95.54	3.2	44,600	4,460	446	44.6	4.46
94.52	3.1	54,800	5,480	548	54.8	5.48

Table 3.18. Discrete Process Sigma Conversion Table (Continued)

Long-Term Yield (%)	Process Sigma (ST)	Defects per 1,000,000	Defects per 100,000	Defects per 10,000	Defects per 1,000	Defects per 100
93.32	**3.0**	**66,800**	**6,680**	**668**	**66.8**	**6.68**
91.92	2.9	80,800	8,080	808	80.8	8.08
90.32	2.8	96,800	9,680	968	96.8	9.68
88.5	2.7	115,000	11,500	1,150	115	11.5
86.5	2.6	135,000	13,500	1,350	135	13.5
84.2	2.5	158,000	15,800	1,580	158	15.8
81.6	2.4	184,000	18,400	1,840	184	18.4
78.8	2.3	212,000	21,200	2,120	212	21.2
75.8	2.2	242,000	24,200	2,420	242	24.2
72.6	2.1	274,000	27,400	2,740	274	27.4
69.2	**2.0**	**308,000**	**30,800**	**3,080**	**308**	**30.8**
65.6	1.9	344,000	34,400	3,440	344	34.4
61.8	1.8	382,000	38,200	3,820	382	38.2
58	1.7	420,000	42,000	4,200	420	42
54	1.6	460,000	46,000	4,600	460	46
50	1.5	500,000	50,000	5,000	500	50
46	1.4	540,000	54,000	5,400	540	54
43	1.3	570,000	57,000	5,700	570	57
39	1.2	610,000	61,000	6,100	610	61
35	1.1	650,000	65,000	6,500	650	65
31	**1.0**	**690,000**	**69,000**	**6,900**	**690**	**69**
28	0.9	720,000	72,000	7,200	720	72
25	0.8	750,000	75,000	7,500	750	75
22	0.7	780,000	78,000	7,800	780	78
19	0.6	810,000	81,000	8,100	810	81
16	0.5	840,000	84,000	8,400	840	84
14	0.4	860,000	86,000	8,600	860	86
12	0.3	880,000	88,000	8,800	880	88
10	0.2	900,000	90,000	9,000	900	90
8	0.1	920,000	92,000	9,200	920	92

Solution:
The first step is to calculate the first pass yield (FPY):

Operation	dpu	FPY
PO #1 (simple)	(85/2000) = 0.0425	(1 – dpu) × 100% = 95.75
PO #2 (complex)	(140/3500) = 0.04	(1 – dpu) × 100% = 96.0

Based on the FPY analysis, the two operations are almost equally good or equally bad. The next step is to calculate DPMO.

PO #1 is simple, but PO #2 is complex; therefore, the first step is to calculate TOFD (total opportunities for defect) for PO #2:

Component/Process	Opportunities for Defects
First Assembly	5
First Assembly w/2 subassemblies	3
Screws	6
Bar code decal	1
Product label decal	1
TOFD	**16**

Now compute dpm and DPMO:

Operation	dpm	DPMO
PO #1 (simple)	42,500	21,250
PO #2 (complex)	40,000	2,500

The above data indicate that the complex operation is performing much better than the simple operation. Yet, if the presence of a defect makes the output of each operation a defective product, then both operations are equally bad.

Example 3.19 Discrete Data

Each component has 8 opportunities for a defect and there are 100 components in the receiving lot. The inspection department decided to perform 100% inspection of the lot and found 40 defects in the received lot. What is the quality level of this lot in the Six Sigma concept? What is the likelihood that a component will have a 0 (zero) defect rate?

Solution:

Let,

n = Number of components in the receiving lot

o = Number of defect opportunities per component

d = Total number of defects per receiving lot

DPO = Defects per opportunities

DPMO = Defects per million opportunities

$$\begin{aligned} \text{DPO} &= d/(n \times o) \\ &= 40/(100 \times 8) \\ &= 0.05 \end{aligned}$$

$$\begin{aligned} \text{DPMO} &= \text{DPO} \times 1{,}000{,}000 \\ &= 0.05 \times 1{,}000{,}000 \\ &= 50{,}000 \end{aligned}$$

See Table 3.18 (Discrete Process Sigma Conversion Table) for the Sigma value (ST) = 3.15. Under the column entitled *Defects per 1,000,000*, check for the value equal to 50,000. There are two nearest values in the column 44,600 and 54,800. Moving horizontally to the reader's left, the next column is *Process Sigma* (ST) and the respective values for 44,600 and 54,800 are 3.2 and 3.1. Therefore, interpolate the *Process Sigma* (ST) value for 50,000 (defects) and the Sigma value is 3.15:

- Probability that the opportunity is not defective:
  = 1 – 0.05
  = 0.95

- Likelihood that any component will contain zero defects:
  = $(0.95)^8$
  = 0.66
  = 66%

based on the assumption that 8 opportunities per component are in series. This concept will now be further explained:

Six Sigma series yield concept. Once the components/processes are in series, the system yield decreases as the number of components/processes increases (see Table 3.19). Table 3.19 shows that if the product has Six Sigma yield metrics (e.g., Situation 4, which has up to 500 opportunities in series), the product is still yielding 99.83% defect-free product. Yet, if the product is in Situation 1, the product quality yield level drops to a very low level in a short time.

Table 3.19. Yield Decreases as Series Complexity Increases

Number of components or Process Steps	System Yield when Components/Processes Are in Series			
	Situation 1 (%)	Situation 2 (%)	Situation 3 (%)	Situation 4 (%)
1	93.32	99.38	99.977	99.99966
3	81.27	98.15	99.93	99.99898
8	57.52	95.15	99.82	99.99728
15	35.45	91.09	99.66	99.9949
25	17.76	85.6	99.43	99.9915
50	3.15	73.27	98.86	99.983
100		53.69	97.73	99.966
200		28.83	95.5	99.932
500		4.46	89.14	99.83

Exercise 3.7: Determining a Single Metric to Compare Incidence of Defects in Two Processes

The Production Manager is interested in using a single metric to compare the incidence of defects in the chassis assembly operation for their inserter system vs. the digital postage machine assembly operation of their Postage Metering division. Defects sample data have been collected:

Operation	Sample Size	Defects
Chassis assembly	400	50
Digital postage machine assembly	1500	125

Description of the chassis assembly operation:

- Assemble 150 components to make a subassembly.
- Assemble 70 components to make a table assembly.
- Assemble two subassemblies with 12 bolts.
- Test the chassis assembly.

Description of the digital postage machine assembly operation:

- Assemble 70 components to make the functional subassembly.
- Attach 10 connection harnesses.

- Attach 6 skin parts.
- Test the final assembly.

Assume an equal level of complexity in both assemblies. Analyze the data and make a recommendation to the Production Manager. Also establish their Sigma performance level.

EPMO

Next is a discussion of EPMO (errors per million opportunities) for a service area. EPMO is a metric for measuring and comparing the performance of distinct administrative, service, or transactional processes. EPMO quantifies the total number of errors or mistakes produced by a process per million iterations of the process. It takes into account the opportunities for that process to have errors or mistakes (TOFE or total opportunities for errors). If an administrative, service, or transactional process is simple, it should not present too many chances for committing errors or making mistakes. Yet, if a process is complicated, cumbersome, difficult, or not well defined, it may present many chances for errors and mistakes.

EPMO = (epm)/(TOFE)

where:

epm = Errors per million

= epu × 1,000,000

epu = Errors per unit

The advantages of using EPMO vs. epm are that EPMO takes into consideration the complexity of the process and the metric lends itself to comparing the performance of different administrative, service, or transactional processes in regard to their level of difficulty. Generally, an auditing method is used to collect data from administrative, service, or transactional processes. The collected sample of data should be large enough to calculate the EPMO. This concept utilization is explained in Example 3.20.

Example 3.20: Utilizing the EPMO Concept

Two types of administrative processes have been audited:

- Generation of invoices in the Billing Department
- Generation of payroll checks in the Payroll Department

Both processes are equally complicated. Opportunities for errors in each process are listed:

Invoice Generation Process

Activity/Component	Opportunities for Errors
Service/product description	1
Service/product quantity	1
Price/unit of service/product	1
Price calculation	1
Total service/product price calculation	1
Applicable discount calculation	1
Net price calculation	1
Invoice payment condition(s)	1
Customer's name	1
Customer's address	1
Customer's identification number	1
Total	**11**

Payroll Check Generation Process

Activity/Component	Opportunities for Errors
Name	1
Address	1
Security number	1
Work hours	1
Overtime hours	1
Social Security taxes	1
401K withholdings	1
Medical and other benefits deduction(s)	1
Federal taxes	1
State taxes	1
Stock options withholding	1
Check amount	1
Pay period	1
Total	**13**

Both processes have been audited. The results are as follows:

Process	Audit Sample Size	Defects
Invoice generation	195	10
Payroll check generation	500	15

Compute epm, EPMO, and the Sigma performance level.

Solution:
For the Invoice Generation Process, the order of calculations would be epm, EPMO, and Sigma performance level:

$$\text{epm} = \text{epu} \times 1{,}000{,}000$$
$$\text{epu} = \text{Number of defects/audited sample size}$$
$$= 10/195$$
$$= 0.051282$$

$$\text{epm} = 0.051282 \times 1{,}000{,}000$$
$$= 51{,}282$$

$$\text{EPMO} = \text{epm/TOFE}$$

For the Invoice Generation Process, TOFE = 11. Therefore,

$$\text{EPMO} = 51{,}282/11$$
$$= 4{,}662$$

Now check for the Sigma performance value in Table 3.18 (Discrete Process Sigma Conversion Table). Under the column entitled *Defects per 1,000,000*, check for the value equal to 4,662. The nearest value in this column is 4,660. Moving horizontally to the reader's left, the next column is *Process Sigma* (ST) and the value is 4.1. Therefore, Sigma performance level is 4.1.

Similar calculations have been done for the Payroll Generation Process. The results are summarized:

Process	epm	EPMO	Sigma Performance
Invoice generation	51,282	4,662	4.1
Payroll check generation	30,000	2,308	4.34

The Payroll Check Generation process is slightly better than the Invoice Generation process, but both processes are performing at a low Sigma level.

Continuous Process Database Metrics

This section will discuss calculating Sigma metrics for the continuous process database.

Assuming the process data have normal distribution, the standard normal distribution has the mean (μ) = 0, and the variance (σ^2) or the standard deviation (σ) = 1, and the area under the density curve is equal to 1. The standard normal distribution is presented in Figures 3.31A and 3.31B. Any value away from the mean is measured in terms of standard deviations. Z is a unit of measure that is equivalent to the number of standard deviations. The Z transformation can be applied as follows:

$$Z = (\text{Data point} - \text{mean})/(\text{Standard deviation})$$

This converts any normal distribution to a standard normal distribution.

The normal probability distribution values are presented in Table 3.20. The probability values of the distribution can be calculated utilizing Microsoft® Excel (MS Excel) logic *Normsdist* (*Z*), and the *Z* value can be obtained for a given probability value using MS Excel logic *Normsinv(Probability Value)*.

The probability values of a normal distribution can also be calculated utilizing MINITAB software, e.g., for a given $Z = 1.96$, the probability value from negative infinity to 1.96 is 0.975. Store the *Z* value in column C1 and use the following logic commands in MINITAB to obtain the probability value 0.975:

> **Calc** > **Probability Distribution** > **Normal** > select **Cumulative Probability** and **Input Column** location C1 > **OK**

Probability value can also be converted to *Z* value utilizing MINITAB software, e.g, for a given probability value of 0.975 (from negative infinity to a *Z* value), the *Z* value is 1.96. Store the probability value 0.975 in column C2 and use the following logic commands in MINITAB to obtain the *Z* value equal to 1.96:

> **Calc** > **Probability Distribution** > **Normal** > Select **Inverse Cumulative Probability** and **Input Column** location C2 > **OK**

The Sigma metric for the continuous data can be calculated as follows:

1. Identify distribution that represents data.
2. Set defects limits.
3. Calculate yield.
4. Convert yield into Sigma value.

As indicated earlier, process data are assumed to have normal distribution; therefore, the next step is to set defect limits. Customer-driven products/services generally have specification limit(s). Beyond these limits product/service is con-

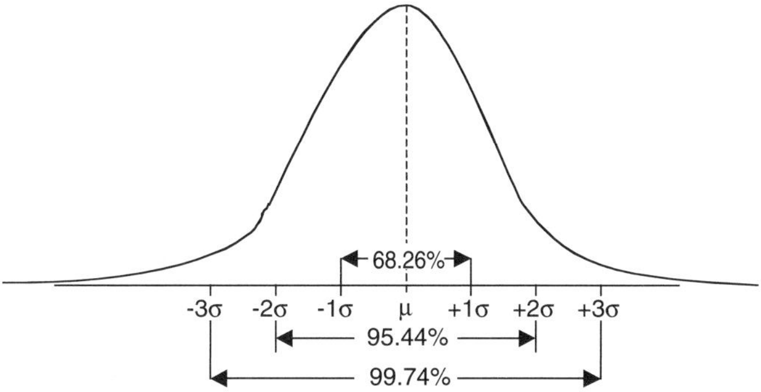

Figure 3.31A. Normal Probability Distribution with σ Values

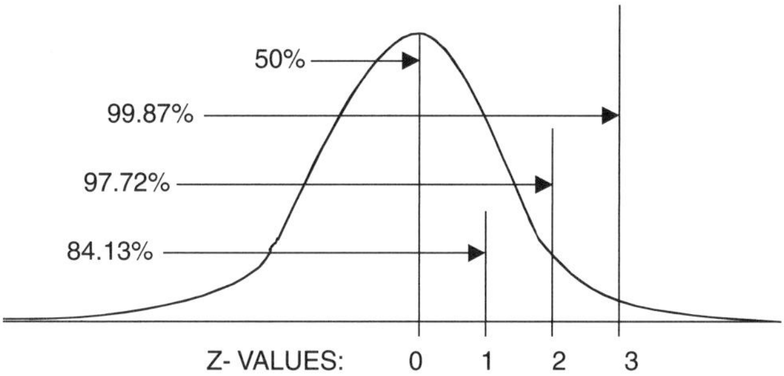

Figure 3.31B. Normal Probability Distribution with Z Values

sidered defective. These limits may be lower specification limits (LSL) and/or upper specification limits (USL). The process of calculating yield and then converting yield into Sigma metrics has been explained with the help of a sample situation presented in Example 3.21.

Example 3.21: Calculating Yield and Then Converting Yield into Sigma Metrics

The Connecticut Truck Manufacturing Company purchases power transmission shafts from a single supplier. The shaft diameter specifications are 50 mm ± 2 mm.

There are 50 power shafts in the latest lot received. Their measured diameters are as follows:

Table 3.20. Cumulative Probabilities of the Normal Probability Distribution (Area Under the Normal Curve from Negative Infinity to Z)

Z	0.00	0.01	0.02	0.03	0.04	0.05	0.06	0.07	0.08	0.09
0.0	0.5	0.5040	0.5080	0.5120	0.5160	0.5199	0.5239	0.5279	0.5319	0.5359
0.1	0.53983	0.5438	0.5478	0.5517	0.5557	0.5596	0.5636	0.5675	0.5714	0.5753
0.2	0.57926	0.5832	0.5871	0.5910	0.5948	0.5987	0.6026	0.6064	0.6103	0.6141
0.3	0.61791	0.6217	0.6255	0.6293	0.6331	0.6368	0.6406	0.6443	0.6480	0.6517
0.4	0.65542	0.6591	0.6628	0.6664	0.6700	0.6736	0.6772	0.6808	0.6844	0.6879
0.5	0.69146	0.6950	0.6985	0.7019	0.7054	0.7088	0.7123	0.7157	0.7190	0.7224
0.6	0.72575	0.7291	0.7324	0.7357	0.7389	0.7422	0.7454	0.7486	0.7517	0.7549
0.7	0.75804	0.7611	0.7642	0.7673	0.7704	0.7734	0.7764	0.7794	0.7823	0.7852
0.8	0.78814	0.7910	0.7939	0.7967	0.7995	0.8023	0.8051	0.8078	0.8106	0.8133
0.9	0.81594	0.8186	0.8212	0.8238	0.8264	0.8289	0.8315	0.8340	0.8365	0.8389
1.0	0.84134	0.8438	0.8461	0.8485	0.8508	0.8531	0.8554	0.8577	0.8599	0.8621
1.1	0.86433	0.8665	0.8686	0.8708	0.8729	0.8749	0.8770	0.8790	0.8810	0.8830
1.2	0.88493	0.8869	0.8888	0.8907	0.8925	0.8944	0.8962	0.8980	0.8997	0.9015
1.3	0.9032	0.9049	0.9066	0.9082	0.9099	0.9115	0.9131	0.9147	0.9162	0.9177
1.4	0.91924	0.9207	0.9222	0.9236	0.9251	0.9265	0.9279	0.9292	0.9306	0.9319

1.5	0.93319	0.9345	0.9357	0.9370	0.9382	0.9394	0.9406	0.9292	0.9306	0.9319
1.6	0.9452	0.9463	0.9474	0.9484	0.9495	0.9505	0.9515	0.9292	0.9306	0.9319
1.7	0.95543	0.9564	0.9573	0.9582	0.9591	0.9599	0.9608	0.9292	0.9306	0.9319
1.8	0.96407	0.9649	0.9656	0.9664	0.9671	0.9678	0.9686	0.9292	0.9306	0.9319
1.9	0.97128	0.9719	0.9726	0.9732	0.9738	0.9744	0.9750	0.9292	0.9306	0.9319
2.0	0.97725	0.9778	0.9783	0.9788	0.9793	0.9798	0.9803	0.9808	0.9812	0.9817
2.1	0.98214	0.9826	0.9830	0.9834	0.9838	0.9842	0.9846	0.9850	0.9854	0.9857
2.2	0.9861	0.9864	0.9868	0.9871	0.9875	0.9878	0.9881	0.9884	0.9887	0.9890
2.3	0.98928	0.9896	0.9898	0.9901	0.9904	0.9906	0.9909	0.9911	0.9913	0.9916
2.4	0.9918	0.9920	0.9922	0.9925	0.9927	0.9929	0.9931	0.9932	0.9934	0.9936
2.5	0.99379	0.9940	0.9941	0.9943	0.9945	0.9946	0.9948	0.9949	0.9951	0.9952
2.6	0.99534	0.9955	0.9956	0.9957	0.9959	0.9960	0.9961	0.9962	0.9963	0.9964
2.7	0.99653	0.9966	0.9967	0.9968	0.9969	0.9970	0.9971	0.9972	0.9973	0.9974
2.8	0.99744	0.9975	0.9976	0.9977	0.9977	0.9978	0.9979	0.9979	0.9980	0.9981
2.9	0.99813	0.9982	0.9982	0.9983	0.9984	0.9984	0.9985	0.9985	0.9986	0.9986
3.0	0.99865	0.9987	0.9987	0.9988	0.9988	0.9989	0.9989	0.9989	0.9990	0.9990

Table 3.21. Descriptive Statistics for Shaft Diameter

Descriptive Statistics for C1				
Variable	**N**	**Mean**	**Median**	
C1	50	50.246	50.000	
Variable	**Tr Mean**	**SD**	**SE Mean**	
C1	50.255	1.054	0.149	
Variable	**Minimum**	**Maximum**	**Q1**	**Q3**
C1	48.000	52.100	49.500	51.000

51, 50, 52, 50, 49.9, 51.5, 49.9, 50, 51, 50.5, 51.5, 50, 52, 51.5, 52.1, 52, 51.9, 52.1, 50, 50, 51, 50.5, 50, 51, 51, 50, 51, 50, 49, 49, 49.5, 48, 49.5, 48.9, 50, 50, 49.5, 48, 49.5, 49, 50, 49, 50, 49, 51, 51.5, 49, 49.5, 50, 50

Utilize the MINITAB tool to:

- Develop a histogram with normal curve.
- Run a process capability analysis to see if the supplier is capable of meeting the engineering specifications of 50 mm + 2 mm.

Solution: Part 1

Enter shaft diameter data in column C1 and use the following commands:

> **Stat** > **Basic Statistics** > **Display Descriptive Statistics** > Select variable **C1** > Click on **Graph** > Select **Histogram of data, with normal curve** > **OK**

A histogram with normal curve will be developed (see Figure 3.32A). Descriptive statistics are presented in Table 3.21.

Solution: Part 2

Now check the process capability of the supplier as per engineering specifications and use tool commands:

> **Stat** > **Quality Tools** > **Capability Analysis (Normal)** > **Select** variable **C1** in **Single Column** > **Subgroup size:** type **50** > **Lower Spec:** type **48** > **Upper Spec:** type **52** > **Options** > **Target (adds CPM to table) 50** > **Calculate statistics using: 6.0 Sigma tolerance** > **OK**

The process capability analysis is presented in Figure 3.32B.

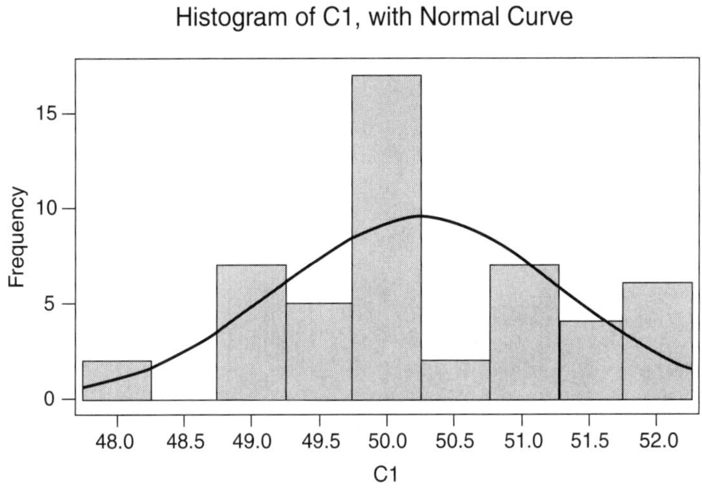

Figure 3.32A. Histogram of C1 with Normal Curve for Shaft Diameter

Under observed performance, none of the shafts in the sample lot is below the LSL, and 2 shafts of 50 shafts in the sample are above the USL. Once this relationship is converted based on 1 million shafts, the number of defective shafts would be 40,000. Therefore, PPM (parts per million) based on the USL is 40,000. Now, looking at Table 3.18, based on 40,000 defects per million, the Sigma metrics value would be approximately 3.25.

Continue the concept of continuous data with the assumption of normal distribution. The next step is to calculate Z value, where Z is a unit of measure that is equivalent to the number of standard deviations a value is away from the mean value. If the value of Z is positive, the location is to the right of the mean value; if the value of Z is negative, the location is to the left of the mean value. The Z value can be calculated as follows:

$$Z = (\text{Data point} - \text{mean value})/(\text{standard deviation})$$

The value of Z helps to convert any normal distribution to a standard normal distribution with mean $(\mu) = 0$ and variance $(\sigma^2) = 1$, $N \sim (0,1)$ and also as $N \sim (\mu, \sigma^2)$. The product/process yield can be presented as follows:

$$\text{Yield} = 1 - \text{Probability of defect}$$

where yield is the percentage of the defect-free product/service produced. The yield concept is graphically presented in Figure 3.33.

Assume that the product has USL at Z equal to 2. Therefore,

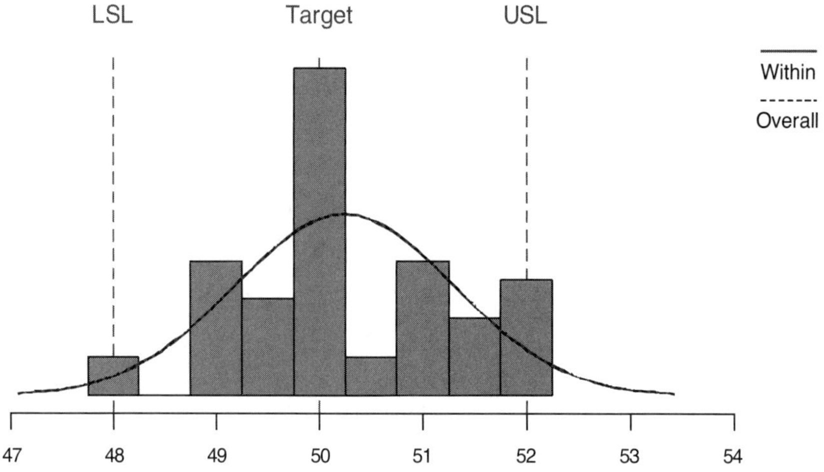

Observed Performance		Exp. "Within" Performance		Exp. "Overall" Performance	
PPM < LSL	0.00	PPM < LSL	16957.79	PPM < LSL	16957.79
PPM > USL	40000.00	PPM > USL	48816.41	PPM > USL	48816.41
PPM Total	40000.00	PPM Total	65774.20	PPM Total	65774.20

Process Data		Potential (Within) Capability		Overall Capability	
USL	52.000	Cp	0.63	Pp	0.63
Target	50.000	CPU	0.55	PPU	0.55
LSL	48.000	CPL	0.71	PPL	0.71
Mean	50.246	Cpk	0.55	Ppk	0.55
Sample N	50	Cpm	0.62		
StDev (Within)	1.05890				
StDev (Overall)	1.05890				

Figure 3.32B. Supplier's Process Capability Analysis for C1 for Shaft Diameter

- Defect-free product/service = 98% and
- Defective product/service = 2%

Now check the Sigma metrics value in Table 3.18 for a 2% defective product/service. The Sigma value is approximately 3.55.

So far how to calculate Sigma metrics for discrete and continuous data have been discussed. These metrics values are *short-term* Sigma values. The *long-term* Sigma value for a process may not stay the same as the value that the team achieved in the short term.

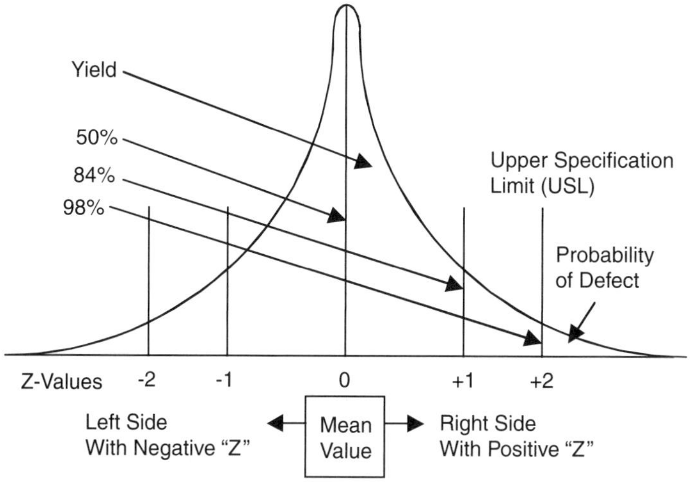

Figure 3.33. Product/Service Yield and Defect Concept

Motorola's 1.5 Sigma Shift Concepts

The plus or minus (± 1.5) sigma shift surfaced when Motorola used it as a worst-case scenario of a significant shift in process average in their explanation of *Why Six Sigma*? Motorola said that a ± 1.5 sigma shift would not be detrimental to their customers' out-of-tolerance percentage if Motorola's processes were designed to have their specification limits at twice the process width or at Six Sigma levels. This concept is presented in Figure 3.34.

The Six Sigma value of 3.4 PPM (parts per million) is defined in Motorola's document entitled *Our Six Sigma Challenge*. According this document, if the design specifications were twice the process width, the process would be extremely robust. Such a process would be robust enough. Even if there were a significant or detrimental shift in average and even if it were as high as +1.5 sigma, a customer would not perceive degradation in product/service quality. In a worst-case scenario, a shift of 1.5 sigma would make an almost 0 defect product/service change to 3.4 PPM. In this case, a customer would only perceive an increase from 0 to 3 defects per million. This result was supposed to be the warranty Six Sigma processes brought to customers and not actual PPM levels for Six Sigma.

After a process has been improved using Six Sigma DMAIC methodology, the process standard deviation and the Sigma value are calculated. DMAIC projects and the related data are generally collected over a short-term period rather than over years. Short-term values generally contain common cause variation. However, long-term data contain common cause variation and special cause variation. Because short-term data generally have no special cause variation, short-

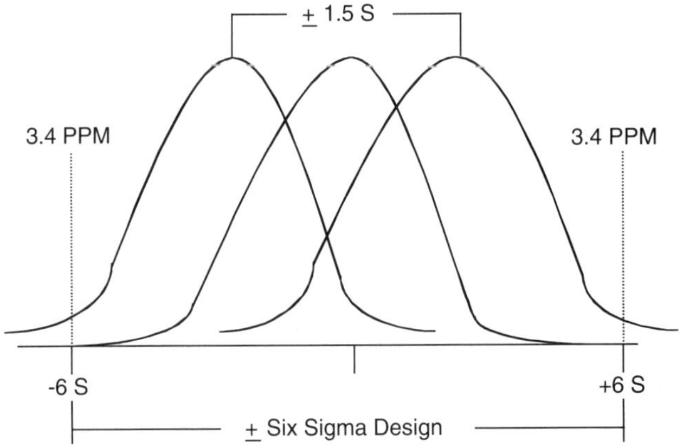

Figure 3.34. Sigma Shift—Long-Term vs. Short-Term Data

term data will typically be of a higher process capability than long-term data. This difference is the 1.5 sigma shift. Once enough process data has been collected, the factor most appropriate for a process can be determined.

Six Sigma concepts are all about improvement. When running processes under statistical control, the user would rather control the input process variables than the usual output product variables. The bottom-line impact of the Six Sigma process is to reduce defects, errors, and mistakes to *zero defects*. Therefore, the objective of Six Sigma process improvement is to reduce variation in the product/process such that the specification limits are at least six standard deviations away from the mean.

The concepts of current Sigma metrics, goal Sigma metrics, and the Sigma shift are now presented together in Example 3.22.

Example 3.22: Current Sigma Metrics, Goal Sigma Metrics, and Sigma Shift

The Connecticut Manufacturing Company is currently manufacturing three products—A, B, and C. Their current and goal manufacturing cycle statistics are presented in Table 3.22. The goal statistics are assumed to be at the short-term Six Sigma metrics level.

Current statistics for all products (A, B, and C) are also shown in a histogram format along with the normal distribution curves (Figures 3.35A, 3.35B, and 3.35C). Calculate the current Sigma metrics for all of the products (A, B, and C).

Table 3.22. The Current and the Goal Manufacturing Cycle Statistics for Products A, B, and C

		Current Statistics		Goal Statistics	
		Manufacturing Cycle (Days)			
Product	Sample Size (N)	Mean	SD	Mean	SD
A	37	30.8	11.33	19.5	3.9
B	34	47.82	21.07	33.0	7.33
C	28	30.32	14.95	23.0	4.5

Solution: Sigma Metric for Product A

The given goal data represent short-term goal statistics. Now, assume the worst-case scenario that the long-term goal statistics may shift by 1.5 σ. Therefore, the longest acceptable manufacturing cycle time utilizing the goal statistics would be:

$$
\begin{aligned}
&= \text{Goal mean} + 4.5\ (\text{goal standard deviation}) \\
&= 19.5 + (4.5 \times 3.9) \\
&= 37.05 \text{ days}
\end{aligned}
$$

Now if the current and goal statistics charts are stacked and both charts are connected with a dashed line, then the left of both distribution curves would be considered as the acceptable manufacturing cycle time area in relation to the given goal (Figure 3.35A). Therefore, calculate the acceptable normal curve area to the left of the dashed line in the current manufacturing cycle curve. Now treat this calculated area as a *Long-Term Yield* value in Table 3.18 and find the corresponding value in the next column *Process Sigma* (ST). The value obtained in the *Process Sigma* (ST) column would be the current Sigma metric for the manufacturing cycle of Product A. Calculation steps are as follows:

Step 1. Calculate the Z score for the current manufacturing cycle at 37.05 days. This is an acceptable limit of the goal manufacturing cycle:

$$
\begin{aligned}
Z &= (37.05 - 30.78)/11.33 \\
&= 0.5534
\end{aligned}
$$

Step 2. Find the probability value at 0.5534 Z from Table 3.20. This value can also be obtained through an MS Excel spread sheet as follows:

NORMSDIST(0.5534) = 0.710005

Step 3. The probability value obtained in Step 2 would be used in the *Long-Term Yield* column of Table 3.18. Then find the corresponding value in the *Process*

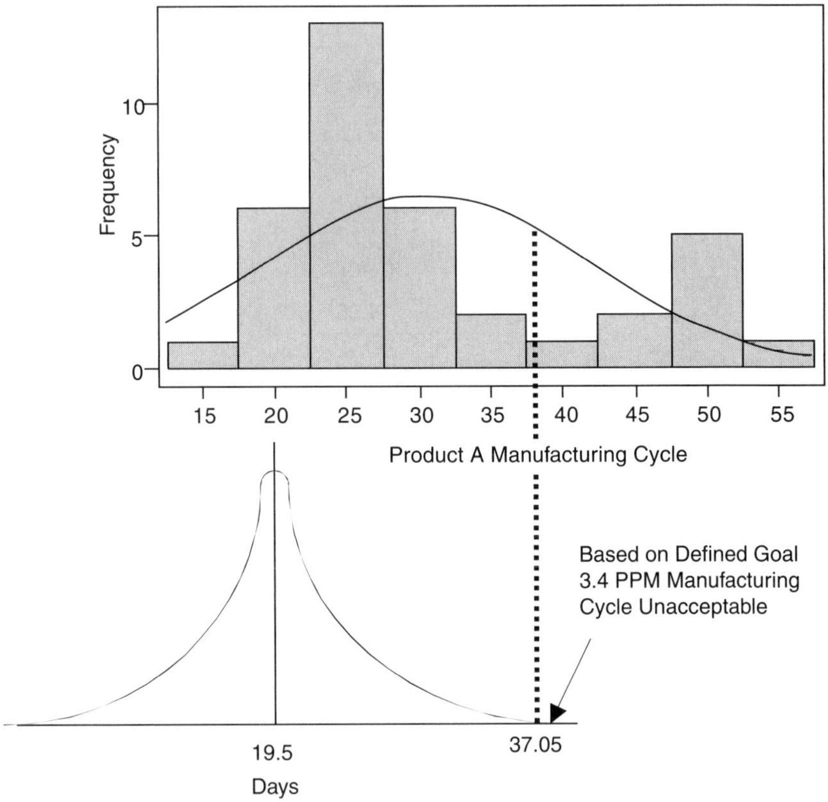

Figure 3.35A. Graphical Presentation of the Manufacturing Cycle for Product A (Histogram with Normal Curve)

Sigma (ST) column in the same table. This value would be approximately 2.06. Therefore, the current manufacturing cycle for Product A is running at 2.06 σ (in relation to the defined goal for the manufacturing cycle. (Current manufacturing cycle Sigma metrics for Products B and C can be similarly calculated.)

3.9 PROCESS CAPABILITY (C_p AND C_pk) AND PROCESS PERFORMANCE (P_p AND P_pk) INDICES

So far process performance that is evaluated through Sigma metrics has been discussed. The higher the Sigma value, the better a process is performing. Another method can be used to evaluate process capability and process performance. This method is also based on statistical measurements: C_p, C_pk, P_p, and P_pk. This

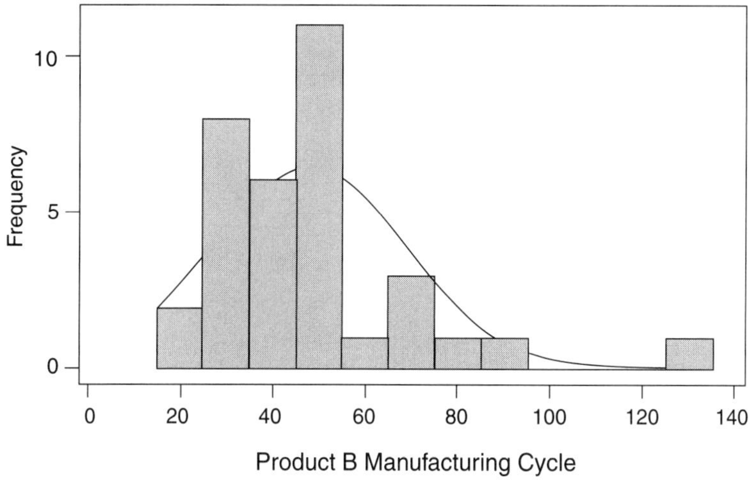

Figure 3.35B. Graphical Presentation of the Manufacturing Cycle for Product B (Histogram with Normal Curve)

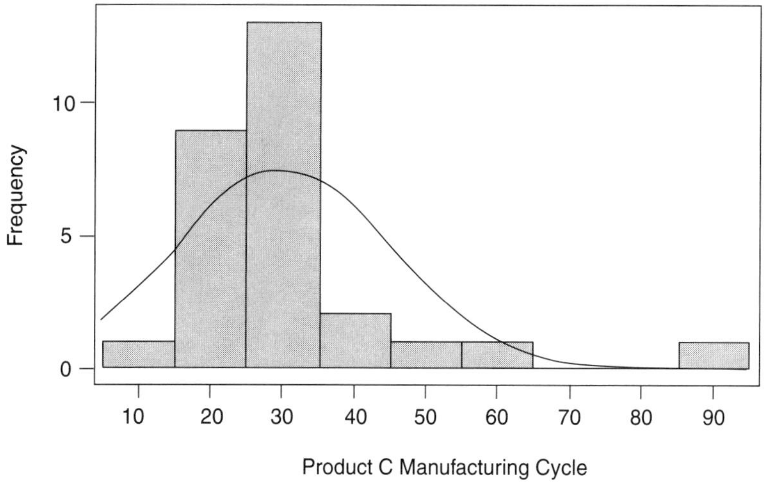

Figure 3.35C. Graphical Presentation of the Manufacturing Cycle for Product C (Histogram with Normal Curve)

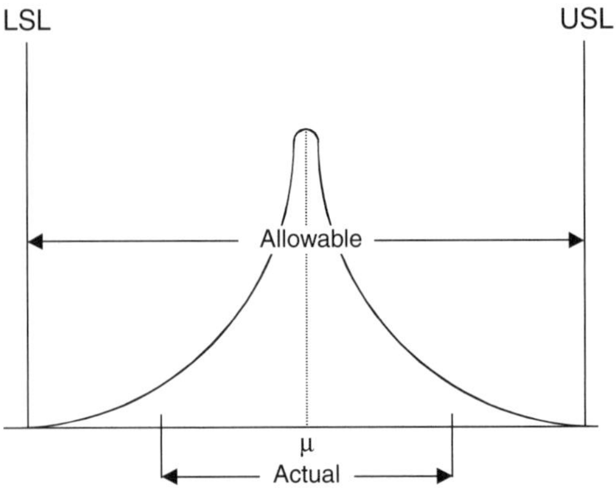

Figure 3.36. Conceptual Presentation of C_p

section will provide a brief discussion of their definitions, interpretations, and calculations.

Process Capability (C_p and C_pk) Index

Two key indices (C_p and C_pk) are used related to technical process capability. They are seldom used in administrative service or transactional processes.

Capability

Capability is defined as the ability of a process to produce product/service within defined specification limits.

Process Potential Index (C_p)

The process potential index measures the potential capability of a process. C_p is defined as the ratio of the allowable spread over the actual spread. This concept is presented in Figure 3.36:

$$C_p = (\text{Allowable spread/Actual spread})$$

$$C_p = (USL - LSL)/6s$$

where:

LSL = Lower specification limit

USL = Upper specification limit

Actual spread is determined from the process data as collected and is calculated six times the standard deviation (6s). Process capability is defined based on the calculated C_p value as follows:

- $C_p < 1$, process is considered potentially *incapable* of meeting specification requirements and
- $C_p \geq 1$, process has the potential to be *capable* of meeting specification requirements

In the Six Sigma process, the specification limits (*LSL* and *USL*) are allowed $\pm 6\sigma$ within the specification limits, and the denominator is still 6s; therefore, $C_p \geq 2.0$. However, a high C_p value does not guarantee that a production process will fall within specification limits because the C_p value does not imply that the *actual* spread must coincide with the allowable spread, i.e., the specification limits. Therefore, C_p is called the process potential and the index commonly used is called process capability index (C_pk).

Process Capability Index (C_pk)

Process capability index measures the ability of a process to create product within specification limits. The value of C_pk is an index, which measures how close a process is running to its specification limits, maintaining the natural variability of the process. Therefore, process capability is defined based on the C_pk value as:

$$C_pk = [Smaller\ of \frac{\bar{X} - LSL}{3s}\ or\ \frac{USL - \bar{X}}{3s}]$$

If,

- $C_pk < 1$, process is referred to as *incapable* of producing the product within specifications and
- $C_pk \geq 1$, process is referred to as *capable* of producing the product within specifications

The value of C_pk would be higher only if the manufacturer were meeting the target consistently with minimum variation. A commonly acceptable minimum value of C_pk is 1.33. Therefore, customers prefer the C_pk value to be 1.33 or higher.

For the Six Sigma process,

$C_pk = 2.0$

because specification limits are $\pm 6\sigma$.

The higher the C_pk, the narrower the process distribution is, as compared to the specification limits, and the more uniform the product is. As standard deviation increases, the C_pk index decreases, which creates the potential to produce product outside the specification limits. C_pk has only positive values.

When $C_pk = 0$, the actual process average matches or falls outside one of the specification limits. The C_pk value will never be greater than C_p, only equal to it when the actual process falls in the middle of specification limits.

Parts per million (PPM) is another process quality metric. PPM applies to:

- Defective product or part (component)
- Defects
- Errors
- Mistakes

Therefore, the metrics can be linked as follows:

- Defects per million
- Errors per million
- Mistakes per million
- Defectives per million
- PPM defective

The standard values for C_p, C_pk, and PPM for $\pm X\sigma$ (Sigma levels) are presented in Table 3.23 (if the product/service data are normally distributed with stability and distribution centered).

Process Performance (P_p) and Process Performance Index (P_pk)

Process performance (P_p) is a simple indicator of the actual process performance, while the process performance index (P_pk) simply tries to verify whether or not the collected sample from the process would meet the specification limits. The logic used to calculate P_pk is the same as that used for C_pk, except that C_pk uses the estimated sigma (s) and P_pk uses the calculated sigma (s_c). Therefore,

$$P_pk = [Smaller\ of\ \frac{\bar{X} - LSL}{3s_c}\ or\ \frac{USL - \bar{X}}{3s_c}]$$

If,

- $P_pk < 1$, actual process is *incapable* of producing the product within specification limits and

Table 3.23. Sample Values for C_p, C_pk, and PPM

Standard Condition	C_p	C_pk	PPM
[± 1 σ] ≅ one sigma	0.33	0.33	317,320
[± 2 σ] ≅ two sigma	0.67	0.67	45,500
[± 3 σ] ≅ three sigma	1.0	1.0	2,700
[± 4 σ] ≅ four sigma	1.33	1.33	63.5
[± 4.5 σ] ≅ four and a half sigma	1.50	1.50	6.9
[± 5 σ] ≅ five sigma	1.67	1.67	0.6
[± 6 σ] ≅ six sigma	2.0	2.0	0.002

- $P_pk \geq 1$, actual process is *capable* of producing the product within specification limits

For the Six Sigma process,

$P_pk = 2.0$

because specification limits are $\pm 6\sigma$.

Differences between C_pk and P_pk. Identified differences between C_pk and P_pk include:

- The value of C_pk is for the short-term; the value of P_pk is for the long-term.
- C_pk references the variation to the specification limits, while P_pk produces an index number for the process variation.
- C_pk can be used to determine how process variation would affect the ability of the process to meet customer needs/requirements (CTQs), while the P_pk measurement would be used to answer, "How much variation is in the process."
- C_pk presents the future capability of the process, assuming that the process remains in a state of statistical control; although P_pk presents past process performance, it cannot be used to predict the future.
- The values of C_pk and P_pk will converge to almost the same value when the process is in statistical control, i.e., both the standard deviations (estimated and calculated) are identical. However, when the standard deviations are distinctly different, the process is out of control.

3.10 SUMMARY

In this chapter, a discussion of the Measure phase of the DMAIC process has been presented with key topics:

- Definition of **Measure**
- Data type
- Data dimension and qualification
- Closed-loop data measurement system
- Flow charting
- Business metrics
- Cause-and-effect diagram
- Failure mode and effects analysis (FMEA) and failure mode, effects, and criticality analysis (FMECA)
- Data collection plan
- Data presentation plan (tables, charts, graphs, and basic statistics)
- Introduction to MINITAB tool
- Determining sample size
- Probabilistic data distributions (normal, Poisson, exponential, binomial, gamma, and Weibull)
- The Central Limit Theorem
- Calculating sigma (discrete and continuous data processes):
  - Defects per million opportunities (DPMO)
  - Errors per million opportunities (EPMO)
  - Sigma shift (long term vs. short term)
- Process capability indices

A project team must perform the following tasks before proceeding to Analyze, the next phase of the DMAIC process:

- Ensure completion of:
  - Selection and team approval of key measures
  - A data collection plan (with a decision made that historical data can be utilized or that data collection is needed)
  - Accounting for long- and short-term process variability
  - Baseline process performance in Sigma metrics
- Identify the following factors:

- Input variables, process variables, and output variables
- Key measures to identify business performance
- Customer CTQs, defect opportunities, and process capability metric
- Charts and processes used for display and communication of process variation
- Gap between current performance and the customer-specified performance
- Any "low-hanging fruit" (i.e., any product/process improvement that is obvious based on preliminary information and which is easy to implement) for immediate remedies to reduce the gap
- Handy quality tool(s) to get through the **M**easure phase

REFERENCES

1. Umble, M. and M.L. Srikanth. 1996. *Synchronous Manufacturing*, Chapter 2. Guilford, CT: Spectrum Publishing.
2. Society of Automotive Engineers/Reliability, Maintainability, Supportability and Logistics Committee. 1993 Jun 18. The FMECA Process in the Concurrent Engineering (CE) Environment. Aerospace Information Report AIR4845. Available at: *http://www.sae.org/technical/standards/AIR4845*.
3. Society of Automotive Engineers. 1993. Failure Mode, Effects and Criticality Analysis. Aerospace Recommended Practice, unpublished paper. Available at *http://www.sae.org/technical/standards/ AIR4845*.
4. Bowles, J.B. and R.D. Bonnell. 1997. Failure Mode, Effects, and Criticality Analysis (What It Is and How to Use It). Presented at the Annual Reliability and Maintainability Symposium, Philadelphia, PA.
5. DOD. 1984 Nov 28. MIL-STD-1629A/Notice 2: Military Standard Procedure for Performing a Failure Mode, Effects and Criticality Analysis. Washington, D.C.: U.S. Department of Defense. Available at *http://www.fmeainfocentre.com/download/MILSTD1629.htm*.
6. Society of Automotive Engineers. 1994 July. Potential Failure Mode and Effects Analysis in Design (Design FMEA) and for Manufacturing and Assembly Process (Process FMEA). Instruction Manual. Surface Vehicle Recommended Practice.

7. Juran, J.M. 2002. *Juran Institute's Transactional Breakthrough Strategy.* Southbury, CT: Juran Institute. Chapter 3 (student material from Black Belt certification training class).
8. Hines, W.W. and D.C. Montgomery. 1992. *Probability and Statistics in Engineering and Management Science, Third Edition.* New York: John Wiley.

4

ANALYZE

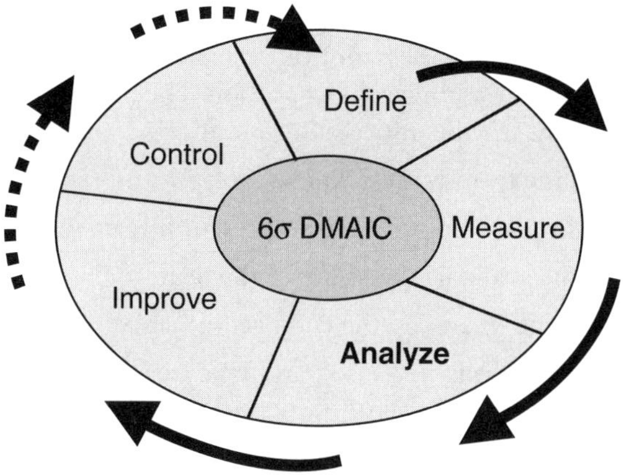

The data collection, sorting, and presentations described in the Measure phase of the DMAIC process were done to assist the team to identify "what is happening to dependent (output) variable (*Y*)." The next phase, known as the Analyze phase, will assist the team to identify "why it is happening." The Analyze phase also identifies root causes and how the input and the in-process variables, also known as independent variables (*X*s), impact the dependent variable (*Y*). Although there may be numerous independent variables, the overall objective of the Analyze phase is to narrow a field of many independent variables (*X*s) to limited (important) ones based on data obtained in the Measure phase. Therefore, it can be said that the Analyze phase attempts to identify the root cause(s) of the major contributor(s) to the problem.

Remember that the output of a process is dependent on the inputs and the in-process. Therefore, mathematically, this can be written as "the output is a function of the inputs and the in-process." Let $X_1, X_2, \ldots, X_n$ be defined as the inputs and the in-process and let Y be defined as an output; then, $Y = f(X_1, X_2, X_3, \ldots, X_n)$.

The responsibility of a Six Sigma team (a Continuous Improvement team) is to identify the inputs and the in-process (Xs), which are known causes of a serious quality problem(s) that is impacting the output (Y), i.e., the process produces bad/poor-quality output (Y). The team is to find a replacement/modification for the current input and/or the in-process, implement the recommended improvements, and put in place the required controls to maintain the required output.

The collected information from the **M**easure (measurement) phase generally provides potential sources of variation. The team then investigates the variations and identifies the most critical variations based on the project objectives. The team would also utilize individual and/or group experiences as well as available graphical/tabular/statistical tools to analyze the information and to "zoom-in" on sources of variation that are impacting team objectives.

So far, the team has been developing theories as to what might be causing the problem. By testing these theories, root causes will be validated. Using a systematic approach in the analysis process is important. Therefore, asking the following questions before analyzing the information is critical:

- What does the team want to know?
- How should the team view and/or present information?
- Which of the available tools should the team use?
- How and from where did the team get information?

Once the information is processed and analyzed, team should ask another question:

- As a team, what have we learned?

Next is a brief analysis of these questions.

What Does the Team Want to Know?

The team should specifically define goals/objectives and the in-process terms. It is important for all team members to participate in the process, e.g., "How do my input and in-process variables (Xs) affect output (Y)?"

How Should the Team View and/or Present Information?

Information can be presented in several ways—descriptively, graphically, and statistically. The team should select the most appropriate way(s) to present information, e.g., present a population distribution of a town by educational level by using a pie chart.

Which of the Available Tools Should the Team Use?

Utilize the following statements to identify the tools for the information sampling, collection, and analyzing plans:

- If the input information can be divided into several categories, utilize multivariable charts, box plots, and main effects plots for the defined categories.
- If the input information is continuous, utilize regression/correlation tools. The regression tool develops a prediction equation between the continuous input variable and the response variable; the correlation tool provides graphical information about the input variables.

Tool selection depends on the type of information and the way questions are presented:

- Regression and correlation tool—Energy utilization in material heating
- Box plots, multivariable charts—Employee composition in a company, e.g., by ethnic background
- Pie chart—Relative contribution/composition of a whole, e.g., a town's population distribution by family
- Control chart—To highlight the average performance and dispersion around the average, e.g., production data about a shaft diameter

These concepts are also presented in Table 4.1 and Figure 4.1.

How and From Where Did the Team Obtain Information?

Typical steps to follow include:

- Identify the input information, e.g., continuous, discrete.
- Develop and explain the plan to team members and all persons who will participate in information collection and/or analysis.
- If planning to utilize the MINITAB software tool, develop a MINITAB information entry sheet according to the sampling plan.
- Identify and assign roles and responsibilities for information collection, entry, storage and processing.
- After processing and analyzing the information, ask the next question: "What have we learned?"

What Has the Team Learned?

- Analyze the data using MINITAB software and check the following points/items for completion. These points have been divided into two groups—question format and statement format. (Some of these

Table 4.1. Analysis Tool Selection—Depending on Question and Data Type

	Y (Output Variable)	
X (Input Variable)	**Continuous Data**	**Discrete Data**
Continuous Data	How does change in input affect change in output? Graphical: Scatter plot Statistical: Regression	How does change in input affect change in output? Statistical: Regression
Discrete Data	**Different Means?** Graphical: Histogram(s) Statistical: t-test, ANOVA	**Different Output?** Graphical: Stratified Pareto diagrams Statistical: Frequency counts, chi-square
	Different Variance? Graphical: Stratified box plots, Multivariable	

points should have been answered based on work previously done. Remaining points will be discussed and answered by the end of this chapter.)

Statement Format Points:

- Identify gaps between the current performance and goal performance.
- Generate list of possible causes (sources of variation).
- Segment and stratify possible causes.
- Prioritize the list of the "vital few" causes.
- Verify and quantify the root causes of variation.
- Determine the performance gap.
- Display and communicate the gap/opportunities in financial terms.

Question Format Points:

- What does the data say about the performance of the business process?

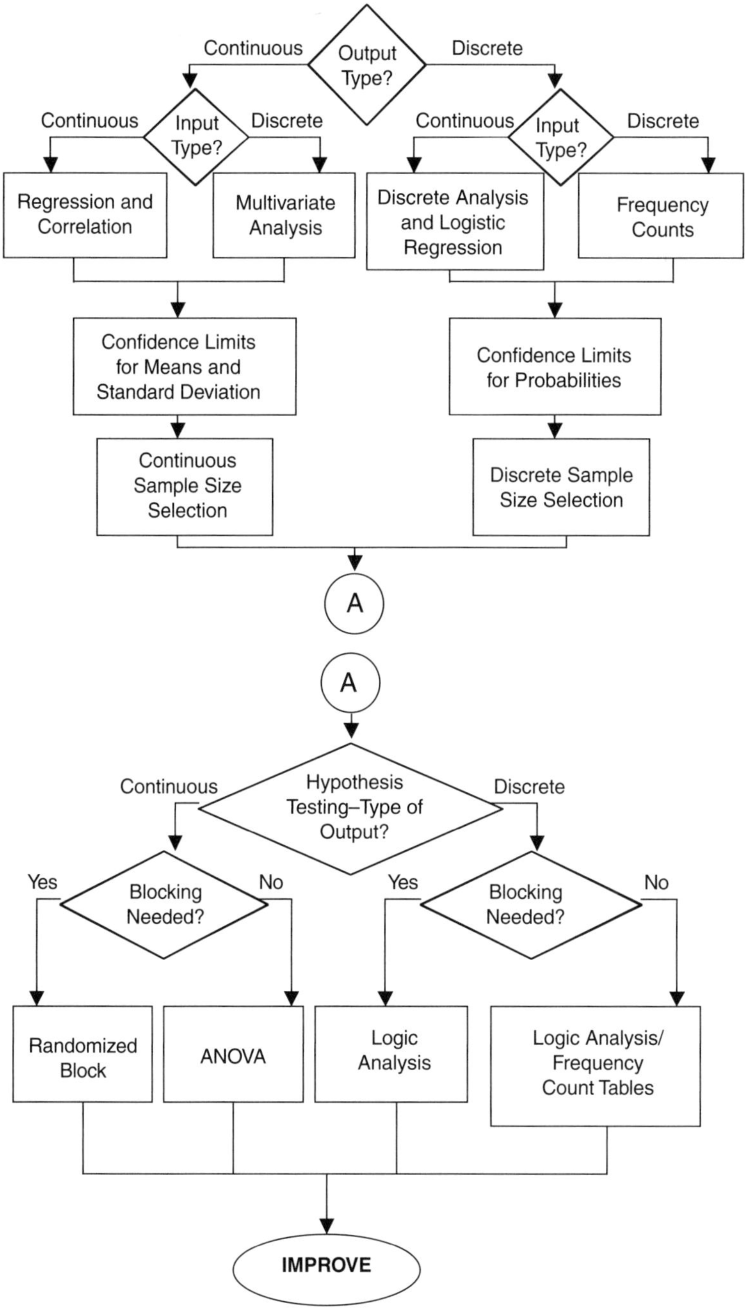

Figure 4.1. An Analyzing Flow Chart

- Did any value-added analysis or "lean thinking" take place to identify some of the gaps shown on the "as is" process map?
- Was a detailed process map created to amplify critical steps of the "as is" business process?
- How was the map generated, verified, and validated?
- What did the team gain from developing a subprocess map?
- What were crucial "moments of truth" on the map?
- Were any cycle time improvement opportunities identified from the process analysis?
- Were any designed experiments used to generate additional insight into the data analysis?
- Did any additional data need to be collected?
- What model would best explain the behavior of output variables in relation to input variables?
- What conclusions were drawn from the team's data collection and analysis?
- How did the team reach these conclusions?
- What is the cost of poor quality as supported by the team's analysis?
- Is the process so severely broken that redesign is necessary?
- What are the rough-order estimates of the financial savings/opportunity for the improvement project?
- Have the problem and goal statements been updated to reflect the additional knowledge gained from the **A**nalyze phase?
- Have any additional benefits been identified that will result from closing all or most of the gaps?
- What were the financial benefits resulting from quick fixes ("low-hanging fruits")?
- What quality tools were used to get through the **A**nalyze phase?

Then,

- State precise and clear conclusions. Update the classified list of input variables for repeat or future analysis.
- Design the next study as appropriate.

Discussing all available tools will not be possible in this book; however, commonly utilized tools will be discussed with examples:

4.1 STRATIFICATION

Stratification is the process of separating data into categories (groups) based on data variation. A specific combination of ranges or variables defines each data category. These characteristics are called the stratification variables. Each stratification variable would have two or more values. One or more variables could be defined in a category. Data stratification is generally needed to estimate a problem source in vastly varied information. Yet, in certain conditions, stratification can be misleading:

- Small differences among groups should not be given undue weight, leading the team to say, "We found it." The team could prematurely identify a cause based on a difference that is insignificant.

- An abnormal group of data is not necessarily the cause of a problem. The team should investigate to find the cause and should not make too much of abnormal data.

Generally, the following steps should be followed in the stratification process:

- Stratify the data into categories. If additional information needs to be collected, the team has to ensure that all potential stratification variables are collected as identifiers.
- Analyze the categorized data for the likely source of a cause. These categories will be used for each stratification chart/graph. These categories may either be a range of values or discrete values.
- Measure and analyze the significant impact of the phenomenon on the process.
- Use bar graphs. They are the most effective method for presenting data. However, other methods are also utilized, e.g., box plots, scatter diagrams.

If the initial stratification does not provide enough evidence for a cause, the team has two options:

- Conduct stratification based on the next key variable within the first variable.
- Go back and stratify all the data based on some other key variable.

If the team decides that the collected information does not represent the process, the team may collect new information. The team should make an effort to collect as much identifying information as they think could possibly prove useful for the stratification process. Then the team will go back to the beginning of the stratification process and complete the stratification process.

Stratification is an information-analysis tool. The information is analyzed according to the stratification factors. A stratification factor is a factor that can be used to separate information into subgroups. Once the team investigates and recognizes a factor as a special cause factor, then that factor is used as a stratification factor. If the stratification process is successful, i.e., if the results give a clear indication that more than one group of data exists, then the team should try to validate their results or try to gain further information to more precisely define the cause. Additional advantages of stratification include:

- May be used as an initial analysis in the DMAIC process to narrow the scope of the project
- May provide significant help in root-cause analysis

Table 4.2A. Manufacturing Cycle Time Raw Data, Calendar Days

2, 5, 10, 2, 5, 11, 3, 6, 11, 4, 7, 11, 4, 8, 10, 3, 6, 12, 2, 5, 10, 2, 4, 13,
3, 5, 12, 2, 6, 14, 1, 7, 10, 3, 8, 11, 2, 5, 12, 3, 6, 14, 1, 6, 11, 5, 9, 9

Table 4.2B. Manufacturing Cycle Time Data by Module, Calendar Days

Raw Data for Module A, Calendar Days:
2, 2, 3, 4, 4, 3, 2, 2, 3, 2, 1, 3, 2, 3, 1, 5
Raw Data for Module B, Calendar Days:
5, 5, 6, 7, 8, 6, 5, 4, 5, 6, 7, 8, 5, 6, 6, 9
Raw Data for Module C, Calendar Days:
10, 11, 11, 11, 10, 12, 10, 13, 12, 14, 10, 11, 12, 14, 11, 9

- Because output is a function of input variables, focus is on input variables
- May identify the issue(s) without getting too deeply into the data collection and analysis processes

Commonly used stratification elements include:

- Cause Category (type)—Complaints from customer/employee, defective product/process
- Time (when)—Frequency of occurrence (daily, weekly, monthly, etc.)
- Location (where)—Supplier site, customer site, domestic, international
- Reporting (who)—Individual, group/department, business

Example 4.1 and the Exercise 4.1 will provide a better understanding of stratification.

Example 4.1: Using Histograms vs. Box Plots for Analyzing Data

A Connecticut manufacturing company produces three modules (A, B, and C) of a product. Management is interested in improving the manufacturing cycle time. A Six Sigma team has been selected for the manufacturing cycle time improvement project. The team has collected manufacturing cycle time data (Table 4.2A). The project team has also decided to plot a histogram to analyze the cycle time (Figure 4.2A).

As the team analyzed the plotted histogram (Figure 4.2A), the team found that the histogram (distribution) had more than one point of concentration, a

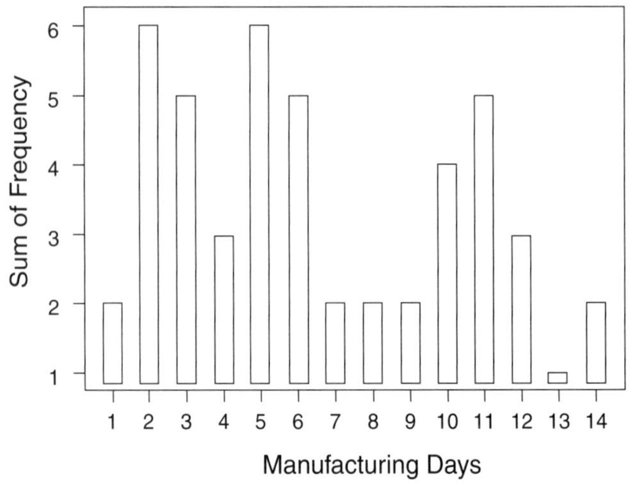

Figure 4.2A. Manufacturing Cycle Time Frequency Histogram for All Systems

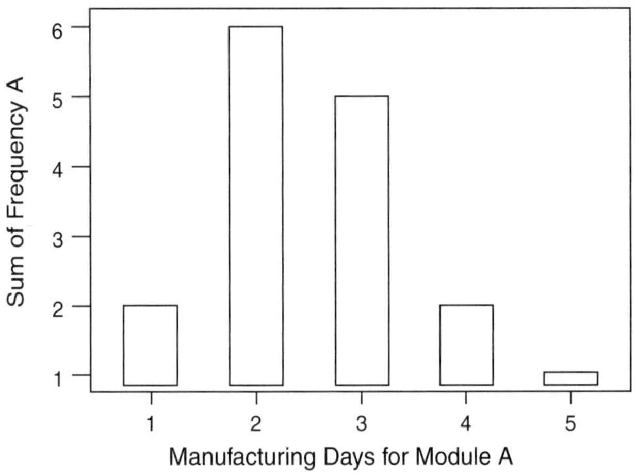

Figure 4.2B. Manufacturing Cycle Time Frequency Histogram for Module A

type of distribution known as "multimodal distribution." (A distribution with a single point of concentration is known as "unimodal distribution.") When multimodal distribution occurs, likely indicated is that either the data are not homogeneous or that the data are from more than one source. Therefore, the team went back and reanalyzed the data and found that all three modules (A,B,

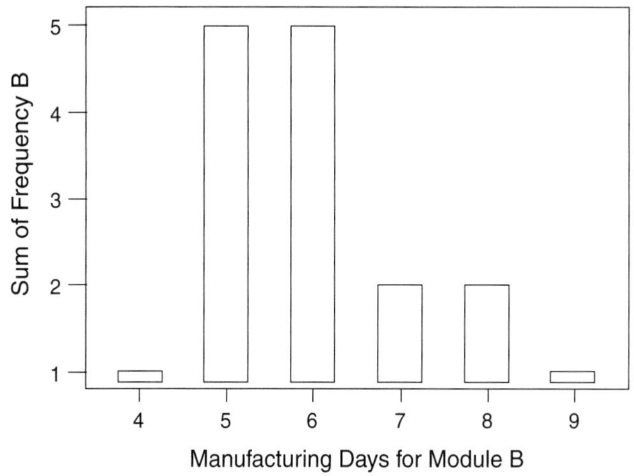

Figure 4.2C. Manufacturing Cycle Time Frequency Histogram for Module B

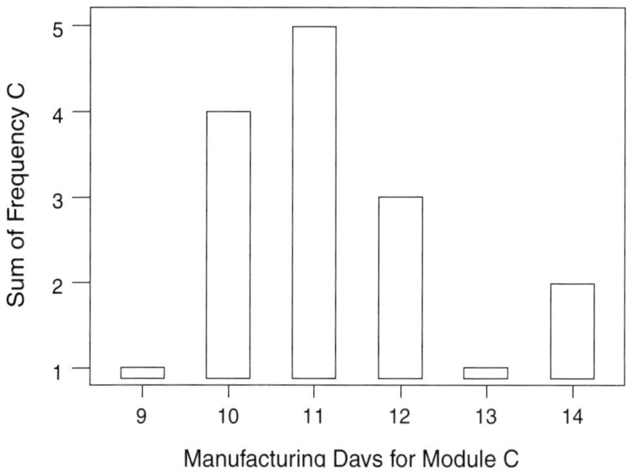

Figure 4.2D. Manufacturing Cycle Time Frequency Histogram for Module C

and C) were produced. So the team sorted the manufacturing cycle time data by module type (Table 4.2B).

Then the manufacturing cycle time data for the three modules (A, B, and C) were plotted in three histograms as shown in Figures 4.2B, 4.2C, and 4.2D. These three histograms clearly show that three modules were manufactured with a

Table 4.2C. Descriptive Statistics when Combining Manufacturing Cycle for All Modules

Variable	N	Mean	Median	
All Systems	48	6.688	6.000	
Variable	**TrMean**	**SD**	**SE Mean**	
All Systems	6.614	3.82	0.552	
Variable	**Minimum**	**Maximum**	**Q1**	**Q3**
All Systems	1.000	14.000	3.000	10.000

Table 4.2D. Descriptive Statistics by Module (A, B, and C)

Variable	Model	N	Mean	Median	TrMean	SD
Manufacturing	6	1	6.0000	6.0000	6.0000	*
Cycle	A	16	2.625	2.500	2.571	1.088
	B	15	6.133	6.000	6.077	1.407
	C	16	11.313	11.000	11.286	1.448
Variable	**Model**	**SE Mean**	**Minimum**	**Maximum**	**Q1**	**Q3**
Manufacturing	6	*	6.0000	6.0000	*	*
Cycle	A	0.272	1.000	5.000	2.000	3.000
	B	0.363	4.000	9.000	5.000	7.000
	C	0.362	9.000	14.000	10.000	12.000

manufacturing cycle time range for module A of 1 to 5 days, for module B of 4 to 9 days, and for module C of 9 to 14 days.

Assuming that the manufacturing cycle time data of the modules are normally distributed, statistical information has been developed and presented in Table 4.2C and Figures 4.2E and 4.2F. What statistical comments do these figures and table provide?

Box plots are very similar to histograms. The box plot tool is useful when working with small sets of data or when comparing several different sets of data, e.g., the individual modules A, B, and C.

This time, manufacturing cycle time data are plotted utilizing the box plot tool (Figure 4.2G) and descriptive statistics are developed (Table 4.2D). This information should lead to the team deriving the same conclusion as reached earlier.

Some definite shortcomings of the stratification process include:

- If small differences exist among the classes of data, a team should not choose a tool based only on stratification. The team should look for other causes—the category itself is not necessarily the cause.
- If collection of more data is required, the team should give extra effort to identifying information that could be useful in stratification.

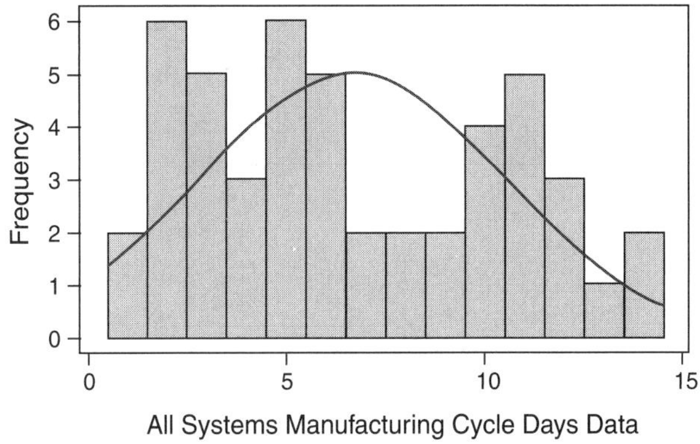

Figure 4.2E. Histogram with Normal Curve for Manufacturing Cycle Frequency for All Modules

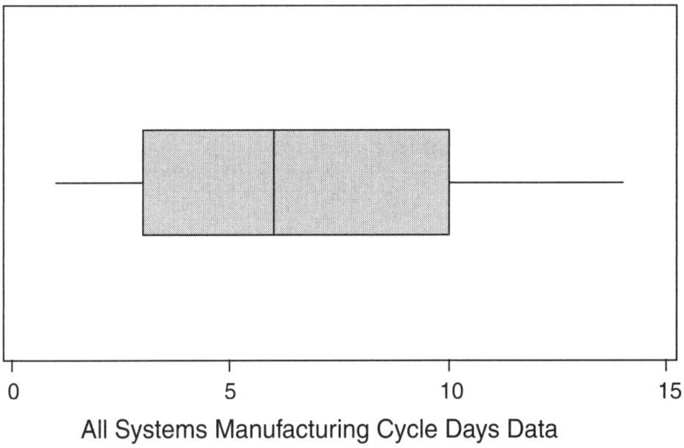

Figure 4.2F. Box Plot for Manufacturing Cycle Time for All Modules

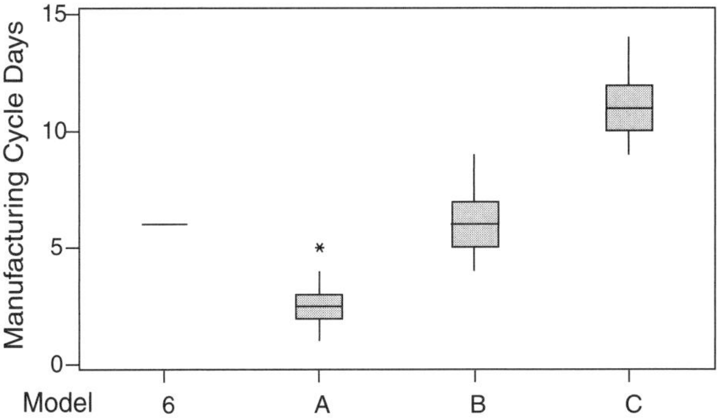

Figure 4.2G. Manufacturing Cycle Time Box Plot by Module (A, B, and C)

Table 4.3A. Manufacturing Cycle Time Data for Product X Before and After Installing Process Improvement

Before		After	
35	47	30	30
38	46	29	32
37	48	31	29
39	40	32	31
40	42	30	30
42	39	29	29
45	38	31	29
40	41	30	30

Table 4.3B. Descriptive Statistics for Product X Manufacturing Cycle Time Before and After Installing Process Improvement

Variable	Model	N	Mean	Median	TrMean	SD
Model	After	16	30.125	30.000	30.071	1.025
Cycle	Before	16	41.063	40.000	41.000	3.732

Variable	Model	SE Mean	Minimum	Maximum	Q1	Q3
Model	After	0.256	29.000	32.000	29.000	31.000
Cycle	Before	0.933	35.000	48.000	38.250	44.250

Exercise 4.1: Creating Box Plots for Before and After Data

A Six Sigma quality improvement team has reduced the manufacturing cycle time of product X. The manufacturing cycle time data are presented in Table 4.3A. Create box plots of the "Before" and "After" data and comment on the team's quality improvement efforts.

Note: The box plot is provided in Figure 4.3 and descriptive statistics may be found in Table 4.3B if access to the tool is unavailable.

Exercise 4.2: Using the Stratification Tool

Use the stratification tool to investigate the following scenarios. Draw a sketch to show how output would be viewed:

1. A company has a help desk to resolve hardware and software problems. Employees are complaining that the help desk takes a long

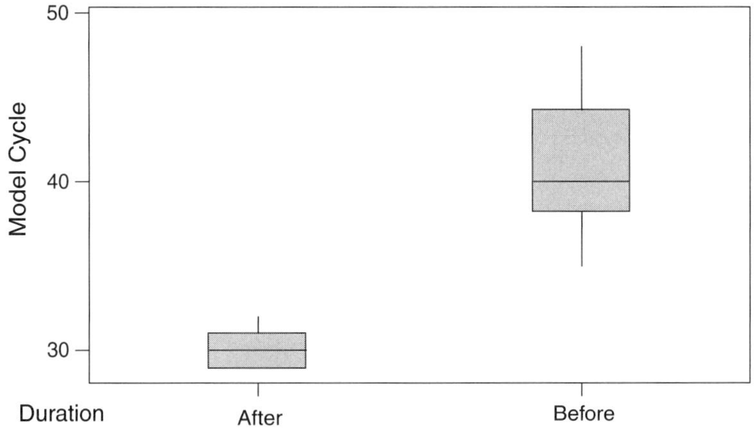

Figure 4.3. Before and After Box Plot for Manufacturing Cycle Time of Product X

time to resolve problems. You have been assigned to investigate the employees' complaints. Based on preliminary communication, your theory is that there may be a time-related element that is creating the long resolution times. You have collected problem resolution time data for 4 weeks and are ready to investigate your theory.

2. A company sells preventive maintenance (PM) contracts to customers who have purchased new equipment. PM services are divided into four regions (East, West, North, and South). Service management at your company suspects that the average PM time between regions is not the same. You have collected 5 weeks of data from all four regions. How would you confirm management's suspicions?

Stratification—The Pareto Chart

The stratification concept can also use a Pareto chart and a cumulative curve. A sample situation is presented in Figure 4.4A. The familiar 80/20 rule (i.e., approximately 20% of the problems cause 80% of poor performance) can also be used. The stratification method can also be utilized if an iterative concept is to go more deeply into a process.

Suppose a company is manufacturing (mostly in an assembly process) four products (A, B, C, and D). These products are manufactured during three shift operations (first, second, and third). Each shift operator has a different level of education (less than high school, high school, and higher than high school) (Figure 4.4B). Nine issues (A, B, C, D, E, F, G, H, and I) have been identified.

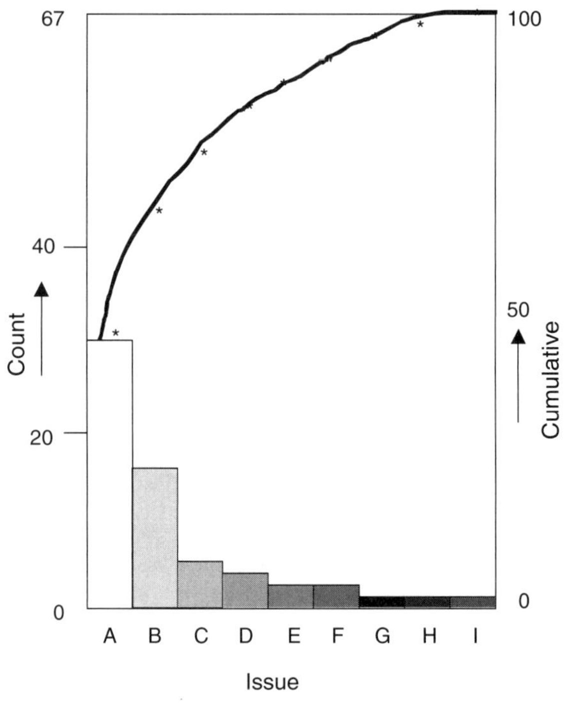

Figure 4.4A. Pareto Chart of Manufacturing Issues

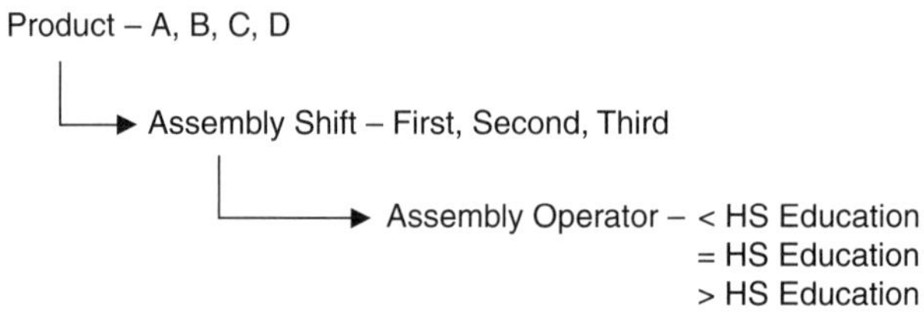

Figure 4.4B. Structural Relationship between Products and Operators

Frequency data for the issues have been collected by operator's education level. A sample Pareto chart has been developed based on an operator's education level being below high school (Figure 4.4A). Similar charts can be developed for operators having the two other education levels (a high school education and a higher than high school education). If these three charts are very similar, then the operator's education level is not a cause of the frequency of these issues.

4.2 HYPOTHESIS TESTING: CLASSIC TECHNIQUES

Statistics plays a critical role in Six Sigma projects. Statistical tools identify the relationship between input variables (*X*s) and the output variable (*Y*). The relationship developed in the Analyze phase of the DMAIC process is *qualitative*. If the qualitative relationship is not strong enough to develop the alternative solutions necessary to achieve the project objective(s), then the team has to develop the *quantitative* relationship. The Design of Experiment (DOE) tool must be utilized to develop a *quantitative* relationship. The DOE tool will be described Chapter 5, *Improve*. These statistical tools validate the root causes of problems (issues).

Think about the following: every member of the project team has a certain image of reality in his/her mind; some of these images may be true, while others may be false; and all members act accordingly. For example, one team member may think that wearing a helmet as a safety precaution when driving/riding a motorcycle reduces fatality rates; therefore, we should provide a sales discount for helmets. Another team member may think that cigarettes cause heart and lung diseases; therefore, we should increase taxes on cigarettes. Similarly, business people have other thoughts (beliefs) about certain things and they make important decisions everyday based on these beliefs.

Now, consider two scenarios. A sugar manufacturing company packages sugar in 5-pound bags because thought at the company is that this size bag is easy to carry and does not create storage problems. A battery manufacturing company provides a battery with an average life of 100 hours because thought at the company is that 100 hours is a good life span for a battery.

In each of these scenarios, and thousands more, people act on the basis of their thoughts/beliefs about reality. An initial thought might be in the form of a simple idea, perhaps with a little thought given to it, but with less thought than would be done if using informed thinking. This thinking might then become a proposition, which possibly could become true; therefore it can be called a hypothesis. Sooner or later, every hypothesis is tested with evidence that either supports or refutes the hypothesis—a process which helps to move a person's image of reality from great uncertainty to less uncertainty.

Hypothesis testing is a systematic approach to assessing beliefs about reality. Hypothesis testing is confronting a belief (such as test/process data that represent an unknown population parameter) with evidence (statistically computed from the test/process data) and then deciding, in relation to the collected data, whether the initial belief (or hypothesis) can be maintained as reasonable and realistic or if it must be rejected as impractical and insupportable.

Therefore, hypothesis testing is an important concept in a Six Sigma process improvement program. For example, process team members might want to know if modified process B has "significantly" improved yield when compared to yield from older process A; if outputs of machines I, II, and III form a homogeneous mass of product; if a quality characteristic of a product is independent of a given condition of production; etc.

Most of the time, collected data are in sample form. It is important to know the mathematical relationship between the sample and the population before any hypothesis testing. Hypothesis testing will be described in the next four subsections.

4.2.1 The Mathematical Relationships among Summary Measures

Most of the time, it is neither practical nor economical to collect population data; therefore, sample data should represent the population. Therefore, a discussion of the mathematical relationship between sample and population follows.

The Relationship of the Sample Mean to the Parent Population

Let

$\bar{X}$ = Sample mean

When selections of sample elements are statistically independent events (typically referred to as "the large-population case"), for a sample of $n \geq 30$ (given that $n < 0.05N$ or normal population and N = population size):

$$Z = \frac{(\bar{X} - \mu_0)}{\sigma_{\bar{X}}}$$

where:

μ_0 = Hypothesized population mean

$$\mu_{\bar{X}} = \mu$$

$$\sigma_{\bar{X}}^2 = \frac{\sigma^2}{n}$$

and

$$\sigma_{\bar{X}} = \frac{\sigma}{\sqrt{n}}$$

When sample elements are statistically dependent events (typically referred to as "the small-population case"), for sample of $n < 30$ ($n \geq 0.05N$ of normal population and N = population size):

$$t = \frac{\left(\bar{X} - \mu_0\right)}{\sigma_{\bar{X}}}$$

$$\sigma^2_{\bar{X}} = \frac{\sigma^2}{n} \frac{\left(N - n\right)}{\left(N - 1\right)}$$

and

$$\sigma_{\bar{X}} = \frac{\sigma}{\sqrt{n}} \sqrt{\frac{(N - n)}{(N - 1)}}$$

where:

$\mu_{\bar{X}}$ = Mean of the sampling distribution

$\sigma^2_{\bar{X}}$ = Variance of sampling distribution

$\sigma_{\bar{X}}$ = Standard deviation of sampling distribution of the sample mean, $\bar{X}$

while:

μ, σ^2, and σ are population mean, variance, and standard deviation, and

N or n are population or sample size, respectively

For the Sampling Distribution of P_0

When selections of sample elements are statistically independent events (typically referred to as "the large-population case"), for $n < 0.05N$:

$$\mu_p = P$$

$$\sigma^2_{P_0} = \frac{P(1 - P)}{n}$$

and

$$s_{P_0} = \sqrt{\frac{P(1 - P)}{n}}$$

When sample elements are statistically dependent events (typically referred to as "the small-population case"), for $n \geq 0.05N$:

$$\sigma^2_{P_0} = \left(\frac{P(1 - P)}{n}\right)\left(\frac{N - n}{N - 1}\right)$$

$$\sigma_{P_0} = \sqrt{\left(\frac{P(1-P)}{n}\right)\left(\frac{N-n}{N-1}\right)}$$

where:

μ_{P_0} = Mean of the sampling distribution

$\sigma^2_{P_0}$ = Variance of sampling distribution

σ_{P_0} = Standard deviation of sampling distribution of the sample proportion, P_0

while:

P is the population proportion and

N and n are population and sample sizes, respectively

The next section (*The Theory of Hypothesis Testing*) will utilize the above-presented relationship.

4.2.2 The Theory of Hypothesis Testing

To illustrate the testing of hypothesis, consider a game. Let a die be shaken in a box and rolled on a table. If an even number turns up, Player X pays Player Y $1.00. If an odd number turns up, Player Y pays Player X $1.00. Umpire Z does the shaking and rolling of the die. If the die is symmetrical and is rolled in a random manner, the theory of probability tells us that, in the long run, we can expect an equal number of even and odd numbers. Under these conditions, the game will be a fair one.

Before the game begins, testing the fundamental hypothesis of symmetry and randomness is desirable. To do this, X and Y agree to have Z roll the die, say, 100 times. If the results agree with the expected results, the game will be played as agreed upon; if not, the proper modifications will be made. Of course, the fundamental question is how close does an agreement with expectations need to be before the hypothesis of symmetry and randomness can be accepted? Consideration of this question leads to the theory of hypothesis testing.

In testing a hypothesis, two types of errors may be made:

- To reject a hypothesis when it is actually *true*—In this case, a *type I* error has been made (also known as *Producer's Risk*). With reference to the illustration, we may conclude after Z rolls the die 100 times, the die is unsymmetrical or is thrown in a biased manner, when actually this is not true.

Table 4.4. Decisions in Hypothesis Testing

	H_0 is True	H_0 is False
Accept H_0	No error	Type II error
Reject H_0	Type I error	No error

- To accept a hypothesis when it is *not true*—In this case, a *type II* error has been made (also known as *Consumer's Risk*). In this case, we may say that the die is symmetrical and is thrown in a random manner, when actually it is not.

This situation is presented in Table 4.4. The probabilities of occurrence of type I and II errors have been given special symbols:

α = P (type I error) = P (reject $H_0|H_0$ is true)

β = P (type II error) = P (accept $H_0|H_0$ is false)

The Trade-Off Concept of α and β

Suppose a null hypothesis is to be tested and definitely unknown is whether the null hypothesis is true or false. Also unknown is whether the sampling distribution resembles part (a) of Figure 4.5 or part (b) of Figure 4.5. Assuming the sampling distribution looks like part (a) of Figure 4.5, and selecting a value of α, a decision rule is developed. This decision rule automatically determines the value of β if H_0 is in fact false. It is clear in Figure 4.5 that for a given sample size, any reduction in α raises β (as the dashed vertical line moves to the right). The opposite is also true: any increase in α lowers β (as the dashed line moves to the left).

Now apply the concept to the sample data statistics presented in Figure 4.5. In part (a) of Figure 4.5, the average paint drying time equals at most 5 hours and is in fact true at a significance level of $\alpha = 0.05$ and, from the sample, standard deviation is equal to 0.6 hour. The critical values are $\overline{X} = 6.0$ hours and $Z = 1.64$. The probability of making a type I error appears to the right of the dashed line.

Part (b) of Figure 4.5 shows the sampling distribution when the null hypothesis is in fact false and when the average drying time is 7.18 hours. The critical value of $\overline{X} = 6$ hours (established on the basis of assuming H_0 to be true) is now shown to be lower than the mean value of the sampling distribution, with the corresponding Z value of –1.96 and the area to the left of this being 0.025. This becomes the probability of making a type II error. Therefore, for any given sample, the selection of α leads to the decision rule and ultimately determines β.

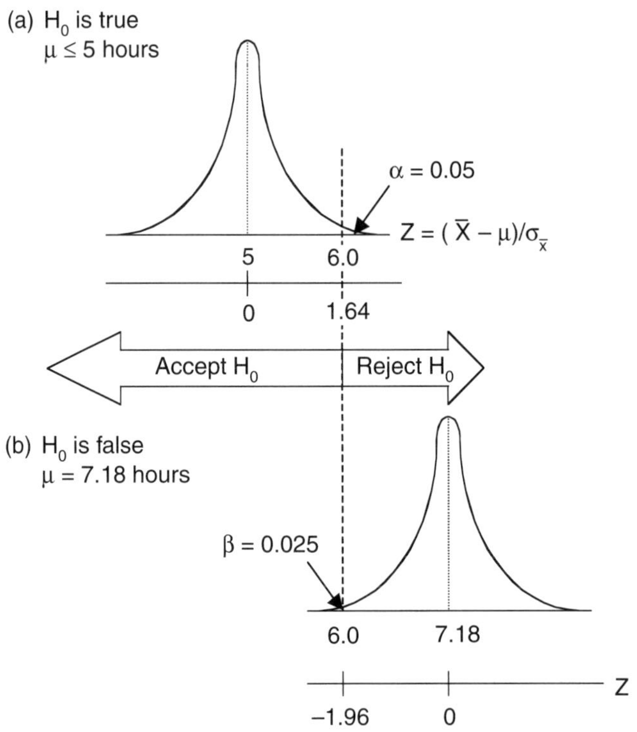

Figure 4.5. Trade-Off between α and β

The Power of the Test

Sometimes working the power of the test is more convenient, where:

$$\text{Power} = 1 - \beta = P\,(\text{reject } H_0 | H_0 \text{ is false})$$

The power of the test is the probability that a false null hypothesis is correctly rejected. Because the results of a test of a hypothesis are subject to error, we cannot "prove" or "disprove" a statistical hypothesis. However, it is possible to design test procedures that control the error probabilities α and β to suitably small values.

The probability of a type I error is often called the significance level or the size of the test. In many tests, α is set at 0.05.

The risk of error of a type II error varies with the actual conditions that exist and can be determined by a statistician only as a function of those conditions. Therefore, the chance of saying that the die is symmetrical and is thrown in an unbiased manner, when actually it is either unsymmetrical or is thrown in an unbiased manner, will vary with the degree of a symmetry or bias.

The relationship between the chance of accepting a hypothesis and the actual conditions that exist is given by the operating characteristic (OC function) for the test. Fortunately, statisticians have worked out formulas or derived tables or have found approximations for the OC functions of many statistical tests, although they are not always in the most desirable form.

Frequently used terms include:

- Null Hypothesis (H_0)—This statement is assumed to be true until sufficient evidence is presented to reject it. Generally, this statement means *no* change or difference.
- Alternate Hypothesis (H_1)—This statement is considered to be true if H_0 is rejected. Generally, this statement means that there is *some* change or difference.
- Type I Error—An error (in communication language) that says there is a difference when actually there is *no* difference. This is the type of error that rejects the H_0 hypothesis when it is in fact true. In business language, it can be defined as *Producer's Risk.*
- Alpha Risk—The maximum risk or chance of making a type I error. This is the greatest level of risk an analyst (or project team) takes in the decision-making process when rejecting the H_0 hypothesis. This probability is always greater than zero and is normally established at 5%.
- Type II Error—An error of not rejecting the H_0 hypothesis when it is in fact false. Simply it says that there is no difference when there actually is a difference. In business language, this can be defined as *Consumer's Risk.*
- Beta Risk—The maximum risk or chance of making a type II error. Simply, it says that the project team is overlooking an effective process or solution to the problem.
- Significant Difference—Describes the results of a statistical hypothesis testing in which the difference is large enough at the defined probability level.
- Power—The probability of correctly rejecting the H_0 hypothesis. It is also utilized to determine if the sample size is large enough to detect a difference in treatments if one exists.
- Test Statistic—Depending on the type of hypothesis testing, the values could be Z, t, F, etc. that represent the feasibility of H_0. Generally, the more acceptable the H_0, the smaller the absolute value of the test

statistic and the greater the probability of observing this value within its distribution.

Hypothesis testing can be two sided or one sided.

4.2.2.1 A Two-Sided Hypothesis

Remembering the die game, the hypothesis is that the die is symmetrical and that it is thrown in a random manner or that the probability of an even number is set at 0.5. Therefore, set the risk of an error of the first type (a type I error) at 0.05 and let us agree that we shall test the die by rolling it 100 times. Take as the statistic for testing the relative frequency of even numbers in 100 rolls of the die. If the relative frequency falls short of the lower acceptance limit P_{La} or exceeds the upper acceptance limit P_{Ua}, we shall reject the hypothesis; if it equals or falls between these limiting values, we shall accept the hypothesis. First, the quantities P_{La} and P_{Ua} have to be determined so that the risk of an error of type I (a) equals 0.05.

$$P_{La} = p - Z_{\alpha/2}(\sigma_P)$$

$$P_{Ua} = p + Z_{\alpha/2}(\sigma_P)$$

In the die example, $p = 0.5$, $\sigma_P = \sqrt{((0.5 \times 0.5)/100)} = 0.05$, $Z_{\alpha/2} = 1.96$. Therefore,

$$P_{La} = 0.5 - 1.96(0.05) = 0.402$$

$$P_{Ua} = 0.5 + 1.96(0.05) = 0.598$$

In other words, if we get *40 or fewer* or *60 or more* even numbers from 100 rolls of the die, we shall *reject* the hypothesis of symmetry and unbiased rolling of the die. If we get *41 to 59* even numbers, we shall *accept* the hypothesis.

If we could have the risk of rejecting our hypothesis when it is true at 0.10, then:

$$P_{La} = 0.5 - 1.645(\sigma_P)$$

$$P_{Ua} = 0.5 + 1.645(\sigma_P)$$

or we could have made it at 0.01 by taking:

$$P_{La} = 0.5 - 2.57(\sigma_P)$$

$$P_{Ua} = 0.5 + 2.57(\sigma_P)$$

4.2.2.2 A One-Sided Hypothesis

Consider a one-tail test applied to an industrial process. Suppose a machining process is producing a component that has historically produced 4% defective components. The manufacturing process has been modified. Has this modification lowered the fraction of defective components? To find the answer, test the hypothesis that there has been no change. Use a sample from the current production process. The setup for the test could be as follows:

- Hypothesis—The current process is operating in a random manner with a fraction defective of 0.04.
- Size of Sample—$n = 500$
- Statistic—The fraction defective in the sample is to be the statistic used in making the test.
- Risk of an Error of the First Type (Type I Error)—Decide to run a risk of 0.05 of rejecting the hypothesis when it is true.
- Acceptance Limits—In this scenario, decide to have only one acceptance limit P_a, which is less than 0.04. If the sample fraction defective is less than P_a, we will reject the hypothesis and conclude that the process modification has lowered the process fraction defective. If the sample fraction defective is equal to or greater than P_a, we will accept the hypothesis. The quantity P_a is to be determined so that the probability that the sample fraction defective will be less than P_a is just 0.05 when the process fraction defective is 0.04.

  To determine the acceptance limit P_a, note that the distribution of sample fraction defective will, because p' is small, be given *approximately* by the Poisson distribution, with n = 500 and $p' = 0.04$. With the help of a Poisson distribution chart/table, obtain the expected number of defective components. At $500P_a = 20$ and $p' = 0.04$, the value from the chart is 13. Therefore, $P_a = 13/500 = 0.026$. If the sample fraction defective is less than 0.026, we reject the hypothesis that the process fraction defective is 0.04.

4.2.3 Hypothesis Testing—Population Mean and the Difference between Two Such Means

Reminder: Define the problem and state the objectives *before* establishing the hypothesis.

Next is to state the null hypothesis (H_0) and the alternate hypothesis (H_1). The hypothesis testing process can be divided into four steps.

Step 1. Select the type of hypothesis:

Hypotheses about a Population Mean—The opposing hypotheses about the value of a population mean μ are typically stated in one of the following three forms by reference to a specified sample mean, μ_0:

Form 1	Form 2	Form 3
H_0: $\mu = \mu_0$	H_0: $\mu \geq \mu_0$	H_0: $\mu \leq \mu_0$
H_1: $\mu \neq \mu_0$	H_1: $\mu < \mu_0$	H_1: $\mu > \mu_0$

Hypotheses about the Difference between Two Population Means—Similarly, the opposing hypotheses about the difference between two population means, μ_A and μ_B, can be written in one of the following three forms:

Form 1	Form 2	Form 3
H_0: $\mu_A = \mu_B$	H_0: $\mu_A \geq \mu_B$	H_0: $\mu_A \leq \mu_B$
H_1: $\mu_A \neq \mu_B$	H_1: $\mu_A < \mu_B$	H_1: $\mu_A > \mu_B$

The above hypotheses can also be stated as:

Form 1	Form 2	Form 3
H_0: $\mu_A - \mu_B = 0$	H_0: $\mu_A - \mu_B \geq 0$	H_0: $\mu_A - \mu_B \leq 0$
H_1: $\mu_A - \mu_B \neq 0$	H_1: $\mu_A - \mu_B < 0$	H_1: $\mu_A - \mu_B > 0$

Step 2. This step depends on one of the above situations and the available information:

- The sample mean, $\overline{X}$, when the hypothesis test involves the population mean
- The difference between two sample means, $\overline{X}_A - \overline{X}_B$, when the test involves the difference between two population means
- An appropriate statistical test based on the assumed probability distribution, Z, t, and F

Step 3. Derive a decision rule that specifies in advance, for all possible values of the test statistic that might be computed from a sample, whether the null hypothesis should be accepted or whether it should be rejected in favor of an alternate hypothesis. Frequently used guidelines include:

- The alpha level (usually 1 to 5%)
- The beta level (usually 10 to 20%)

Table 4.5A. Collected Sample Data of Sheet Metal Thickness, Inches

0.0100	0.0102	0.0099	0.0102	0.0090	0.0109	0.0095	0.0107
0.0095	0.0107	0.0102	0.0093	0.0095	0.0095	0.0109	0.0103
0.0092	0.0104	0.0094	0.0098	0.0102	0.0096	0.0100	0.0093
0.0104	0.0094	0.0097	0.0107	0.0099	0.0098	0.0099	0.0106
0.0100	0.0099	0.0105	0.0100	0.0097	0.0100	0.0090	0.0090

Step 4. Select a sample, compute the test statistic, and confront it with the decision rule.

Example 4.2: Computing the Z-Test and Confidence Interval of the Mean (using MINITAB Software)

A sheet metal producer needs to manufacturer aluminum sheets of 0.01-inch thickness with a population standard deviation of 0.0005. Accordingly, the quality inspector at the firm will test the quality of manufactured sheets by measuring the thickness in a simple random sample of manufactured sheets (see Table 4.5A for sample data). Use a one-sample Z to compute a confidence interval and perform a hypothesis test of the mean when population standard deviation (σ) is known.

For a two-tailed one-sample Z:

H_0: $\mu = \mu_0$

H_1: $\mu \neq \mu_0$

where:

μ = Population mean

μ_0 = Hypothesized population mean

Solution:

1. Choose **Stat** > **Basic Statistics** > **1-Sample Z**
2. Variables: Enter the column(s) containing samples
3. Sigma: Enter population σ value ($\sigma = 0.0005$ in this example)
4. Test mean: (0.01 in this example)
5. **Graph:** Optional (histogram of data and dot plot of data in this example)
6. **Options:** Confidence level, range 1 to 100; default value, 95 (used 95). Alternative: 3 choices (used "not equal" in this example)

Table 4.5B. Descriptive Statistics of Sheet Thickness Sample Data—Z Test

One-Sample Z: Sheet Thickness, Inches

Test of mu = 0.01 vs. mu not = 0.01
Assumed sigma = 0.0005

Variable	N	Mean	SD	SE Mean
Sheet Thickness	40	0.009918	0.000526	0.000079

Variable	95.0% CI	Z	P
Sheet Thickness	(0.009763,0.010072)	−1.04	0.297

The confidence interval is calculated as follows:

$$\bar{X} - Z_{\alpha/2}(\sigma/\sqrt{n}) \quad \text{to} \quad \bar{X} + Z_{\alpha/2}(\sigma/\sqrt{n})$$

and

$$Z = (\bar{X} - \mu)/(\sigma/\sqrt{n})$$

Descriptive statistics for the sample data are presented in Table 4.5B. The dot plot and histogram of the sample data are presented in Figures 4.6A and 4.6B, respectively.

Interpreting the results: The test statistic, Z for testing if the population mean equals 0.0100, is –1.04. Because the P-value of 0.297 is greater than the selected α-value (0.05), there is significant evidence that μ is equal to 0.0100; therefore, we accept H_0 in favor of μ being equal to 0.0100.

Example 4.3: Using the One-Sample t-Test and Confidence Interval

Utilize the sample data from Example 4.2 (see Table 4.5A). Assume that the population standard deviation is not known.

Use one-sample t to compute a confidence interval and perform a hypothesis test of the mean when the population standard deviation, σ, is unknown.

For a two-tailed one-sample t:

H_0: $\mu = \mu_0$

H_1: $\mu \neq \mu_0$

where:

μ = Population mean

μ_0 = Hypothesized population mean

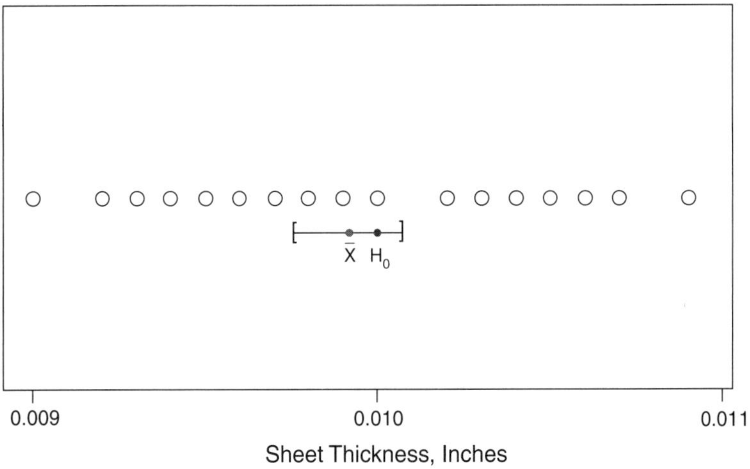

*With Ho and 95% Z-confidence interval for the mean, using sigma = 0.00050000.

Figure 4.6A. Dot Plot of Sheet Thickness Sample Data*

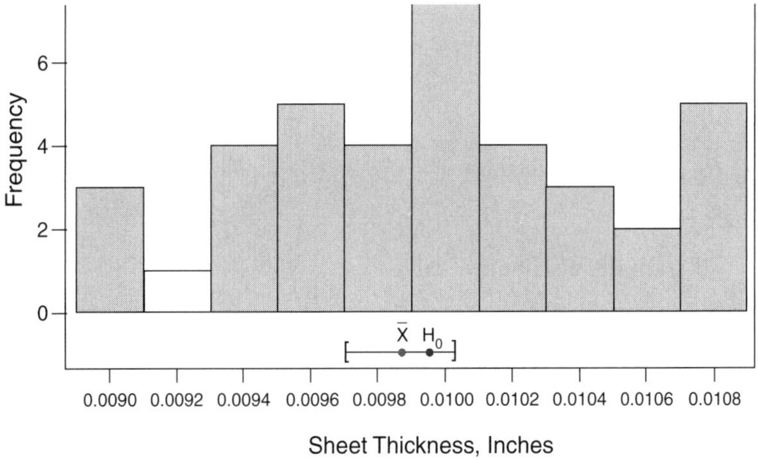

*With Ho and 95% Z-confidence interval for the mean, using sigma = 0.00050000.

Figure 4.6B. Histogram of Sheet Thickness Sample Data*

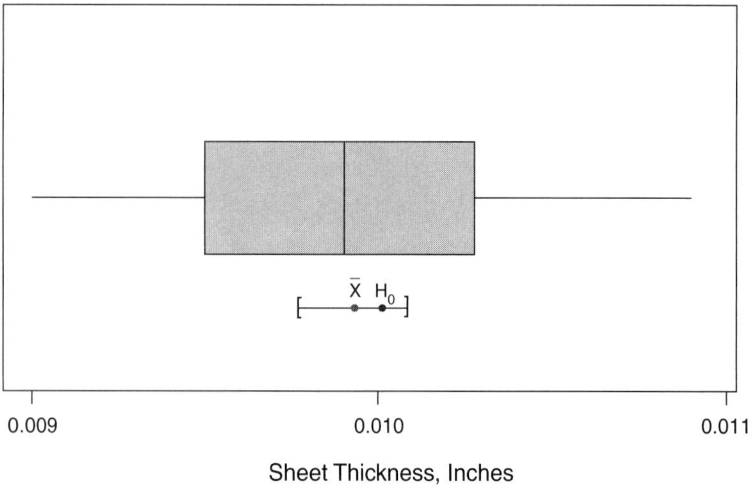

*With Ho and 95% t-confidence interval for the mean.

Figure 4.6C. Box Plot of Sheet Thickness Sample Data*

The confidence interval is calculated as follows:

$\bar{X} - t_{\alpha/2}(s/\sqrt{n})$ to $\bar{X} + t_{\alpha/2}(s/\sqrt{n})$

where:

$\bar{X}$ = Mean of sample data

s = Sample standard deviation

n = Sample size

$t_{\alpha/2}$ = Value from t-distribution table

where:

α is $(1 - \text{confidence level})/100$ and degrees of freedom are $(n - 1)$ and

$t = (\bar{X} - \mu_0)/(s/\sqrt{n})$

The descriptive statistics of the sheet thickness sample data are presented in Table 4.5C. See Figure 4.6C for the box plot. (A write-up of the process for this example would be the same as for Example 4.2.)

Table 4.5C. Descriptive Statistics of Sheet Thickness Sample Data—T Test

One-Sample T: Sheet Thickness, Inches

Test of mu = 0.01 vs. mu not = 0.01

Variable	N	Mean	SD	SE Mean
Sheet Thickness	40	0.009918	0.000526	0.000083

Variable	95.0% CI	T	P
Sheet Thickness	(0.009749,0.010086)	–0.99	0.327

Interpreting the results: The test statistic, T for H_0: $\mu = 0.0100$, is calculated as –0.99 and the P-value of this test, or the probability of obtaining more extreme value of the test statistic by chance if the null hypothesis was true, is 0.327. This is called the attained significance level (or P-value). Therefore, accept H_0 if the acceptable α level ($\alpha = 0.05$) is lower than the P-value or 0.327.

4.2.4 Hypothesis Testing—Proportion Mean and the Difference between Two Such Proportions

This process is very similar to the process in Section 4.2.3. Examples will be given in this section to explain the concept. The following application of a proportion concept is to compute a confidence interval and perform a hypothesis test. For a two-tailed test of a proportion:

H_0: $P = P_0$ vs. H_1: $P \neq P_0$

where:

P = Population proportion

P_0 = Hypothesized value

Data can be in either of two forms: raw or summarized:

- Raw data—All data must be of the same type: numeric, text, or date/time. (MINITAB default logic defines the lowest value as *failure* and the highest value as *success*. This logic can be reversed.)
- Summarized data—Identify the number of trials and one or more values for the number of successes. (MINITAB software performs a separate analysis for each success value.)

Example 4.4: Explaining the Process with MINITAB Software

Utilizing the Summarized Data Concept

A hospital leadership team needs to know if 98% percent of the drug dosages prepared by a machine weigh precisely 50 milligrams. A random sample of 500 dosages was collected; 485 dosages were found to be of correct weight. Test the hypothesis at a 95% confidence level that the sample represents the expected machine performance. Use MINITAB software.

Step 1. Formulate two opposing hypotheses:

H_0: $P = 0.98$
H_1: $P \neq 0.98$

Step 2. Select a test statistic—The standard normal deviate for the sample proportion:

$$Z = \frac{\left(\hat{P} - P_0\right)}{\sqrt{\dfrac{P_0(1 - P_0)}{n}}}$$

where:

$\hat{P}$ = Observed probability = X/n, where X is the observed number of successes in n trials

P_0= Hypothesized probability

n = Number of trials

Step 3. Derive a decision rule—The expected level of significance is equal to 0.05, where $\pm Z_{\alpha/2} = \pm 1.96$ (because this is a two-tailed test) and the confidence interval is:

$$\hat{P} \pm Z_{\alpha/2}\sqrt{\frac{\hat{P}_0(1-\hat{P}_0)}{n}}$$

MINITAB commands:

1. Chose **Stat > Basic Statistics > 1 Proportion.**
2. Choose **Summarized data.**
3. In **Number of trials**, enter 500. In **Number of success**, enter 485.
4. Click **Options.**
5. In **Test proportion**, enter 0.98.
6. From **Alternative**, choose **not equal.** Click **OK** in each dialog box.

A session window output of descriptive statistics is presented in Table 4.6.

Table 4.6. Descriptive Statistics of Drug Dosages Sample Data

Test and CI for One Proportion

Test of p = 0.98 vs. p not = 0.98

Sample	X	N	Sample p	95.0% CI	Exact P-Value
1	485	500	0.970000	(0.951002, 0.983114)	0.147

Interpreting the results: The P-value of 0.147 suggests that the data are consistent with the null hypothesis (H_0: P = 0.98), i.e., the proportion of drug dosages prepared by the machine is equal to the required proportion of 0.98. The sample represents the expected machine performance. Therefore, the null hypothesis can be accepted.

Testing the Hypothesis and Confidence Interval of Two Proportions
For a two-tailed test of two proportions:

H_0: $P_1 - P_2 = P_0$ vs. H_1: $P_1 - P_2 \neq P_0$

where:

P_1 and P_2 are the proportions of success in populations 1 and 2, respectively

P_0 is the hypothesized difference between the two proportions

Data can be in two forms: raw or summarized.

Select the Z statistic for normal distribution assumption. Based on the defined level of significance, calculate the confidence interval and test the hypothesis.

4.3 HYPOTHESIS TESTING: THE CHI-SQUARE TECHNIQUE

Section 4.2 has demonstrated the importance of "normal" distribution and the "t" distribution for purposes of estimating population parameters and/or testing hypotheses about them. In situations when these distributions cannot be used, the chi-square technique is used. Four major applications of the chi-square technique will be discussed:

- Testing the independence of two qualitative population variables
- Making inferences about more than two population proportions

- Making inferences about a population variance
- Performing goodness-of-fit tests to assess the possibility that sample data are from a population that follows a specified type of probability distribution

4.3.1 Testing the Independence of Two Qualitative Population Variables

Generally, qualitative variables are not expressed numerically because they differ in type rather than in degree among the fundamental units of a statistical population. Situations are numerous when it is important to know if two such variables are statistically *independent* of one another (the probability of occurrence of one variable is unaffected by the occurrence of the other) or if these variables are statistically *dependent* (the probability of occurrence of one is affected by the occurrence of the other). The list of situations would be endless, e.g., the variables between heart attacks and smoking, saturated food intake and cholesterol, system failure and prior year of service, customer arrival at a bank and the time of the day, etc.

The procedural steps and an example will follow the mathematical logic of the model. Let the observed data be presented in r rows and c columns, creating the $r \times c$ table; and

O_{ij} = Observed value in cell ij, i = 1, 2, ..., r, and j = 1, 2, ..., c

E_{ij} = Expected value in cell ij

Then,

E_{ij} = ((Total of row i) × (total of column j))/(total number of observations)

The total χ^2 is calculated as follows:

$$\chi^2 = \sum_i \sum_j \frac{\left(O_{ij} - E_{ij}\right)^2}{E_{ij}}$$

$$(r - 1) \times (c - 1) = \text{Degrees of freedom}$$

Steps in the procedure are:

Step 1. State the practical problem and formulate two opposing hypotheses:

H_0: The two variables are independent

H_1: The two variables are dependent

Step 2. Select a test statistic; in this situation:

$$\chi^2 = \sum_i \sum_j \frac{\left(O_{ij} - E_{ij}\right)^2}{E_{ij}}$$

Step 3. Derive a rule, e.g., needing to set a significance level of $\alpha = 0.05$ and knowing degrees of freedom $(r-1)(c-1)$, the critical value of $\chi^2_{\alpha,\text{df}}$ from the chi-square table:

"Accept H_0 if calc $\chi^2 <$ table $\chi^2_{\alpha,\text{df}}$" or

"Reject H_0 if calc $\chi^2 >$ table $\chi^2_{\alpha,\text{df}}$"

Next, translate the statistical conclusion into process (simple) language (see Example 4.5).

Example 4.5: Comparing Gender to Soft Drink Consumption

If soft drink consumption is customer-gender related, then different advertisements must be created for men's and women's magazines. Therefore, a soft drink producer wants to know if the gender of consumers is independent of their preferences for four brands of soft drinks. A test of independence will be conducted at the 5% significance level based on the sample data presented in Table 4.7A:

Step 1. Formulate two opposing hypotheses:

H_0: Gender and soft drink preference are independent variables

H_1: Gender and soft drink preference are dependent variables

Step 2. Select a test statistic:

$$\chi^2 = \sum_i \sum_j \frac{\left(O_{ij} - E_{ij}\right)^2}{E_{ij}}$$

Step 3. Derive a decision rule:

Given: $\alpha = 0.05$ and 3 degrees of freedom (2 genders and 4 types of soft drink)

Step 4. Select the provided sample data, compute the test statistic, and test it with the decision rule.

Table 4.7A. Sample Data of Soft Drink Preference by Gender

Gender	Soft Drink Preference	Gender	Soft Drink Preference
M	A	M	B
F	A	M	B
F	A	M	B
F	A	M	B
F	A	M	B
F	A	M	B
F	A	M	B
F	B	M	B
F	B	M	B
F	B	M	B
F	C	M	B
F	A	F	C
M	A	M	C
F	A	F	D
M	A	M	C
F	A	F	D
M	A	M	C
F	A	F	D
M	A	M	C
F	A	F	D
M	A	M	C
F	A	F	D
M	A	M	C
F	A	M	C
M	A	M	C
F	A	M	D
M	A	M	D
F	A	M	D
M	B	M	D
F	A	F	D
F	D		

Table 4.7B. Tabulated Statistics for Soft Drink Preference by Gender

Gender	A	B	C	D	All
F	16	3	2	7	28
	11.48	6.89	4.59	5.05	28.00
	1.34	–1.48	–1.21	0.87	—
M	9	12	8	4	33
	13.52	8.11	5.41	5.95	33.00
	–1.23	1.36	1.11	–0.80	—
All	25	15	10	11	61
	25.00	15.00	10.00	11.00	61.00
	–	—	—	—	—

Chi-square = 11.445, df = 3, P-value = 0.010
One cell with expected counts less than 5.0

Note: Rows: gender; columns: soft drinks.

Use MINITAB software to analyze the above data:

1. Open the software and enter the data:
   Column C1—Gender
   Column C2—Soft drink preference
2. Choose **Stat** > **Table** > **Cross Tabulation**
3. In **Classification variable**, enter Gender, Soft drink preference
4. Check **Chi-Square analysis** and then choose **Above and std. residual**; Click **OK**

MINITAB output of tabulated statistics for the soft drink preferences by gender is presented in Table 4.7B. From the table, $\chi^2_{0.05,3} = 7.815$.

Interpreting the results: The output data contain the observed frequency counts, the expected frequencies, and the standardized residual or contribution to the χ^2 statistic, where:

Standard residual = (Observed count – Expected count)/√(Expected count)

The P-value of the test, 0.010, indicates that there is evidence for an association between the variables Gender and Soft drink preference. Therefore, accept the alternate hypothesis:

$\chi^2_{calculated} = 11.45$ (see Table 4.7B) and from the chi-square table, $\chi^2_{0.05,3} = 7.815$

Table 4.7C. Soft Drink Users—Classified by Gender

	Type of Soft Drink				
Gender	**A**	**B**	**C**	**D**	**Total**
Male	9	12	8	4	33
Female	16	3	2	7	28
Total	25	15	10	11	**61**

Therefore, since $\chi^2_{calculated} > \chi^2_{table}$, reject H_0 and accept the H_1 hypothesis. This is another way to test the hypothesis (as stated in Step 3). One of the eight cells shows an expected frequency of less than 5, but this number is less than the 20% threshold. If the number is close to the 20% threshold, interpret the results with caution.

Another way to test census data for statistical independence is to use:

Step 1. Set up a contingency table for the Example 4.5 data as presented in Table 4.7C. The table classifies the data according to two or more categories (e.g., four types of soft drinks: A, B, C, and D) and these categories are associated with the qualitative variables (e.g., two variables: male and female) that may or may not depend on each other statistically.

Step 2. Next, develop sums for the rows and columns and sums for grand totals.

Step 3. Now think about the special multiplication law for independent events when events A and B are independent, if P(A and B) = P(A) × P(B).

Step 4. Now consider the problem from above, where the frequency for any particular pair of attributes can be found by multiplying the respective frequencies for those two individual attributes and dividing the product by the total number of units observed. For example, female users of soft drink B:

= ((Total female users of soft drink) × (total users of soft drink B))/(total sample size)

= (28 × 15)/61 = 6.9

The female users of soft drink B in Table 4.7C are 3; therefore, gender and soft drink performance are *dependent* variables.

However, under these circumstances, since the population frequencies are unknown and only sample data are available, this type of test will not work. There are many joint probabilities that may then fail to equal the product of the relevant unconditional probabilities due to sampling error and not because of any statistical dependence between the two qualitative variables of interest in the population.

Table 4.8A. Collected Sample Data from PC Integration Line

	Integration Line Speed (Units per Hour)					
PC Quality	**A = 30**	**B = 35**	**C = 40**	**D = 45**	**E = 50**	**Total**
(1) Defective	4	5	5	6	7	27
(2) Acceptable	46	45	45	44	43	223
Total	50	50	50	50	50	**250**

Therefore, under such circumstances the chi-square technique finds its first application.

4.3.2 Making Inferences about More than Two Population Proportions

One effectively assumes that certain proportions (i.e., females among all high school teachers or males among all taxi drivers) are the same for all categories of some variable when expected frequencies are being calculated for the various cells of a contingency table. The same technique that allows testing for the independence of two qualitative population variables can also be used to test if a number of population proportions are equal to each other or if they are equal to any predetermined set of values. The above identified logic will be used in Example 4.6.

Example 4.6: Comparing Integration Line Speeds for Personal Computers

Consider the process of manufacturing personal computers. Business leaders are interested in testing the hypothesis that the proportion of defective units (PCs) produced will be the same for each of five possible integration speeds. The quality group at the company has been asked to perform a test at the 1% significance level, taking 5 samples of 50 PCs each, while different integration line speeds are being maintained. The collected data are presented in Table 4.8A.

The statistical testing process will follow these steps:

Step 1. Formulate two opposing hypotheses:

H_0: The population proportion of defectives is the same for each of 5 integration line speeds, i.e., $P_1 = P_2 = P_3 = P_4 = P_5 = 0.05$ (given)

H_1: The population proportion of defectives is not the same for each of 5 integration line speeds, i.e., at least one of the equalities in H_0 does not hold true

Table 4.8B. Chi-Square Test Output for Sample Data in Table 4.8A

	Chi-Square Test					
PC Quality	**A**	**B**	**C**	**D**	**E**	**Total**
(1)	4 5.4	5 5.40	5 5.40	6 5.40	7 5.40	27
(2)	46 44.60	45 44.60	45 44.60	44 44.60	43 44.60	223
Total	50	50	50	50	50	**250**

Chi-square = 0.363 + 0.030 + 0.030 + 0.067 + 0.474 + 0.044 + 0.004 + 0.004 + 0.008 + 0.057 = 1.080

df = 4; P-value = 0.898

Note: Expected counts are printed below observed counts.

Step 2. Select a test statistic:

$$\chi^2 = \sum_i \sum_j \frac{\left(O_{ij} - E_{ij}\right)^2}{E_{ij}}$$

Step 3. Derive a decision rule:

Given: $\alpha = 0.01$ and 4 degrees of freedom, 2 possible product (PC) qualities, and 5 possible integration line speeds:

$$1 \times 4 = 4 \text{ df}$$

Step 4. Select the samples, compute the test statistic, and confront it with the decision rule.

Enter the collected sample data need in MINITAB as follows:

A	B	C	D	E
4	5	5	6	7
46	45	45	44	43

1. Choose **Stat > Tables > Chi-Square Test.**
2. In columns containing the table, enter **A B C D E**. Click **OK.**
3. Chi-square test output is presented in Table 4.8B.

From the chi-square table, $\chi^2_{0.01,4} = 13.277$

Interpreting the results: The P-value of 0.898 indicates that there is *no* strong evidence that the units defective and the integration line speed are related. Therefore, accept the null hypothesis. If a cell had an expected count less than 5, and even with significant P-value for these data, interpret the results with skepticism. To be more confident of the results, repeat the test with or without modifications.

4.3.3 Making Inferences about a Population Variance

The sample variance s^2 is an unbiased estimator of the population variance σ^2 provided that the selections of sample elements are statistically independent events. Probabilities of the sample variance can be established with the help of χ^2 distributions. Since:

$$s^2 = \frac{\sum X^2 - n\bar{X}^2}{n-1}$$

and the converted value in the chi-square with $(n - 1)$ degrees of freedom are as follows:

$$\chi^2 = \frac{s^2(n-1)}{\sigma^2}$$

where:

s^2 = Sample variance

n = Sample size

σ^2 = Population variance

and the probability interval for the sample variance, s^2:

$$\left(\frac{\sigma^2\chi_L^2}{n-1}\right) \le s^2 \le \left(\frac{\sigma^2\chi_U^2}{n-1}\right)$$

where:

$\chi_L^2 = \left(\frac{s_L^2(n-1)}{\sigma^2}\right)$ lower chi-square value and

$\chi_U^2 = \left(\frac{s_U^2(n-1)}{\sigma^2}\right)$ upper chi-square value

and the confidence interval for the population variance, σ^2:

$$\left(\frac{s^2(n-1)}{\chi_U^2}\right) \le \sigma^2 \le \left(\frac{s^2(n-1)}{\chi_L^2}\right)$$

where:

χ_U^2 = Value of χ^2 variable with $(n - 1)$ degrees of freedom such that larger values have a probability of $\alpha/2$

χ_L^2 = Value of χ^2 variable with $(n - 1)$ degrees of freedom such that smaller values have a probability of $\alpha/2$

$\alpha = 1 -$ confidence level

As an example, consider a process at a food packing company. The company is filling bags. The weight of these bags is normally distributed with a population standard deviation of $\sigma = 2$ ounces (oz). (Therefore, the population variance is $\sigma^2 = 4$ oz squared). A simple random sample of 25 bags is taken from this population. Calculate the probability of finding a sample variance between 3 and 5 oz squared:

Given: $s_L^2 = 3$ and $s_U^2 = 5$

First calculate χ_L^2 and χ_U^2:

$$\chi_L^2 = \left(\frac{s_L^2(n-1)}{\sigma^2}\right)$$

$$= (3(25 - 1))/4$$
$$= 18$$

$$\chi_U^2 = \left(\frac{s_U^2(n-1)}{\sigma^2}\right)$$

$$= (5(25 - 1))/4$$
$$= 30$$

Now find the χ^2 probability values from the chi-square table for the given $\chi^2 = 18$ at 24 degrees of freedom; the probability value is approximately 0.80. Similarly for the calculated $\chi^2 = 30$ at 24 degrees of freedom, the probability value is approximately 0.20. Therefore, the area of about $(0.8 - 0.2 = 0.6)$ lies between these values, and the value of 0.6 is also the probability of finding a sample variance between 3 and 5 oz squared in this example.

Similarly, the limits below and above the specified percentage of all possible s^2 values can also be calculated. Take the above example, at 5% each limit (lower and upper) with 24 degrees of freedom:

$\chi^2_{0.95,24}$ = 13.848 (the lower χ^2 value from the chi-square table)

$\chi^2_{0.05,\,24}$ = 36.415 (the upper χ^2 value from the chi-square table)

Therefore:

$$s_L^2 = \left(\frac{\sigma^2 \chi_L^2}{n-1}\right)$$

$$= (4 \times 13.848)/(25 - 1)$$
$$= 2.31$$

$$s_U^2 = \left(\frac{\sigma^2 \chi_U^2}{n-1}\right)$$

$$= (4 \times 13.415)/(25 - 1)$$
$$= 6.07$$

Therefore, 5% of all s^2 values would lie below 2.31, another 5% would lie above 6.07, and 90% would lie between these two values. Next, continue the above example with some modifications:

- New sample size, n = 30 food bags
- Sample variance, s^2 = 3 oz squared

What is the 90% confidence interval of σ^2?

Since α = 0.10, and degrees of freedom = 29, then from the chi-square table:

$\chi_U^2 = \chi^2_{0.05,\,29} = 42.557$

$\chi_L^2 = \chi^2_{0.95,\,29} = 17.708$

and the σ^2 interval can be calculated as follows:

$$\left(\frac{3(30-1)}{42.557}\right) \le \sigma^2 \le \left(\frac{3(30-1)}{17.708}\right)$$

$$2.04 \le \sigma^2 \le 4.91$$

Therefore, with 90% confidence, the food bags' variance can be said to be between 2.04 and 4.91 oz squared, and the food bags' standard deviation is between 1.43 and 2.22 oz.

Testing the Hypothesis about the Population Variance

These hypotheses could be one-sided or two-sided, and the one-sided one could be a lower-tailed or upper-tailed hypothesis. Three examples present varieties of these hypotheses: Example 4.7, a lower-tail hypothesis test; Example 4.8, an upper-tail hypothesis test; and Example 4.9, a two-tail hypothesis test.

Example 4.7: Using a Lower-Tail Hypothesis Test

This lower-tail hypothesis test will use an airline's booking area waiting-line policy as an example. Airline management would like to introduce the concept of a single-line policy that directs all passengers to enter a single waiting line in the order of their arrival and that in turn would direct them to different check-in counters. Airline management thinks a single-line policy will decrease waiting-time variability. However, some critics of management claim that variability would be at least as great with a single-line policy as with a policy of multiple independent lines, which in the past had a standard deviation of $\sigma_0 = 8$ minutes per customer checking in. A hypothesis at the 2% significance level is to settle the issue. The hypothesis is to be based on the experience of a random sample of 30 customers subjected to the new policy.

Next, formulate two opposing hypotheses:

H_0: Single waiting-line's variance would be equal to or greater than 64 minutes squared ($\sigma^2 \geq 64$)

H_1: Single waiting-line's variance would be less than 64 minutes squared ($\sigma^2 < 64$)

and the test statistics:

$$\chi^2 = \left(\frac{s^2(n-1)}{\sigma_0^2} \right)$$

The concept of deriving the decision policy is presented in Figure 4.7A.

Given: A desired significance level of $\alpha = 0.02$ and $n - 1 = 29$ degrees of freedom, value from the chi-square table, $\chi^2_{0.98,\,29} = 15.574$ (this is a lower-tail test)

Therefore, the decision rule must be:

Accept H_0 if $\chi^2_{\text{calculated}} > 15.574$

A sample was collected, test statistics were computed, and the results were tested with the decision rule. After taking a sample of 30 passengers, the standard deviation was computed and $s = 3$ minutes. Now compute the test statistic:

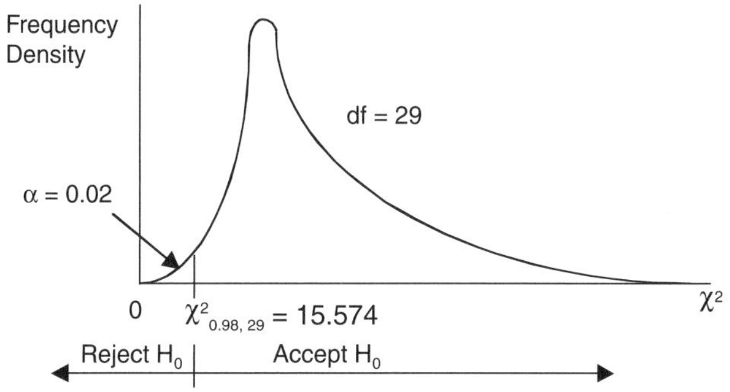

Figure 4.7A. Hypothesis Testing Decision Rule (Lower-Tail Test)

$$\chi^2 = \left(\frac{s^2(n-1)}{\sigma_0^2} \right)$$
$$= (3^2)(30 - 1)/64$$
$$= 4.08$$

This result suggests that the null hypothesis should be rejected. At a 2% significance level, the sample result is statistically significant. The observed divergence from the hypothesized value of $\sigma_0 = 8$ minutes is unlikely to be the result of chance factors operating during sampling. It is more likely to be the result of management being right—a single waiting line feeding into several check-in counters does reduce waiting-time variability.

Example 4.8: Using an Upper-Tail Hypothesis Test

This upper-tail hypothesis test will use the variation of a digital postage meter as an example. A manufacturer of postage metering equipment is bringing out a new model of a digital meter (the meter is used for weighing an envelope, calculating postage, and stamping the calculated postage on the envelope). The standard deviation of the postage calculation on the old model was $\sigma_0 = 0.5$ cents. A hypothesis test at the 5% significance level is to be conducted to support the manufacturer's claim that the new meter's variability is equal to or less than that of the old model. The test involves collecting 25 readings from known postage requirements.

Formulate two opposing hypotheses:

H_0: New digital postage meter variance would be equal to or less than 0.25 cents squared ($\sigma^2 \leq 0.25$)

H_1: New digital postage meter variance would be greater than 0.25 cents squared ($\sigma^2 > 0.25$)

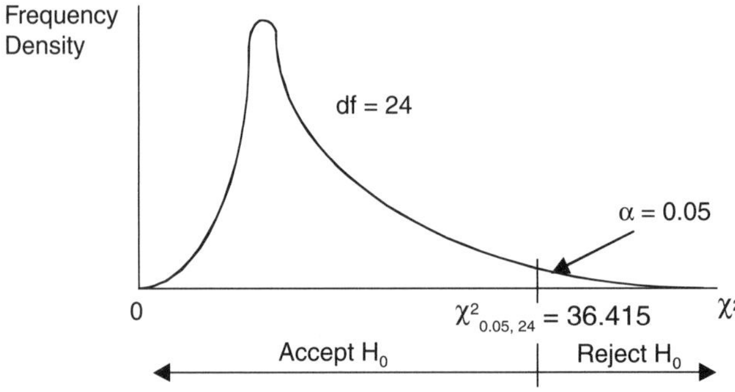

Figure 4.7B. Hypothesis Testing Decision Rule (Upper-Tail Test)

and the test statistics:

$$\chi^2 = \left(\frac{s^2(n-1)}{\sigma_0^2}\right)$$

The concept of deriving the decision policy has been presented in Figure 4.7B.

Given: A desired significance level of $\alpha = 0.05$ and $(n - 1) = 24$ degrees of freedom, value from the chi-square table, $\chi^2_{0.05,\ 24} = 36.415$ (this being an upper-tail test)

Therefore, the decision rule must be:

Accept H_0 if $\chi^2_{\text{calculated}} \leq 36.415$

A sample was collected, test statistics were computed, and the results were tested with the decision rule. After taking a sample of 25 postage meter stamping readings, the standard deviation was calculated and $s = 0.3$ cents.

Now compute the test statistic:

$$\chi^2 = \left(\frac{s^2(n-1)}{\sigma_0^2}\right)$$

$$= (0.32\ (25 - 1))/0.52$$

$$= 8.64$$

This result suggests that the null hypothesis should be accepted. At the 5% significance level, the sample result is statistically insignificant. The new digital postage meter is equal to or better than the old one as claimed by the manufacturer.

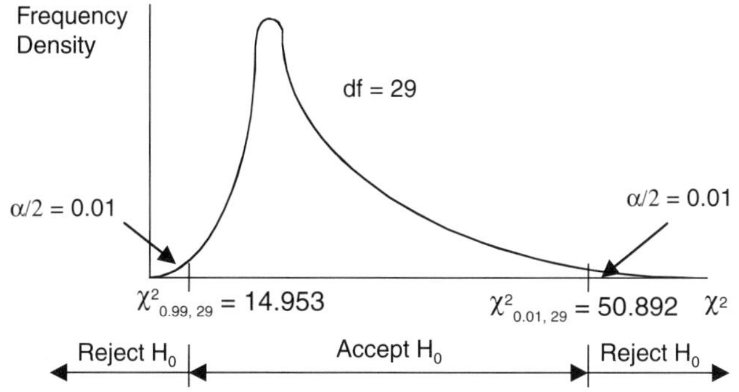

Figure 4.7C. Hypothesis Testing Decision Rule (Two-Tail Test)

Example 4.9: Using a Two-Tail Hypothesis Test

This two-tail hypothesis test will use the diameter of a fuel tank lid in an aircraft as an example. An aircraft manufacturer is concerned about the variability in the lid diameter for a lid that is used to seal the fuel system. The fuel system is located inside the aircraft's wings. Only a narrow range of lid diameter is acceptable. If the lid fits too tightly, the lid will prevent air from entering the fuel system as the fuel is being consumed, creating a vacuum and ultimately causing the wing structure to collapse. A lid that fits too loosely can allow fuel to be sucked out of the fuel system during flight, which is equally undesirable for flight safety. Therefore, a test at the 2% significance level is to be conducted with a random sample of 30 fuel system lids to see if the variance of lid diameters is equal to 0.0001 inch squared as specified by designers.

Formulate two opposing hypotheses:

H_0: Fuel system's lid diameter variance would be equal to 0.0001 inch squared ($\sigma^2 = 0.0001$)

H_1: Fuel system's lid diameter variance would not be equal to 0.0001 inch squared ($\sigma^2 \neq 0.0001$)

and the test statistics:

$$\chi^2 = \left(\frac{s^2(n-1)}{\sigma_0^2} \right)$$

The concept of deriving the decision policy is presented in Figure 4.7C.

Given: A desired significance level of $\alpha = 0.02$ and a two-tail test; the lower and the upper critical χ^2 values must be established (0.01 of the area under the χ^2 distribution lies below and above each of these values)

Therefore, the values from the chi-square table:

$$\chi^2_{0.99,\,29} = 14.953 \text{ and } \chi^2_{0.01,\,29} = 50.892$$

The decision rule must be:

Accept H_0 if $14.953 \leq \chi^2 \leq 50.892$

A sample of 30 lids was collected, test statistics were computed, and the results were tested with the decision rule. The calculated standard deviation was $s = 0.01$ inch, and the computed value of the test statistic equals:

$$\chi^2 = \left(\frac{s^2(n-1)}{\sigma_0^2}\right)$$

$$= ((0.01)^2\,(30 - 1))\,/\,0.0001$$

$$= 29$$

This result suggests that the null hypothesis should be accepted. At the 2% significance level, the sample result is not statistically significant. Therefore, the fuel system lids meet specifications.

4.3.4 Performing Goodness-of-Fit Tests to Assess the Possibility that Sample Data Are from a Population that Follows a Specified Type of Probability Distribution

This test compares the shape of two distributions: discrete and continuous probability. One distribution describes sample data and the other describes hypothesized population data. The test has a limited objective of identifying only the family to which the sample data distribution belongs, or it might go further and identify a particular member of that family. For example, the null hypothesis might be general: "The sample data come from a normally distributed population." The null hypothesis could also be more specific: "The sample data come from a normally distributed population with a mean of 50 and a standard deviation of 3."

It is important to note that a null hypothesis can clearly be false in many different ways, e.g., the sample data might come from all types of populations that are normally distributed, but have different population parameters than those specified, or from populations that are not normally distributed. Therefore, calculating the β risk (accepting that the null hypothesis is false) for a goodness-of-fit test is difficult unless one first specifies in what particular way the null

Table 4.9A. Collected Sample Data of Housing Code Violations in Rental Properties

Number of Possible Violations per Apartment	Observed Frequency, O_i
0	29
1	50
2	65
3	35
4	30
5	21
6	12
7	8
Total observations	**250**

hypothesis is false. If a fairly large sample is taken, a good approach is to protect against a type II error.

We know that knowledge of the underlying population distribution is important whenever statistical procedures are used to rely on sample data. For example, if one wants to build a queuing model, he/she might want to ensure that the underlying population values were Poisson-distributed. If one were interested in small-sample hypothesis testing with the help of the t distribution, he/she would grind out unnecessary information unless the *underlying population* values were normally distributed.

Sample data in Example 4.10 are used to make inferences about the underlying population distribution. It is highly unlikely that a single sample would provide a perfect match between the two distributions (sample distribution and population distribution), but on average, when many samples are taken, it is expected that the sample data will reveal the nature of the population distribution.

Example 4.10: Using Goodness of Fit to the Binomial Distribution

An inspector from the property code department of a city has investigated landlords for compliance with housing codes. The inspector has collected a random sample from 250 apartments. The data reveal that apartments have code violations ranging from 0 to 7. The inspector wants to conduct a hypothesis test at the 5% significance level to determine if the sample is from a population in which the number of actual violations per apartment is a binomially distributed random variable. The collected sample data are shown in Table 4.9A. Process steps include:

Step 1. Formulate two opposing hypotheses.

Since the binomial distribution parameter is not given, the inspector has to estimate the probability of success parameter p (number of city code violations). We know that the mean of a binomial random variable is $n \times p$, where n is the number of possible outcomes. Therefore, p can be calculated as follows:

$$n \times p = \left(\frac{0(29) + 1(50) + 2(65) + 3(35) + 4(30) + 5(21) + 6(12) + 7(8)}{250} \right)$$

$$= 638/250$$
$$= 2.552$$

and $p = 2.552/7 = 0.365$.

Now state the null and the alternate hypotheses as:

H_0: The number of violations per apartment in the city apartment population is binomially distributed with the probability of success in any one trial of $p = 0.365$

H_1: The number of violations per apartment in the population of all city apartments is not correctly described by H_0

Step 2. Select a test statistic.

Using the chi-square statistic:

$$\chi^2 = \sum \frac{(O_i - E_i)^2}{E_i}$$

The following is a sample calculation for the expected frequency. Binomial probability density function, $f(X)$ is presented as follows:

$$f(X) = \left(\frac{n!}{X!(n - X)!} \right) p^X q^{n-X}$$

In this example, X = number of possible violations per apartment and X takes values 0, 1, 2, …, 7:

$p = 0.365$ and

$q = (1 - p) = (1 - 0.365) = 0.635$

When $X = 0$:

$f(X = 0) = ((7!)/(0!\,.\,7!)) \times (0.365)^0 \times (0.635)^7$

$f(X = 0) = 0.0416$

The expected frequency (if H_0 is true) when $X = 0$ is equal to $0.0416 \times 250 = 10.4$.

When $X = 1$:

$f(X = 1) = ((7!)/(1!\,.\,6!)) \times (0.365)^1 \times (0.635)^6$

$f(X = 1) = 0.1675$

The expected frequency when $X = 1$ is equal to $0.1675 \times 250 = 41.9$.

Remaining calculations can be done as presented above.

Step 3. Derive the decision rule.
First establish the expected frequencies for the various numbers of possible violations per apartment, assuming H_0 is true. Calculate the binomial probability value (or check in binomial table) for each possible violation (0, 1, 2, 3, 4, 5, 6, and 7) per apartment for given $n = 8$ and $P = 0.365$. Now calculate the expected frequency (E_i, $i = 0, 1, 2, \ldots, 7$) for each possible apartment violation by multiplying the calculated probability by the total number of observations (250). *Note:* Keep the expected frequency value of 5 or higher by combining adjacent classes as needed.

Next establish the number of degrees of freedom (*df*):

df = number of classes (adjusted) – 1 – number of estimated parameters

Binomial distribution has only one parameter and the given desired significance level of $\alpha = 0.05$ and the adjusted df. Find the χ^2 value from the chi-square table. Compute the test statistic and then confront it with the decision rule. If the calculated value (χ^2_{cal}) is less than the table value (χ^2_{table}), accept the null (H_0) hypothesis; otherwise reject the null hypothesis.

Next, perform a chi-square goodness-of-fit test using MINITAB software. Since the population distribution is assumed to be binomial, the first activity is to calculate the expected number of outcomes for the binomial case:

1. Enter the possible outcomes 0, 1, 2, 3, 4, 5, 6, and 7 in a work sheet under **Outcomes** and enter observed frequency in the next column (C2) under **Observed**
2. Choose **Calc** > **Probability Distribution** > **Binomial**
3. In **Number of trials**, enter 7; in **Probability of success**, enter 0.365
4. Choose **Input Column**, then enter *Outcomes*; in **Optional storage**, enter *Probs* to name the storage column; click **OK**
5. Choose **Calc** > **Calculator**
6. In **Store result in variable**, enter *Expected* to name the storage column
7. In **Expression**, enter *Probs*250*; click **OK**

Table 4.9B. Goodness of Fit Test Output

Outcome	Observed	Probability	Expected	Chi-Square	Cumulative Probability	P-Value
0	29	0.041631	10.4077	372.923	1	0
1	50	0.167505	41.8768			
2	65	0.288851	72.2127			
3	35	0.276721	69.1802			
4	30	0.159060	39.7650			
5	21	0.054857	13.7142	} 16.5577		
6	12	0.010511	2.6277			
7	8	0.000863	0.2158			

Next, calculate the χ^2 statistics and P-value:

1. Choose **Calc** > **Calculator**
2. In **Store result in variable**, enter *Chisquare* to name the storage column
3. In **Expression**, enter SUM((*Observed-Expected)***2/*Expected*); click **OK**
4. Choose **Calc** > **Probability Distribution** > **Chi-Square**
5. Choose **Cumulative probability** and in **Degrees of freedom**, enter 4 [The degrees of freedom value is equal to the number of (adjusted) classes minus one and minus one parameter (6 – 1 – 1 = 4).]
6. Choose **Input column** and enter *Chisquare*; in **Optional storage**, enter *CumProb* to name the storage column; click **OK**
7. Choose **Calc** > **Calculator**
8. In **Store result in variable**, enter *Pvalue* to name the storage column
9. In **Expression**, enter 1 – *CumProb*; click **OK**

The work sheet output is presented in Table 4.9B.

The *P*-value of 0.00 associated with the χ^2 statistic of 372.923 indicates the binomial probability model with $p = 0.365$ is probably not a good model for this experiment (test), i.e., the observed number of outcomes is not consistent with expected number of outcomes using a binomial model. Therefore, reject the null hypothesis.

Other examples of a goodness-of-fit test include:

- Normally Distributed Population—A financial analyst would like to determine if the daily volume of New York Stock Exchange is still normally distributed with a mean of 50 million trades and a standard deviation of 5 million trades.
- Uniformly Distributed Population—A business management team of a house cleaning service wants to know if service requests are spread evenly over the six business days of a business week. Accordingly, this information will be used to set work schedules for employees.

Therefore, chi-square tests are used for:

- Goodness of Fit—To test if the sample data have the same distribution as expected
- Test of Independence—To test if the samples are from the same distribution

Limitations when using the chi-square test include:

- Use discrete data. Use no ranking or variable data.
- Observations must be independent.
- The chi-square test works best with five or more observations in each cell. Cells may be combined (to make a larger range) to pool observations.

Exercise 4.3: Determining the Distribution of Passengers Arriving at a Luggage Checkout

An airline manager wants to determine if the Poisson distribution can describe the number of hourly passenger arrivals at the luggage checkout area. A test at the 1% level of significance is to be conducted. A simple random sample over 48 hours has been collected (Table 4.9C).

Based on prior experience of the airline manager, the passenger mean arrival rate is four passengers per hour, assuming the Poisson probability distribution. Perform a detailed analysis to verify the summary information in Table 4.9D.

Based on the summary information in Table 4.9D, the *P*-value of 0.640743 associated with the χ^2 statistic of 6.05793 indicates that the Poisson probability model with $\lambda = 4$ (mean passenger arrival rate per hour) is probably a good model for this experiment, i.e., the observed number of outcomes is consistent with expected number of outcomes using a Poisson model. Give an opinion of these comments.

Next is a discussion of ANOVA (the analysis of variance), which takes this type of analysis one step further.

Table 4.9C. Collected Sample Data from Luggage Checkout Area

Number of Passenger Arrivals per Hour to Luggage Checkout Area	Observed Passenger Frequency
0	0
1	1
2	5
3	8
4	13
5	9
6	7
7	3
8 or more	2

4.4 ANALYSIS OF VARIANCE (ANOVA)

Reengineering and/or redesigning processes are a natural part of the responsibilities of any Six Sigma team. As discussed in the previous section, the normal probability distribution (for large samples) and the Student's t-distribution (for small samples) are ideally suited to assist in performing any desired hypothesis test about the comparative magnitudes of two population means. This section will take this type of analysis a step further. The means of more than two quantitative populations will be compared, leading to the conclusion that such extended comparisons are not performed well using the earlier procedures.

Consider two situations. In one, a production manager wants to test if the average daily throughput differs among six possible production methods. In the other, a store manager wants to know if average sales vary among five alternatives: newspaper ads, TV ads, window displays, type of packaging, and price levels.

Tempting as it may be, it is unwise to string together the results of several two-sample tests. Therefore, an analysis of variance (ANOVA) table will assist in determining the effect of multiple input variables on a response.

Analysis of variance (commonly known as ANOVA) is a statistical technique especially designed to test if the means of more than two quantitative populations are equal. If the equality of only two means is tested, then the test will yield the same results as the normal distribution or the t-distribution discussed in the previous section. The ANOVA technique involves taking an independent simple random sample from each of several populations of interest and then analyzing the data. Similar to the t-test, the ANOVA test also assumes that the sampled popula-

Table 4.9D. Goodness of Fit Test Output Summary

Probability Density Function: Poisson with mu = 4.00000

x	P(X = x)	x	P(X = x)	x	P(X = x)
0.00	0.0183	3.00	0.1954	6.00	0.1042
1.00	0.0733	4.00	0.1954	7.00	0.0595
2.00	0.1465	5.00	0.1563	8.00	0.0298

Outcome	Observed	Probability	Expected	Chi-square	Cumulative Probability	P-Value
0	0	0.018316	0.87915	6.05793	0.359257	0.640743
1	1	0.073263	3.51660			
2	5	0.146525	7.03321			
3	8	0.195367	9.37761			
4	13	0.195367	9.37761			
5	9	0.156293	7.50209			
6	7	0.104196	5.00139			
7	3	0.059540	2.85794			
8	2	0.051100	2.45280			

tions are normally distributed and have identical variances. The ANOVA test is quite robust with respect to the normality assumption. Some moderate departure from the normality assumption causes little change in the results, but any violation of the equal-variances assumption will seriously affect the validity of the test.

The basis of the above assumptions is typical because the entire development of the test is from the sample data of two independent estimates of what is assumed to be the common variance, σ^2, of the populations of interest:

- The first estimation of σ^2 is based on the variation among the sample means and is denoted by s_t^2. This is an unbiased estimate of σ^2 only if the population means are in fact equal.
- The second estimation of σ^2 is based on the variation of the individual sample observations within each sample and is denoted by s_e^2. This is a weighted average of the individual sample variances.

The ratio of s_t^2/s_e^2 would be close to 1, if and only if, the population means are equal to each other. If the value of this ratio diverges from 1, then the probability would be greater that the population means are not equal to each other. In principle, this ratio of squares can take any value between zero and positive infinity. Therefore, ANOVA helps test hypotheses about the equality of means.

Two types of problem analysis are commonly used:

- *One-Factor* ANOVA or *One-Way* ANOVA—A *completely randomized design* uses *randomization* as a control device. This design creates *one* treatment group for each treatment and assigns each experimental unit to one of these groups by a random process. In the end, only *one* factor (the treatment) is considered as possibly affecting the variable of interest. Analysis of this type of problem is referred to as one-factor ANOVA or one-way ANOVA. (See Chapter 5, *Improve*; Section 5.3, *Introduction to Design of Experiments*, for further discussion of this concept.)
- *Two-Factor* ANOVA or *Two-Way* ANOVA—A *randomized block design* uses *blocking* as an additional control device. It divides the available experimental units into specifically different, but internally homogeneous blocks and then randomly matches each treatment with one or more units within any given block. This treatment is believed to have an effect within any one block only, but also possible is observing potential differences for any given treatment among blocks. An analysis of this type of problem is referred to as two-factor ANOVA or two-way ANOVA. (Any statistics textbook may be consulted for additional details.)

One-Way ANOVA

Examples can facilitate understanding the concept of one-way ANOVA.

Example 4.11: Analyzing Rice Yield

In a 1-year study, 20 experimental plots in which rice was grown were observed. Then 5 plots were randomly selected for each group, and all 20 plots were divided into 4 groups. Four different types of fertilizer (1, 2, 3, and 4) were applied, one in each group of five plots. Determine whether four different types of fertilizer are equally effective at a 5% significance level or if they are not. A completely randomized plot design was developed. The rice yield data were measured in pounds (Table 4.10A). To analyze the data, formulate the opposing hypotheses:

H_0: The mean pounds of rice yield for all 5 plots in which fertilizer type 1 was applied are the same as those for the application of fertilizers 2, 3, and 4, i.e., $\mu_1 = \mu_2 = \mu_3 = \mu_4$

Table 4.10A. Collected Sample Data of Rice Yield from Plots

Treatment, i (Type of Fertilizer Applied)	Plot, j					Total	Sample Mean
	1	2	3	4	5		
1	19	15	22	17	19	92	$\bar{X}_1 = 18.4$
2	20	25	21	19	22	107	$\bar{X}_2 = 21.4$
3	18	12	17	16	16	79	$\bar{X}_3 = 15.8$
4	20	17	16	15	15	83	$\bar{X}_4 = 16.6$

Grand Mean: $\bar{X} = 18.05$

H_1: The mean rice yield from at least one of plot group is different from the others, i.e., at least one of the equalities does not hold

The body of the table has four rows ($r = 4$) and five columns ($c = 5$) in which rice yield data have been stored. Study the yield variation in the sample data. This variation has two components:

- Variation among rows: Explained by fertilizer treatments
- Variation within rows: Due to error

Variation among rows: explained by fertilizer treatments. The variation among the $r = 4$ sample means ($\bar{X}_1, \bar{X}_2, \bar{X}_3$, and $\bar{X}_4$) that summarize the data associated with each of the fertilizer treatments is known as *explained variation* or *treatment variation*. This variation is not attributable to chance, but to inherent differences among the treatment populations. (Remember from an earlier discussion that the measurement of this variation constitutes the first estimate, s_t^2, of the population variance, σ^2.) This estimate is based on several considerations:

Given: The assumed normality of the sampled populations, the sampling distribution of each sample mean, $\bar{X}_i$, where, $i = 1, 2, 3$, and 4 represents treatments, will be normally distributed:

Let:

$\sigma^2_{\bar{X}_i}$ = Variance among treatment population, $i = 1, 2, 3, 4$

σ^2 = Population variance

then,

$$\sigma^2_{\bar{X}_i} = \left(\frac{\sigma_i^2}{n_i}\right)$$

Assume: Equality of population variances, i.e.: $\sigma_1^2 = \sigma_2^2 = \sigma_3^2 = \sigma_4^2$ and equal sample sizes $(n_1 = n_2 = n_3 = n_4)$

Then the value of $\sigma^2_{\bar{X}_i}$ is the same for each i, and sample size in each treatment is equal to column (c).

Therefore:

$$\sigma^2 = n\sigma^2_{\bar{X}} = c\sigma^2_{\bar{X}} \text{ and } \bar{\bar{X}} = \text{Grand mean}$$

The variance of the sample distribution of $\bar{X}$ can be calculated as:

$$\sigma^2_{\bar{X}} \cong s^2_{\bar{X}} = \frac{\sum(\bar{X}_i - \bar{\bar{X}})^2}{(r-1)}$$

From previous equations,

$$\sigma^2 = c\sigma^2_{\bar{X}} \cong \left(\frac{c\sum\left(\bar{X}_i - \bar{\bar{X}}\right)^2}{\left(r-1\right)}\right)$$

and

$$c\sum(\bar{X}_i - \bar{\bar{X}})^2 = \text{Treatments sum of squares (or TSS)}$$

For the sample data,

$$\begin{aligned} \text{TSS} &= 5[(18.4 - 18.05)^2 + (21.4 - 18.05)^2 + (15.8 - 18.05)^2 \\ &\quad + (16.6 - 18.05)^2] \\ &= 92.05 \end{aligned}$$

and the degrees of freedom (df) associated with the estimation of σ^2 with the help of the variation among sample means. Therefore,

$$\text{df} = r - 1 = 4 - 1 = 3 \text{ (in the example)}$$

σ^2 can be estimated from the sample data, as follows:

$$\sigma^2 \cong \left(\frac{c\sum(\bar{X}_i - \bar{\bar{X}})^2}{(r-1)}\right)$$

This is known as treatments mean square (TMS) and also as explained variance and is identical to the population variance estimate symbolized by s_t^2 above.

In the example,

$$\begin{aligned} TMS = s_t^2 &= TSS/(r-1) \\ &= 92.05/(4-1) \\ &= 30.68 \end{aligned}$$

Variation within rows: due to error. The variation of the sample data within each of the $r = 4$ rows (or samples) about the respective sample mean is known as *unexplained variation* or *residual variation* or simply as (experimental or sampling) *error* and it is attributed to chance. As noted above, the measurement of this variation constitutes a second estimate, s_e^2, of the population variance, σ^2, and this estimate is based on the considerations that from each of the treatment samples (i), a sample variance can be derived as follows:

$$s_i^2 = \frac{\sum (X_{ij} - \bar{X}_i)^2}{n_i - 1}$$

where:

X_{ij} = Sample observations in row i and column j

$\bar{X}_i$ = Mean of sample i, where i = 1, 2, 3, and 4

n_i = number of observations in sample i

To obtain a single estimate of σ^2, take the weighted average of the i sample variances,

$$\sigma^2 \cong \frac{\sum\sum (X_{ij} - \bar{X}_i)^2}{(c-1)r} = \text{Error mean square (EMS) or explained variance}$$

$$= s_e^2$$

and

$\Sigma\Sigma(X_{ij} - \bar{X}_i)^2$ = Error sum of squares (ESS)

$(c - 1) \times r$ = df

Calculations for the ESS are presented in Table 4.10B. Based on the Table 4.10B data:

Table 4.10B. Error Sum of Squares Data

Treatment i	Observation 1	2	3	4	5	Total
$(X_{1j} - \bar{X}_1)^2$	$(19 - 18.4)^2 = 0.36$	11.56	12.96	1.96	0.36	27.2
$(X_{2j} - \bar{X}_2)^2$	$(20 - 21.4)^2 = 1.96$	12.96	0.16	5.76	0.36	21.2
$(X_{3j} - \bar{X}_3)^2$	$(18 - 15.8)^2 = 4.84$	14.44	1.44	0.04	0.04	20.8
$(X_{4j} - \bar{X}_4)^2$	$(20 - 16.6)^2 = 11.56$	0.16	0.36	2.56	2.56	17.2

$$\text{ESS} = 27.2 + 21.2 + 20.8 + 17.2 = 86.4$$

$$\text{df} = (c - 1) \times r = (5 - 1) \times 4 = 16$$

$$\sigma^2 \simeq \text{EMS} = s_e^2$$

For the example:

$$\text{EMS} = 86.4/16 = 5.4$$

The ANOVA Table

An ANOVA table shows for each source of variation, the sum of squares (SS), the degrees of freedom (df), and the ratio of the sum of squares to the df. The ratio of the sum of squares is called the *mean square* and it is the desired estimate of the population variance. The last row of the table is called the *Total Sum of Squares* or *Total SS,* which can be calculated independently by summing the squared deviations of each individual sample observation from the mean of all observations (grand mean).

In a one-way ANOVA table,

Total SS = TSS + ESS and

Total df = $(r - 1) + (c - 1)r = rc - 1$

A one-way ANOVA table for the sample data is presented in Table 4.10C.

The F Distribution

The ratio s_t^2/s_e^2 is equal to TMS/EMS and would be close to 1 whenever the null hypothesis of equal population means was true. This ratio is used as the ANOVA test statistic and is denoted by *F*. The probability distribution of *F* helps in deciding if any given divergence of *F* from 1 is significant enough to warrant the rejection of the null hypothesis of equal population means. In contrast to the *t* and χ^2

Table 4.10C. One-Way ANOVA Table for Fertilizer Treatment on Rice Yield

Source of Variation	SS (1)	df (2)	Mean Square (3) = (1) / (2)	Test Statistic (4)
Treatments	92.05	r – 1 = 3	TMS = 92.05/3 = 30.68	F = 30.68)/(5.4) = 5.68
Error	86.4	(c – 1)r = 16	EMS = 86.4/16 = 5.4	
Total	178.45	19		

statistics, the F statistic is associated with a *pair* of degrees of freedom and not *single* degrees of freedom.

In this example, a Table 4.10C value of $F_{\alpha=0.05,\mathrm{df}(3,16)} = 3.24$ and the calculated $F_{\mathrm{cal}} = 5.68$, since $F_{\mathrm{cal}} > F_{\mathrm{table}}$. Therefore, reject the null hypothesis and conclude that the four fertilizers do have different effects.

Mathematical Model

Now put this concept into a mathematical format. Suppose we have t different levels of a single factor (treatment) that we wish to compare. The observed response for each of the t treatments is a random variable.

Let:

Y_{ij} = Under ith treatment jth observation taken

and also consider the case where there is an equal number of observations, n, on each treatment. Now, the model can be described as follows:

$$Y_{ij} = \mu + \tau_i + \varepsilon_{ij}$$

where:

$i =$ 1, 2, 3, …, t (number of treatments)

$j =$ 1, 2, 3, …, n (number of observations)

μ = Overall mean

τ_i = Parameter associated with the ith treatment (the ith treatment effect)

ε_{ij} = Random error

Note that Y_{ij} represents both the random variable and its realization. For model testing, the model errors are assumed to be normally and independently distributed random variables with mean zero and variance σ^2. The variance σ^2 is assumed constant for all levels of the factor.

Mathematical Hypotheses:

H_0: τ's = 0 (Null hypothesis assumes the treatment term is zero)

H_1: $\tau_i \neq 0$ (For at least one i)

Conventional Hypotheses:

H_0: $\mu 1 = \mu 2 = \ldots = \mu_{i=t}$

H_1: At least one μ_i is different

ANOVA Steps:

Step 1. State the problem.

Step 2. Model assumptions:

- Treatment response means are independent and normally distributed:
  - The experiment run must be randomized.
  - The sample size must be good.
  - Run a normality test on the collected data. When using MINITAB software: **Stat > Basic Stats > Normality Test**
- Homogeneity test of population variances should be equal across all levels of factors:

Therefore, for σ:

H_0: $\sigma_{\text{population1}} = \sigma_{\text{population2}} = \ldots$; and

H_1: At least two are different

Step 3. State the hypotheses.

Step 4. Develop an ANOVA table.

Step 5. Check that the errors of the model are independent and normally distributed. Ways to check include:

- Run a normality check on error terms.
- Plot residuals against fitted values.
- Randomize runs during the experiment.
- Ensure adequate sample size.
- Plot a histogram of error terms.

Step 6. Interpret the P-value and/or the F-statistic for the factor or treatment effect.

For example:

At $\alpha = 0.05$, P-value < 0.05, then reject H_0.

Otherwise, assume the null hypothesis is true. The test performer must evaluate P-value before making any decision.

In the case of F-statistic:

If $F_{calculated} < F_{table}$, then accept the H_0

Otherwise, assume the alternate hypothesis is true.

Step 7. Calculate epsilon squared for the treatment and error terms.

$\varepsilon^2_{treatment}$ = (Treatment SS)/(Total SS)

ε^2_{error} = (Error SS)/(total SS)

Note: The epsilon-square (ε^2) statistic is not universally acceptable. This statistic is a guideline of the significance of treatment effect. It is also a measure of variation of the output in relation to input.

Step 8. Translate the technical output from the test into simple language.

Now, work with the same example (Example 4.11), using MINITAB software and following the ANOVA steps.

Step 1. State the problem:

- A scientist would like to know whether all fertilizer treatments could affect rice yield equally or if they will not.
- Plot the data. Plotting the collected data is important. Two data plots (dot plots and box plots) have been developed using the collected sample data (Figures 4.8A and 4.8B, respectively). These plots present pictorial views of the sample data.

Step 2. Model assumptions:

- Run the normal probability plot to check that response means are independent and normally distributed (Figure 4.8C).
  - Generally run randomize runs during the experiment and data collection.
  - Ensure that sample size is adequate (sample >30). Sample size in this example = 20.
  - Run a normality test on the data:

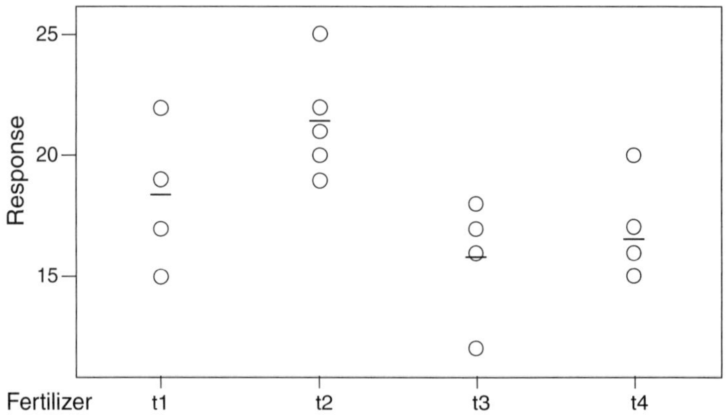

*Group means are indicated by lines

Figure 4.8A. Dot Plot of Fertilizer Treatment on Rice Yield*

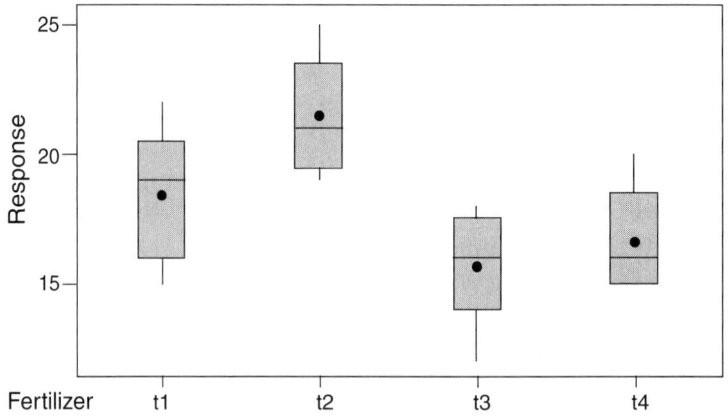

*Means are indicated by solid circles.

Figure 4.8B. Box Plot of Fertilizer Treatment on Rice Yield*

- Use MINITAB software: **Stat** > **Basic Stats** > **Normality Test**.
- The Anderson-Darling normality test is used here.

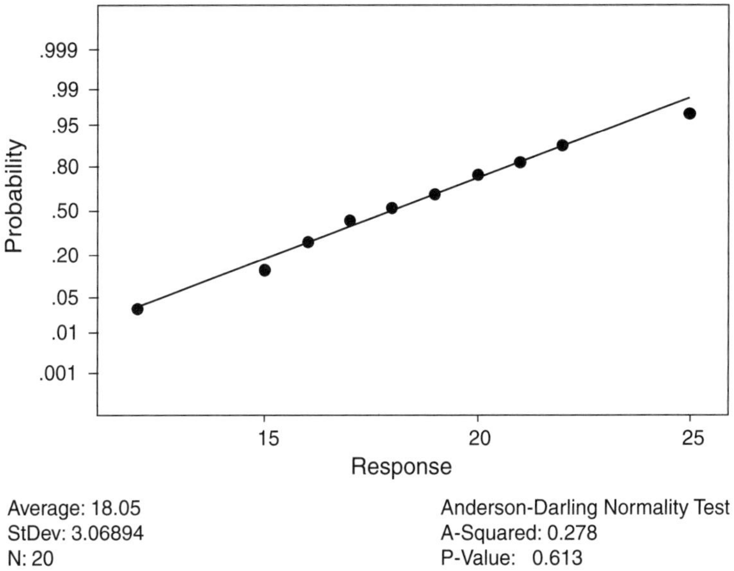

Figure 4.8C. Normality Test using Anderson-Darling Test

- Perform homogeneity of variance analysis to check that the population variances are equal across all levels of treatment (factor). The assumption of equal variance generally holds if the number of observations for each treatment is the same. MINITAB data are presented in Table 4.10D and Figure 4.8D.

For s:

H_0: $s_{population1} = s_{population2} = s_{population3} = s_{population4}$

H_1: At least two are different

Step 3. State the hypotheses:

H_0: $\mu_{ferti1} = \mu_{ferti2} = \mu_{ferti3} = \mu_{ferti4}$

H_1: At least two fertilizer treatments are different

or

H_0: τ's = 0 (null hypothesis assumes the treatment term is zero)

H_1: τ's $\neq 0$

Table 4.10D. Equal Variance Test Data

Response: Response
Factor: Fertilizer
Confidence Level: 95.0000

Lower	Sigma	Upper	N	Factor Levels
1.37662	2.60768	10.8186	5	t1
1.21534	2.30217	9.5512	5	t2
1.20382	2.28035	9.4606	5	t3
1.09470	2.07364	8.6030	5	t4

Note: Bonferroni confidence intervals for standard deviations.

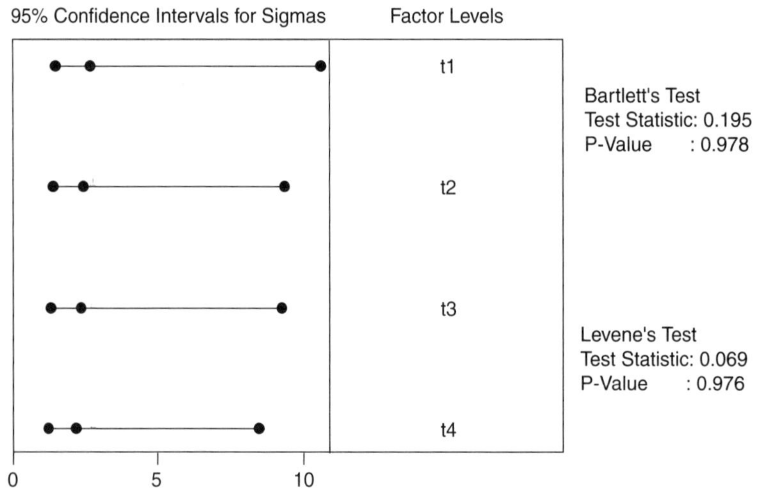

Figure 4.8D. Homogeneity of Variance Test for Rice Yield

- Null hypothesis—Average rice yield from each plot is the same or fertilizer treatments will not have a significantly different yield from plots.
- Alternate hypothesis—At least one fertilizer treatment will affect average rice yield.

Step 4. Develop an ANOVA table. The developed ANOVA table is presented in Table 4.10E.

- Use MINITAB software: **Stat** > **ANOVA** > **Oneway** ...

Note: Store residuals and fits for later use.

Table 4.10E. One-Way ANOVA Table—Rice Yield vs. Fertilizer Treatment

	Analysis of Variance for Response				
Source	**df**	**SS**	**MS**	**F**	**P**
Fertilizer	3	92.55	30.85	5.71	0.007
Error	16	86.40	5.40		
Total	**19**	**178.95**			

				Individual 95% CIs for Mean Based on Pooled SD
Level	**N**	**Mean**	**SD**	-----+---------+---------+---------+-
t1	5	18.400	2.608	(------*-------)
t2	5	21.400	2.302	(------*-------)
t3	5	15.800	2.280	(-------*------)
t4	5	16.600	2.074	(------*-------)
				-----+---------+---------+---------+-
Pooled SD = 2.324				**15.0 18.0 21.0 24.0**

Step 5. Check that errors of the model are independent and normally distributed. Three graphs have been plotted (Figures 4.8E, 4.8F, and 4.8G). The graph plotted in Figure 4.8E checks the residual normality. The histogram plotted in Figure 4.8F should appear as a bell curve, but in this example the bell curve shape can be ignored because the sample is small (<30). Figure 4.8G shows that the residuals should be random about 0 (zero) without trends. The graph in Figure 4.8G investigates if the mathematical model fits equally for low to high values of the fit.

Step 6. Interpret the *P*-value and/or the *F*-statistic for the factor or treatment effect. For example:

At $\alpha = 0.05$, *P*-value< 0.05, reject H_0

Otherwise, assume the null hypothesis is true.

An analysis of variance for treatment response is presented in Table 4.10F. When group sizes are equal, $\sigma^2_{pooled} = (\sigma_1^2 + \sigma_2^2 + \sigma_3^2 + \sigma_4^2)/4$; this value in Table 4.10F is 5.40. The table value of F ($F_{a=0.05,df(3,16)}$) is 3.24; the calculated value from Table 4.10F is 5.71.

Since the $F_{calculated} > F_{table}$, therefore, the null hypothesis is rejected.

Another check for the hypothesis test is the *P* test. Since $\alpha = 0.05$ and the calculated value of *P* is 0.007, at least one group mean is different. Therefore, again

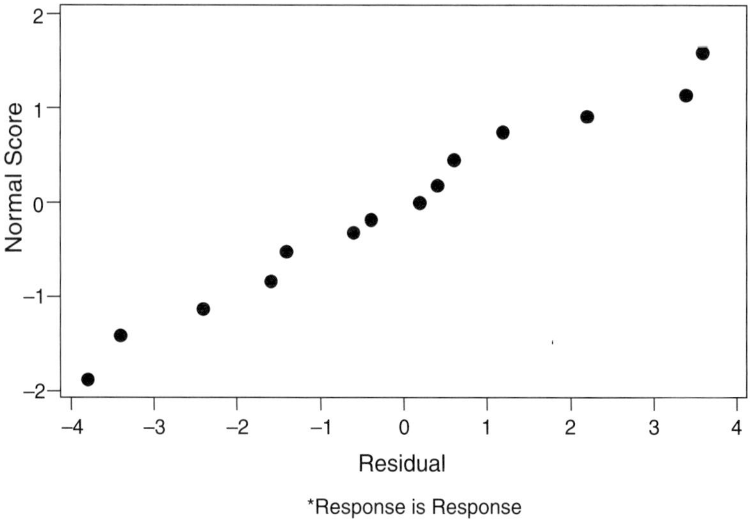

Figure 4.8E. Normal Probability Plot of the Residuals*

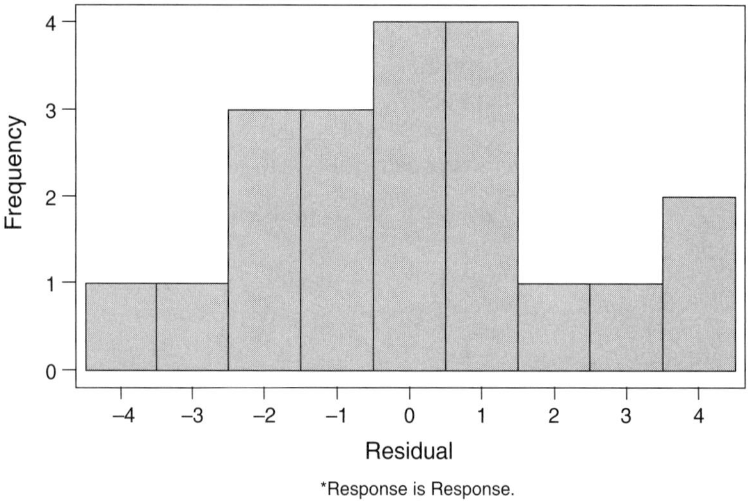

Figure 4.8F. Histogram of Residuals*

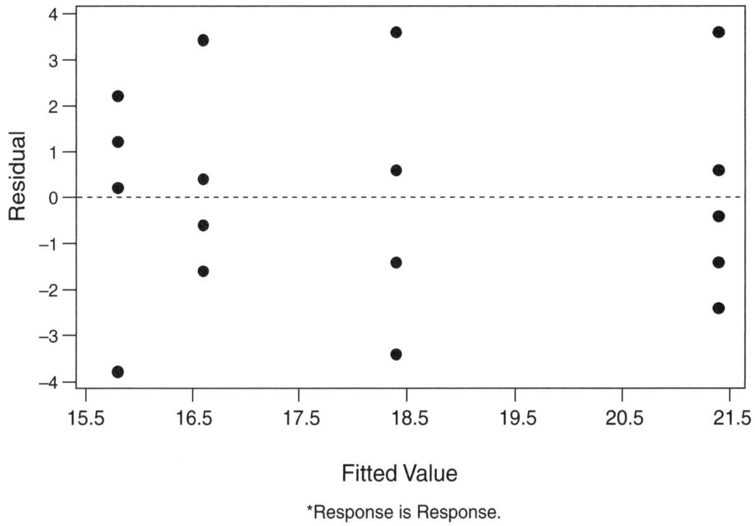

Figure 4.8G. Residuals vs. Fitted Values*

the null hypothesis that all the group means are equal is rejected. At least one fertilizer treatment mean is different.

Step 7. Calculate epsilon squared for the treatment and error terms:

$$\varepsilon^2_{\text{treatment}} = (\text{Treatment SS})/(\text{Total SS})$$

$$\varepsilon^2_{\text{treatment}} = (92.55)/(178.95) = 0.52$$

Therefore, 52% of the variation in rice yield can be explained by fertilizer treatment.

Step 8. Translate the technical output from the test into simple language, e.g.: "We have found that fertilizer treatment does affect rice yield. Fertilizer treatment two provides the highest yield."

Exercise 4.4: Comparing Average Cost of Market Basket Goods in Four Cities

A nonprofit organization wants to test, at the 1% level of significance, if the average cost of a given market basket of goods is the same in four cities (Boston, Chicago, Dallas, and Los Angeles). A random sample of eight stores in each of the cities has provided the data (see Table 4.11 for average cost of a given market

Table 4.10F. Analysis of Variance for Treatment Response

	Analysis of Variance for Response				
Source	**df**	**SS**	**MS**	**F**	**P**
Fertilizer	3	92.55	30.85	5.71	0.007
Error	16	86.40	5.40		
Total	19	178.95			

basket by city in dollars). Perform the desired test by the organization, showing computations along with an ANOVA table.

Exercise 4.5: Comparing Average Sales by Display Used in Department Stores

An advertising department in a clothing outlet company uses four displays (A, B, C, D) in their department stores to advertise a product. The advertising department wants to determine if average sales are the same regardless of which display is used to advertise a product. Independent random samples of stores using displays A, B, C, and D, respectively, provided monthly sales in dollars (Table 4.12). Perform the desired test at the 5% level of significance, showing computations and an ANOVA table. List the assumptions.

To continue establishing a qualitative relationship between the independent variables (*X*s) and the dependent variable (*Y*), simple regression and correlation will now be discussed.

4.5 REGRESSION AND CORRELATION

Once the variables in any study can be analyzed, using a systematic process, it is possible to find that the value of one variable is associated with the value of another variable. For example, consider the linkage (relationship) between repair frequency and the age of a machine or how output varies with input, revenue varies with price, education level varies with starting compensation, price varies with product demand (or supply), etc. This type of list has no end, but one thing is clear: having knowledge and understanding of these types of relationships would be very useful to project leaders, researchers, and decision makers.

Understanding relationships enables prediction of the value of one variable based on knowledge about another variable. Regression and correlation analysis supports such an endeavor once the following are established:

- The type of relationship that exists between variables
- The strength of these relationships

Table 4.11. Sample Data of a Given Market Basket (Average Cost in Dollars)

Store	Boston (1)	Chicago (2)	Dallas (3)	Los Angeles (4)
1	70.05	71.95	70.55	51.25
2	68.35	76.15	69.10	68.45
3	67.85	69.75	65.10	55.20
4	74.05	73.35	70.15	57.30
5	77.45	68.35	60.25	55.65
6	63.92	75.15	59.35	53.25
7	69.35	77.50	62.45	53.20
8	73.65	68.04	67.35	72.15

Table 4.12. Sample Data of Monthly Sales from Eight Stores

Display	Monthly Sales, $							
A	131	130	135	140	130	119	105	101
B	171	190	192	206	251	99	89	81
C	55	67	90	78	45	53	70	52
D	101	115	99	125	140	155	174	130

Important: The techniques presented in this section are designed to determine the existence and strength of association between variables. These techniques are not able to prove anything about the possible cause-and-effect relationships. For example, if unemployment is high, colleges and universities will show high enrollment. Yet, in fact, the opposite might be true or neither variable might be causally related to the other variable, despite this association.

However, knowing about an association such as this would be very helpful in allowing an estimation to be made, e.g., to estimate an *unknown* unemployment level from a *known* value of college and university enrollment. This *association knowledge* among variables would also be useful as a first step in a broader investigation of cause-and-effect relationships. In general, finding the systematic association between two variables frequently provides initial support to further study of the cause-and-effect relationship.

Definitions of frequently used terms include:

- Regression Analysis—A statistical method with key focus on establishing an equation that allows the unknown value of one variable to be estimated from the known value of one or more other variables

- Regression Equation—A prediction equation that could be linear or curvilinear, which allows the unknown value of one variable to be estimated from the known value of one or more other variables
- Regression Line—In regression analysis, a line that summarizes the relationship between an independent variable, *X*, and a dependent variable, *Y*, while also minimizing the errors made
- Coefficient of Determination: r^2—Measures how well the estimated regression line fits the sample data or the amount of variation explained by the regression equation
- Coefficient of Correlation: $\sqrt{r^2} = r$—The square root of the sample coefficient of determination, which is a common alternative index of the degree of association between two quantitative variables
- Coefficient of Determination (Adjusted): r^2(Adj)—The r^2(Adj) for degrees of freedom (If a variable is added to an equation, r^2 will almost always get larger, even if the added variable is of no real value.)

Simple regression analysis and simple correlation analysis will now be discussed:

- Simple Regression Analysis—A method in which a single variable is used to estimate the value of an unknown variable
- Simple Correlation Analysis—A statistical method in which a key focus is the establishment of an index that provides, in a single number, an instant measure of the strength of association between two variables (Depending on the value of this measure (0 to 1), how closely two variables move together can be determined and, thereby, with what degree of confidence one variable can be estimated with the help of the other.)

4.5.1 Simple Regression Analysis

In regression analysis, there are two types of variables, *X* and *Y*. The value of a variable assumed *known* is symbolized by *X* and is referred to as the *independent variable* or *predictor variable*. In contrast, the value of the variable assumed *unknown* is symbolized by *Y* and is referred to as the *dependent variable* or *predicted variable*.

The relationship between these *X* and *Y* variables can be *deterministic* or *stochastic*. If the relationship is precise, exact, or *deterministic*, the value of *Y* is uniquely determined whenever the value of *X* is specified. In contrast, the relationship can be an imprecise, inexact, or *stochastic*, in such a way that many possible values of *Y* can be associated with any one value of *X*. Only the deterministic model will be discussed in this section.

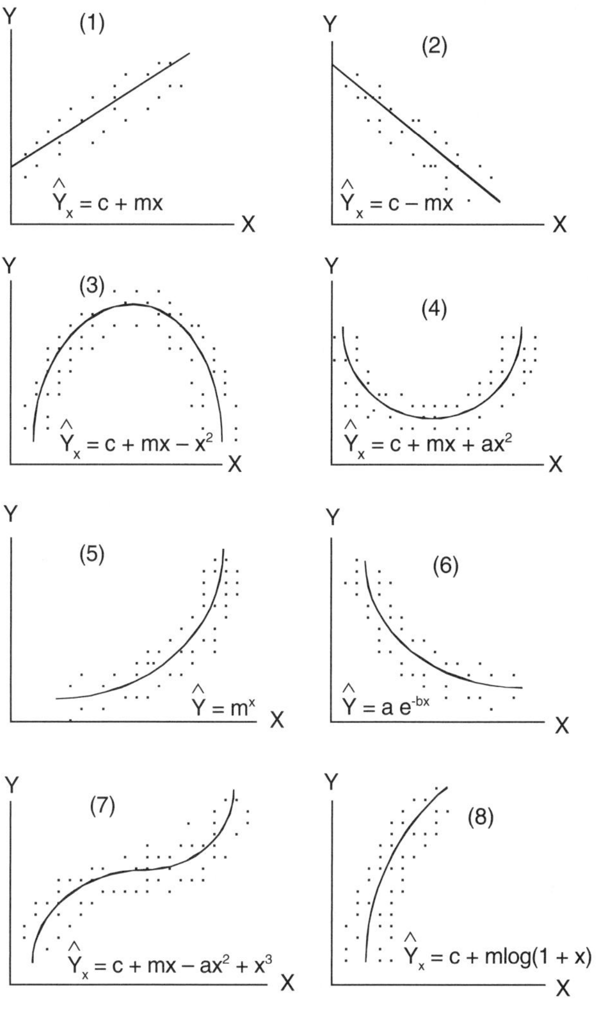

Figure 4.9. Relationships between X and Y

Figure 4.9 contains panels of the alternative relationships between *X* and *Y*. Each dot in the graphs represents a hypothetical pair of observations about an independent variable *X* and a dependent variable *Y*. The lines summarize the nature of their relationship.

Panel (1) is described by the equation $Y = c + mX$. In this particular example, *X* and *Y* are variables, while c is the vertical intercept and m is the slope of the straight line. Both c and m are defined as constants. The slope could be positive or negative. For example, Panel (2) presents a straight regression relationship, but with a negative slope. In Panel (1), as the value of the dependent variable *Y* increases with the larger values of the independent variable *X*, there is said to be a *direct* relationship. The slope of this regression line is positive and is represented by m. If instead, as in Panel (2), the value of the dependent variable *Y* decreases with the larger values of the independent variable *X*, there is said to be an *inverse* relationship and the value of m is negative.

Panels (1) and (2) present a linear relationship and Panels (3) through (8) present curvilinear relationships. In addition, the relationship in Panels (1), (5), and (8) could be defined as *direct*; or it could be *inverse*, as presented in Panels (2) and (6); or it could be a *combination* of direct and inverse as presented in Panels (3), (4), and (7). Of course, the values of the constants (a, c, and m) do differ from one equation to the next.

Essential: Carefully check the following elements when plotting collected data:

- Properly Identify the *X* and the *Y* Variables—Analyze the variables correctly for potential cause and effect. The process (independent) variable, as the predictor, is on the *X* axis and the output (dependent) or process performance variable, as the response, is on the *Y* axis. *Important*: When plotting data, a common mistake is mixing up the *X* and *Y* variables.
- Properly Scale a Scatter Diagram—To have a proper interpretation of data, it is important to use, to the fullest possible extent, both the *X* and *Y* axes to cover all the collected data. Improper scaling of any axis can result in an obscured pattern. Divide the space on each axis so that data plotting and data reading are facilitated.
- Pair Data Correctly—The *X* and *Y* variables must be paired before plotting, i.e., there must be a logical correspondence between the data to appropriately study the correlation.

Finding the Regression Line—The Method of Least Squares

Fitting the data to a line in a scatter diagram is known as the *method of least squares* (also least squares method), a commonly used approach. The line is developed so that the sum of the squares of the vertical deviations between the line and the individual data plots is minimized. These vertical deviations represent the errors associated with using the regression line to predict *Y* with the help of *X*. Figure 4.10 shows the nature of the squares and the sum of these squares is being minimized.

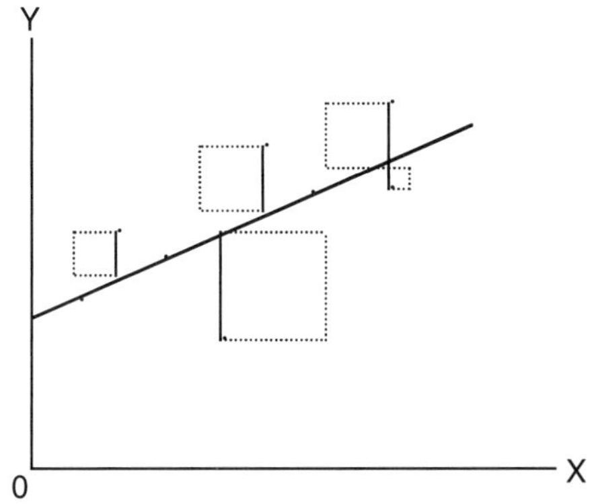

Figure 4.10. The Method of Least Squares

A regression line from the sample data calculated by the least squares method is known as the simple regression line or *estimated* regression line. The value of parameters c and m in its equation:

$$\hat{Y}_X = c + mX$$

are referred to as the estimated regression coefficients, and their values can be estimated as follows:

$$m = \frac{\sum X_i Y_i - \left(\frac{\sum X_i \sum Y_i}{n}\right)}{\sum X_i^2 - n\left(\frac{\sum X_i}{n}\right)^2}$$

$$c = \left(\frac{\sum Y_i}{n}\right) - m\left(\frac{\sum X_i}{n}\right)$$

where:

m = Slope of the estimated regression line

c = Intercept of the estimated regression line

X_i = Observed values of the independent variable

Y_i = Associated observed values of the dependent variable

$i = 1, 2, 3, \ldots, n$ number of observations

as presented in Example 4.12.

Example 4.12: Using the Least Squares Method to Develop a Regression Equation

Twenty sample data points and in-process information are presented in Table 4.13A. Based on the available information:

$$\begin{aligned}\bar{X} &= \Sigma X_i / n \\ &= 240/20 \\ &= 12\end{aligned}$$

$$\begin{aligned}\bar{Y} &= SY_i / n \\ &= 475/20 \\ &= 23.75\end{aligned}$$

$$m = \frac{\sum X_i Y_i - \left(\frac{\sum X_i \sum Y_i}{n}\right)}{\sum X_i^2 - n\left(\frac{\sum X_i}{n}\right)^2}$$

$$\begin{aligned} &= (6392 - ((240 \times 475)/20)) \,/\, (3262 - 20(240/20)^2) \\ &= 692/382 \\ m &= 1.812\end{aligned}$$

$$c = \left(\frac{\sum Y_i}{n}\right) - m\left(\frac{\sum X_i}{n}\right)$$

$$\begin{aligned} &= (475 \,/\, 20) - 1.812\ (12) \\ c &= 2.006\end{aligned}$$

Therefore, the regression equation is:

$$Y_i = 2.006 + 1.812\ X_i$$

If the developed regression equation is utilized, the estimated values for the dependent variable (Y) can be obtained. The three selected points are where $X = 8$, 12, and 15 and the calculated $Y = 16.5$, 23.75, and 29.19, respectively. Now the collected data values can be compared with the estimated values in Table 4.13B.

Example 4.13: Using MINITAB Software—The Estimated vs. the True Regression Line

Imagine a scatter diagram for the population, not just a sample. For each and every value of X, there would be a value of Y, but there would be a multitude of

Table 4.13A. Utilizing the Least Squares Method to Establish the Regression Line

Count, i	X_i	Y_i	X_iY_i	X_i^2
1	2	5	10	4
2	4	9	36	16
3	8	25	200	64
4	8	9	72	64
5	8	20	160	64
6	12	20	240	144
7	13	25	325	169
8	14	30	420	196
9	14	25	350	196
10	15	30	450	225
11	10	25	250	100
12	12	25	300	144
13	12	26	312	144
14	12	22	264	144
15	11	18	198	121
16	15	26	390	225
17	21	45	945	441
18	16	35	560	256
19	16	25	400	256
20	17	30	510	289

Table 4.13B. Projected and Actual Values of Dependent Variable in Relation to Independent Variable

	Dependent Variable Y	
Independent Variable X	Actual Collected Value Through Sample	Estimated Value Through the Regression Equation
8	25, 9, 20	16.5
12	20, 25, 26, 22	23.75
15	30, 26	29.19

data points. The least squares regression line that might be derived from such data is called the *population* regression line or the *true* regression line. This line might be described by an equation:

$$E(Y) = \alpha + \beta X$$

where:

$E(Y)$ = Expected value of Y for any given X

and

α and β are the true regression coefficients:

α = Vertical intercept of the regression line

β = Slope of the regression line

These population parameters are the values that are of real interest rather than the sample or estimated regression coefficients (c and m), which, as a result of sampling error, may seriously distort the true underlying relationship between X and Y. Statisticians have devised ways to make inferences concerning the true regression line from sample data, but the validity of these inferences rests on some or all of the following assumptions:

1. The values of X are known without error, and the different sample observations about Y that are associated with any given X are statistically independent of each other.
2. Every population of Y values is normally distributed. Because each of these normal curves of Y values is associated with a specific value of X, each curve is referred to as a *conditional probability distribution* of Y and is said to have a *conditional mean* of $Y(\mu_{Y.X})$ and a conditional standard deviation of Y $(\sigma_{Y.X})$.
3. All conditional probability distributions of Y have the same conditional standard deviation of Y. This value $(\sigma_{Y.X})$ is also referred to as the *population standard error of the estimate.* The assumption is that the scatter of observed Y values above and below each conditional mean is the same.
4. All the conditional means $(\mu_{Y.X})$ lie on a straight line that is the true regression line and is described by the equation:

$$E(Y) = \mu_{Y.X} = \alpha + \beta X$$

Using Example 4.13, suppose an estimate is needed of the value of the conditional mean, $\mu_{Y.X}$, such as $\mu_{Y.10}$, the mean starting salary of all those in the population from which Example 4.13 sample data were drawn, when the individuals have 10 years of education. Assume that any point on the sample regression line is an estimate of the point on the population regression line. Let $\mu_{Y.10}$ be a point on the population regression line that can be estimated using a least squares sample regression line:

$$\begin{aligned} Y_{X\text{-}estimated} &= c + mX \\ &= -\,6.67531 + 2.90166\,X \end{aligned}$$

Therefore,

$$\begin{aligned} Y_{10\text{-}estimated} &= -\,6.67531 + 2.90166\,(10) \\ &= 22.34 \end{aligned}$$

This is the best point estimate of $\mu_{Y.10}$ that is available. If a different sample had been drawn, a different regression equation would have been estimated and thus would have produced a different point estimate of $\mu_{Y.10}$. This degree of uncertainty about the value of $\mu_{Y.X}$ can be made explicit by presenting an interval estimate, not a point estimate. In regression analysis, a confidence interval within which a population parameter is being estimated typically is referred to as a *prediction interval.*

Estimating a Prediction Interval for $\mu_{Y.X}$

This estimation applies to both small and large samples. The following information is in a summary form. (Refer to any statistics textbook for additional details.)

- $\mu_{Y.X}$ for a small sample (n <30):

$$\mu = \bar{X} \pm \left(t\sigma_{\bar{X}}\right)$$

$$\sigma_{\bar{X}} = s / \sqrt{n}$$

$$\mu_{Y.X} = \hat{Y}_X \pm t\sigma_{\hat{Y}_X}$$

$$\sigma_{\hat{Y}_X} \cong s_{Y.X}\sqrt{\frac{1}{n} + \frac{\left(X - \bar{X}\right)^2}{\sum X^2 - n\bar{X}^2}}$$

$$\mu_{Y.X} = \hat{Y}_X \pm \left(t_{\alpha/2} . s_{Y.X}\sqrt{\frac{1}{n} + \frac{\left(X - \bar{X}\right)^2}{\sum X^2 - n\bar{X}^2}}\right)$$

- $\mu_{Y.X}$ for a large sample:

$$\mu_{Y.X} = \hat{Y}_X \pm \left(Z_{\alpha/2} \left(\frac{s_{Y.X}}{\sqrt{n}} \right) \right)$$

Now that simple regression analysis, which establishes a precise equation that links two variables, has been discussed, the next section will discuss simple correlation analysis, which will establish a general index about their strength of association.

Example 4.13 (Continued): Applying the Least Squares Method

Use the least squares method to determine the estimated regression line for education level and starting salary for survey data in Table 4.14A.

Solution:
Use MINITAB software:

1. Always try to plot the data as shown in Figure 4.11A:
   Graph > Plot
2. Obtain a prediction equation (regression data are found in Table 4.14B):
   Stat > Regression > Fitted Line Plot initially plotted the linear regression graph in Figure 4.11B.
   Check options:
   - **Display Confidence Band**
   - **Display Prediction Band**
   - Use the default confidence level at 95%.

Interpreting the results: Data have fit using the *linear* model. The R^2 (from Table 4.14B) indicates that the education level accounts for 86.7% of the variation in the annual starting salary (coefficient of determination, R^2, and the R^2(Adj) with the calculated value of 86.2%, will be discussed in the next section). In Figure 4.11B, the lines labeled CI are the 95% confidence limits for the annual starting salary, and the lines labeled PI are the 95% prediction limits for new observations.

A visual inspection of the plot reveals that the sample data are not evenly spread about the regression line, implying that there is a systematic lack-of-fit. Therefore, in the next regression analysis, try the fit in the quadratic model. Output from MINITAB software is presented in Table 4.14C and Figure 4.11C.

Interpreting the results: The *quadratic* model appears to provide a better fit to the data (see Figure 4.11C). The R^2 indicates that the education level accounts for 96.1% of the variation in the annual starting salary (with R^2(Adj) = 95.8%)

Table 4.14A. Sample Data—Starting Salary for Different Levels of Educational Background

Individual	Education Level, Grade	Annual Starting Salary, $K
A1	6	15
A2	6	17
A3	6	14
A4	6	16
A5	8	15
A6	8	18
A7	10	20
A8	10	22
A9	12	24
A10	12	25
A11	12	23
A12	14	28
A13	14	26
A14	14	28
A15	14	29
A16	15	30
A17	15	35
A18	15	34
A19	16	38
A20	16	40
A21	16	39
A22	16	41
A23	16	43
A24	17	46
A25	17	48
A26	18	53
A27	18	54
A28	20	57

Table 4.14B. Linear Regression Analysis Statistics for Sample Data

The regression equation is

Annual Start = –6.67531 + 2.90166 Education Level, Grade

S = 4.76578	R-Sq = 86.7%	R-Sq(adj) = 86.2%

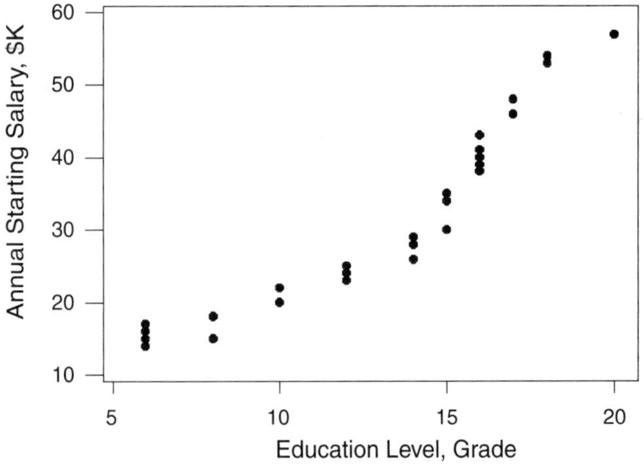

Figure 4.11A. Graphical Presentation of Collected Data

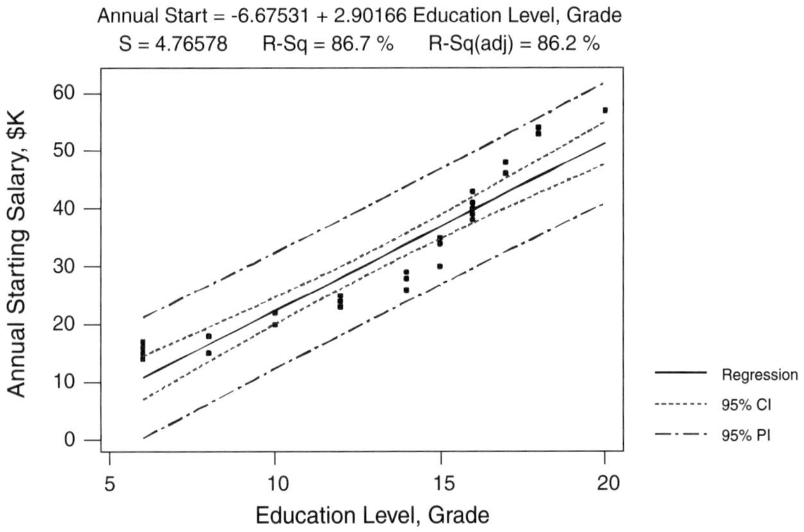

Figure 4.11B. Linear Regression Plot with Confidence Interval

Table 4.14C. Polynomial Regression Analysis Statistics for Sample Data

The regression equation is **Annual Start = 25.7852 – 3.20207 Education Level, Grade** **+ 0.252643 Education Level, G**2**		
S = 2.62107	R-Sq = 96.1%	R-Sq(adj) = 95.8%

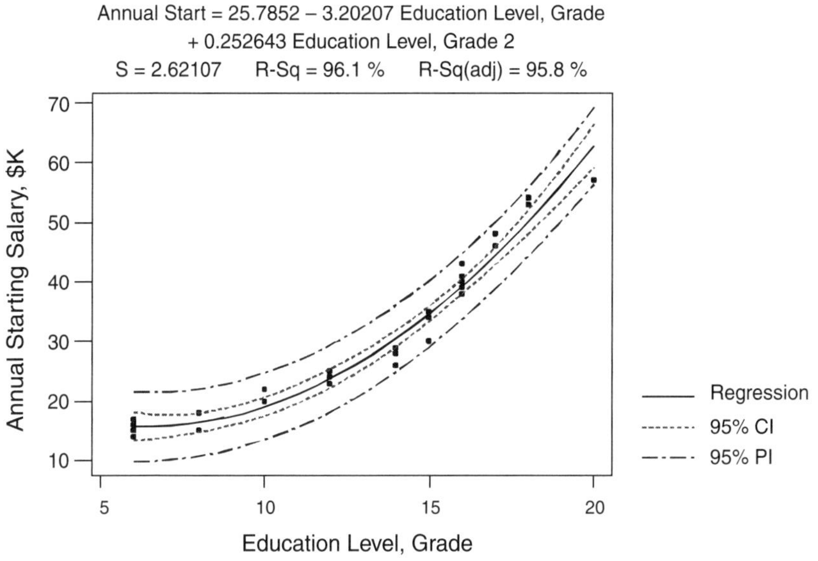

Figure 4.11C. Polynomial Regression Plot of the Sample Data

(see Table 4.14C). A visual inspection of the plot reveals that the data are evenly spread about the regression line, implying that there is no systematic lack of fit (Figure 4.11C).

4.5.2 Simple Correlation Analysis

Simple correlation analysis establishes a general index about the strength of association between two variables. The panels in Figure 4.12 show from zero (no) correlation to perfect correlation. Although there are several different indices of association between quantitative variables, only two will be discussed—the coefficient of determination and the coefficient of correlation.

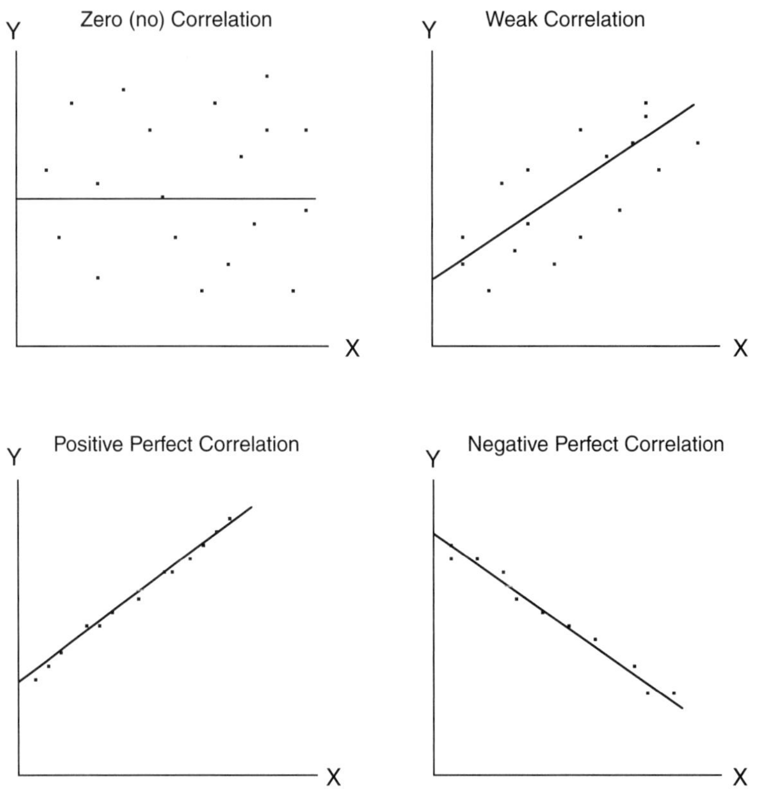

Figure 4.12. Different Degrees of Correlation

The Coefficient of Determination (r^2)

This coefficient is a measure of how well the estimated regression line fits the sample data. This coefficient is equal to the proportion of the total variation in the values of the dependent variable Y. This relationship is as follows:

Total Variation = Explained Variation + Unexplained Variation

The relationship can also be presented as:

Total Sum of Squares = Regression Sum of Squares + Error Sum of Squares

or $TSS = RSS + ESS$.

$$\sum\left(Y-\bar{Y}\right)^2=\sum\left(\hat{Y}_X-\bar{Y}\right)^2+\sum\left(Y-\hat{Y}_X\right)^2$$

where:

Y_s = Observed values of dependent variable Y

$\bar{Y}$ = Mean of dependent variable

$\hat{Y}_X$ = Estimated value of Y for a given value of independent variable X

r^2 = Explained variation/Total variation = RSS/TSS

$$r^2 = \frac{\sum\left(\hat{Y}_X - \bar{Y}\right)^2}{\sum\left(Y - \bar{Y}\right)^2}$$

Since, Total $SS - ESS = RSS$, therefore,

$$r^2 = (TSS - ESS)/TSS = 1 - (ESS/TSS)$$

$$r^2 = 1 - \frac{\sum\left(Y - \hat{Y}_X\right)^2}{\sum\left(Y - \bar{Y}\right)^2}$$

and a sample coefficient of determination (an alternate formula in relation to the regression equation):

$$r^2 = \frac{c\sum Y + m\sum XY - n\bar{Y}^2}{\sum Y^2 - n\bar{Y}^2}$$

where additional variables:

n = Sample size

c = Intercept of regression equation

m = Slope of regression equation

The Coefficient of Determination Adjusted [r^2(Adj)]

As defined earlier, r^2 is adjusted for the degrees of freedom. If a variable is added to an equation, r^2 will almost always get larger, even if the added variable is of no real value. Therefore, to compensate for this:

$$r^2 = \frac{ErrorSS/(n-m)}{TSS/(n-1)}$$

where:

m = Number of coefficients fit in the regression equation

The Coefficient of Correlation (*r*)

The square root of the sample coefficient of determination, $\sqrt{r^2}$, is a common alternative index of the degree of association between two quantitative variables. The coefficient *r* takes on absolute values between 0 and 1. The positive or negative value of *r* denotes a direct relationship or an inverse relationship between *X* and *Y*, respectively. Therefore, when:

$r = 0$ → No correlation
$r = +1$ → Perfect correlation between directly related variables
$r = -1$ → Perfect correlation between inversely related variables

The following is Pearson's formula for calculating r without prior regression analysis (also known as Pearson's Sample Coefficient of Correlation):

$$r = \frac{\sum XY - n\bar{X}\bar{Y}}{\sqrt{\left(\sum X^2 - n\bar{X}^2\right)\left(\sum Y^2 - n\bar{Y}^2\right)}}$$

where:

Xs = Observed values of the independent variable

$\bar{X}$ = Mean of independent variable

Ys = Observed associated values of the dependent variable

$\bar{Y}$ = Mean of dependent variable

n = Sample size

Similarly, *r*(Adj) is the square root of the coefficient of determination adjusted.

Example 4.13 (Continued): Applying the Coefficient of Determination and the Coefficient of Correlation

Now analyze the coefficient of determination and the coefficient of correlation of the sample in Example 4.13. When developed in a linear regression equation:

$r^2 = 0.867$ and r^2(Adj) = 0.862 (this r^2 is adjusted for degrees of freedom)

In other words, 86.2% of the total variation in *Y* (annual starting salary) was observed. Therefore, *r*(Adj) = 0.928, indicates that the annual starting salary is strongly correlated with education level.

When using a quadratic regression equation:

$r^2 = 0.961$, r^2(Adj) = 0.958, and *r*(Adj) = 0.979

This clearly shows that the quadratic equation is better fitted than the linear fitted equation.

Tools have been presented in this chapter to establish a qualitative relationship between the independent variables (*X*s) and the dependent variable (*Y*). The following are the general comments related to the *coefficient of determination* and the *coefficient of correlation*:

- As a regression equation is developed, the value of r^2 will tell which of the three—linear, quadratic, or cubic—regression is a better-fit equation. (If there is a poor or a no-linear relationship, then the value of r^2 will be low, but this does not mean that there is no curvilinear relationship.)
- Statisticians prefer to use r^2 rather than r as a measure of association because fairly high absolute values of r (e.g., $r = 0.70$) can give a false impression that a strong association exists between *Y* and *X* (but in this case, $r^2 = 0.49$; thus, the association of *Y* with *X* explains less than half of the variation of *Y*). Only at the extreme values of *r*, when $r = \pm 1$ or when $r = 0$ (under these situations, $r = r^2$) does the value of *r* directly convey what proportion of the variation of *Y* is explained by *X*.
- The correlation coefficient measures only the *strength* of a statistical relationship between two variables. A strong statistical relationship between *X* and *Y* need not imply a causal relationship. Perhaps *Y* causes *X*; perhaps *X* causes *Y*; or perhaps each is part cause/part effect of the other. Perhaps the two variables move together by pure chance. Therefore, the existence of a high-positive or -negative correlation between two variables that have no logical connection with one another is commonly known as a *nonsense correlation* or *spurious correlation*.

Exercise 4.6: Developing a Regression Equation

The quality group in a manufacturing company has collected sample data from a welding department and wants to establish a relationship between weld diameter (in inches) and the shear strength (in pounds) of weld. Develop a regression equation; obtain the coefficient of determination and the coefficient of correlation. Provide data with comments. See Table 4.15 for the collected sample data.

Exercise 4.7: Determining an Estimated Regression Equation and the Coefficient of Correlation

A realtor wants to establish the relationship between the number of weeks houses are on the market prior to sale and the asking price. Sample data are provided in

Table 4.15. Sample Data from a Welding Department

Weld Diameter, Inches	Shear Strength, Pounds
0.190	680, 710, 700
0.200	800, 825
0.209	780, 810
0.215	885, 975, 1025
0.230	1100, 1000, 1055
0.250	1030, 1200, 1150, 1300
0.265	1175, 1300, 1250

Table 4.16. Determine an estimated regression equation and the coefficient of correlation. Also provide comments.

4.6 SUMMARY

Establishing the qualitative relationship between the independent variables (*X*s) and the dependent variable (*Y*) has been described. This relationship will assist with the development of alternate process improvement solutions.

Also discussed were important questions that assist with the definition of the importance of critical data. Qualitative analysis tools were also presented along with examples to demonstrate their capabilities. The tools discussed included:

- Stratification
- The Classic Technique of Hypothesis Testing
  - Mathematical Relationships among Summary Measures
  - The Theory of Hypothesis Testing
  - The Testing of Hypothesis—Population Mean and the Difference between Two Such Means
  - The Testing of Hypothesis—Proportion Mean and the Difference between Two Such Proportions
- The Chi-Square Technique of Hypothesis Testing
  - Testing the Independence of Two Qualitative Population Variables
  - Making Inferences about More than Two Population Proportions
  - Making Inferences about a Population Variance

Table 4.16. Real Estate Sales Related Data

Asking Price, $K	Weeks to Sale
40	6.5
198	8.6
160	6.8
199	10.6
200	14.0
250	15.0
201	8.6
260	15.0
250	12.1
360	19.0
280	9.0
240	12.5
220	9.5
400	27.0

    - Performing Goodness-of-Fit Tests to Assess the Possibility that Sample Data Come from a Population Following a Specified Type of Probability Distribution
- Analysis of Variance (ANOVA)—One-Way ANOVA
    - Analysis of Variance Concept with Example
    - Mathematical Model
    - ANOVA Steps
- Regression and Correlation
    - Definition of Key Terms
    - Simple Regression Analysis
    - Simple Correlation Analysis

Before proceeding to the next phase, **I**mprove, of the DMAIC process, a project team should check the following:

- As information is processed and analyzed, identify gaps between the current performance and the goal performance.
- Root cause analysis should have led to verifying and quantifying the causes of variation and should have included:
    - A list of possible causes or the sources of variation

  - A list and prioritizing of the issues or sources of variation by using a Pareto chart
- Root cause analysis should have led to quantifying the gap/opportunity.

Questions may be used as a guide to determine the appropriate application tool for information and process analysis:

- What does the information say about the performance of the business process?
- Was any value-added, non-value added, and waste activities analysis done to identify some of the gaps in the "as is" process map?
- Was a detailed process map created to reveal the critical steps of the "as is" process?
- What procedure was used in generating, verifying, and validating the process map?
- Was any additional useful information obtained through detailed subprocess mapping?
- Were any cycle time improvement opportunities identified through the process analysis?
- Did the team think that additional information should have been collected during analysis?
- Which tool would best explain the behavior of output (dependent) variable(s) in relation to input (independent) variables?

Questions may also be used as a guide to quantify the gap/opportunity:

- What team is estimating the cost of poor quality?
- Is the process so broken that a redesign is required?
- If the team judges that the project is not a DMAIC process project, would the project lend itself to a DMADV project?
- What are the latest estimates of the financial savings/opportunities for the improvement project? Where easy benefits can be obtained through "quick fixes"?
- Was the project mission statement updated as the team went through the **A**nalyze phase?

5

IMPROVE

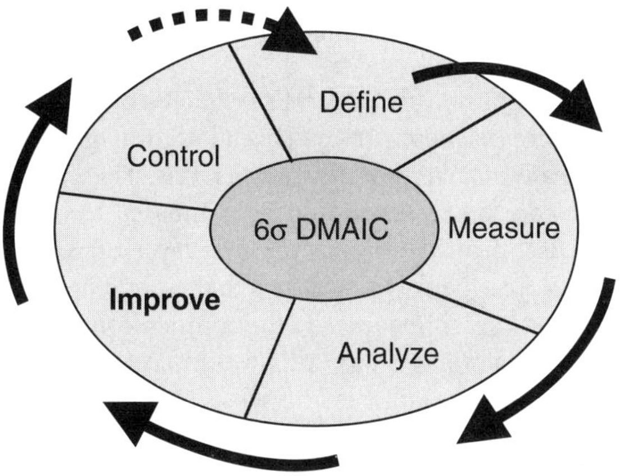

The most important phase is **I**mprove because this phase focuses on reducing the amount of variation found in a process. Reduction of variability is the solution to many processes problems (e.g., in a manufacturing process). Although some reengineering programs promote the concept of tearing down the functional silos and rebuilding process groups from scratch, other businesses believe that they should start where they are organizationally and build on current successes and modify current processes. These businesses strongly rely on the interwoven concepts of defect reduction, which encourage employees to rely more on each other and cycle time reduction, which eliminates unnecessary, non-value-adding and waste steps from processes.

Yet, Six Sigma requires more than a financial investment. Businesses must have a plan, the required resources, the commitment of everyone, especially business leaders, and uncompromising metrics. Along with these elements, businesses must also set aggressive goals for a defined path and hold people accountable (both internal and external). Commonly utilized goals and commitments include having:

- A totally satisfied customer
- A commitment to a common language throughout the business
- A commitment to common and uniform quality measurement techniques throughout the business
- Improvement goals based on uniform metrics
- Goal-directed incentives for both employees and management
- Common training material on "why," "how," and "when" to achieve a goal

No one set of procedures can be used when following Six Sigma methodology. Every business is different and must consider its strengths and weaknesses and then leverage them accordingly.

Typically, a quantitative understanding of customer satisfaction can be achieved through surveys. These surveys should identify gaps between customer needs and the company's current performance levels. Then through benchmarking, the company's core processes should be compared to another best-in-class performer. This is useful in identifying the first layer of goals that are needed. Imagine that a company is performing at less than a four sigma level and that the competition is close to a six sigma level. Is the competition 2000 times better than the company? (A comparison such as this would certainly get the attention of leaders of the business.) In a mathematical sense, six sigma is a known quality. As improvements are implemented, quality improves and everyone's expectations go up. As customers' perceptions about a business change, quality at the business is driven to a level never before thought possible to achieve.

Businesses exist in which the corporate culture is fear-based and mistakes are not tolerated. As a result, employees try to hide defects. Six Sigma programs can help these employees to minimize defects and the business will also flourish.

If one speaks with Six Sigma champions, they will identify numerous issues to count, measure, benchmark, and improve regardless of the type of the business, e.g., whether it is a physician's office or a storage space rental company. Within any business, all types of variations can be found, e.g., from warehousing, security, and personnel policies to cafeteria management.

If any business is not improving, that business will eventually fail. Six Sigma is a philosophy of continuous improvement. As improvements are made, the business is driven in a direction of achieving its goals. Often improvement ideas come from customers; therefore, talk to customers and find out what they consider to be defects. Work on big defects first. Try to find out why they happen and how to permanently correct them.

Businesses that are satisfied with their current quality levels simply do not understand the real challenge of quality. Businesses that are satisfied should investigate the defect levels their customers are experiencing as well as the internal defects that cause rework, additional inspections, and higher product costs. Only when a business fully assesses itself can improvements really begin.

Improvement strategies could include:

- The team applying the concept of process reengineering to determine the solution (depending on team's current level of process knowledge and the additional information collected so far)
- In a systematic approach, the team examining the vital *X*s (independent variables) as they relate to the process to determine the best approach for developing a process/solution to produce an output to meet customer needs
- The team determining the process/solution under the given constraints (depending on the team's total knowledge and understanding of the process/solution)
- The team incorporating different combinations of reengineering, statistical, and quality tools

After giving consideration to the above list, the key step in the **I**mprove phase is to evaluate the team's improvement strategy.

The team should begin the **I**mprove phase by going through reengineering of the process/solution. The team should reengineer the current process and then generate alternatives to find the best process/solution under the given constraints. If the team does not have enough confidence to relate the independent variables (*X*s) with the dependent variable (*Y*), then the team could set up a design of experiments (DOE) to develop a quantitative relationship between the inputs and the output under the given constraints and modify the selected alternative according to the specific requirements of the process/solution. A DOE develops graphs and a regression equation that will allow the team to determine the best possible combination under the given constraints and operational settings.

It is possible that team's project will include a combination of both types of essential *X*s (alternatives and factors). In this situation, the team would use improvement strategies for the specific key *X*s that may result in more than one proposed process/solution. An improvement strategy flowchart will be presented (see Figure 5.1). Sources of variation include:

- A level of good communication with employees
- Employees knowing what they are supposed to do

- Employees having access to business policies, guidelines, procedures, and quality standards—Employees must understand this information and should be required to follow policies, procedures, etc. If employees have issues with and/or are unclear about any policy, procedure, etc., they must have a contact source. Employees should understand the consequences of failing to meet requirements.
- Employees having the requirement of sampling their work and having the time allocated for these activities—Employees should also be required to record the results of their sampling.
- Supervisors maintaining individual employee performance records
- Employees being evaluated in quantitative terms in relationship to business goals and having a correction mechanism in place to correct deficiencies

Therefore, the first improvement activity could be process reengineering and then developing improvement strategies for the factors and alternatives. This chapter will discuss the following topics:

5.1 Process Reengineering
5.2 Guide to Improvement Strategies for Factors and Alternatives
5.3 Introduction to the Design of Experiments (DOE)
  5.3.1 The Completely Randomized Single-Factor Experiment
  5.3.2 The Random-Effect Model
  5.3.3 Factorial Experiments
  5.3.4 DOE Terminology
  5.3.5 Two-Factor Factorial Experiments
  5.3.6 Three-Factor Factorial Experiments
  5.3.7 2^k Factorial Design
    5.3.7.1 2^2 Design
    5.3.7.2 2^3 Design
5.4 Solution Alternatives
5.5 Overview of Topics
5.6 Summary
References

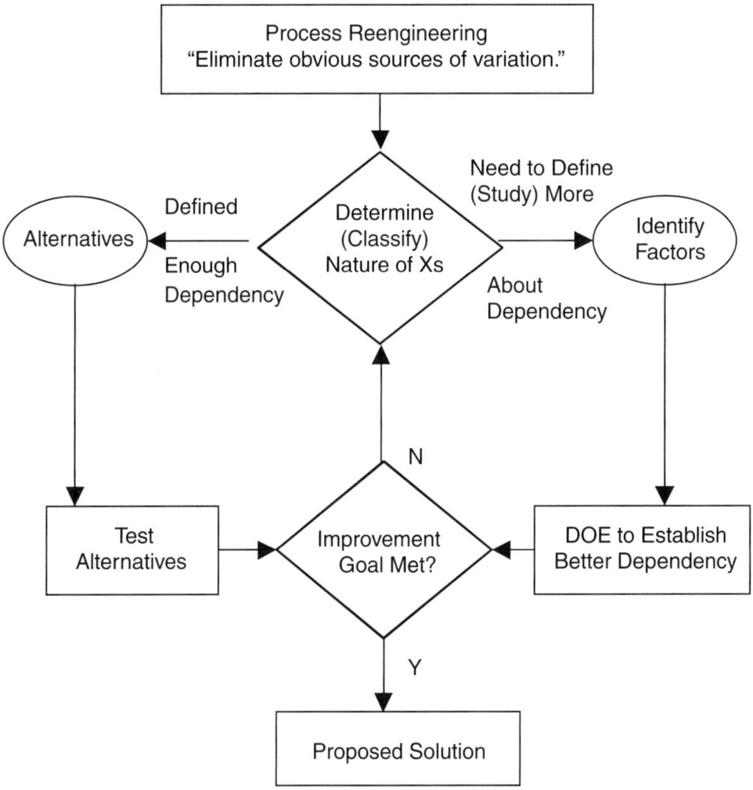

Figure 5.1. Evolution of Improvement Strategy

5.1 PROCESS REENGINEERING

Reengineering is a process (Figure 5.1) in which unnecessary tasks are eliminated, tasks are combined or reordered, information is shared among all the workforce involved in a process, and process improvements can be realized by reducing cycle time and cost and improving process accuracy, service, and flexibility. A *process* consists of diverse tasks and it crosses existing organizational boundaries that are managed by functional managers.

Process Centering

Process centering is the first step in *process reengineering*, steps which start the business on the road to process centering.[1] Critical steps are required in naming a process:

- Boundries—A typical process *crosses* existing organizational boundaries:
  - A "rule of thumb" is that if a process does not make more than two people angry, it is not a process.
  - Many businesses simply rename a functional unit as a process.
  - Process identification requires an ability to look horizontally across the whole organization, from the outside, rather than from the top down.
- Awareness—Include personnel levels from top executives to employees at the lowest levels (e.g., the manufacturing floor of a product company) to ensure that all employees in the business are aware of the process and its importance to the business:
  - Employees must recognize their process by name, must clearly understand the inputs and outputs to the process, and must also understand their relationship to the process.
  - Process participants must link themselves to the whole process (up and down).
  - Each participant is not to perform only his/her duties, but also to watch, understand, and support the process as necessary.
- Process Measurement—Every business must have a method for measuring a participant's performance in completing the process.
- Process Management—Focus at the business must continue on all processes so that employees remain attuned to the needs of the changing business environment:
  - One-time improvements are of little value unless the entire process is addressed.
  - A process-centered business must strive for ongoing process improvement.

A process resource analysis is presented in Example 5.1.

Example 5.1: A Quick Process Resource Analysis

This business has a traditional, quite rigid hierarchical organization (Worker → Supervisor → Manager → Director → Vice President → . . .). Each process follows the chain of command. For example, a customer makes a payment on his invoice. The employee receiving the customer's payment is responsible for determining if the payment was received "on-time" or if it is "late." The accounts receivable department is responsible for determining whether the payment is for the correct amount or if it is not. If a data entry employee notices anything unusual, he/she must take the issue to his/her supervisor, then the supervisor takes the issue to his/her manager, etc. When a customer inquires about a payment, he/she has to go through several employees to get all the information needed, a procedure that makes the customer unhappy. How should this business improve its payment receiving process?

Solution:
Business leadership must think "out of the box," be creative, and establish fewer organizational layers by cross-training employees in several areas:

- Contract interpretation
- Customer billing and how it is done
- Customer payments and how they should be made
- Correct payment amount
- Knowledge (limited) of account auditing
- Communication methods with field sales (about contract)

Easy access to customer accounts should be provided to customer service (customer contact) employees.

Process Activities
The next step is analyzing process activities. Every process is a group of activities to achieve an objective. Process activities can be divided into three categories:

- Value-Adding Work—Work for which a customer is willing to pay
- Non-Value-Adding Work—Activities which create no value for the customer, but are required to get value-adding work done
- Waste—Work that neither adds any value for a customer nor is required to get the value-adding work done

A simple concept of process reengineering is to eliminate *waste*, minimize *non-value-adding work*, and improve/modify/reprocess *value-adding work*. Businesses utilize significant amounts of resources to eliminate waste, which provides benefits, but not enough benefits for a business in the competitive global market. By simply eliminating waste activities, the business organization structure is unchanged. Non-value-adding work is also used as the "glue" that binds together value-adding work in a conventional process. Typically, non-value-adding activities fall into several categories:

- Checking
- Reporting
- Controlling
- Supervising
- Liaising
- Reviewing

Value-adding work is generally divided into very small tasks that require limited knowledge and experience to complete. Supervisors/checkers are used to monitor these activities (monitoring activities are non-value-adding work), e.g., reviews, managerial audits, checks, approvals, etc. Although value-adding workers are generally less skilled and lower paid, their activities make a process complex. Their activities add expense. Adding complexity to a process makes the process error-prone and difficult to understand. Although non-value-adding activities have been justified on the basis that they "make the process work," they are also a source of:

- Errors
- Misunderstanding
- Miscommunication
- Squabbles
- Reconciliation
- Inflexibility
- Rigidity
- Telephone calls
- Headaches
- Delay

Because simply eliminating these activities would not allow the process to function, it is therefore necessary to *design* non-value-adding work through *reorganizing* the value-adding work. This process is often called *reengineering* or *process reengineering*. Example 5.2 presents a situation in which specific employee qualifications are based on an identified process.

Example 5.2: Employee Qualifications for an Identified Process

Company XYZ has an opening for a customer service representative (CSR).[2] List the qualities needed and knowledge requirements for this open position.

Solution:

The responsibility of a CSR is to resolve a customer's problem. A CSR must focus on the outcome rather than on any single activity. Therefore, a CSR must be proficient in several distinct types of activities and must have knowledge of multiple disciplines. Specific qualities and requirements of a CSR include:

- Must be able to speak with customers and have the competency to use sophisticated software programs
- Must have sufficiently developed "people" skills
- Must grasp the essentials of a customer's request for service
- Must have sufficient knowledge of company products and services to recommend solutions for customer problems
- Must have a sense of the "art and science" of working with company resources

- Must be able to judge priority situations and assign priorities correctly to certain customers, e.g., during a busy time such as an emergency
- Must be able to train prospective employees for the CSR position, providing sufficient information about company products and services to allow new a CSR to recommend solutions to customers

If a selected candidate does not have these qualities, but is capable of learning them, the company should provide all required training to the candidate before he/she begins to function as a CSR.

Analyzing the Process

Once the process reengineering team understands the basics of a process and the quality requirements of the participating employees, the next step is to analyze the process for reengineering. A process-centered job could have several characteristics, e.g.:

- Free of non-value-adding work
- Big and complex
- Covers a range of tasks. Requires job holder to understand the "big picture:"
  - Business goals
  - Customer needs
  - Process structure

As non-value-adding work is eliminated (e.g., it is often minimized), the job becomes:

- Substantive
- Increasingly difficult (as a consequence of becoming substantive)
- Challenging
- Of higher intensity

and job responsibilities become:

- Results-oriented
- A route to personal autonomy
- Having the authority to make decisions

Reengineering jobs may have two types of employees—professionals and workers. A *professional* is responsible for achieving results rather than performing tasks, e.g., attorneys, architects, accountants, physicians, etc. are responsible for achieving results. A professional's "world view" consists of three categories—customer, results, and process. A professional must have a reservoir of knowledge and an appreciation for the application of this knowledge to different situations. Characteristics as a professional include:

- Has required education and training
- Does not necessarily work according to predefined instructions
- Is directed toward a goal and has been provided with significant latitude
- Must be a problem solver
- Must be able to cope with unanticipated and unusual situations without "running to management" for guidance
- Is a constant learner, not only in the classroom, but also in professional life
- Must be competitive, with energy directed from inside the organization to outside
- Must have a professional career that concentrates on knowledge, capability, and influence

A *worker* recognizes personal responsibility based on three different categories—boss, activity, and task, e.g, workers can be sales representatives, customer service representatives, etc.

When an employee considers moving to a process-oriented environment, key questions come to mind:

- Will I succeed in this new type of work?
- What job title will I have?
- How and how much will I be paid?
- What are the prospects for future growth?

Process-centered work and a process-centered environment transform workers into professionals, with all the advantages and disadvantages this change implies.

A High-Level Listing of Process Reengineering Steps

Step 1. Define the Process to Be Analyzed:

- Identify the process that the team will analyze for improvement.
- Describe the process in enough detail for each activity to be identified as value-added, non-value-added, and waste.

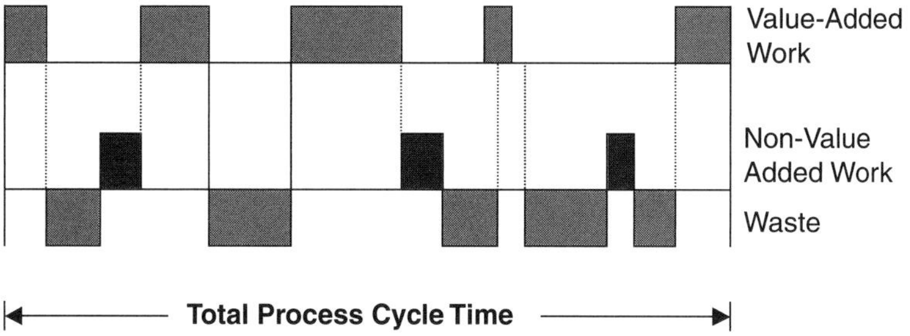

Figure 5.2. Graphic Presentation of a Process into Activity Classifications

- Identify process starting and ending points.

Step 2. Map Process Flow:

- Prepare all step-by-step process flow maps by tracing all process steps in sequence, as well as resources, functions, time, distance, etc.

Step 3. Define Process Activities:

- Define process flow, identifying each detailed step in the process and using common sign conventions:

  O Process/Operation

  ⇨ Transport/Move

  □ Inspect

  △ Store

  D Wait/Delay

Step 4. Analyze Throughput (Distance Traveled, Cycle Time):

- Some of the most important measurements that impact quality, inventory, cost, and customer satisfaction are measurements of the speed with which a process is completed and in which the throughput is made.

Calculate value ratios and process documentation as presented in Figure 5.2:

Value-added work ratio = (Value-added work time)/(Total process cycle time)

Non-value-added work ratio = (Non-value-added work time)/(Total process cycle time)

Waste ratio = (Waste time)/(Total process cycle time)

Summarize process cycle statistics as applicable:

- Activities statistics (value-added, non-value-added, waste)
- Distance traveled
- Delay/wait time
- Resources statistics
- Average cycle time

Generate ideas to eliminate waste and minimize non-value-added work:

- Utilize brainstorming concept to generate ideas.

Step 5. Test Feasibility of the Selected Idea:

- Because implementation of the selected idea is required, a feasibility test is critical.

Step 6. Implement Idea and Develop User Procedure Document:

- While implementing the selected idea, develop the user procedure-document.

Step 7. Record Results Achieved or Demonstrated:

- Summarize achieved results as well as expected results. If expected results are different, provide an explanation.

Exercise 5.1: Simplifying a Warehouse Material Receiving and Stacking Process: Process Reengineering[2]

A warehouse layout is presented in Figure 5.3. Material receiving process flowcharts are provided in Figures 5.4 (parts A through G). Analyze the warehousing problem, following the outline presented earlier. Propose an improved material receiving and stacking process.

Project guidance: This is not a typical warehouse such as would be found in a parts manufacturing facility warehouse (i.e., components). These warehouses are also not as technologically advanced as those found in a manufacturing facility. The quality of material received in these warehouses also varies significantly.

Typically, there are two staging areas: one is on the receiving dock and the second is on the manufacturing side of the business just outside the warehouse. Generally, the material received needs to be quality-checked before it can be stacked in the warehouse. Most of the production material is a common type of material and it is supplied to several machines at the same time. Once material is

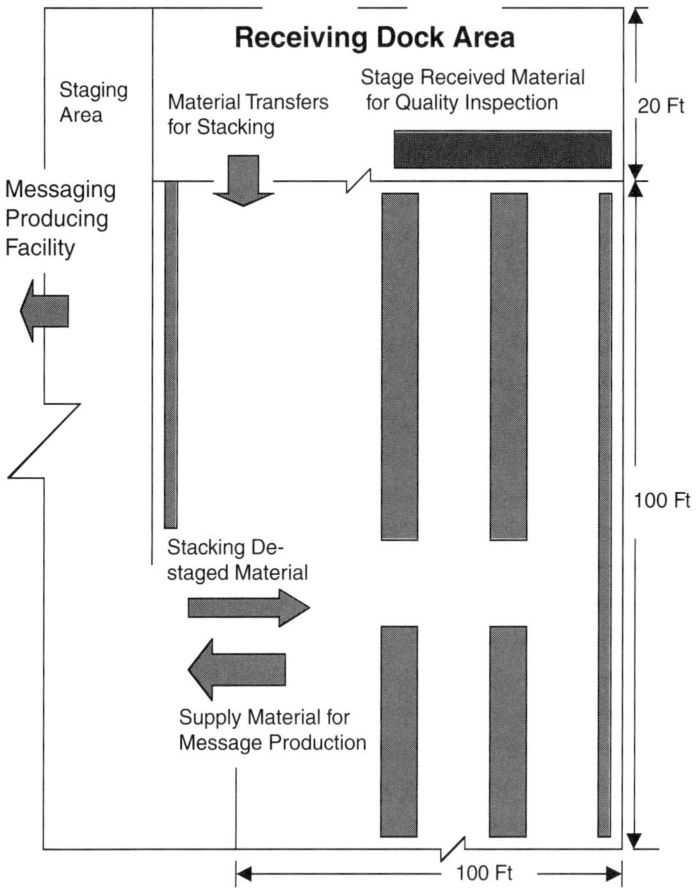

Figure 5.3. Warehouse Layout

retrieved from the warehouse for production, the material is staged in a second staging area. The material handling workforce then supplies the material to individual production machines from the second staging area. The warehouse layout with the receiving dock and the two staging areas is presented in this exercise.

The duration of certain activities is provided as a range of time. In order to calculate cycle time, use the average duration for these activities. While reading the description of these activities, note that certain activities are a combination of two or more activities (as described earlier in Section 5.1, *Process Reengineering*). Classify these activities into value-added, non-value-added, and waste based on the main action (function) performed during the defined activity time.

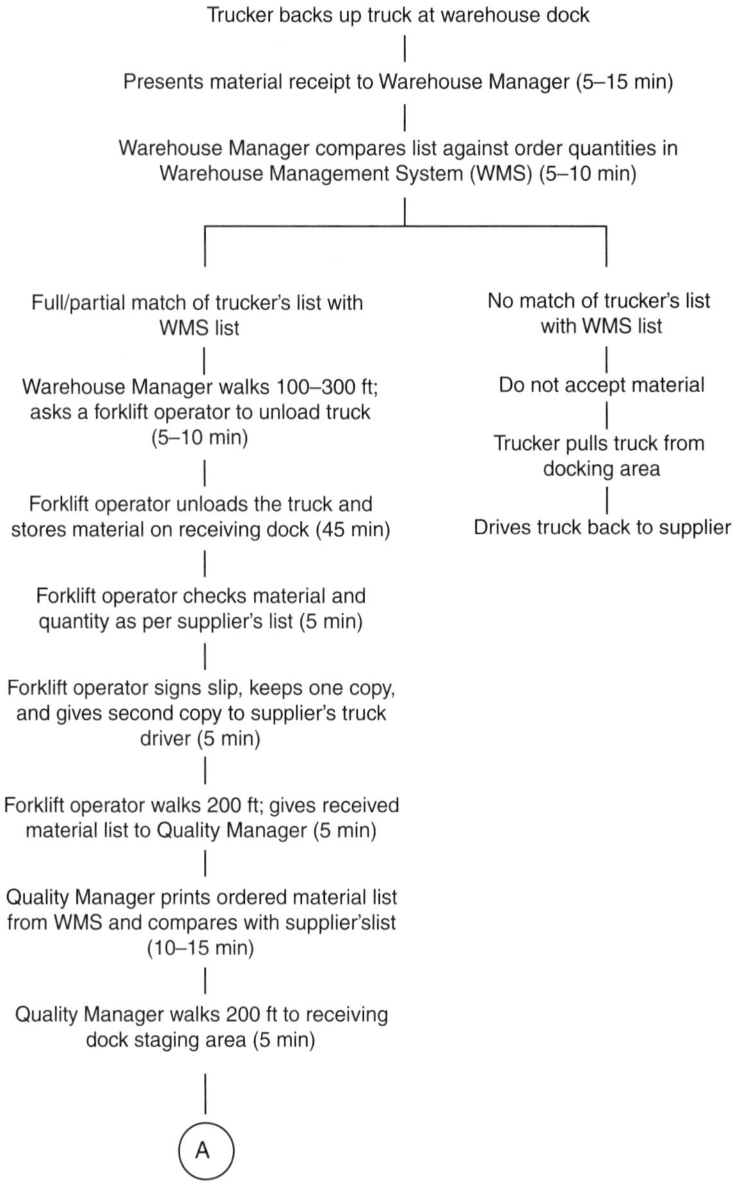

Figure 5.4 (Parts A to G). Warehouse Material Receiving and Stacking Process Flowchart

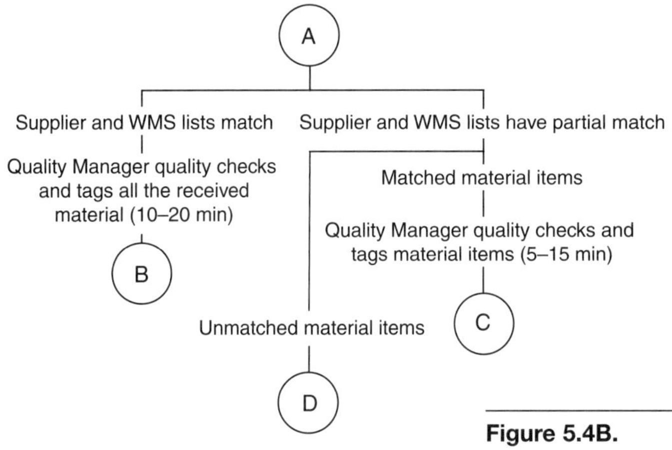

Figure 5.4B.

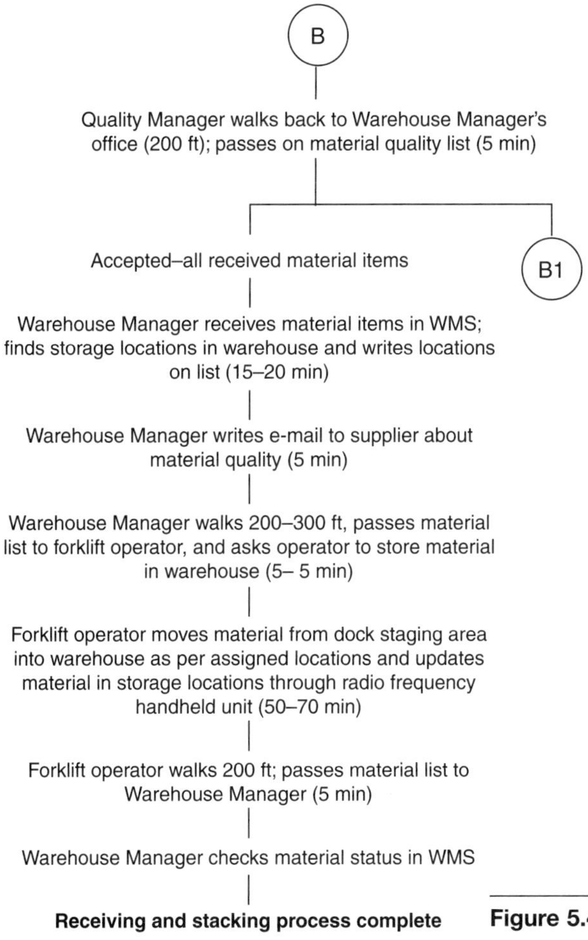

Figure 5.4C.

B1

Partially Accepted–all received material items

Warehouse Manager receives material items in WMS; finds storage locations in warehouse and writes locations on list (15–20 min)

Warehouse Manager writes an e-mail to supplier about material quality and expects supplier to pick-up rejected material by following working day (5 min)

Warehouse Manager walks 200–300 ft; passes material list to forklift operator; asks operator to store accepted material in warehouse (5–15 min)

Forklift operator moves only accepted material from dock staging area into warehouse as per assigned locations and updates material in storage locations with radio frequency handheld unit (50–70 min)

Forklift operator walks 200 ft; passes material list to Warehouse Manager (5 min)

Warehouse Manager checks material status in WMS

Supplier truck arrives the following working day; Warehouse Manager asks forklift operator to load rejected material in truck and get trucker's signature for material received (15–50 min)

Receiving and stacking process complete

Figure 5.4D.

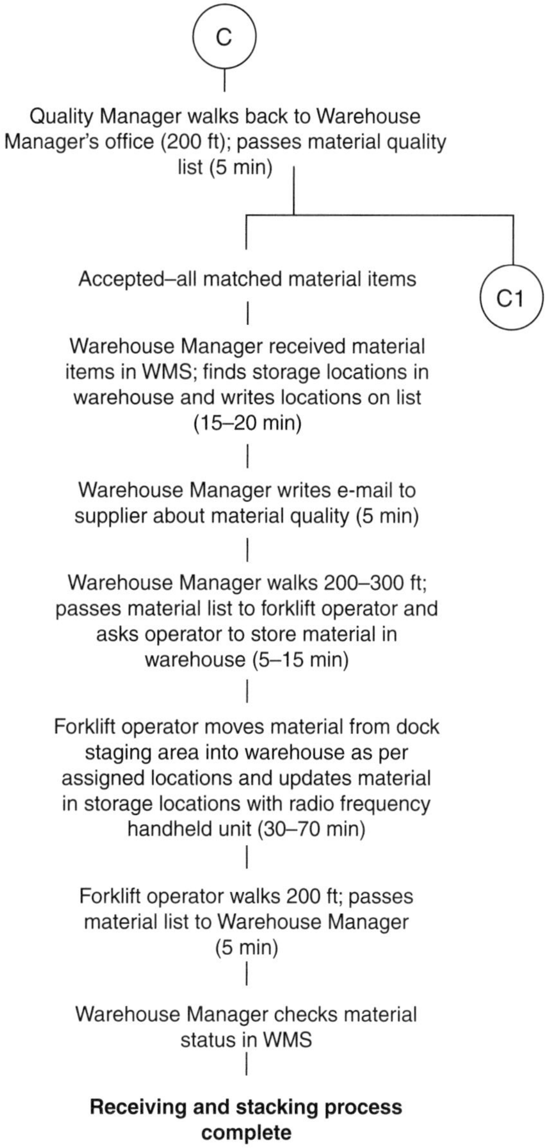
C
Quality Manager walks back to Warehouse Manager's office (200 ft); passes material quality list (5 min)
Accepted–all matched material items
C1
Warehouse Manager received material items in WMS; finds storage locations in warehouse and writes locations on list (15–20 min)
Warehouse Manager writes e-mail to supplier about material quality (5 min)
Warehouse Manager walks 200–300 ft; passes material list to forklift operator and asks operator to store material in warehouse (5–15 min)
Forklift operator moves material from dock staging area into warehouse as per assigned locations and updates material in storage locations with radio frequency handheld unit (30–70 min)
Forklift operator walks 200 ft; passes material list to Warehouse Manager (5 min)
Warehouse Manager checks material status in WMS
Receiving and stacking process complete

Figure 5.4E.

C1

Partially Accepted — all matched material items

Warehouse Manager receives material items in WMS; finds storage locations in warehouse and writes locations on list (15–20 min)

Warehouse Manager writes e-mail to supplier about material quality and expects supplier to pick-up rejected material by following working day (5 min)

Warehouse Manager walks 200–300 ft; passes material list to forklift operator and asks operator to store accepted material in warehouse (5–15 min)

Forklift operator moves only accepted material from dock staging area into warehouse as per assigned locations and updates material in storage locations with radio frequency handheld unit (30–70 min)

Forklift operator walks 200 ft; passes material list to Warehouse Manager (5 min)

Warehouse Manager checks material status in WMS

Supplier truck arrives the following working day; Warehouse Manager asks forklift operator to load rejected material in truck and get trucker's signature for material received (15– 50 min)

Receiving and stacking process complete

Figure 5.4F.

Figure 5.4G.

5.2 GUIDE TO IMPROVEMENT STRATEGIES FOR FACTORS AND ALTERNATIVES

As the team went through the Analyze phase of identifying the relationship between independent variables (*X*s) and the dependent variable (*Y*), along with applying the concept of process reengineering, the team would decide whether the $Y = f(X)$ relationship has been defined enough or not. Two identified conditions will be discussed:

Condition 1. Dependency *has been* sufficiently defined so that the team can develop alternatives:

- Various independent scenarios can be developed that must be tested.
- Risk assessment will be needed for each scenario.
- Alternatives will need testing either through pilots or through simulation.
- Alternatives will need evaluation, with selection of the *best alternative* under the given constraints

Possible issues include:

- Process Flow—Optimize process flow issue under the given/modified/improved constraints.
- Lack of Standardized Process/Operation—Standardize the process as much as possible.
- Specific Problem Identified—Develop a good practical solution to the problem.

Possible alternatives include:

- Brainstorming ideas
- Benchmarking and best practices
- Mistake checking (monitoring)
- Making pilot tests
- Process mapping and reengineering
- Process simulation

Condition 2. Dependency *has not been* sufficiently defined. The team will need to further define (or study) the dependency of *Y* on factor *X*s. Possible methods to define dependency include:

- Run simulation or design of experiment (DOE).
- Optimize significant factors under the given constraints.
- Develop a prediction equation/mathematical model.

Factors can be *continuous* or *discrete*, but risk assessment is critical in both situations.

- If factors are *continuous*, and the team needs to develop a model to predict process behavior and to solve the issue, team will need to develop a *mathematical model.*
- If factors are *discrete*, and can be set at different levels, the team will need to determine the best possible combination with identified factor values (levels) under the given constraints.

When dependency *has not been* defined sufficiently, two tools are commonly used:

- Design of experiments (DOE)
- Simulation

If the project team is not confident about the relationship between independent variables and the dependent variable, then the next step is to design and conduct a DOE (see Section 5.3, *Introduction to the Design of Experiments*).

Before moving on to the next section, consider the four scenarios in Exercise 5.2. These scenarios have been developed to identify an improvement strategy for each scenario.

Exercise 5.2: Identifying Factors and Alternatives and Determining Improvement Strategies

Instructions: In the following scenarios, determine if each scenario is based on factors or alternatives. Determine the improvement strategy that should be implemented.

Case 1. To Improve Average Patient Treatment Time in an Emergency Room
A Six Sigma team has completed a project to improve treatment time in an emergency department of a hospital. The team identified critical *X*s for fast treatment as:

- Attending physican
- Diagnostic equipment

The team modeled the relationship of these factors to average treatment time required to treat emergency room patients. They used two-way ANOVA (analysis of variance) with existing data to develop a useful model. The team used the model to assess the impact of each factor on treatment time and to assess interation of the factors with each other. This type of analysis helped them to develop an alternate solution.

❑ Factors

or

❑ Alternatives?

Any improvement strategy?

Case 2: To Improve Product Demand that Will Lead to Increased Revenue
A Six Sigma team project has examined methods to improve demand for a product, which would increase revenue. To attract potential customers, the team decided to educate them about the products that are offered by the company. The team also tried to identify key *X*s to improve demand:

- Product price
- Customer income
- Customer taste

To solve the problem, the team needed to model the relationship of these key *X*s to product demand and determine which key *X*s would eventually increase revenue to the level that is required to meet the target of business leadership. They used multiple regression analysis with historical data to develop a useful model. The team used the model to assess the relative impact of each key *X* on demand and then developed an alternative solution based on the analysis of information.

- ❑ Factors

  or

- ❑ Alternatives?

Any improvement strategy?

Case 3. To Reduce Process Variation and Cycle Time for Assembling Electromechanical Products

A Six Sigma team project is to reduce process variation, assembly, and test cycle time for electromechanical products. Work flow analysis showed that four separate processes had evolved in different assembly and test areas as a result of upgraded products. However, existing processes had not been documented or standardized. Frequent delays occurred from part shortages as well as from excess inventory of the wrong parts.

After observing the process for each model, the team decided to develop a generic work flow diagram for all products and, subsequently, to modify this common process to fit the individual products. The team worked with process engineers from each product group to build and validate a generic work flow process chart. Then, the cross-functional process team developed, tested, and implemented process instructions that were tailored to each product being assembled and tested.

- ❑ Factors

  or

- ❑ Alternatives?

Any improvement strategy?

Case 4. To Increase the Number and Quality of Service Contract Leads for a Service-Providing Business

A Six Sigma team has as a project to increase the number and quality of service leads for a service-providing business. The team reviewed service calls from the previous year. They determined that the business lost a large number of desirable customers to competitors due to prospective customers receiving incomplete service information. The team decided to attract potential customers by providing them with better information about the services that are available. They developed methods to accomplish this:

- Mass mailing of printed service literature
- Testomonials from existing customers
- Calls to customers of competitors
- Advertising a quick service-response time

Evaluation of data from the trials showed that advertising a quick service-response time generated the most service business.

- ❑ Factors

  or

- ❑ Alternatives?

Any improvement strategy?

5.3 INTRODUCTION TO THE DESIGN OF EXPERIMENTS (DOE)

If the premise that new knowledge is most often obtained by careful analysis and that interpretation of data is accepted, then paramount is giving considerable thought and effort to planning data collection so that maximum information is obtained with the least expenditure of resources.

What is an experiment? Different definitions are available for the word *experiment*. For our purposes, consider an experiment to be "a planned inquiry to obtain new facts or to confirm or deny the results of previous experiments, where such inquiry would aid the team in the decision process." Some conducting experiments might comment that the results of this "experiment" are remarkably well-behaved and that they exhibit little of the variation with which they have to contend. However, these results will serve the purposes of the team. For example, the objective of this "experiment" is to compare the speed of two machines. The objective can be stated in two ways: "Is there *any difference* in speed?" and "To test the hypothesis that there is *no difference* in speed." The second stated objective, which is related to the first, is to estimate the size of the difference in speed. Almost all experiments are carried out for one or both of these objectives: testing the hypothesis and estimating the differences in the effect of various treatments.

Experiments are performed in all disciplines—engineering, scientific, financial, and marketing—and are a major part of the discovery and learning process. Decisions that are made based on the results of an experiment are dependent on how the experiment was conducted. Therefore, the design of an experiment (DOE) plays a major role in the problem solution.

What is a design of an experiment? A DOE is a formal plan for conducting an experiment. It includes the choice of responses, factors, levels, blocks, and treatments and also allows for planned grouping, randomization, repetition, and/or replication. DOE identifies how factors (independent variables, *X*s) individually and in combination affect the process and its output (dependent variables, *Y*s). A DOE develops a mathematical relationship and determines the best configuration or combination of independent variables, *X*s. A DOE is a most efficient tool.

Analysis of the results from a DOE is not difficult, especially if computer-based tools such as MINITAB software are utilized. Because computing technology is inexpensive and easily available, computer-based tools are the best way to conduct experiments. *Remember*: The best analysis in the world cannot rescue a poorly designed experiment.

DOE accomplishes the following:

- Identifies significant *X*s and also helps the team to narrow a list to the most potential *X*s and their impact on the process.
- Develops a quantitative relationship between *X*s and *Y*s.
- Identifies interactions among *X*s and if any interactions affect *Y*s, helping the team in their decision-making process.
- Identifies the best values of *X*s to optimize *Y*s for the defined process constraints.

5.3.1 The Completely Randomized Single-Factor Experiment

Begin with considering how an experiment would be designed for testing the differential effect of raw material of the same specifications from different suppliers on the output product quality. Although this concept has already been discussed in Chapter 4 (***A**nalyze*), some additional mathematical detail will now be given.

Suppose there are m different suppliers of the same material that are to be compared (a single-factor treatment). The product output for the raw material (treatments) of each of the m suppliers is a random variable. Observed data are presented in Table 5.1, where:

Y_{ij} = the jth observation (output product quality) taken under treatment i (material supplier i)

$i = 1, 2, 3, \ldots, m$

$j = 1, 2, 3, \ldots, n$ (number of observations)

Observations presented in Table 5.1 are the *linear statistical model*, where:

$$Y_{ij} = \mu + \tau_i + \varepsilon_{ij}$$

μ = Overall mean (parameter common to all treatments)

Table 5.1. Data for One-Way Classification ANOVA

Treatment, i (Supplier Material)	Observation, j (Output Product Quality)	Totals	Averages
1	Y_{11} Y_{12} ... Y_{1n}	$Y_{1.}$	$\bar{Y}_1$
|			
m	Y_{m1} Y_{m2} ...Y_{mn}	$Y_{m.}$	$\bar{Y}_m$

τ_i = ith treatment effect (parameter associated with the ith treatment)

ε_{ij} = Random error component

For hypothesis testing, the model errors are assumed to be normally and independently distributed random variables with mean zero and variance σ^2 [abbreviated as NID(0, σ^2)]. The variance σ^2 is assumed constant for all levels of the factor. The above model equation is known as the *one-way classification analysis of variance* (ANOVA) because only one factor is investigated.

In the *fixed-effect model*, the treatment effects τ_1 are usually defined as deviations from the overall mean, so that:

$$\sum_{i=1}^{m} \tau_i = 0$$

Therefore, to test the equality of the *m* treatments (material suppliers) effects, the appropriate hypotheses are:

H_0: $\tau_1 = \tau_2 = \ldots = \tau_m = 0$

H_1: $\tau_i \neq 0$ for at least one i

The process logic is the same as that in Chapter 4, ***A**nalyze.*

5.3.2 The Random-Effect Model

In several situations, the factor of interest could be a large number of possible levels. Suppose a Six Sigma team was interested in drawing conclusions about the entire population of factor levels. If the team had selected m of these levels from the population of factor levels, then the team could say that the factors were random factors. Since the levels of the factor actually used in the experiment were chosen randomly, the conclusions reached would be valid for the entire population of factor levels. The team would assume that the population of factor levels is either of infinite size or large enough to be considered infinite.

The linear statistical model uses the same equation, but in this case, it is called the *components of variance* or the *random-effect* model:

$$Y_{ij} = \mu + \tau_i + \varepsilon_{ij}$$

where:

τ_i and ε_{ij} are independent random variables

If the variance of τ_i is σ_τ^2, then the variance of any observation is

$$V(Y_{ij}) = \sigma_\tau^2 + \sigma^2$$

where:

σ_τ^2 and σ^2 are variance components

In order to test hypotheses in this model, requirements are that:

$\{\varepsilon_{ij}\}$ are NID$(0, \sigma^2)$ and

$\{\tau_i\}$ are NID$(0, \sigma_\tau^2)$ and that:

τ_i and ε_{ij} are independent

The assumption, that the $\{\tau_i\}$ are independent random variables, implies that the unusal assumption of:

$$\sum_{i=1}^{m} \tau_i = 0$$

from the fixed-effect model, does not apply to the random-effect model.

The sum of squares identity is the same:

$$SS_{Total} = SS_{Treatment} + SS_{Error}$$

and the appropriate testing hypotheses are:

$$H_0\text{: } \sigma_\tau^2 = 0$$

$$H_1\text{: } \sigma_\tau^2 > 0$$

- Null hypothesis, if $\sigma_\tau^2 = 0$, all treatments are identical.
- Alternate hypothesis, if $\sigma_\tau^2 > 0$, then there is variability between treatments.

$(SS_{Error}/\sigma^2) \sim$ Chi-square distribution with $(N - m)$ degrees of freedom, where N = total number of observations, m = total number of treatments

and under the null hypothesis,

$(SS_{Treatment}/\sigma^2) \sim$ Chi-square distribution with $(m - 1)$ degrees of freedom

Since both random variables are independent, therefore, under the null hypothesis, the ratio:

$$F_0 = \frac{\left(\frac{SS_{Treatment}}{m-1}\right)}{\left(\frac{SS_{Error}}{N-m}\right)}$$

$$F_0 = \frac{MS_{Treatment}}{MS_{Error}}$$

where:

$F \sim \text{df}((m - 1), (N - m))$

Usually estimating the variance components (σ^2 and σ_τ^2) in the model is needed. The procedure used to estimate σ^2 and σ_τ^2 is called the *analysis of variance.* The procedure consists of equating the expected mean squares to their observed value in the analysis of variance table and solving for the variance components. When equating observed and expected mean squares in the one-way classification random-effect model, the following is obtained:

$MS_{Treatment} = \sigma^2 + n\sigma_\tau^2$

where:

n = Number of replicates and

$MS_{Error} = \sigma^2$

Therefore, the estimators of the variance components are

$\hat{\sigma}^2 = MS_{Error}$

$\hat{\sigma}_\tau^2 = (MS_{Treatment} - MS_{Error})/n$ and

$\hat{V}(Y_{ij}) = \hat{\sigma}_\tau^2 + \hat{\sigma}^2$

For unequal sample size, replace n in the above equation with n_0,

$$n_0 = \frac{1}{m-1}\left[\sum_{i=1}^{m} n_i - \frac{\sum_{i=1}^{m} n_i^2}{\sum_{i=1}^{m} n_i}\right]$$

Note: Sometimes the analysis of variance method produces a negative estimate of the variance component. Since variance components are by definition non-negative, a negative estimate of the variance component is troublesome. Some solutions include:

- Accept the estimate and use it as a proof that the true value of the variance component is zero, assuming that sampling variation has created the negative estimate. This has some intuitive appeal, but it will disturb the statistical properties of other estimates.
- Reestimate the negative variance component with a method that always yields non-negative estimates.
- Consider the negative estimate as evidence that the assumed linear model is not correct. Another study with an assumption of a more appropriate model may be needed.

This concept will now be presented in Example 5.3.

Example 5.3: A Single-Factor Experiment Involving the Random-Effect Model

A company that manufactures window screen materials weaves screen material on a number of looms. The company is interested in determining loom-to-loom variability in tensile strength of the screen material. Tensile strength of the screen material has been varying between 86 and 104 psi, with an average tensile strength of 95 psi. The minimum requirement is 90 psi. A process engineer has redesigned the production process to reduce variation in the tensile strength to between 90 and 100 psi.

To validate the production process, the process engineer has set up an experiment to investigate the tensile strength of the screen material. The process engineer selects four looms at random and makes four strength determinations on

Table 5.2A. Sample Data from Four Screen Looming Machines

Screen Looming Machine	Observations (Window Screen Material Tensile Strength, psi)					
SLM	1	2	3	4	**Total**	**Mean**
SLM1	95	96	91	98	380	95
SLM2	96	95	90	97	378	94.5
SLM3	99	97	93	99	388	97
SLM4	98	95	92	96	381	95.25
					1527	95.44

Table 5.2B. One-Way ANOVA Data for Screen Looming Machines

One-Way ANOVA: Observation (Tensile vs. Screen Looming Machines, SLM)

Analysis of Variance for Observation

Source	**df**	**SS**	**MS**	**F**	**P**
Screen L	3	14.19	4.73	0.58	0.639
Error	12	97.75	8.15		
Total	15	111.94			

Level	**N**	**Mean**	**SD**
SLM1	4	95.00	2.94
SLM2	4	94.50	3.11
SLM3	4	97.00	2.83
SLM4	4	95.25	2.50

Individual 95% CIs for Mean Based on Pooled SD

```
-----+---------+---------+---------+-
       (-----------*-----------)
    (-----------*-----------)
                (-----------*-----------)
        (-----------*-----------)
-----+---------+---------+---------+-
   92.5      95.0      97.5     100.0
```

Pooled SD = 2.85

screen material samples chosen at random from each loom. The collected data are presented in Table 5.2A.

Solution:

MINITAB software was utilized to develop an ANOVA table as presented in Table 5.2B.

The F table value at $\alpha = 0.05$, and df (3, 12) is equal to 3.49. Since $F_{calculated} < F_{table}$, therefore, the manufacturing process on these loom machines is not significantly different.

The process standard deviation can be estimated as follows:

$$\hat{\sigma}_\tau^2 = (MS_{Treatment} - MS_{Error})/n$$
$$= (4.73 - 8.15) / 4$$
$$= -0.855$$
$$\hat{V}(Y_{ij}) = \hat{\sigma}_\tau^2 + \hat{\sigma}^2$$
$$= -0.855 + 8.15$$
$$= 7.295$$

The estimated process standard deviation is:

$$\hat{\sigma}_Y = \sqrt{\hat{V}(Y_{ij})}$$
$$= \sqrt{(7.295)}$$
$$= 2.7$$

The pooled standard deviation (SD) using MINITAB software is 2.85 as shown in an ANOVA table (see Table 5.2B).

5.3.3 Factorial Experiments

When there are several interesting independent factors (*X*s) for an experiment, a factorial design should be used. Factors vary together in these experiments. A factorial experiment indicates that in each complete trial or replicate of the experiment, all possible combinations of the levels of the factors are investigated.

The following discussion will illustrate a simple factorial experiment. There are two factors *P* and *Q*, with *p* levels of factor *P* and *q* levels of factor *Q*. Each replicate would have all *pq* treatment combinations. The effect of a factor is defined as the change in response produced by a change in the level of this factor. This change is called the *main effect* because it refers to the independent factors in the study. Consider the data related to *P* and *Q* factors as presented in Table 5.3.

The main effect of factor *P* is the average difference of outputs between the levels $(P_2 - P_1)$ or:

$$P = ((35 + 45) / 2) - ((15 + 25) / 2)$$
$$= 20$$

i.e., changing factor *P* from level 1 to level 2 creates an average response increase of 20 units. Similarly, the main effect of factor *Q* is:

Table 5.3. Factorial Experiment with Two Factors

	Factor Q	
Factor P	Q_1	Q_2
P_1	15	25
P_2	35	45

Table 5.4. Factorial Experiment with Interaction

	Factor Q	
Factor P	Q_1	Q_2
P_1	15	25
P_2	35	0

$$Q = ((25 + 45) / 2) - ((15 + 35) / 2)$$
$$= 10$$

Sometimes, there is a difference in response between the levels of one factor and the levels of the other factor. Sample data are presented in Table 5.4. At Q_1 level of Q, while changing P from level from P_1 to P_2, the P effect is:

$$P = 35 - 15 = 20$$

Similarly, at Q_2 level of Q, while changing P level from P_1 to P_2, the P effect is:

$$P = 0 - 25 = -25$$

and the main effect of P is:

$$P = ((35 + 0)/2) - ((15 + 25)/2)$$
$$= -2.5$$

The impact is greater when the effect of P is examined at different levels of factor Q, but the main effect is not that significant. Therefore, knowledge of the PQ interaction is more useful than knowledge of the main effect. Sometimes a significant interaction may hide the significance of main effects. The data presented in Tables 5.3 and 5.4 are also presented graphically in Figures 5.5A and 5.5B, respectively.

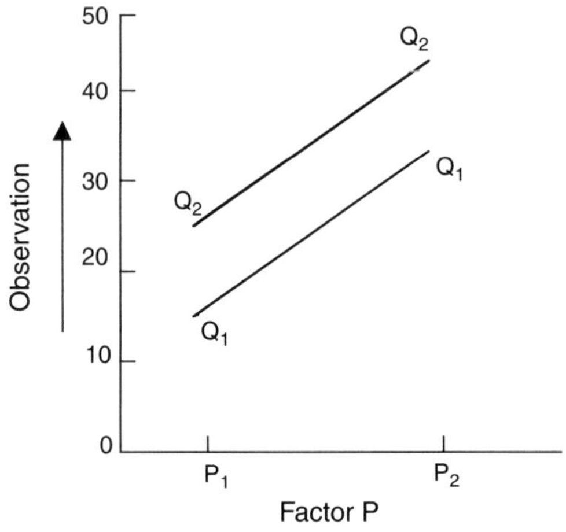

Figure 5.5A. Two-Factors Experiment with No Interaction (Using Table 5.3 Data)

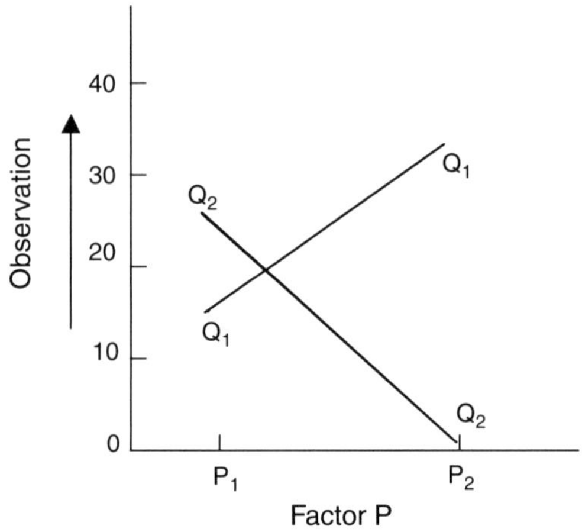

Figure 5.5B. Two-Factors Experiment with Interaction (Using Table 5.4 Data)

5.3.4 DOE Terminology

Definitions of commonly used terms include:

- Independent Variable—Independent variables, variable Xs, are commonly known as factors. A factor may be discrete or continuous. If the factor is discrete, factor levels would naturally exist, which would be used in the experiment. If a factor is continuous, it must be classified into two levels: low and high.

- Dependent Variable—The value of the dependent variable is assumed to be unknown and is symbolized by *Y*. The dependent variable is often called the response variable.
- Factor—A factor is an input in the experiment and could be a controlled or an uncontrolled variable whose impact on a response is being studied in the experiment. A factor might be qualitative (e.g., different operators, machine types) or might be quantitative (e.g., distance in feet or miles, time in minutes).
- Level—Levels are the input values of a factor being studied in an experiment. Levels should be set far enough apart that effects on the dependent variable *Y* can be detected. Levels are generally referred to as "–1" and "1." A level is also known as a *treatment*. Therefore, each level is a treatment.
- Factorial $k1 \times k2 \times k3$ ...—Factorial $k1 \times k2 \times k3$ ... is a basic description of a factorial experiment design. Each *k* represents a factor and the value of *k* is the number of levels of interest for that factor, e.g., a $3 \times 2 \times 2$ design indicates that there are three input variables (factors). One input has three levels and the other two have two levels.
- Experimental Run (Test Run)—An experimental run is one or more observations of the output variable for a defined level of input variable(s).
- Treatment Combination—Identifying the experiment runs using a set of specific levels of each input variable is known as treatment combination. A full experiment uses all the treatment combinations for all the factors, e.g., a $3 \times 2 \times 2$ factorial experimental design will have 12 possible treatment combinations in the experiment.
- Repetition—Repetition is running more than one experiment consecutively using the same treatment combinations.
- Replication—In replication, the same experimental setup is used more than once with no change in the treatment levels to collect more than one data point. Replicating an experiment allows the user to estimate the residual or experimental error.
- Balanced Design—In a balanced design, each level for any one factor is repeated the same number of times for all possible combination levels of the other factors, e.g., a factorial design of two factors (A and B) and two levels (–1, 1) will have four runs as shown in Table 5.5.

Table 5.5. Factorial Design Runs for 2 × 2

Run	Factors → A	B
1	–1	–1
2	1	–1
3	–1	1
4	1	1

- Unbalanced Design—A designed experiment that does not meet the criteria of balanced design is known as an unbalanced design, e.g., a design in which each experimental level for any one factor is not repeated the same number of times for all possible levels of the other factors.

5.3.5 Two-Factor Factorial Experiments

The easiest type of factorial experiment is considered to be a situation in which there are only two factors (e.g., A and B). Assuming "a" levels of factor A and "b" levels of factor B, let there be n replicates of the experiment and let each replicate contain all ab treatment combinations. The two-factor factorial is a completely randomized design in which any observation may be described by the linear model that follows:

$$Y_{ijk} = \mu + \tau_i + \beta_j + (\tau\beta)_{ij} + \varepsilon_{ijk}$$

where:

Y_{ijk} = ijth observation in the kth replicate

$i = 1, 2, \ldots, a$

$j = 1, 2, \ldots, b$

$k = 1, 2, \ldots, n$

μ = Overall mean effect

τ_i = Effect of the ith level of factor A

β_j = Effect of the jth level of factor B

$(\tau\beta)_{ij}$ = Effect of interaction between A and B

ε_{ijk} = A NID$(0, \sigma^2)$ random error component

Because two factors are under study, the process used is called a two-way analysis of variance. Therefore, to test:

Table 5.6. ANOVA Table for a Two-Way Classification, Fixed-Effect Model

Source of Variation	Sum of Squares	Degrees of Freedom	Mean Square	F_0
A treatments	SS_A	a – 1	$MS_A = SS_A/(a-1)$	MS_A/MS_E
B treatments	SS_B	b – 1	$MS_B = SS_B/(b-1)$	MS_B/MS_E
Interaction	SS_{AB}	(a – 1)(b – 1)	$MS_{AB} = SS_{AB}/(a-1)(b-1)$	MS_{AB}/MS_E
Error	SS_E	a b(n – 1)	$MS_E = SS_E/(a\,b)(n-1)$	
Total	SS_T	abn - 1		

H_0: $\tau_i = 0$ (no row factor effects)

H_0: $\beta_j = 0$ (no column factor effects)

H_0: $(\tau\beta)_{ij} = 0$ (no interaction effects)

This would lead to an ANOVA table for the two-way classification with fixed-effect model as presented in Table 5.6.

F distribution with:

- Numerator degrees of freedom = The number of degrees of freedom for the numerator mean square
- Denominator degrees of freedom = $ab(n-1)$

Detailed statistical logic may be found in any DOE textbook.

Commonly followed steps to set up and run an experiment include:

Step 1. Select project's dependent variable, *Y*.

Step 2. Select independent variables, *X*s.

Step 3. Select the test levels for each independent variable (*X*).

Step 4. Perform risk analysis.

Step 5. Select the design and set up the experiment.

Step 6. Run the experiment and collect data.

Step 7. Analyze data.

Step 8. Perform statistical testing, e.g., hypothesis testing, prediction model, etc.

Step 9. Draw conclusions and complete confirmation runs.

This concept is explained by Example 5.4.

Table 5.7A. Collected Data: 3 × 3 Factorial Experiment with Four Replications

	Temperature (°F)					
Material	**Low**		**Medium**		**High**	
1	131	150	35	41	21	69
	75	175	79	76	81	59
2	149	187	135	123	26	69
	160	127	107	116	58	45
3	137	109	173	121	95	105
	170	159	151	140	83	61

Example 5.4: A Two-Factorial Experiment

This experiment involves a storage battery used in the launching mechanism of a shoulder-fired ground-to-air missile. Three material types are used in the test battery plates. The objective is to recommend a battery that is relatively unaffected by ambient temperature. The output response from the battery is expected to be maximum voltage. Three temperature levels were used in the test, and a factorial experiment with four replications was designed to run the experiment. The collected data are presented in Table 5.7A (the body of the table is maximum voltage data or battery output response). As a hired consultant, what plate material would you recommend?

Solution:

- Dependent variable—Battery output response in voltage
- Independent variables—Material and temperature (three levels for each)

The MINITAB software tool is used to analyze the relationship between independent and dependent variables through the factorial design. Assuming that the independent variables are fixed, test:

H_0: $\tau_i = 0$ (no material effects)

H_0: $\beta_j = 0$ (no temperature effects)

H_0: $(\tau\beta)_{ij} = 0$ (no interaction effects)

Divide the corresponding mean square by mean square error. Each of these ratios would follow an F distribution with degrees of freedom given in Table 5.6. An ANOVA table was developed with MINITAB software (Table 5.7B).

Table 5.7B. ANOVA Information for 3 × 3 Factorial Experiments for Example 5.4

Factorial Design: General Factorial Design

Factors:	**2**	**Factor Levels:**	**3, 3**
Runs:	**36**	**Replicates:**	**4**

General Linear Model: Battery Voltage vs. Material, Temperature (°F)

Factor	**Type**	**Levels**	**Values**
Material	Fixed	3	1 2 3
Temperature	Fixed	3	1 2 3

Analysis of Variance for Battery, using Adjusted SS for Tests

Source	**df**	**Seq SS**	**Adj SS**	**Adj MS**	**F**	**P**
Material	2	11084.7	11084.7	5542.3	8.80	0.001
Temperature (°F)	2	38280.5	38280.5	19140.3	30.40	0.000
Material/ Temperature (°F)	4	9471.3	9471.3	2367.8	3.76	0.015
Error	27	16998.5	16998.5	629.6		
Total	**35**	**75835.0**				

Since table $F_{0.05,2,27} = 3.35$ and $F_{0.05,4,27} = 2.73$, the conclusion is that material type and temperature levels affect battery output voltage (a *significant* interaction); futhermore, there is also an interaction *between* these factors. A graph of the battery output voltage averages vs. the type of battery plate material at three different temperatures (low, medium, and high) has been plotted in Figure 5.6A.

Plate Material 3 provides a higher voltage output for a wider temperature range. There is an interaction between Materials 2 and 3 at a low temperature and between Materials 1 and 2 at a high temperature.

Model Adequacy Checking

Residuals from a factorial experiment are important in assessing model adequacy. Residuals are the differences between the observations and the corresponding cell averages:

$$E_{ijk} = Y_{ijk} - \overline{Y}_{ij}$$

The normal probability plot of the voltage residuals is shown in Figure 5.6B. This plot has tails that do not fall exactly along a straight line passed through the center of the plot. This indicates that there are some potential problems with the normality assumption, but that the deviation from normality does not appear severe.

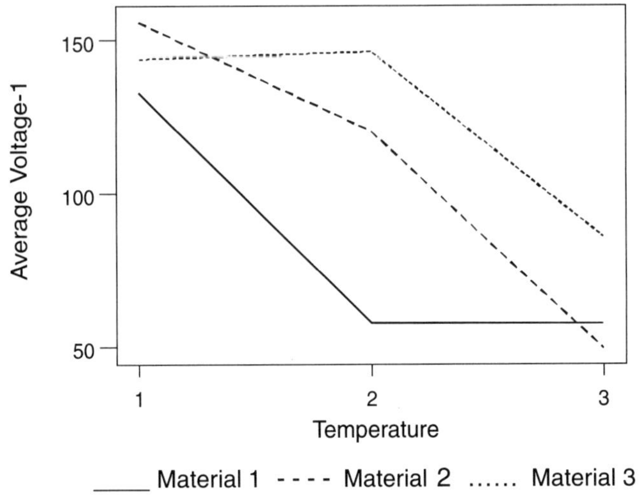

Figure 5.6A. Battery Output Average Voltage for Different Plate Materials and Ambient Temperatures

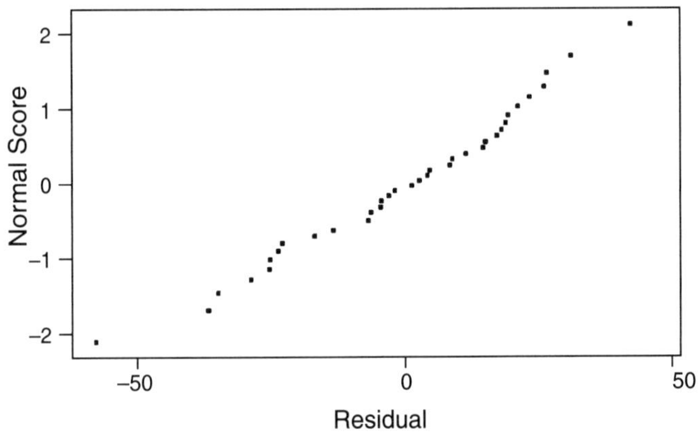

Figure 5.6B. Normal Probability Plot of the Residuals (Response Is Battery)

A plot of the residuals vs. the battery output voltages is shown in Figure 5.6C. In this case, there is some randomness at high voltage output. The plot of residuals against the voltage output is shown in Figure 5.6D. Here, there is good randomness in data. Since the experimental data closely follow the model, the recommendation would be to use Material 3 for the battery plate.

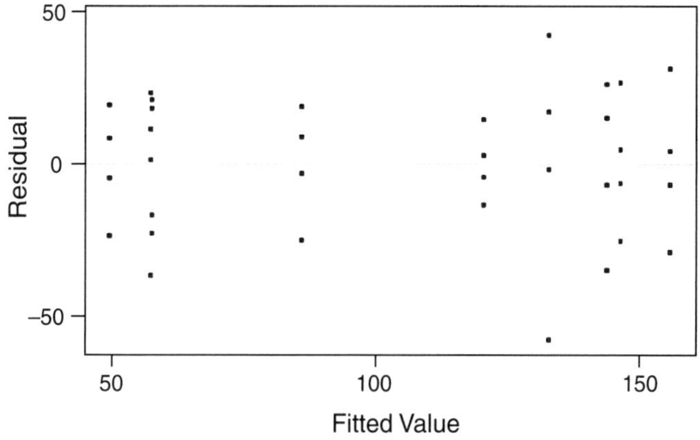

Figure 5.6C. Residuals vs. Battery Output Voltage: Residuals vs. Fitted Values (Response Is Battery)

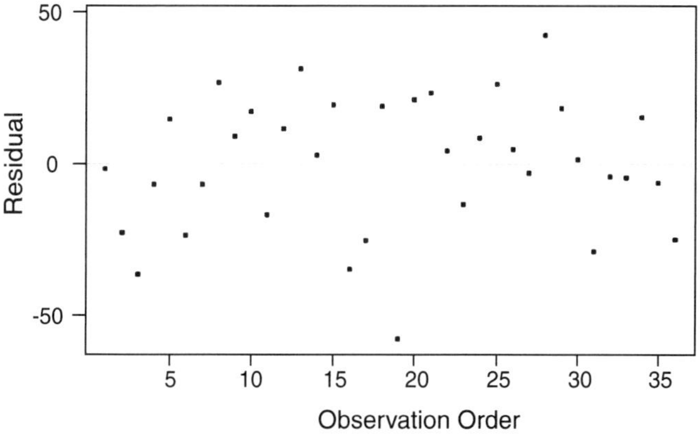

Figure 5.6D. Random Plot of Residuals vs. Battery Output: Residuals vs. Order of the Data (Response Is Battery)

Exercise 5.3: Investigating the Effect of Glass Type and Phosphor on Television Screen Brightness

Investigate the effect of two factors (glass type and phosphor) on the brightness of a television screen. The response variable to be measured is the current necessary (in microamps) to obtain a specified brightness level. The collected data are presented in Table 5.8. Analyze the data and draw conclusions, assuming that both factors are fixed.

Table 5.8. Collected Data: Two-Factors Impact on Product (Television Screen)

	Phosphor Type		
Glass Type	1	2	3
1	280	300	290
	290	310	285
	285	295	290
2	230	260	220
	235	240	225
	240	235	230

5.3.6 Three-Factor Factorial Experiments

Many experiments involve more than two factors. As an example, let there be three factors—A, B, and C—and let there be "a" levels of factor A, "b" levels of factor B, and "c" levels of factor C. There would be abc × n total observations if there were n replicates of the complete experiment. The following equation represents a three-factor mathematical model with the assumption that A, B, and C are fixed:

$$Y_{ijkl} = \mu + \tau_i + \beta_j + \gamma_k + (\tau\beta)_{ij} + (\tau\gamma)_{ik} + (\beta\gamma)_{jk} + (\tau\beta\gamma)_{ijk} + \varepsilon_{ijkl}$$

where:

$i = 1, 2, \ldots, a$

$j = 1, 2, \ldots, b$

$k = 1, 2, \ldots, c$

$l = 1, 2, \ldots, n$

There must be at least two replicates ($n \geq 2$) to compute an error sum of squares. The F-tests on main effects and interactions follow directly from the expected mean squares. The ANOVA table is presented in Table 5.9.

The following are computing formulas for the sums of squares:

$$SS_T = \sum_{i=1}^{a}\sum_{j=1}^{b}\sum_{k=1}^{c}\sum_{l=1}^{n} Y_{ijkl}^2 - \left(\frac{Y_{....}^2}{abcn}\right)$$

$$SS_A = \sum_{i=1}^{a} \frac{Y_{i...}^2}{bcn} - \frac{Y_{....}^2}{abcn}$$

$$SS_B = \sum_{j=1}^{b} \frac{Y_{.j..}^2}{acn} - \frac{Y_{....}^2}{abcn}$$

$$SS_C = \sum_{k=1}^{c} \frac{Y_{..k.}^2}{abn} - \frac{Y_{....}^2}{abcn}$$

$$SS_{AB} = \sum_{i=1}^{a}\sum_{j=1}^{b} \frac{Y_{ij..}^2}{cn} - \frac{Y_{....}^2}{abcn} - SS_A - SS_B$$

$$= SS_{subtotals(AB)} - SS_A - SS_B$$

$$SS_{AC} = \sum_{i=1}^{a}\sum_{k=1}^{c} \frac{Y_{i.k.}^2}{bn} - \frac{Y_{....}^2}{abcn} - SS_B - SS_C$$

$$= SS_{subtotals(AC)} - SS_A - SS_C$$

$$SS_{BC} = \sum_{j=1}^{b}\sum_{k=1}^{c} \frac{Y_{.jk.}^2}{an} - \frac{Y_{....}^2}{abcn} - SS_B - SS_C$$

$$= SS_{subtotals(BC)} - SS_B - SS_C$$

$$SS_{ABC} = \sum_{i=1}^{a}\sum_{j=1}^{b}\sum_{k=1}^{c} \frac{Y_{ijk.}^2}{abcn} - \frac{Y_{....}^2}{abcn} - SS_A - SS_B - SS_C - SS_{AB} - SS_{AC} - SS_{BC}$$

$$= SS_{subtotals(ABC)} - SS_A - SS_B - SS_C - SS_{AB} - SS_{AC} - SS_{BC}$$

The error sum of squares may be found by subtracting the sum of squares for each main effect and the interaction from the total sum of squares, which could be presented as:

$$SS_E = SS_T - SS_{subtotals(ABC)}$$

Obviously, factorial experiments with three or more factors are complicated and will require several runs, particularly if some of the factors have several levels (e.g., more than two). Therefore, using a certain class of factorial designs (2^k) is common if all factors are at only two levels. These designs are extremely easy to set up and analyze. Example 5.5 demonstrates how to utilize this model. (Subsection 5.3.7 will explain 2^k Factorial Design.)

Table 5.9. ANOVA Table for a Three-Factor Fixed-Effect Model

Source of Variation	Sum of Squares	Degrees of Freedom	Mean Square	Expected Mean Squares	F_0
A	SS_A	(a – 1)	MS_A	$\sigma^2 + \frac{bcn\sum\tau_i^2}{a-1}$	$F_0 = MS_A/MS_E$
B	SS_B	(b – 1)	MS_B	$\sigma^2 + \frac{acn\sum\beta_j^2}{b-1}$	$F_0 = MS_B/MS_E$
C	SS_C	(c – 1)	MS_C	$\sigma^2 + \frac{abn\sum\gamma_k^2}{c-1}$	$F_0 = MS_C/MS_E$
AB	SS_{AB}	(a – 1)(b – 1)	MS_{AB}	$\sigma^2 + \frac{cn\sum\sum(\tau\beta)_{ij}^2}{(a-1)(b-1)}$	$F_0 = MS_{AB}/MS_E$
AC	SS_{AC}	(a – 1)(c – 1)	MS_{AC}	$\sigma^2 + \frac{bn\sum\sum(\tau\gamma)_{ik}^2}{(a-1)(c-1)}$	$F_0 = MS_{AC}/MS_E$
BC	SS_{BC}	(b – 1)(c – 1)	MS_{BC}	$\sigma^2 + \frac{an\sum\sum(\beta\gamma)_{jk}^2}{(b-1)(c-1)}$	$F_0 = MS_{BC}/MS_E$
ABC	SS_{ABC}	(a – 1)(b – 1)(c – 1)	MS_{ABC}	$\sigma^2 + \frac{n\sum\sum\sum(\tau\beta\gamma)_{ijk}^2}{(a-1)(b-1)(c-1)}$	$F_0 = MS_{ABC}/MS_E$
Error	SS_E	abc(n – 1)	MS_E		σ^2
Total	SS_T	abcn – 1			

Example 5.5: Analyze the Level of Significance of Three Factors

A processing engineer is studying the surface finish of a component that is produced in a turning department. Three key factors affect the surface finish of the component—tool feed rate (A), depth of cut (B), and tool angle (C). All three factors have been assigned two levels and two replicates of a factorial design to collect the data for the experiment setup. Surface finish data are presented in coded form in Table 5.10A. In-process data are presented in Table 5.10B. Analyze the data and state at which level of significance these factors are significant.

To test the data, set the null hypotheses:

H_0: $\tau_i = 0$ (no tool feed rate effect)

H_0: $\beta_j = 0$ (no depth of cut effect)

H_0: $\gamma_k = 0$ (no tool angle effect)

H_0: $(\tau\beta)_{ij} = 0$ (no interaction effect of tool feed rate and depth of cut)

H_0: $(\tau\gamma)_{ik} = 0$ (no interaction effect of tool feed rate and tool angle)

H_0: $(\beta\gamma)_{jk} = 0$ (no interaction effect of depth of cut and tool angle)

H_0: $(\tau\beta\gamma)_{ijk} = 0$ (no interaction effect of all three factors—tool feed rate, depth of cut, and tool angle)

The following analysis shows the relation of the data with the model. (This analysis can easily be done using MINITAB software.)

$$SS_T = \sum_{i=1}^{a}\sum_{j=1}^{b}\sum_{k=1}^{c}\sum_{l=1}^{n} Y_{ijkl}^2 - \left(\frac{Y_{....}^2}{abcn}\right) = 1998 - ((176)^2/16) = 62$$

$$SS_A = \sum_{i=1}^{a}\frac{Y_{i...}^2}{bcn} - \frac{Y_{....}^2}{abcn} = ((79)^2 + (97)^2/8) - ((176)^2/16) = 20.25$$

$$SS_B = \sum_{j=1}^{b}\frac{Y_{.j..}^2}{acn} - \frac{Y_{....}^2}{abcn} = ((82)^2 + (94)^2/8) - ((176)^2/16) = 9$$

$$SS_C = \sum_{k=1}^{c}\frac{Y_{..k.}^2}{abn} - \frac{Y_{....}^2}{abcn} = ((83)^2 + (93)^2)/8) - ((176)^2/16) = 6.25$$

$$SS_{AB} = \sum_{i=1}^{a}\sum_{j=1}^{b}\frac{Y_{ij..}^2}{cn} - \frac{Y_{....}^2}{abcn} - SS_A - SS_B$$

$$= (((40)^2 + (39)^2 + (42)^2 + (55)^2)/4) - ((176)^2/16) - 20.25 - 9 = 12.25$$

$$SS_{AC} = \sum_{i=1}^{a}\sum_{k=1}^{c}\frac{Y_{i.k.}^2}{bn} - \frac{Y_{....}^2}{abcn} - SS_A - SS_C$$

$$= (((37)^2 + (42)^2 + (46)^2 + (51)^2)/4) - ((176)^2/16) - 20.25 - 6.25 = 0$$

$$SS_{BC} = \sum_{j=1}^{b}\sum_{k=1}^{c}\frac{Y_{.jk.}^2}{an} - \frac{Y_{....}^2}{abcn} - SS_B - SS_C$$

$$= (((38)^2 + (44)^2 + (45)^2 + (49)^2)/4) - ((176)^2/16) - 9 - 6.25 = 0.25$$

$$SS_{ABC} = \sum_{i=1}^{a}\sum_{j=1}^{b}\sum_{k=1}^{c}\frac{Y_{ijk.}^2}{abcn} - \frac{Y_{....}^2}{abcn} - SS_A - SS_B - SS_C - SS_{AB} - SS_{AC} - SS_{BC}$$

$$= (((18)^2 + (22)^2 + (19)^2 + (20)^2 + (20)^2 + (22)^2 + (26)^2 + (29)^2)/2) - ((176)^2/16) - 20.25 - 9 - 6.25 - 12.25 - 0 - 0.25$$

$$= 1.0$$

$$SS_E = SS_T - SS_{subtotals(ABC)}$$

$$= 62 - 49 = 13$$

An ANOVA table is presented in Table 5.11. The following factors are significant in Table 5.11: [a]Tool Feed Rate (A) is significant at 1%; [b]Depth of Cut (B) and the interaction of Tool Feed Rate and Depth of Cut (AB) are significant at 5%; and [c]Tool Angle (C) is significant at 10%.

5.3.7 2^k Factorial Design

The 2^k factorial design is very useful if each factor is at two levels. Because each complete replicate of the design has 2^k runs or treatment combinations, the arrangement is known as 2^k factorial design. 2^k factorial designs have a greatly simplified statistical analysis. 2^k designs also form the basis of many other useful designs. The logic of two- and three-factors design will now be described.

5.3.7.1 2^2 Design

The simplest type of 2^k design is the 2^2. If there are two factors, e.g., *A* and *B*, and each factor is at two levels, generally these levels are assumed as *low* and *high* of the factor. A graphical design of 2^2 factorial is shown in Figure 5.7. The $2^2 = 4$ runs form the corners of the square. Two types of notations are used in combinations:

- Treatment Combination—This combination is represented by lowercase letters. If the letter is present, then the corresponding factor is run at its high level in that treatment combination; if the letter is absent, the factor is run at its low level. For example, treatment combination a indicates that factor *A* is at the high level. A treatment combination with both factors at the low level is represented by (1).
- Factorial Effect—The coefficients of factorial effects are always either +1 or −1.

The effects of interest in the 2^2 design are the main effects *A* and *B* and the two-factor interaction *AB*. The letters (alphanumeric) (1), *a*, *b*, and *ab* also represent the total of all *n* observations taken at these design points. The main effect of:

Table 5.10A. Coded Surface Roughness Data for Example 5.5

	Depth of Cut (B)				
	0.020 in. Tool Angle (C)		0.035 in. Tool Angle (C)		
Tool Feed Rate (A)	**12°**	**22°**	**12°**	**22°**	$Y_{i...}$
15 in./min	10	12	9	11	
	8	10	10	9	79
Subtotal	18	22	19	20	
25 in./min	9	10	12	15	
	11	12	14	14	97
Subtotal	20	22	26	29	
B × C Totals $Y_{.jk\cdot}$	**38**	**44**	**45**	**49**	**Y.... = 176**

Table 5.10B. In-Process Coded Surface Roughness Data for Example 5.5

A × B Totals $Y_{ij..}$			A × C Totals $Y_{i.k.}$		
	B			C	
A	0.020	0.035	**A**	12	22
15	40	39	15	37	42
25	42	55	25	46	51
$Y_{.j..}$	**82**	**94**	$Y_{..k.}$	**83**	**93**

- A = (Average observations on the right side) – (Average observations on the left side)
  $= ((a + ab)/2n) - ((b + (1))/2n)$
  $= (1/2n)\,[a + ab - b - (1)]$

Similarly, the main effect of

- $B = (1/2n)\,[b + ab - a - (1)]$

and

- $AB = (1/2n)\,[ab + (1) - a - b]$

Table 5.11. ANOVA for Example 5.5

Source Variation	Sum of Squares	Degrees of Freedom	Mean Square	F_o	F_{table}
Tool Feed Rate (A)	20.25	1	20.25	12.462[a]	$F_{0.01,1,8} = 11.26$
Depth of Cut (B)	9	1	9	5.538[b]	$F_{0.05,1,8} = 5.32$
Tool Angle (C)	6.25	1	6.25	3.486[c]	$F_{0.10,1,8} = 3.46$
AB	12.25	1	12.25	7.538[b]	$F_{0.05,1,8} = 5.32$
AC	0	1	0	0	
BC	0.25	1	0.25	0.154	
ABC	1.00	1	1.00	0.615	
Error	13.00	8	1.625		
Total	**60.0**	**15**			

[a]Tool feed rate (A) is significant at 1%; [b]depth of cut (B) and interaction of tool feed rate and depth of cut (AB) are significant at 5%; [c]tool angle (C) is significant at 10%.

The quantities in brackets are known as *contrasts*, e.g., the A contrast is

$$\text{Contrast}_A = a + ab - b - (1)$$

Table 5.12 can be used to determine the sign (plus or minus) for each treatment combination for a particular contrast. The column headings are the main effects A and B and AB interaction, with I representing the total. The row headings refer to the treatment combinations. *Important*: The sign in the AB column is the product of the signs from columns A and B. The sum of squares for A, B, and AB can be obtained as follows:

$$SS = (\text{contrast})^2/(n\Sigma(\text{contrast coefficients})^2)$$

Therefore,

$$SS_A = [a + \text{ab} - b - (1)]^2/4n$$

$$SS_B = [b + ab - a - (1)]^2/4n$$

$$SS_{AB} = [ab + (1) - a - \text{b}]^2/4n$$

The ANOVA is completed as usual with SS_T degrees of freedom $(4n - 1)$ and SS_E degrees of freedom $4(n - 1)$.

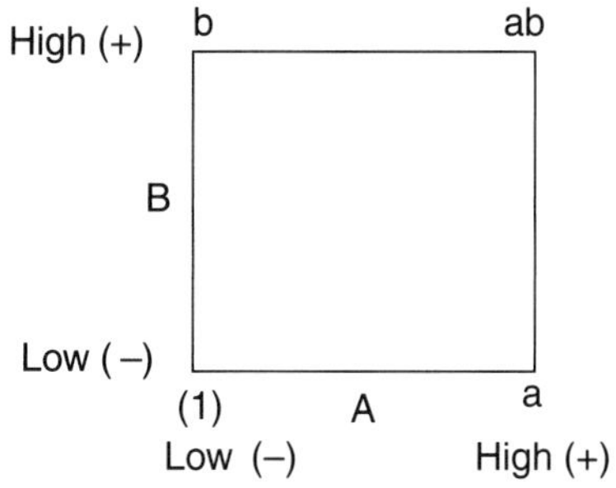

Figure 5.7. 2^2 Factorial Design

5.3.7.2 2^3 Design

The 2^2 design method presented in Section 5.3.7.1 for a factorial design with k = 2 factors each at two levels can easily be increased to more than two factors. In this section, the increase is to $k = 3$ factors, each at two levels. This design allows three main effects to be estimated (A, B, and C), with three two-factor interactions (AB, AC, and BC) and a three-factor interaction (ABC).

Table 5.13 contains the signs (plus and minus). In Table 5.13, the lowercase letters (1), *a*, *b*, *c*, *ab*, *ac*, *bc*, and *abc* represent the total of all *n* replicates at each of the eight treatment combinations in the design. The main effect of factors and interactions is as follows:

$$\mathrm{A} = (1/4n)\ [a + ab + ac + abc - b - c - bc - (1)]$$

$$\mathrm{B} = (1/4n)\ [b + \mathrm{ab} + bc + abc - a - c - ac - (1)]$$

$$\mathrm{C} = (1/4n)\ [c + ac + bc + abc - a - b - ab - (1)]$$

$$\mathrm{AB} = (1/4n)\ [ab + (1) + abc + c - b - a - bc - ac]$$

$$\mathrm{AC} = (1/4n)\ [ac + (1) + abc + b - a - c - ab - bc]$$

$$\mathrm{BC} = (1/4n)\ [bc + (1) + abc + a - b - c - ab - ac]$$

$$\mathrm{ABC} = (1/4n)\ [abc - bc - ac + c - ab + b + a - (1)]$$

As the team defines and uses the DOE tool, the team will be able to develop a better understanding of the distinctions between independent variables (*X*s) and the dependent variable (*Y*). At this point, the team must be in a position of having enough information to generate alternative solutions.

Table 5.12. Signs for Effects in 2^2 Design

Treatment Combination	Factorial Effect			
	I	A	B	AB
(1)	+	−	−	+
a	+	+	−	−
b	+	−	+	−
ab	+	+	+	+

Table 5.13. Signs for Effects in 2^3 Design

Treatment Combination	Factorial Effect							
	I	A	B	AB	C	AC	BC	ABC
(1)	+	−	−	+	−	+	+	−
a	+	+	−	−	−	−	+	+
b	+	−	+	−	−	+	−	+
ab	+	+	+	+	−	−	−	−
c	+	−	−	+	+	−	−	+
ac	+	+	−	−	+	+	−	−
bc	+	−	+	−	+	−	+	−
abc	+	+	+	+	+	+	+	+

Exercise 5.4: Analyzing Revenue and Factors that Impact Sales Revenue

A sales organization is analyzing its revenue data. The factors impacting its sales revenue are presented in Table 5.14A. As a hired consultant, based on the information provided in Tables 5.14B and 5.14C, provide recommendations.

5.4 SOLUTION ALTERNATIVES

As a Six Sigma team progresses through the analyzing phase of a project in which the team must identify objectives and alternative solutions for the product/process to achieve the defined goals/objectives, the entire improvement process may be summarized into three stages:

Table 5.14A. Factors Impacting Sales Revenue

Factor	Level	
	Low	**High**
Sales Representative's Participation	No	Yes
Sales Representative's Experience	$\leq$1 year	$>$5 years
Existing or New Customer	Existing	New
Advertising	No	Yes
Sales Promotion	No	Yes

Table 5.14B. Sales Information for Scenario 1

Scenario 1:

(A) X_1: Sales Representative's Participation
(B) X_2: Existing or New Customer
(C) X_3: Advertising

X_1	X_2	X_3	Y_1	Y_2
–	–	–	15	14
+	–	–	25	26
–	+	–	27	28
+	+	–	28	30
–	–	+	20	19
+	–	+	22	23
–	+	+	17	16
+	+	+	29	30

Table 5.14C. Sales Information for Scenario 2

Scenario 2:

(A) X_1: Sales Representative's Experience
(B) X_2: Existing or New Customer
(C) X_3: Sales Promotion

X_1	X_2	X_3	Y_1	Y_2
–	–	–	15	15
+	–	–	25	26
–	+	–	24	25
+	+	–	27	28
–	–	+	20	19
+	–	+	29	30
–	+	+	24	25
+	+	+	28	29

Table 5.15. Summarized Process Stages

Investigate Should Lead to Developing Alternative Solutions	Evaluate and Propose	Implement
• Process Mapping • Brainstorming • Creative Thinking • CTQs • Cause-and-Effect Diagram • FMEA • Benchmarking • Process/Product Cost Analysis • Problem Solving Process	• Information Collection: Qualitative and/or Quantitative • Graphing Tools • Analyzing Tools: Hypothesis Testing–Classical, Chi-Square, ANOVA, Regression, and Correlation • Criteria-Based Decision Matrix • Develop Alternatives • Cost/Benefit Analysis • Risk Analysis • Pilot Testing Alternatives • Cost/Benefit Analysis • Propose Best Alternative	• Resource Training • Resource Upgrading • Schedule/Work Breakdown Structure • Control Plan • Implementation

- Investigate
- Evaluate and Propose
- Implement

Key elements of these stages are presented in Table 5.15.

Another way of looking at the improvement process is to ask, "What constitues the bottom line of a Six Sigma project?" Some answers might include:

- To Generate Alternate Solutions—Team will need to either analyze the historical data or first collect the data and then analyze it (or a combination of both) to develop the alternative solutions. In the process, the team will need to identify constraints. The team might be able to benchmark similar processes and eliminate unrealistic or infeasible alternatives.

- To Assess Risk—The team will need to assess risk as it relates to alternative solutions and their impact on customers, the business, employees, federal, state, and local regulations, and the bottom line of the business.
- To Perform an Initial Study to Test Alternatives—An initial study may be accomplished using a small-scale experiment or by using pilot projects.
- To Evaluate and Select the Best Alternative to Meet/Exceed the Defined Objectives—As the team is solving a problem, it is important for team members to understand how their processes have evolved to the current state and to try to utilize this information to develop a comprehensive solution to the problem. This might require testing several alternatives. Because different tools are used in individual businesses for identifying, evaluating, and selecting alternative solutions, the team should check the type of tools used in its business. If the team feels comfortable with these tools, the team can utilize them. As the team goes through the improvement process, it is critical that it remains focused on the critical input variables (Xs) as identified in the **A**nalyze phase.

5.5 OVERVIEW OF TOPICS

This section will provide a brief overview of topics that have been discussed in previous chapters.

Investigate
The investigation concept is described in detail in Chapters 1, 2, and 3. Selected topics are now briefly discussed.

Process Mapping—Process mapping is generally utilized for:

- Developing and understanding a process/workflow
- Identifying alternative processes
- Eliminating redundancies, loops, waste and non-value-added activities, and delays
- Consolidating activities to streamline the process
- Facilitating resources planning

Process mapping should be developed by actual users as well as Six Sigma team members. These mappings should be analyzed. Then a real (or actual) process map should be developed. An actual process map should lead to an improved process map.

Brainstorming—One of the easiest ways to generate a high volume of ideas is by using brainstorming sessions. Concepts could be applied to generate alternatives. Mathematical/statistical tools are also a source of generating alternatives. They may be used to test the alternatives developed from brainstorming. Rules commonly followed during brainstorming session include:

- Make no judgment, analysis, or criticism of the ideas.
- Capture all ideas.
- Build on the ideas and creativity of others.
- Encourage participation by all team members.
- Limit the session. Keep the time frame short (typically 15 to 25 minutes).

Creative Thinking—The key to creative thinking is that "rules and regulations" should not stop anyone from asking questions. The team should ask questions about each element/activity of the process/product. Think about several questions while keeping the customer's needs and expectations in mind:

- Why has the activity been performed? Can it be eliminated?
- Who performs the activity? Can someone else perform it?
- Where has the work been done? Can it be done somewhere else?
- What resources are required? Where else could resources be found?
- Under what conditions is work done? Can those conditions be changed?
- What is the value added by the work? Can it be improved?

Key thought-generating questions include:

- Why? → Substitute/Eliminate?
- Who? → Sources to Substitute?
- How? → Process Change/Modify/Eliminate?
- When? → Present/Future?
- What? → Optional/Required/Eliminate?

CTQs—The product or process performance characteristics must satisfy customers. Therefore, it is important to define CTQs (critical to quality characteristics) for customers. Defining customer CTQs, requires a three-step process: Identify → Research → Translate. This process delivers:

- Prioritized internal and external customer lists; also identifies stakeholders
- Prioritized customer needs
- CTQs to support customer needs

Ensure that all information (company and customer) is in the same language. Then compare team research output with the customers' suggested needs and wants and prepare a gap analysis. This gap analysis will lead to CTQs. Simple guidelines to translate customer requirements into needs and wants include:

- State customer needs and wants.
- Have measurable terms in CTQs.
- Reflect a positive attitude in written text.
- Confirm or verify needs and wants with customers.
- Write simply and in complete sentences. Ensure specific issues are addressed.

Cause-and-Effect Diagram—A cause-and-effect diagram is an analysis tool that provides a systematic way to look at effects and the causes that create or contribute to those effects. Cause-and-effect listings are also useful to summarize knowledge about the process. A cause-and-effect diagram is designed to assist a team in categorizing all (sometimes many) potential causes of problems or issues in an orderly way and identifying root causes.

FMEA—FMEA is an iterative process. It is used for system design, manufacturing, maintenance, and failure detection. Key functions include:

- Identifying unacceptable effects that prevent achieving design requirements
- Assessing the safety of system components
- Identifying design modifications and corrective action needed to mitigate the effects of a failure on the system

FMEA helps to keep each responsible group focused on its responsibilities as the product goes through its life cycle. In the FMEA process, the system is treated as a "black box" with only its inputs and the corresponding outputs specified.

Benchmarking—Benchmarking involves sharing process and business information about one company with other company. Most businesses have developed procedures to manage and monitor the company's involvement in benchmarking visits. Before planning a visit to any external business, consult business management at your company about these policies and procedures. A benchmarking process will assist in:

- Measuring business performance or processes at a business against the best-in-class practices of other businesses
- Determining how other businesses achieve their performance levels
- Providing information to improve one's own performance

Process/Product Cost Analysis—Every business has its own methods to analyze process/product costs that should be followed. Follow the company's already-developed costing guidelines. Basic rules in a costing process can include:

- Keeping cost data as realistic as possible
- Utilizing the same logic for the present process/product as well as for the developed alternatives without adding any unrealistic cost factors, e.g., a cost element in overhead applies to one very specific process/product, but this cost element is distributed over all processes/products
- Comparing all cost data (present process/product and alternatives) in present dollars and before taxes (federal and state)

Problem-Solving Process—In many situations, a problem-solving process is designed to find a simpler or faster procedure that will result in an improvement. During a problem-solving process, listening to and acting upon the suggestions of employees who are closely involved with the process/product is important. These employees could provide information that would help the team to make a decision quickly. Commonly used steps in the problem solving process include:

- Identifying the problem area and defining the problem (issue)
- Collecting background data and designing focused questions (Apply the concepts presented in Chapters 2, 3, and 4—**D**efine, **M**easure, and **A**nalyze. Develop questions starting with "what" and "how." "What" questions are used to identify process/product elements. "Why" questions are used to solve the issue/problem.)
- Identifying employees who should participate in the discussion (Diversity in the team is critical to get new ideas. Team size should be limited to no more than 12 members.)

- Identifying a meeting facilitator so that he/she may do his/her "homework" before the meeting
- Conducting a problem-solving session and providing team members with all necessary information 1 week before the session
- Identifying and obtaining (reserving) all supportive material so that it is available at the time of the meting
- Communicating problem-solving recommendations to all interested parties and implementing the recommendation according to a developed schedule
- Recognizing the problem solving team for its achievements

Evaluate and Propose

Once process/product issues have been identified, the next steps are collecting information, utilizing presenting tools to present the collected information, and utilizing analyzing tools to analyze the collected information. Detailed supportive material about these topics may be found in Chapters 3, 4, and 5. Selected topics are now briefly discussed.

Risk Analysis—Before conducting any pilot testing, evaluate the risks (safety and security) associated with each alternative in relationhip to:

- Customers—Impact in relationship to current exposure: alternatives must provide better safety and security.
- Employees—Safety and security issues are similar to customers.
- Compliance—Depending on the location (usage) of the product/ service, compliance must satisfy local and global safety and security requirements.
- Business Goals—Selected alternatives should be in line with business goals/objectives.

Evaluate risk associated with any alternative by:

- Identifying risks, e.g., safety, security, market share, technical quality, etc.
- Analyzing the risks
- Planning, communicating, and obtaining business/compliance authority approval before testing pilot alternatives
- Tracking and maintaining risk data

A team should evaluate risk at several stages of a DMAIC process. At this point, only testing risk(s) are to be evaluated/questioned. Risk analysis will be required again when the selected alternative is implemented to improve the process/product.

The Simulation Tool—Simulation is a powerful analyzing tool. Important characteristics of the tool include:

- Simulation can be used with a detailed process model to determine how the process output (Y) would respond to changes in the process structure, inputs (Xs), and/or neighboring independent variables (Xs).
- Simulation can be used to test alternative solutions. The simulation events can be discrete or continuous:
  - Discrete Events Simulation—Discrete events occur at distinct points in time. These events control process performance.
  - Continuous Simulation—A simulation utilized if process parameters change continuously.
- Simulation can be used:
  - To identify intricate and specific issues in the existing or proposed process
  - To develop a model realistically close to the real situation/process
  - To predict the behavior of the process under varying conditions (constraints)
- Simulation can help the team to generate process data that might be needed to make decisions about the design and the operations of the process.
- Simulation might not solve a specific problem, but it can help the team to identify problems and evaluate alternative solutions through quantitative information under a variety of conditions.
- A simulation model is "virtual reality." Different process situations will need different types of simulation.

Simulation model development is the most time-consuming activity in the simulation process. If the model developed is not a fairly accurate representation of reality, the model will be of no benefit. *Remember*: "Garbage in, garbage out." Model steps may be linear, simultaneous, or iterative. A sample linear model is presented in Figure 5.8.

Pilot-Testing Alternatives—Pilot testing involves testing, at a small scale, of all or part of a proposed solution to better understand the proposed solution and to learn how to achieve a more-effective full-scale implementation. Pilot testing can be in the following categories:

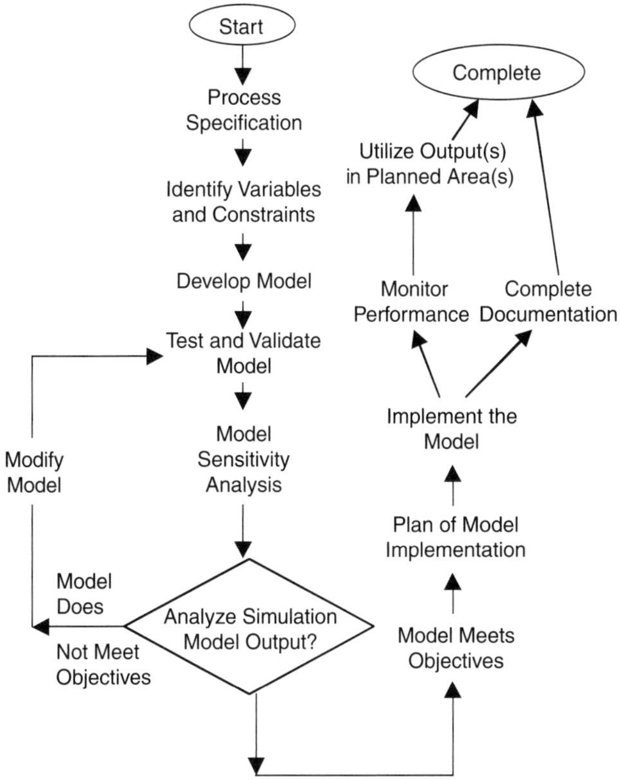

Figure 5.8. Flow Chart: Simple Linear Simulation Model

- To test the complete solution
- To test isolated elements of a solution and/or isolated locations
- To test for robustness

Several activities generally support pilot testing and a successful program:

- Communicating periodically with business leadership to obtain leadership's full support
- Developing a detailed plan for pilot testing
- Selling the pilot plan to all associated employees who will be affected by it
- Training associated employees
- Monitoring pilot implementation

- Analyzing pilot information utilizing proper statistics
- Designing a closed-loop system to improve/adjust the proposed solution
- Assessing execution of the pilot

Cost/Benefit Analysis—Key elements of a cost/benefit analysis include:

- Buy-In—As other employees (not members of the team, e.g., financial, sales, design, service) participate in cost/benefit analysis and accept the data, their buy-in and support for the project will be generated.
- Communication—A formal cost/benefit analysis should be communicated in financial terms. Describe the project to the financial group and other interested parties so that they can evaluate it the project makes good business "sense" or if it does not.
- Calculations—A cost/benefit analysis may include calculations such as net present value, cashflow, internal rate of return, return on equity, payback period, and other financial information of interest.
- Refined Data—Cost/benefit data at this stage of a project should be refined when compared to the estimated data that was available when the project statement was developed.

The importance of a cost/benefit analysis is to identify all benefits—tangible, intangible, and/or both. Identifying all benefits is essential. A cost/benefit analysis allows determination of whether or not a project has a clear financial payback. Benefits should be aligned with the business metrics and should be tracked accordingly. Experience has shown that teams generally underestimate the impact of their projects. Utilize the financial department at the business to ensure that all data concerning all benefits realized from this project have been collected.

Guidelines for a cost/benefit analysis typically involve a simple process, although an individual business/workplace may require additional information to meet its requirements:

- Estimate benefits to be gained
- Estimate implementation and operating costs for the improved product/process
- Determine net financial improvements
- Identify intangible benefits

Therefore,

Total improvement = Net financial benefits + Intangible benefits
= (Tangible benefits – Implementation costs) + Intangible benefits

The team should prepare a cost/benefit analysis with the help of the financial department. Guidelines include:

- Direct Savings/Benefits—Determine the impact and appropriate measurements for the activities/process/product. Use standard or average rates as they apply in the business and obtain savings/benefits data.
- Financial Benefits—Financial benefits from a project are possible only after successful implementation of the team's recommended improvements. Therefore, subtract implementation costs from tangible benefits or financial gains as projected (estimated) above. Even if intangible benefits are not measureable for financial purposes, intangible benefits are generally considered to be favorable outcomes that justify the value of the project.
- Prepare a Formal Financial Cost/Benefit Analysis—A formal financial cost/benefit should be prepared for the selected solution. It should update the financial opportunity derived from the project, which was estimated in the **D**efine phase and refined in the **A**nalyze phase. The formal final financial analysis must include intangible benefits derived from the project.

A simple pay-off matrix is shown in Table 5.16. A pay-off matrix will help the team to evaluate the alternative solutions in relationship to the efforts required and the benefits anticipated. *Important*: All the team members should share the same operational definitions of high and low.

Implement

The next step is to implement the selected alternative to meet project objectives. Before implementing the selected alternative, examine:

- Resources Training—Review understanding of the process to be implemented with all affected employees. Answer their questions and eliminate their concerns. Analyze the employee knowledge base to determine if any training is needed before implementing the recommended solution.
- Resource Upgrading—Resources other than employees include facility, equipment, technology, etc. Review these resources, e.g., address safety issues. Equipment and/or the facility may need to be upgraded to meet local, state, and federal safety requirements.

Table 5.16. Pay-Off Matrix

Benefits		Effort: Low	Effort: High
	High	Accepted Alternative for Continuation	Rescope/Reconsider Alternative
	Low	Reject Alternative	Reject Alternative

- Schedule and Work Breakdown Structure—As the workforce undergoes training, employees must also have training for the improved process so they understand the process structure. Process breakdown/structure is generally a good tool for training and a reference point for the process owners. An implementation schedule is also a good management tool. Project implementation should be tracked against the developed schedule.
- Control Plan—Relating gains achieved from a Six Sigma project is important. (Several elements that help to retain the gains will be discussed in detail in Chapter 6, *Control.*)

During project implementation, the team must monitor project progress and also listen to comments and concerns of participating employees. If the implementation plan progresses smoothly, the project team and other participating employees will see the improvements. It is critical to monitor the implementation schedule, process improvements, financial benefits, and input from participating employees. The financial benefits of implementing Six Sigma projects are generally very attractive—increased revenue, improved business margin, reduced cycle time, and higher inventory turns. A cost/benefit exercise is presented in Exercise 5.5.

Exercise 5.5: Analyzing Costs vs. Benefits

The XYZ division of a corporation produces an electromechanical, software-controlled product. The XYZ division does not manufacture any components. Outside suppliers and sister divisions of XYZ supply the components. The XYZ product is an integrated and tested system that is made up of three modules: A, B, and C. These three modules (A, B, and C) are assembled and tested at XYZ division. The total manufacturing process at XYZ division is presented in Figure 5.9. Material costs are as follows:

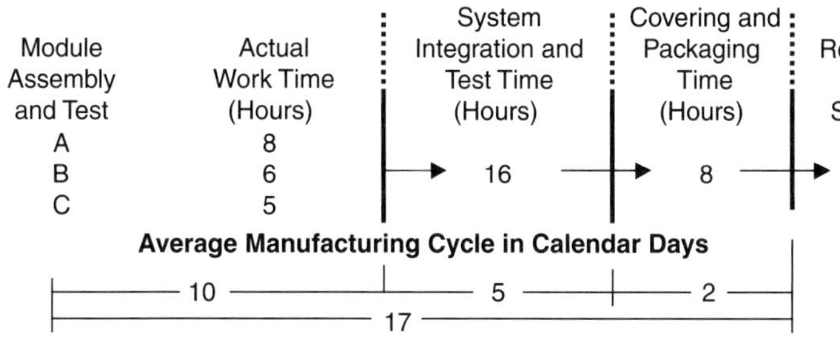

Figure 5.9. Total Manufacturing Process for a Product at XYZ Division of a Corporation

Module A = $15K per unit

Module B = $3K per unit

Module C = $2K per unit

The Six Sigma team has investigated and analyzed historical data for the total manufacturing cycle and has found two critical issues with highest priority:

- Technical support in the module assembly and test areas is not available when needed due to poor scheduling.
- Parts shortages exist on the manufacturing floor because suppliers are missing delivery dates.

Improvement has been proposed by the team:

- Modify the current supplier contract from 6 months to 2 years. This will guarantee quality on-time parts delivery with a 1% reduction in material cost. Because workers will not have to wait for parts, estimates are that the assembly and test work will be reduced by 15%.
- Purchase and install scheduling software to improve the chances of technical resource availability in the module assembly and test areas. The scheduling software will cost $20K. Installation and training costs would be $5K.

Once the above-listed improvements are implemented, the team has estimated that the manufacturing cycle time for assembly and test areas will be reduced by 25%.

Additional information includes:

- Wage rate for assembly and test workers—$5/hour
- Benefit cost for assembly and test workers—25% of wage rate

- Annual inventory carrying cost—12%
- Total manufacturing overhead—300% percent of workers' wage rates
- Annual capital borrowing cost—8%
- Annual inflation adjustment rate—3%
- Annual production forecast—180 systems

Develop a cost/benefit analysis and state assumptions.

Conceptual Summary

Discussion so far has been about the process from project proposal through to implementation of the recommended solution. As the Six Sigma team worked on the project from the Define phase through the implementation of the recommended solution to achieve the stated project goals, the team needs to consider several questions:

- How does the solution address the root cause(s) of the problem?
- How did the team generate alternative solutions?
- What criterium(a) did the team use to evaluate potential solutions?
- What did the team develop as a "should be" process map (incorporating changes in the process)?
- How would the team manage cultural aspects required for successful change. Has the team mobilized support?
- What level of risk assessment was done before the pilot/small-scale project test?
- Was the solution tested as a pilot process or on a small scale? What was learned from the test?
- If the solution has many components, did the team test some isolated elements? As an example, if the team's solution is to implement a company-wide communication network, a few elements of the system can be selected from different sections of the business to evaluate performance, which would help the team to determine whether or not there will be any conflicts with the existing network.
- How robust is the proposed system or process? What happens when the system is overloaded with inputs or unexpected events? What instructions are provided to users? How well does the alternative solution perform under adverse conditions? As an example, if the team were testing a call center in the communication network, and they could load the network with an excessive number of calls to determine whether or not some new bottlenecks had been created, how

could the excessive load be relieved? Examining robustness could create a next level of issues that need to be addressed/resolved.

- What are potential problems? Does the team have a backup plan if "things go wrong?"
- What is the implementation plan? How would the team know whether or not the plan has been followed?
- Can team members explain their cost/benefit analysis including assumptions the team made to others?

5.6 SUMMARY

In the first five chapters, four phases of the DMAIC process have been discussed—**D**efine, **M**easure, **A**nalyze, and **I**mprove. This chapter has discussed the **I**mprove phase. Improvement means "reducing variation or improving a process;" therefore, process improvement solutions have been discussed. Starting with the improvement strategy led to establishing a quantitative relationship between the independent variables (Xs) and the dependent variable (Y). The tool used for relationship establishment was DOE (the design of experiments). Several steps developed alternative solutions, selected the most appropriate solution to meet/exceed the goals/objectives of the Six Sigma project, and then implemented the selected process improvement. Topics discussed in this chapter include:

- Improvement Strategy
- Process Reengineering
- Guide to Improvement Strategies for Factors and Alternatives
- Introduction to Design of Experiments
  - Completely Randomized Single-Factor Experiment
  - The Random-Effect Model
  - Factorial Experiments
  - Design of Experiments Terminology
  - Two-Factor Factorial Experiments
  - Three-Factor Factorial Experiments
  - 2^k Factorial Design
- Solution Alternatives
  - Investigate
  - Evaluate and Propose
  - Implement
- Conceptual Summary

A project team should determine if the following steps were followed before proceeding to Control, the next phase of the DMAIC process:

- Generate and test possible alternatives so that a proper selection can be made to meet/exceed the project goals/objectives. Key in-process elements that should have been followed include:
  - Analysis and testing
  - Development of process map
  - Cost/benefit analysis
  - Testing the improvement alternatives with small-scale/pilot solution implementation
  - Implementation of any process modification required based on the pilot data and analysis
- Design the implementation plan. Then implement the selected improvement process. The implementation plan should include workforce training, resources upgrading, schedule/work breakdown structure, and a control plan. Always have a contingency plan in case implementation does not go as planned.
- Monitor (a team responsibility):
  - How possible alternative solutions have been developed
  - Tools that have been used to tap into the creativity and encouragement of participants
  - Tools that have been used to select the best alternative
  - The type of criteria the team has developed to test and evaluate potential alternatives
  - The assumptions that have been made in the cost/benefit analysis
  - The basic guidelines that have been used in risk analysis
  - If there were any constraints (technical, governmental, cultural, or other) that could have forced the team to reject certain alternative solutions
  - How the pilot test was run, the data were collected and analyzed, and conclusions were drawn
  - The lessons learned, if any, from the pilot that have been incorporated into the design of the full-scale solution
  - How good the implementation plan has been
  - How good the process map/design has been and any issues or concerns
  - How well the selected solution has eliminated/minimized key sources of variation

- Tools that were most useful during the **I**mprove phase of the DMAIC process
- Different elements of communication that were necessary to support the implementation of the selected solution
- How process owner(s) have monitored the implementation plan and recognized its intended improvements
- The team's contingency plan to handle any potential problems during implementation

Once the project has been implemented and is performing as planned, the next question that comes to mind is, "What kind of control measures are needed to ensure that the implemented solution stays successful? This question will be answered in Chapter 6.

REFERENCES

1. Hammer, M. 1996. *Beyond Reengineering*. New York: Harper Collins.
2. Kumar, D. 2003. *Lean Manufacturing Systems*. Unpublished.

6

CONTROL

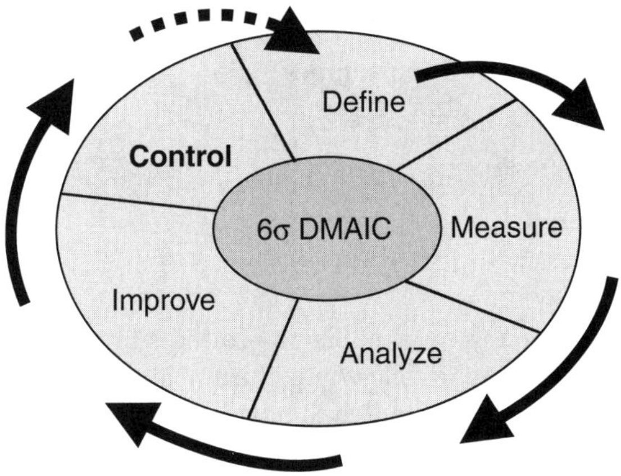

A Six Sigma team's responsibility does not end once a recommended solution has been implemented. At this point, the project represents a "milestone" accomplishment, yet significant effort still will be required to take the project to completion. The team has the responsibility of leading/guiding several activities, which are critical for project completion:

- 6.1 Self-Control
- 6.2 Monitor Constraints
- 6.3 Error Proofing
  - 6.3.1 Employee Errors
  - 6.3.2 The Basic Error-Proofing Concept
  - 6.3.3 Error-Proofing Tools

Retaining the gains made from a Six Sigma project is important. Concepts and ideas that the team may need to follow/implement will now be presented. A combination of these ideas may be required to retain the improvements made.

6.1 SELF-CONTROL

Once a recommended solution has been implemented, the team must think about the following questions:

- Is the implemented solution capable of meeting the expected project goals?
  - Is the project holding Six Sigma metrics goals?
  - Are data from the implementation solution validating the expected relationship between the independent variables (*X*s) and the dependent variable (*Y*)?
  - Is the process stable and under control?
- Is the process not stable enough and still changing? If so, should the team intervene or not?

- Do employees (workers) have the necessary knowledge, experience, and tools? Are they capable of meeting expected performance levels?
- Do workers have the authority to make the required adjustments without any major administrative "red tape?"
- Do workers understand their responsibilities and goals? Have their targets been clearly spelled out?
- Are any feedback mechanisms in place so that workers know how well they are doing in relationship to expectations?

If the answers to the above questions are generally "yes" or "positive," the business has been providing what is known as "self-control" or the optimal conditions for the process.

Self-control also implies that workers understand the basic elements of their jobs and have been motivated to expend their efforts to change and improve the results of their efforts. Therefore, the "bottom line" is that workers have become their own feedback loop. If employees are provided with responsibilities and authority over their surroundings, they receive a higher status and a form of "ownership."

Other important questions include:

- Do workers (who now "own" the process) have the resources and an awareness of documentation? As an example, several documents and displays should be accessible to workers. Workers should also know how to use these documents:
  - Written process/product specifications
  - Service conformity standards and work instructions
  - Same document edition (or version) at all locations
  - A display of defective products and services for educational purposes
  - Policy and procedures about deviation from the standard
- Do workers have mechanisms in place to know about their performance in relationship to standards?
  - Feedback mechanisms
  - Performance metrics
  - Quality inspectors/examiners
- Do workers have the resources required to improve their performance if they have been performing below the expected standard?
  - Periodic measurement of product/process quality
  - A guide to improve worker performance

Provide as much quality control to the operating workforce as possible. This provides the shortest feedback loop. It also requires that the process implemented by system designers be capable of meeting product quality goals. Employee empowerment, i.e., for the employees responsible for the process, is another important factor for designers to consider when designing controls in the system. Employee self-control means that workers understand the key elements of their jobs and are motivated to expend their efforts to change and/or improve the results of their efforts. The bottom line is that workers become their own feedback control (improvement) loop. Therefore, workers must understand their job assignments and think that they are the part of the process/system, which results in a sense of "ownership" for employees.

Resources are constraints in any business/process. How resources are utilized is key for any business to succeed in a globally competitive market.

Exercise 6.1: Self-Assessing a Process

- Select a work process you perform and briefly describe it.
- What is the expected result(s) of the process?
- What metrics do you use to measure the performance of your process?
- What kind of feedback mechanism do you use to correct your process?
- What level of self-control responsibility and authority do you have?

6.2 MONITOR CONSTRAINTS

Several constraints impact a process/product. The impact of all constraints is not equal. Generally recognized constraints include:

- Material
- Process
- Technology
- Workforce
- Equipment
- Metrics
- Information
- Training
- Environment
- Utilities

Many businesses measure resource utilization and wait until the output is generated before action is taken, which is often too late. Controls should be placed within the process. To produce a better-quality product, controls must be put into effect well before the output is produced.

Deciding exactly which constraints to select can be difficult for the team. The team is well advised to identify the most critical constraints (or vital few) and give these constraints appropriate attention. Then, select one constraint that is more important than all of the others. Once a constraint is selected, analyze the impact of the selected constraint on:

- The process
- The constraint's performance
- The processed output

As an example, the constraint selected is "workforce." The workforce is required to support the process. The workforce must be dynamic and must adjust according to process change. The workforce must also have the skills and experience to support an ever-changing process. Worker training, feedback for error correction, and job rotation are critical elements to maintain a high workforce performance level.

As another example, select as the constraint "material," which is one of the key input elements in an SIPOC process. The combination of input elements and in-process activities produces the output to meet customer needs. To have quality material for the process, material quality must be maintained at the supplier's workplace.

A Six Sigma team needs to answer key questions about monitoring:

- What should I (the team) monitor?
- Where should I (the team) monitor?
- How do I (the team) monitor?
- When do I (the team) monitor?

What Should I (the Team) Monitor?

All monitoring should be centered on a specific resource that the team wants to monitor. Monitoring does not work without a feedback loop. Resource monitoring is a combination of:

- Process features
- Product features
- Side effects of process and/or product features

Process Features—Most monitoring is utilized to evaluate process features that most directly affect the product, e.g., coolant chemistry in a turning machine is utilized to keep tool temperature low enough to achieve the surface finish on a part; ink in an ink jet printer is used for printing addresses on envelopes; etc. Several process features become candidates for monitoring subjects as a means of eliminating or minimizing failures. These monitoring elements are generally selected based on historical data, FMEA analysis, and/or research data. These process features-related monitors are linked to the decision question, "Should the process be run or stopped?"

Product Features—Some monitors are utilized by evaluating the product's features, e.g., copying paper must be at a certain minimal weight to be utilized in a copying machine. Therefore, the major activity is an inspection to check product specifications or objectives. This type of activity is generally performed at defined product phases in which breakdowns may have occurred in the production process.

Side Effects of Process and/or Product Features—These features generally do not affect the product, but they may create side effects, e.g., certain activities in the backyard of a house may be offensive to the neighborhood; chemical leaks from a plant may create threats to the environment; etc.

Where Should I (the Team) Monitor?

Constraint review stations are usually designed to provide evaluations and/or early warnings at several phases:

- Before starting on a significant, irreversible activity, e.g., a preflight check that astronaut goes through before mission control allows an astronaut team to take off for a space project mission
- At changes of responsibility and/or authority, a time at which either one or both are transferred from one organization to another
- After creation of a critical quality feature
- At the site of dominant process variables
- At areas that allow an economical/financial evaluation to be made

Generally, a flowchart of the process is very useful in identifying a group of constraints within appropriate monitoring stations. Key areas to set up monitors include:

- At the start of a significant, irreversible activity
- When authority changes
- After creation of a critical quality feature
- At the site of dominant process variables

How Do I (the Team) Monitor?

The feedback loop is a tool used to monitor the actual performance of a process/product and to keep it performing as designed (known as a closed-loop system). A feedback loop flow chart is presented in Figure 6.1.

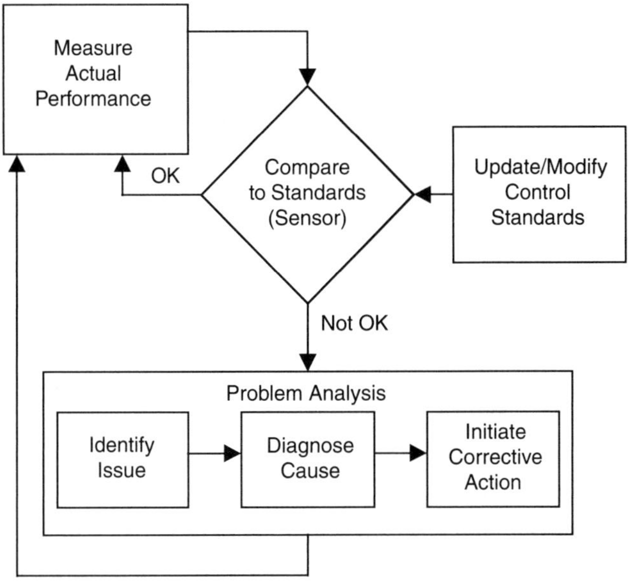

Figure 6.1. Feedback Loop Flow Chart

Components of a feedback loop ("sensor," problem analysis) could be a combination of mechanical, electrical, software, and employees. Feedback loops are an integral part of the process design and control system. They keep the process performing as designed, e.g., a thermostat, a fuel gauge in automobile, etc. The flow of information and activities within a feedback loop includes the following:

- Actual performance of the operating process is first measured.
- The results or outputs of the process are compared against an established standard or control target. The tool used to measure the process is usually referred to as the "sensor."
- Based on the established objectives/guidelines, a decision is made about whether there is adequate conformity or not. The decision-maker is generally called a "judge" or "umpire." If performance meets or exceeds established guidelines, the process continues to run.
- If performance does not meet the target, the umpire begins analyzing to identify the problem, diagnose the causes, and to initiate a series of activities that will adjust the process and restore conformance. Performance is brought in line with the target. Operation of the feedback loop continues as long as the process stays within the guidelines.

When Do I (the Team) Monitor?

The timing of process monitoring is critical. It can take place at several stages as a process progresses. Commonly used stages include:

- At the start of a process
- During the process
- During supporting operations

At the Start of a Process—Results of a monitored process are used to decide whether or not to start the process, e.g., preflight takeoff process checks. Generally, monitoring involves:

- Following preparatory steps to get ready for a process—Usually, the product/process supplier provides these steps.
- Evaluating the start monitoring information to determine whether, if started, the process will meet the goals
- Verifying that the criteria have been met
- Assigning preparatory responsibility—This assignment is a function of quality goals. As criticality and/or complexity become greater, the probability of assigning the task to a specialist/supervisor/consultant instead of a typical worker becomes greater.

During the Process—Monitoring during a process is very common. These monitors check the process at different stages. The different types of monitors should be stipulated in the process:

- Running Monitors—This form of monitoring takes place periodically during operation of the process.
- Product Feature Monitors—This type of monitoring is utilized at different stages of product production and performs several functions:
  - Understanding product quality goals
  - Evaluating product quality as the product is produced
  - Evaluating the above information and deciding whether to continue the process or to stop the process

Commonly used elements in a process-monitoring matrix include:

- The subject and unit of measure
- The type of sensor
- The frequency of measurement
- Sample size
- Criteria

- Action to be taken
- Location/assigned to

Process-Monitoring Summary—Key monitoring functionality requirements include:

- Individuals responsible for monitoring must know what they are supposed to do.
- Goals and targets must be defined. They must also be made available to responsible parties.
- The feedback performance system must be immediate (or at least take place quickly).
- Process monitoring resources must have the capability and the means to regulate process outcomes.
- Process users need a capable process and the tools, training, and authority to regulate the process.

During Support of the Operation—In some processes, supporting equipment, the facility, etc. must be closely monitored to maintain product quality, e.g., print room temperature and relative humidity to maintain good-quality printing.

Exercise 6.2: Developing a Process Monitoring Matrix

Using the process described in Exercise 6.1, develop a process monitoring matrix. Be prepared to explain the rationale for why the chosen monitoring subjects are dominant variables.

6.3 ERROR PROOFING

Error proofing is an area in which a Six Sigma team must commit resources to retain gains from the project. Employees are a major source of error. Following several fundamental rules can help to avoid errors:

- Build Quality into the Process—A quality inspection after processing the material simply sorts between good and bad parts.
- Do Not Think about Excuses—Think about how to do the job right the first time.
- Do Not Do Anything Wrong Knowingly. Do It Right, Now—Eliminate all reasons why a process is being done "wrong."

- Errors and Defects Can be Reduced to Zero by a Team Effort—Zero errors and defects cannot be achieved by one person. All employees in the business must be part of the team to eliminate errors and defects.
- Teams Are Better than Individuals—Individual creativity is important, but a team effort is more valuable. Teamwork is the key for business success.
- Seek Out the True Cause of an Error or Defect—Should an error or defect occur, continually ask, "Why did the error or defect occur?" Ask this question until the root cause is discovered. Then ask, "How do we fix it?" Then implement the solution.

Analyzing and understanding how a business approaches employee errors is critical. Basic rules and tools are available to handle human errors. These tools will be presented in sections that follow.

6.3.1 Employee Errors

Each businesses approaches employee errors differently. Some use a positive approach and others use a negative approach:

Positive Approach: Errors and Defects Can Be Eliminated	**Negative Approach: Errors and Defects Will Happen**
– Ask "why?" and find "how?"	– Blame somebody
– Create a positive environment	– Employees make errors
– Develop an error-free process	– Detect through inspection
– Build supplier/customer partnership	– Inspect all the material at receiving

Errors are made by all levels of employees. The causes of employee errors are numerous:

- There are no written or visual standards.
- Employees are not analyzing issues correctly.
- Employees jump to conclusions before finding the root cause.
- Employees are untrained.
- Employees ignore business standard procedures.
- Employees use a decision-making process slowly.
- Equipment is not capable of meeting product/service specifications.

- Employees are overloaded.
- Employees are physically at the workplace, but mentally somewhere else.

Techniques exist to reduce and control errors:

- If employees lack essential skills to prevent errors, then errors are:
  - Specific
  - Unavoidable
  - Consistent
  - Definitely unintentional

  Solutions are:
  - To identify areas where employees need training.
  - To train the employees in required skills.
  - To show employees exactly what they should do differently.
  - To redesign the process if necessary to incorporate essential knowledge.
- If employees are making errors unknowingly and are not giving their full attention in the decision process, possible reasons could be that:
  - They are physically present, but mentally absent.
  - Physiological and/or psychological issues may exist.
  - Errors may be random.

  Solutions could be:
  - To install checkpoints at critical locations
  - To help employees to resolve personal issues
- If employees are making errors, communication might be inadequate:
  - Standard procedures could be conflicting and/or standard procedures may not have been updated according to market requirements.
  - No employee performance metrics are in place.
  - Employees are not allocated/assigned to jobs according to their skills and experience. Resolve these issues by:
    - Updating standard procedures
    - Establishing performance metrics
    - Reassigning work

6.3.2 The Basic Error-Proofing Concept

Following fundamental rules can improve the error-proofing concept:

- Describe the error or defect the employee has made and provide the statistics, if available, to the employee.
- Identify areas where there is the potential for error/defect and find ways to minimize the areas where an error/defect has already occurred.
- Instruct employees to follow standard procedures.
- Establish checks and balances to minimize errors.
- Find the root cause(s) of errors by asking "why?" Find a solution by asking "how?"
- Use brainstorming sessions to find ideas to resolve errors/defects.

6.3.3 Error-Proofing Tools

Guidelines for designing a tool with the objective of minimizing errors/defects include:

- If a tool detects an error while the error is being made, the tool is considered to be a *good* tool.
- If a tool can predict a defect before the next operation, the tool is considered to be a *better* tool.
- If a tool makes occurrence of an error impossible, the tool is considered to be a *best* tool.

Although numerous tools are available for error proofing, commonly used tools include:

- Sensors
- Checks and balances
- Templates
- Standard procedures/guides/references
- Sequence checks
- Critical condition indicators
- Mistake proofing
- A redesign process
- Create error-preventing devices:
  - Simple process

- Quick feedback loop
- Focused application
- Team of the right employees

These tools help businesses to reduce errors. Yet, two simple ways to minimize errors are:

- Prevent errors
- Mitigate errors

Prevent Errors—Errors may be prevented in several ways:

- Eliminate the possibility of errors. Install/utilize a tool that would prevent a system user from reaching a stage in which as error could occur, e.g., an automobile will not start until it is in "park." This type of tool is generally known as "eliminate error possibility."
- Delegate responsibility. An "easy way out" is to delegate the necessary responsibility to make decisions to someone else. Generally, this is not a good tool, but some employees may take advantage of it.
- Facilitate tasks. A very commonly used tool (concept) is to facilitate tasks. Achieving this concept can include:
  - Task matching to an individual's ability
  - Task stratification
  - Task specialization
  - Task identification using different colors
- Detect errors. An error-detection tool is a commonly used tool, e.g., a smoke detection alarm.

Mitigate Errors—A variety of mitigating tools are available, e.g, the "auto file saving" feature in Microsoft Office® software. Prevention guidelines include:

- Universal involvement in defect prevention
- Process improvement to eliminate, simplify, and/or combine operations/activities/processes
- On-time production of products/services to minimize chances of error
- Production based on demand or no extra production

If the team is not successful at maintaining process improvement gains using these tools and techniques, the next step is to utilize the SPC tool (statistical process control).

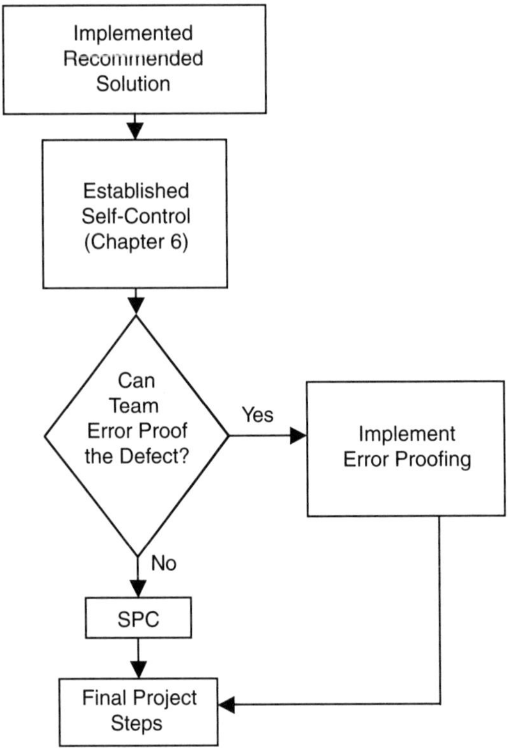

Figure 6.2. Control Flow Chart

Exercise 6.3: Identifying Error-Proofing Devices

- What are four error-proofing devices used at your workplace/business?
- Categorize these error-proofing devices as prevention or mitigation.
- Develop the answers on a flip-type chart for presentation.

6.4 STATISTICAL PROCESS CONTROL (SPC) TECHNIQUES

At this point in the project, the team has implemented the recommended solution and has also established a self-control process. The team has also used some error-proofing processes, but finds that maintaining the gains is difficult. Therefore, the next step for the team is to implement the statistical process control (SPC) tool. A decision-process flow chart (a control flow chart) is presented in Figure 6.2.

SPC is a problem-solving tool that may be applied to any process. SPC reflects a desire of all individuals in the business/product/process group for a continuous improvement in quality by the systematic reduction of variability. Although several available SPC tools are listed below, only the SPC control chart tool of SPC will be discussed. (Some of these tools have already been discussed in previous chapters.)

- Cause-and-effect diagram
- Check sheet
- Defect-concentration diagram
- Histogram
- Pareto chart
- Scatter diagram

In the 1920s, Walter A. Shewhart of Bell Telephone Laboratories was a pioneer in the SPC field. Since World War II, W. Edward Deming and Joseph M. Juran have been leaders in spreading statistical quality-control methods.

A control chart is a statistical device primarily used for studying, analyzing, and controlling repetitive processes. Control charts have key purposes:

- To define the goal or standard for a process that business leaders are striving to attain
- To be used as a tool for attaining the defined goal
- To be used as a tool for evaluating whether or not a goal has been achieved

Therefore, a control chart is a tool to be used for product/process specifications, production, and inspection as needed to link and make interdependent these phases in any business environment. The control chart tool of SPC will now be discussed in several subsections.

6.4.1 Causes of Variation in a Process

Primarily, variation is of two types—chance and special (or assignable). *Chance variation* is due to inherent interaction among input resources. Industry recognizes that certain variations in the quality of product are due to chance variations and that little can be done other than revise the process. This chance variation is the sum of the effects of an entire complex of chance causes. In this complex of causes, the effect of each cause is slight and no major part of the total variation can be traced to a single cause. The key to minimizing chance variations is to focus on a fundamental *process change.*

In addition to chance variation in quality, other variations are due to *assignable causes.* These variations are relatively large and are attributable to special (assignable) causes. Input resources are typically the main source of assignable variations. Assignable variations are generally unpredictable and are not "normal." Investigating the specific data points (information) related to the special variation is important. Develop solution(s) for a special variation, implement the most appropriate solution, and check the variation again. In summary, there are two types of variations:

- Chance
- Assignable Causes—Usually assignable-cause variations are due to:
  - Differences in equipment, people, material, process/technology, and facility
  - Differences in each of these factors over time
  - Differences in their relationships to each other

Once the cause(s) of variation in a process is known, the next step is to determine the SPCs impact on control of process performance.

6.4.2 Impact of SPCs on Controlling Process Performance

Control limits in a control chart are generally based on establishing ± 3 sigma limits for the variable being measured. These control limits are *not customer specification limits.* A control chart serves several purposes:

- To define a goal or standard for a process with upper and lower control limits, e.g., something a business might be striving to attain
- To be used as a tool for attaining the defined goal
- To be used as a judging tool of whether or not a goal has been reached
- To allow identification of unnatural (nonrandom) patterns in process variables
- To track processes and product parameters over time

Advantages and disadvantages of using a control chart include:

Advantages:

- Effective in defect prevention
- A proven technique in quality and productivity improvement
- Provides process capability information
- A good diagnostic tool
- Can be used for independent and dependent variables

Table 6.1. Qualitative Classification of Process Control Activities

Category 1 —	Implemented improvement *will eliminate* error condition from occurring; may be a long-term corrective action from error-proofing or design changes	**BEST** ↑
Category 2 —	Implemented improvement *will detect* when error condition occurs; "raising the flag" will stop the equipment/process so that defect will not move forward	
Category 3 —	If every participant is fully trained and understands *SPC charts*, once a chart signals a problem, everyone must understand SPC rules and agree to stop process for special issue identification	
Category 4 —	Audit or *inspection 100%*; generally a short-term solution	
Category 5 —	Same as Category 3 *except participants do not have authority to implement corrective action*; team will need approval from management	
Category 6 —	Just to implement standard operating procedure; generally this type of action is difficult to maintain	
Category 7 —	Utilization of *warning signals* to detect defects; frequency of ignoring these signals is generally high	
Category 8 —	Implementing SPC without training the participants	↓ **WORST**

Disadvantages:

- Not a simple tool; all users must be well trained and must participate in a continuing education (training) program
- Correct data must be collected
- Tool parameters (mean, standard deviation, range) must be calculated correctly
- User must have good knowledge of how to analyze charts correctly

Process control activities can also be classified qualitatively from *best* to *worst* as shown in Table 6.1.[1]

6.4.3 Control Chart Development Methodology and Classification

Typical steps are used to develop and analyze a Shewart control chart:

1. Select the appropriate response variable to chart.
2. Establish a rationale of data collection frequency for a subgroup and an appropriate sample size.
3. Select the appropriate control chart for the data.
4. Establish the data collection system.
5. Calculate the centerline and control limits (upper and lower).
6. Plot the data.
7. Check for out-of-control (OOC) conditions. A basic guideline includes:
   - One or more data points outside the 3-sigma control limits
   - Two of three data points outside the 2-sigma limit
   - Four of five data points outside the 1-sigma limit
   - Several consecutive data points (six to eight) on one side of the centerline
   - Once the process leaders have defined the warning limits, and if one or more points are in the "neighborhood" of a warning limit, then this suggests the need to collect more data immediately to check for the possibility of the process being out of control.
8. Interpret findings, investigate cause(s) for variation, and propose and implement solution.

Control Chart Classification

Control charts are classified for measurements (continuous) and attributes (discrete), depending on if the observations on the quality characteristic are *measurements* or *enumeration* data. As an example, we may choose to measure the diameter of a hole in a component, e.g., with a micrometer, and utilize these data to develop a control chart for measurement. On the other hand, we may judge each unit of this product as either defective or not defective and use the fraction of defective units found or the total number of defects in relation to a control chart for attributes. Classification of a control chart is presented in Figure 6.3. The following is a short description of control charts:

- X & MR Chart—This chart is also known as an *individuals* and a *moving-range* chart. This chart plots each *individual collected value* per product and a *moving average*. This chart is similar to a X-bar & R chart.

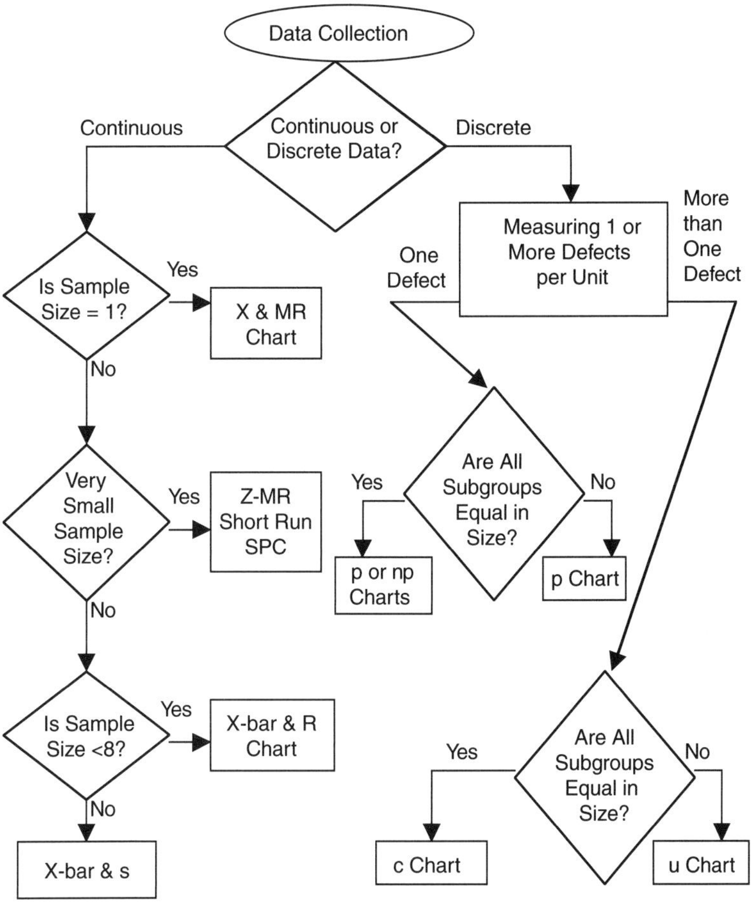

Figure 6.3. Control Chart Classification

- Xbar & R Chart and Xbar & Sigma Chart—Control chart development over an *average* quality is known as an X-bar chart. Range (R) charts measure the gain or loss of uniformity within each subgroup that represents the variability in the response over time. R charts are based on the range of values within each subgroup. Process variability is tracked through sigma charts that are based on the standard deviation (SD) within each subgroup.
- p Chart—This is a simple chart that is used to track the number of nonconforming units for a constant sample size as well as for a variable sample size.

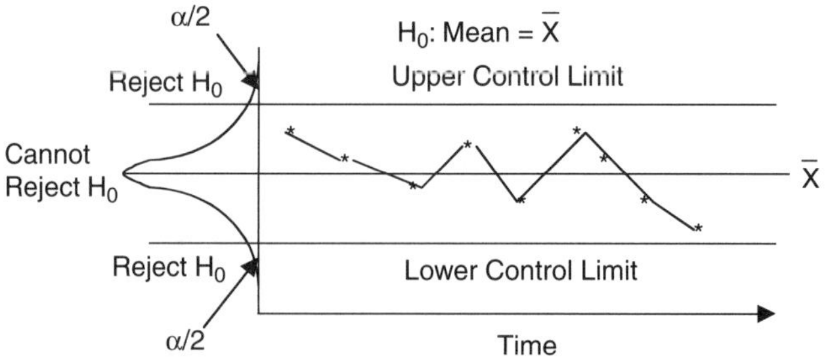

Figure 6.4. Control Chart Hypothesis Testing

- c Chart—This is a simple chart that is used to track the number of defects per unit with the assumption that the sample size is constant.
- u Chart—A u chart is similar to a c chart with the assumption that the sample size is both fixed and variable.

Control Chart Hypothesis Testing

The hypothesis testing concept is presented in Figure 6.4. Lower control limit (LCL) and upper control limit (UCL) represent the boundaries for the nonrejection area of H_0 and the areas that lie outside these limits represent H_0 rejection areas at α level of significance.

Assuming that the process mean and standard deviation (SD), e.g., μ and σ, are known, and, furthermore, assuming that the quality characteristic follows the normal distribution, let $\bar{X}$ = sample mean based on random sample of size n.

Then, the probability is $(1 - \alpha)$ that the mean of such random sample will fall between $\mu + Z_{\alpha/2}(\sigma/\sqrt{n})$ and $\mu - Z_{\alpha/2}(\sigma/\sqrt{n})$.

6.4.4 Continuous Data Control Charts

This subsection will describe several charts that present the Continuous Data and Box-Cox Transformation Methods.

Continuous Data for Individuals

Collected (measured) data for the *individuals* must be tested for normality before using the calculated lower (LCL) and upper control limits (UCL) based on standard formulas. If the distribution is skewed on either side (positive or negative), the control limits for individuals must be calculated based on area distribution tables. The theoretical limits will be calculated using standard deviations (SDs) from the mean. Values of X and R can have substantial variability because there is only one individual value per subgroup. The number of subgroups should be large, e.g., 100 or more.

Box-Cox Transformation

Box-Cox transformation is a commonly used method to normalize data. Box-Cox transformation will manipulate non-normal data and suggest the appropriate factor to be used to change the collected data into normal data. Yet, correcting non-normal data is not always necessary unless the data are *highly* skewed. Control charts work well even if the data are not normally distributed; therefore, according to Wheeler[2] and Wheeler and Chambers,[3] transforming data are not required if the data are used in control charts. Therefore, a user must use care when deciding to use Box-Cox transformation.

MINITAB software can provide Box-Cox transformation of data in two situations:

- Individual observations or subgroup data
- Power transformation for other conditions—Xbar, R, S, Xbar-R, Xbar-S, individual moving range, EWMA, moving average, Z-MR, etc. (Details are available in books on MINITAB.)

Individual Observations or Subgroup Data Transformation—This is good procedure for positive data only. The MINITAB procedure is as follows:

Step 1. Choose the commands **Stat** > **Control** > **Box-Cox transformation**. The menu screen will come up.

Step 2. Choose one of the following:

- If subgroups or individual data are in one column, enter the data column in **Single Column**. In **Subgroup size**, enter a subgroup size or a column of subgroup indicators. If data are individual observations, enter a subgroup size of 1.
- For a subgroup in rows, enter a series of columns in **Subgroups across rows of**.

Step 3. At this point, a command can be used in one of the following ways:

- To establish the best lambda (λ) value for the transformation, click **OK**.
- To establish the best λ value for the transformation, transform the data, and store the transformed data in the column(s) you specify. To do this, in **Store transformed data in**, enter a column (or columns) in which to store the transformed data, and then click **OK**.
- To transform the data with a λ value, enter and store the transformed data in a column (or columns) you specify. To do this, in **Store transformed data in**, enter column(s) in which to store the transformed

data. Click **Options**, in **Use lambda**, enter a value. Click **OK** in each dialog box.

Box-Cox transformation estimates the λ value, which minimizes the standard deviation (SD) of a standardized transformed variable.

When:

$\lambda \neq 0$, the resulting transformation is Y^{λ}

$\lambda = 0$, the resulting transformation is $\log_e Y$

Some specific relationships[4] for the different values of λ are presented in Table 6.2A.

The sample data in Table 6.2B are used to show how to use the MINITAB tool to obtain the λ value. A sample of gas mileage data for 70 automobiles was collected and reorganized in range groups as presented in Table 6.2B.

Gas mileage frequency data for the automobiles are plotted and presented in Figure 6.5A in histogram form, which shows that the mileage frequency data are skewed to the right. A second chart is presented in Figure 6.5B, which is a Box-Cox plot for the λ values.

Interpreting the Box-Cox λ plot: The "Last Iteration Information" table (in Figure 6.5B) contains the best estimate of λ, which is Est = 0.562, Low = 0.506, and Up = 0.618. A 95% confidence interval for the "true" value of λ is designated by vertical lines on the graph in Figure 6.5B. Although the best estimate of λ is 0.562, in practical situations, a λ value is wanted that corresponds to an understandable transformation, such as the square root (for $\lambda = 0.5$). In this example, the value of $\lambda = 0.5$ is a reasonable choice because it falls within the 95% confidence interval. All λ values in the 95% confidence interval are less than or equal to the horizontal dashed line in Figure 6.5B. Therefore, any λ value that has a standard deviation close to the dashed line is also reasonable to use for the transformation. In this example, this corresponds to an interval of 0.2 to 1.1.

MINITAB Charts

MINITAB software can provide four types of continuous data control charts:

- Moving Average Chart—Unweighted moving averages
- Exponentially Weighted Moving Average Chart (EWMA)—Exponentially weighted moving averages
- Cumulative Sum Chart (CUSUM)—Cumulative sum of the deviations of each sample value from the target value
- Zone Chart—Assigns a weight to each point, depending on its distance from the centerline, and plots the cumulative scores

Table 6.2A. Developed Transformation Values for Some Specific λ Values

Lambda Value (λ)	Transformation
–1	1/Y
–0.5	$1/(Y)^{0.5}$
0	Log_e Y
0.5	$(Y)^{0.5}$
2	Y^2

Source: Based on Nutter, J., W. Wasserman, and M. Kutner. 1990. *Applied Linear Statistical Models: Regression, Analysis of Variance, and Experimental Designs, Third Edition.* Chicago: Richard D. Irwin.

Table 6.2B. Grouped Automobile Performance Data, Miles per Gallon

9, 10, 11
14, 15, 15, 16
20, 21, 19, 20, 21, 21, 20
24, 25, 25, 26, 24, 25, 27, 24, 25, 25, 26, 24
30, 31, 30, 32, 29, 30, 30, 31, 32, 29, 30, 30, 32, 29, 31, 30, 32, 33, 28, 29, 30
34, 34, 35, 36, 35, 34, 36, 37, 34, 34, 35, 36, 35
30, 40, 39, 41, 42, 39,

Moving Average Chart—This chart contains *moving averages*, which are averages calculated from artificial subgroups created from consecutive observations. In this case, the observations can be either individual measurements or subgroup means. A moving average chart can be developed utilizing MINITAB software. Generally, a moving average chart is not preferred over an EWMA chart because a moving average chart does not weight observations as an EWMA chart does.

Exponentially Weighted Moving Average Chart—An exponentially weighted moving average chart (EWMA) contains exponentially weighted moving averages. Each EWMA point incorporates information from all of the previous subgroups or observations. An EWMA chart can be custom tailored to detect any size shift in a process. Therefore, EWMA charts are often used to monitor in-control processes to detect small shifts away from the target. The following logic is used to generate an EWMA chart:

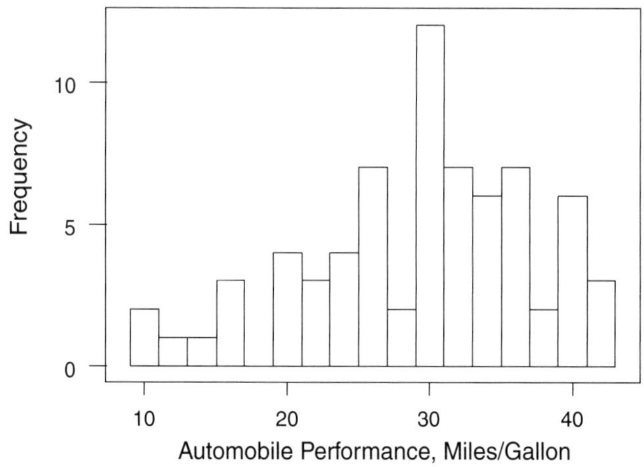

Figure 6.5A. Frequency Histogram: Automobile Performance, Miles per Gallon

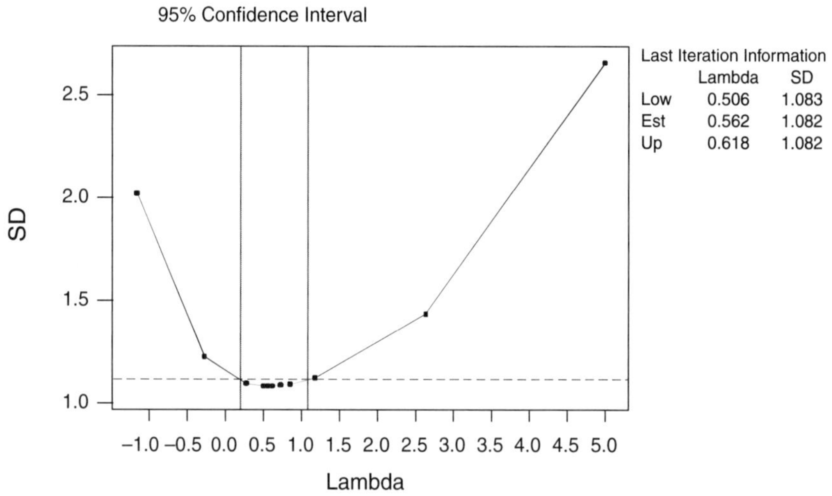

Figure 6.5B. Box-Cox Plot for the Lambda (λ) Values

Table 6.3. Individual Measurements for Selected Subgroups

Subgroup	1	2	3	4	5	6	7	8
Measurement	13	8	7	9	12	6	8	10

Let:

Z_i = Data group i

then,

$$Z_i = w\overline{X}_i + (1 - w)\, Z_{i-1}$$

or the general expression:

$$Z_i = w\overline{X}_i + w(1 - w)\overline{X}_{i-1} + w(1 - w)^2\overline{X}_{i-2} + \ldots + w(1 - w)^{i-1}\overline{X}_1 + (1 - w)^i\overline{X}_0$$

where:

w = Weight

$\overline{X}_i$ = Mean of subgroup i

$\overline{X}_0$ = Mean of all data

Example 6.1: Developing an EWMA Chart

Use the eight individual measurements as presented in Table 6.3 to develop an EWMA chart, using the weight factor of 0.25.

Solution:

The chart in Figure 6.6 has been developed using MINITAB software. The commands are as follows:

Stat > Control chart >EWMA

The data are stored in one column "Subgroup Mean," therefore, select

Single Column: "Subgroup Mean"

Weight for EWMA: 0.25

OK

Figure 6.6 is based on the following calculations, which are performed by MINITAB software in the background:

Mean of all the data:

$$\overline{X}_0 = (13 + 8 + 7 + 9 + 12 + 6 + 8 + 10)/8$$
$$= 9.125$$

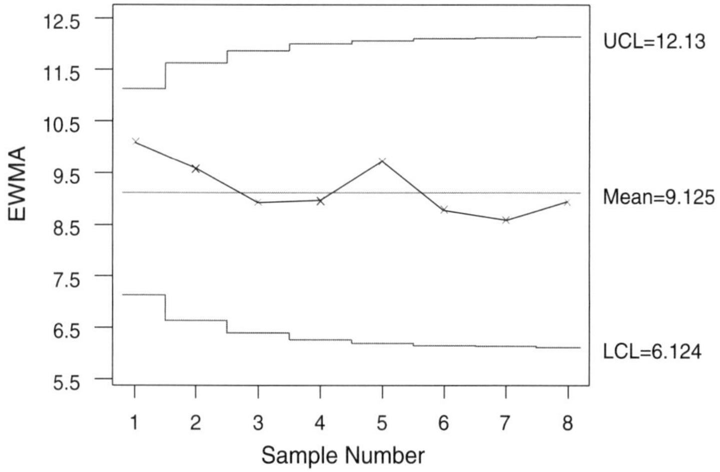

Figure 6.6. EWMA Chart for Subgroups

$$Z_i = w\bar{X}_i + (1 - w)\, Z_{i-1}$$

$$Z_1 = w\bar{X}_1 + (1 - w)\, \bar{X}_0$$

$$Z_1 = (0.25)\,(13) + (1 - 0.25)(9.125) = 10.094$$

$$Z_2 = w\bar{X}_2 + w(1 - w)\,\bar{X}_1 + (1 - w)^2\,\bar{X}_0$$

$$Z_2 = (0.25)(8) + (0.25)(1 - 0.25)(13) + (1 - 0.25)^2(9.125) = 9.57$$

Similarly, the remaining values as presented here may be checked: $Z_3 = 8.93$; $Z_4 = 8.95$; $Z_5 = 9.71$; $Z_6 = 8.78$; $Z_7 = 8.59$; and $Z_8 = 8.94$.

Cumulative Sum Chart—A cumulative sum chart (CUSUM) plots the cumulative sums of the deviations of each sample value from the target value. The CUSUM plotted chart is based on the subgroup means or the individual observations. Once a process is in-control, a CUSUM chart (as well as an EWMA chart) is a good device to use to detect small shifts from the target. Detailed explanations as well as instructions about developing a CUSUM chart may be found in a MINITAB tool book.

Zone Chart—A zone chart is a hybrid of the $\bar{X}$ (or individuals) chart and the CUSUM chart. Zone charts are usually preferred over $\bar{X}$ charts because zone charts are simple. Detailed explanations and instructions about developing a zone chart may be found in a MINITAB tool book.

Other Charts—Other continuous data control charts include:

- Z-MR Chart
- Xbar and R Chart
- Xbar and s Chart

Z-MR Chart—If enough data do not exist in each run to produce good estimates of process parameters, use a Z-MR chart. Measurement data are standardardized by subtracting the mean to the center of the data, then dividing by the standard deviation ($Z = (X - \mu)/\sigma$). Standardizing allows data collected from different runs to be evaluated by interpreting a single control chart.

The MINITAB tool can be used to estimate the process means and the standard deviations:

- Estimating the Process Mean—A Z-MR chart estimates the mean for each different component or product separately. It pools all the data for a common component and obtains the average of the pooled data. The result is an estimate of μ for that component.
- Estimating the Process Standard Deviation—A Z-MR chart provides four methods for estimating σ, the process standard deviation (SD) (Table 6.4). Details of the four methods may be found in a MINITAB book.

Generally, the *By component* method (see Table 6.4) is a good choice when a team has very short runs and wants to combine runs of the same component to obtain a more reliable estimate of σ. If the runs are sufficiently long, the *By component* method can also provide good estimates of σ.

The estimation method choosen by a team will be determined by assumptions that the team is willing to make about the variation of their process. Guidance for selection is presented in Table 6.4. A Z-MR chart estimates the mean for each different component or product separately. The mean of a component is calculated in a Z-MR chart by averaging all the data for that component. This average is the estimate of μ for that component.

Example 6.2: Developing a Z-MR Chart

A machining department produces a power transmission shaft in batches of three units. Shaft diameter data were collected from five runs as presented in Table 6.5. Develop a Z-MR chart from the data.

Solution:
A Z-MR chart has been developed using the MINITAB tool. The chart is presented in Figure 6.7.

Table 6.4. The Process Standard Deviation's Estimating Methods

Method	When ...	Which does this ...
Constant: pool all data	All output from process has the same variance regardless of size of measurement	Pools all data across runs and components to obtain a common estimate of σ
Relative to size: pool all data, use log (data)	Variance increases in a fairly constant manner as size of measurement increases	Takes natural log of data, pools transformed data across all runs and all components, and obtains a common estimate of σ for transferred data; natural log tranformation stabilizes the variation in cases where variation increases as size of measurement increases
By component: pool all runs of same component/ batch	All runs of a particular component or product have same variance	Combines all runs of same component or product to estimate σ
By run: no pooling	Cannot assume all runs of a particular component or product have same variance	Estimate σ for each run independently

Xbar and R Charts—Xbar and R charts are generally utilized to track the process level and process variation for a sample size less than 8, while Xbar and s charts are used for larger samples. A user analyzing the charts will be able to detect the presence of special causes.

In MINITAB, Xbar and R charts base the estimate of the process variation σ on the average of the subgroup ranges. A user can also use a pooled standard deviation or enter an historical value for σ.

The Xbar and R charts are utilized to analyze several critical points:

- The Xbar chart shows how a process is working and where the process is centered.
- If there is an impact of natural variation only, the Xbar chart will show that the center of the process is not shifting significantly.

Table 6.5. Sampled Collected Data for Shaft Diameter

Job Run, #	Shaft Diameter, in.
1	2.012
1	2.005
1	2.050
2	2.010
2	2.070
2	2.090
3	2.015
3	2.019
3	2.052
4	2.035
4	2.045
4	2.030
5	2.040
5	2.010
5	2.035

- If the Xbar chart shows a trend in which the center of the process is moving gradually up or down, a good probability exists that this movement is due to assignable causes.
- If the Xbar chart is erratic and out of control, then something is changing the center rapidly and inconsistently.
- If the Xbar chart and R chart are both out of control, first look for the issues affecting the R chart.
- If the R chart is out of control, it can affect the Xbar chart as well. If the R chart is out of control, this is also an indication that something is not operating in a uniform manner.
- If the R chart is narrow, the product is uniform.

Example 6.3: Developing Xbar and R Charts

The camshaft department of a bus manufacturing company manufactures a power transmission shaft that is 25 ± 0.1 in. long. The bus assembly department is complaining that the power transmission shaft is not produced to specifications. As a result of the complaints, management wants to run Xbar and R charts to monitor the length characteristic of the shaft.

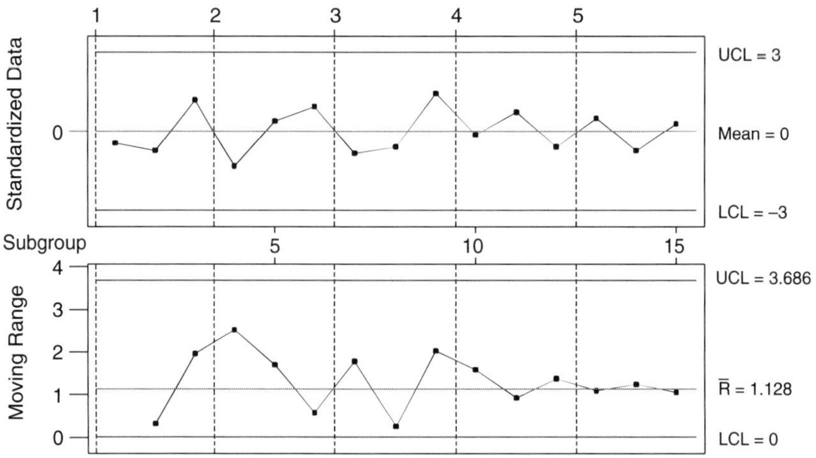

Figure 6.7. Z-MR Chart for Shaft Diameter

The data in Table 6.6 have been collected in ten subgroups with five data points in each subgroup. Develop Xbar and R charts and test as follows:

- One point or less that is more than 3 sigma from the centerline
- Six points in a row, all increasing or all decreasing
- Two out of three points that are more than 2 sigma from the centerline (while all of these three points are on the same side)
- Four out of five points that are more than 1 sigma from the centerline (on same side)

Solution:
Xbar and R charts have been developed using MINITAB software with $\pm 3\sigma$ control limits in Figure 6.8.

Interpreting the results: The centerline on the Xbar chart is at 25.03, implying that the process is falling within the specification limits. The centerline on the R chart, 0.105, is slightly larger than the maximum allowable variation of ± 0.1 in. This excess may indicate variability in the process.

Two additional groups of charts have been developed using MINITAB software. They are presented in Figures 6.9 and 6.10 (Xbar and R charts with $\pm 2\sigma$ control limits and $\pm 1\sigma$ control limits, respectively).

Xbar and s Chart—Although Xbar and R charts are used for smaller samples, Xbar and s charts are typically used to track process variation for sample sizes

Table 6.6. Length Data for Shaft

Subgroup	Shaft Length, in.				
1	25.02,	25.00,	25.05,	24.95,	24.99
2	25.07,	25.12,	24.99,	24.98,	25.05
3	24.98,	25.01,	25.07,	25.04,	24.99
4	24.95,	24.99,	24.98,	24.99,	25.05
5	25.02,	25.01,	25.05,	25.07,	25.02
6	25.09,	25.01,	25.07,	25.05,	25.06
7	25.02,	25.01,	25.09,	25.11,	25.12
8	24.97,	24.95,	24.99,	25.05,	25.09
9	24.99,	24.95,	25.01,	25.05,	24.98
10	25.12,	25.04,	25.01,	24.99,	25.00

larger than seven. Because both charts are plotted together, a user can track both the process level and the process variation at the same time, as well as detect the presence of special causes. (No example is presented here, but MINITAB software can be used to plot Xbar and s charts.)

6.4.5 Discrete Data Control Charts

Discrete data control charts are similar in structure to continuous data control charts, except that these charts plot statistics from *count data* rather than from *measurement data*, e.g., a product may be compared against a standard and classified as being either defective or not defective. The number of defects may also classify products.

A process statistic, e.g., the number of defects, is plotted vs. sample number or time in variables control charts. The centerline represents the average statistic. The upper (UCL) and lower control limits (LCL) are drawn, by default, 3 σ above and below the centerline.

A process is in-control when most of the points fall within the bounds of the control limits and the points display no nonrandom patterns.

The p, c, and u charts will now be discussed.

- p Chart
- p Chart with Varying Sample Size
- c Chart
- u Chart
- u Chart with Varying Sample Size

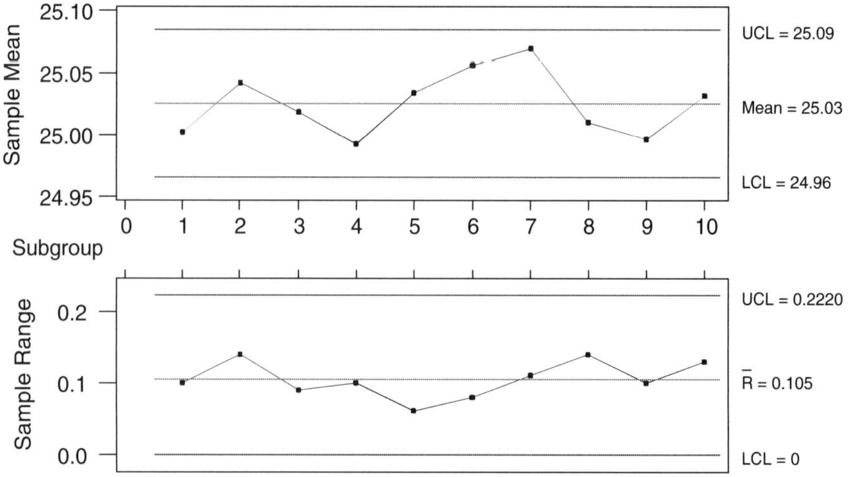

Figure 6.8. Developed Xbar and R Chart for Shaft Length

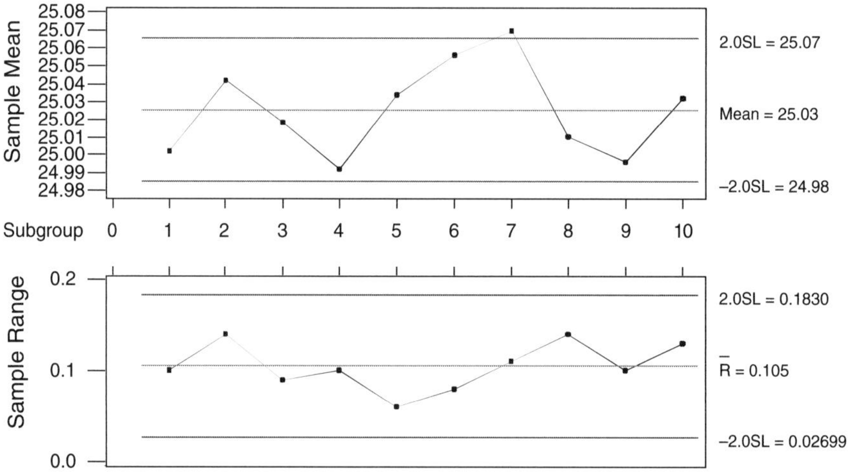

Figure 6.9. Additional Xbar and R Chart for Example 6.3 at ± 2.0SL

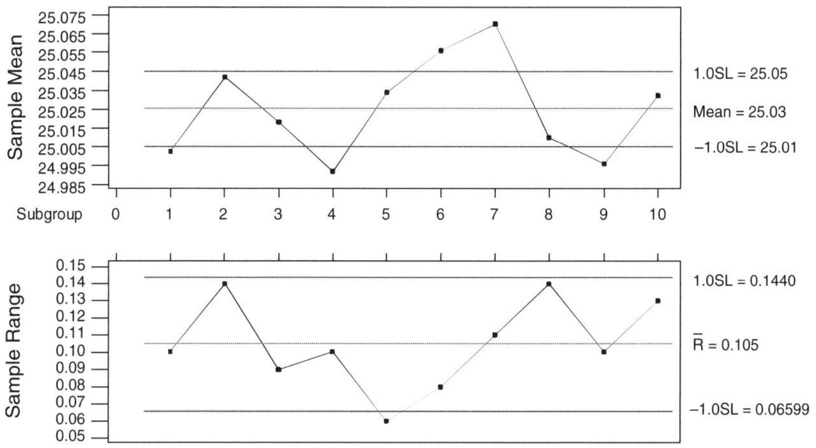

Figure 6.10. Additional Xbar and R Chart for Example 6.3 at ± 1.0SL

The p Chart—A p chart is drawn from the *proportion defective* data, when a product is classified as either defective or nondefective based on comparison with the standard. This concept provides economy and simplicity in an inspection operation, e.g., checking the length of a rod with a "go/no go" gauge and accepting or rejecting the rod would be much easier and more economical than using some other type of measuring device. *Important*: These control charts require a large sample size compared to their measurement counterparts. *Proportion defective* is defined as the number of defectives divided by the subgroup size. A p chart tracks the proportion defective and detects the presence of special causes. Assumed is that the number of defectives for one subgroup will follow binomial distribution with parameters n and p.

Let:

D = Number of defective units in a random sample of n units

p = Fraction defective

then, $p_{estimated} = D/n$ and the variance of $p_{estmated} = \sigma^2_{p\text{-}estimated}$

$$\sigma^2_{p\text{-}estimated} = p(1-p)/n$$

Therefore, $\sigma^2_{p\text{-}estimated}$ may be estimated as:

$$\sigma^2_{p-estimated} = \frac{P_{estimated}(1-P_{estimated})}{n}$$

Table 6.7. Receiving and Inspection Data for Part X for a Two-Week Period (Fixed Sample Size)

Lot Size:	100	100	100	100	100	100	100	100	100	100
Part Failed:	5	6	7	8	9	7	5	6	7	6

The centerline and control limits for the proportion defective (fraction defective) can be calculated as follows:

Let:

m = Number of samples and

n = Number of units in a sample (as defined earlier)

then,

$$\bar{p} = \frac{\sum D}{m \times n}$$

and

$$UCL = \bar{p} + 3\sqrt{\frac{\bar{p}(1-\bar{p})}{n}}$$

$$LCL = \bar{p} - 3\sqrt{\frac{\bar{p}(1-\bar{p})}{n}}$$

Example 6.4: Developing a p Chart with MINITAB Software

Part X has quality issues. Receiving and Inspection receive part X from a supplier daily. Data for received lots for the last 2 weeks are presented in Table 6.7. Develop a p chart utilizing the MINITAB software tool.

Solution:

$\bar{p} = (5 + 6 + 7 + 8 + 9 + 7 + 5 + 6 + 7 + 6)/(10 \times 100)$

$= 0.066$

$UCL = 0.066 + 3 \times \sqrt{((0.066)\ (1 - 0.066))/100}$

$= 0.1405$

$LCL = 0$

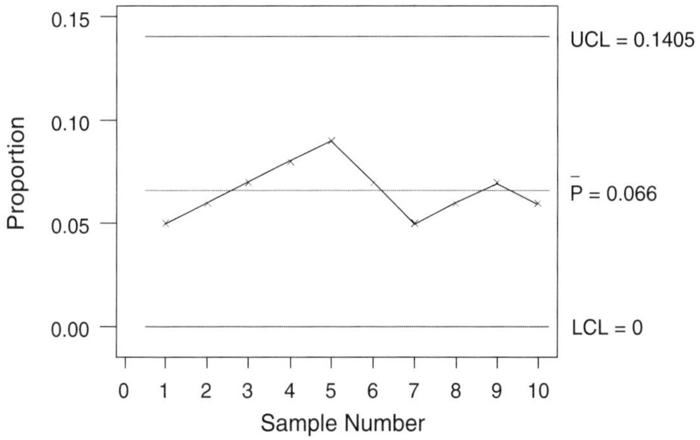

Figure 6.11. p Chart for Receiving Part Quality with Fixed Sample Size

The chart developed with MINITAB software is presented in Figure 6.11. All samples are in control. From a Six Sigma quality improvement point of view, the Sigma metrics is at 3.0 sigma, indicating room for improvement still exists. Appropriate steps should be taken to investigate the process and determine root causes of variation. Once defect types are known, process changes should be implemented.

The p Chart with Varying Sample Size—The previous section that described the p chart was greatly simplified because the sample size taken was constant. In many situations, having a fixed sample size is not necessary.

Let:

D_i = Number of defective units in a random sample of n_i units, $i = 1, 2, ..., m$

n_i = Number of units in sample i

m = Total number of samples

p_i = Fraction defective in sample i

then,

$p_i = D_i / n_i$

The centerline and control limits for the fraction defective chart can be calculated as follows:

Let:

$\bar{p}$ = Centerline

then,

$$\bar{p} = \frac{\left(\sum \frac{D_i}{n_i}\right)}{m}, i = 1, 2, \ldots, m$$

Because MINITAB software calculates the value of $\bar{p}$ based on a simple average, the above logic is based on simple average calculations. *Important*: A simple average of the fraction defective per unit of each sample is not taken. To work with these data, a weighted average must be taken. The weighted average can be calculated as follows:

Let:

M = Total unit count in m samples

$= \Sigma n_i$, i = 1, 2, 3, . . ., m

Then,
$$\bar{p} = \sum_i \left[\left(\frac{n_i}{M}\right) p_i\right], i = 1, 2, \ldots, m$$

Control limits for the p chart are as follows:

$$UCL = \bar{p} + 3\sqrt{\frac{\bar{p}(1 - \bar{p})}{\frac{M}{n}}}$$

$$LCL = \bar{p} - 3\sqrt{\frac{\bar{p}(1 - \bar{p})}{\frac{M}{n}}}$$

Control limits for each sample can be calculated as follows:

Table 6.8. Receiving and Inspection Data for Part for a Two-Week Period (Varying Sample Size)

Lot Size:	100	115	95	120	118	99	105	120	119	110
Part Failed:	5	6	7	8	9	7	5	6	7	6

$$UCL_{-pi} = \bar{p} + 3\sqrt{\frac{\bar{p}(1-\bar{p})}{n_i}}$$

$$LCL_{-pi} = \bar{p} - 3\sqrt{\frac{\bar{p}(1-\bar{p})}{n_i}}$$

This logic has been applied in Example 6.5.

Example 6.5: Developing a p Chart with a Variable Sample Size (n)

Part X has some quality issues. Receiving and Inspection receives part X from a supplier daily. Data for received parts for the last 2 weeks are presented in Table 6.8. Develop a p chart utilizing the MINITAB software tool.

Solution:
If the centerline is based on a simple average, then,

$$\bar{p} = \frac{\left(\sum \frac{D_i}{n_i}\right)}{m}$$

$$= (5+6+7+8+9+7+5+6+7+6)/(100+115+95+120+118+99+105+120+119+110)$$

$$= 66/1101$$

$$= 0.05995$$

If the centerline is based on a weighted average, then,

$$\bar{p} = \sum_i \left[\left(\frac{n_i}{M}\right) p_i\right]$$

The in-process data are presented in Table 6.9. The weighted $p = 0.0601$.

Table 6.9. In-process Data for the Weighted $\bar{p}$ Calculation

n_i	100	115	95	120	118	99	105	120	119	110
D_i	5	6	7	8	9	7	5	6	7	6
p_i	0.05	0.052	0.074	0.067	0.076	0.071	0.048	0.05	0.059	0.055
$p_{i\text{-est}}$	0.00454	0.00543	0.00639	0.0073	0.00815	0.00638	0.00458	0.00545	0.00638	0.0055

The p chart's upper control limit (UCL) is calculated using a simple average (since MINITAB software is used):

$$UCL = \bar{p} + 3\sqrt{\frac{\bar{p}(1-\bar{p})}{\frac{M}{m}}}$$

$$= 0.05995 + 3 \sqrt{((0.05995(1 - 0.05995))/(1101/10))}$$

$$= 0.1278$$

Similarly, $LCL = 0$.

Control limits can be calculated for each sample.

Sample 1. Where, $n_1 = 100$.

Then,

$$UCL_{-p1} = \bar{p} + 3\sqrt{\frac{\bar{p}(1-\bar{p})}{n1}}$$

and

$$UCL_{-p1} = 0.05995 + 3 \sqrt{((0.05995(1 - 0.05995))/100)}$$

$$= 0.13117$$

and

$$LCL_{-p1} = 0$$

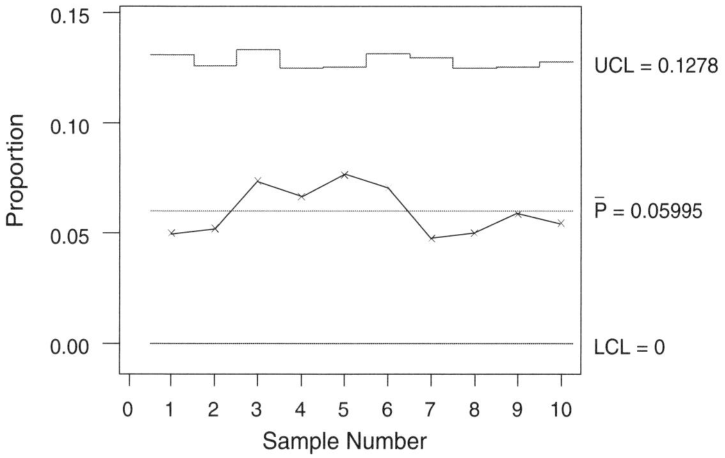

Figure 6.12. p Chart for Receiving Part Quality with Variable Sample Size

Sample 2. Where, $n_2 = 115$.

$$UCL_{-p2} = 0.12636$$

and

$$LCL_{-p2} = 0$$

Similarly, the control limits for the remaining samples can be calculated.

A chart developed with MINITAB software is presented in Figure 6.12. All samples are in control. From a Six Sigma quality improvement point of view, the Sigma metrics is at 3.0 sigma, indicating room for improvement still exists.

The c Chart—At times, controlling the *number of defects* in a unit product is more critical than controlling the *proportion defective* (fraction). In this circumstance, a c chart should be used (as a control chart) for defects, e.g., when producing a roll of sheet material, controlling the number of defects per foot is important. When the number of defects is linked to a per-unit-of-measurement situation, then the Poisson distribution model should be used with parameter λ. Both the mean and variance of this distribution are also λ.

Let:

c_i = Number of defects in unit i, $i = 1, 2, 3, \ldots, n$

n = Number of units used in the test

Table 6.10. Sample Data of Identified Components' Characteristics

Component	Identified Defective Characteristics	Count of Defective Characteristics
1	2, 4, 1	3
2	1, 4, 5	3
3	1, 2	2
4	2, 4	2
5	2, 3, 4, 5	4
6	1, 2, 3	3
7	4, 5	2
8	3, 4, 5	3
9	2, 3, 4	3
10	1, 2	2
11	4	1
12	3, 5	2
13	1, 2, 5	3
14	1, 2, 4	3
15	2, 3, 4	3
16	3, 4	2
17	1, 2, 4, 5	4
18	2, 4, 5	3
19	1, 3, 4	3
20	3, 5	2

Then, the centerline of the control chart is

$$\bar{c} = \frac{\sum c_i}{n}$$

and

$$UCL = \bar{c} + 3\sqrt{\bar{c}}$$

$$LCL = \bar{c} - 3\sqrt{\bar{c}}$$

are the upper and the lower control limits, respectively. See Example 6.6 for how to develop a c chart.

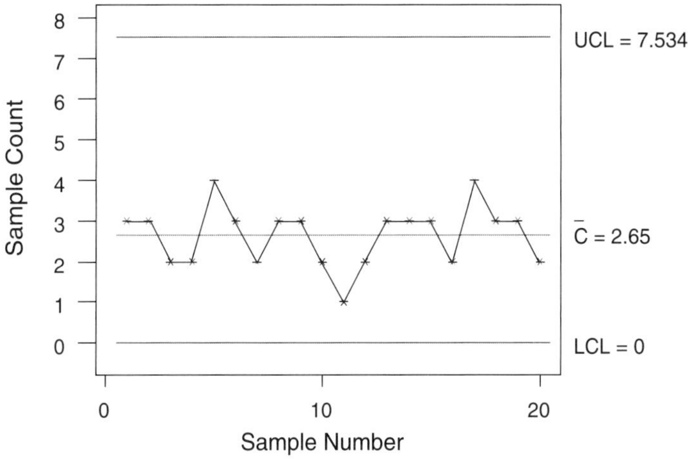

Figure 6.13. c Chart for Several Specification Characteristics Failure

Example 6.6: Calculating the Centerline and Control Limits for a c Chart and Plotting the Chart using MINITAB

A manufactured component has five identified characteristics to be inspected (1, 2, 3, 4, and 5). Inspection data are presented in Table 6.10. The data identify results of inspecting the characteristics of 20 components. Calculate the centerline and control limits for a c chart. Plot the chart using MINITAB software.

Solution:
The centerline of the control chart is $\bar{c}$:

$$\bar{c} = 53/20 = 2.65$$

and the upper (UCL) and lower (LCL) limits are

$$UCL = 2.65 + 3\sqrt{2.65} = 7.534$$

$$LCL = 2.65 - 3\sqrt{2.65} = 0$$

The c chart is plotted using MINITAB software (Figure 6.13). Based on the plotted chart, the process appears to be under control. However, 2.65 defective characteristics per component out of five is too many. The process could be improved.

The u Chart—The u chart is utilized when sample defects data are collected from n components in the sample. Working with the number of defects per unit rather than with the total number of defects is preferable.

Table 6.11. Sample Data of Component's Characteristics

Sample	Sample size, n	Number of Characteristics Unacceptable	Defects per Unit
1	7	5	0.717
2	7	7	1.000
3	7	6	0.857
4	7	4	0.571
5	7	8	1.143
6	7	10	1.429
7	7	6	0.857
8	7	9	1.286
9	7	11	1.571
10	7	4	0.571
11	7	7	1.000
12	7	8	1.143
13	7	5	0.717
14	7	9	1.286
15	7	10	1.429

Let:

n = Number of units in the sample

c = Total number of defects in the sample

u = Average number of defects per unit

m = Number of samples

where: $u1, u2, u3, \ldots, u_m$ are defects per unit for sample $i = 1, 2, 3, \ldots, m$, respectively.

Then,

$\overline{u}$ = Centerline on the u chart

and

$$\overline{u} = \frac{1}{m}\left(\sum u_i\right), \text{ i} = 1, 2, 3, \ldots, \text{m}$$

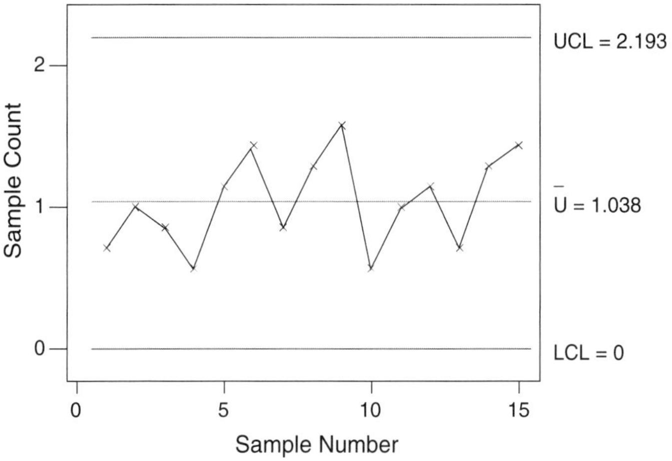

Figure 6.14. u Chart of Characteristics Failure per Unit for Selected Components

and the control limits,

$$UCL = \bar{u} + 3\sqrt{\frac{\bar{u}}{n}}$$

$$LCL = \bar{u} - 3\sqrt{\frac{\bar{u}}{n}}$$

Example 6.7. Developing a u Chart

A u chart is to be constructed for the component characteristics data in Table 6.11. There are seven components in each sample (n = 7). Calculate the centerline, UCL, and LCL for a u chart. Utilize the MINITAB software tool to plot the u chart.

Solution:
The centerline for the u chart:

$$\bar{u} = (1/15)\,(15.577) = 1.0385$$

The upper (UCL) and lower (LCL) control limits:

$$UCL = 1.0385 + 3\sqrt{(1.0385/7)} = 2.194$$

$$LCL = 1.0385 - 3\sqrt{(1.0385/7)} = 0$$

The plotted u chart (utilizing the MINITAB software tool) is presented in Figure 6.14.

The u Chart with Varying Sample Size—In the previous section, the u chart was greatly simplified because a constant sample size was taken. In many situations, having a fixed sample size is not necessary. Therefore, a u chart with variable sample size can be used.

Let:

n_i = Sample size for sample i, $i = 1, 2, 3, \ldots, m$

m = Number of samples

c_i = Total number of defects in sample i

u_i = Defects per unit in sample i

Then:

$u_i = c_i / n_i$

Therefore, $u_1, u_2, u_3, \ldots, u_m$ are the defects per unit for i = 1, 2, 3, . . ., m samples, respectively.

MINITAB software calculates the simple average to draw the centerline, but technically the weighted average is required.

Let:

$\bar{u}$ = Centerline of the u chart with varying sample size

Then, based on the simple average:

Let:

M = Total unit count in m samples
$= \Sigma n_i$, $i = 1, 2, 3, \ldots, m$

$\bar{u} = (\Sigma c_i)/M$

and based on the weighted average:

$$\bar{u} = \sum_i \left[\left(\frac{n_i}{M} \right) u_i \right], \text{ i} = 1, 2, 3, \ldots, m$$

The upper (UCL) and lower (LCL) control limits for each sample are

Table 6.12. Sample Data of Component's Characteristics with Varying Sample Size

Sample Number	Sample Size	Number of Defects	Weighted Defects per Unit	UCL	LCL
1	5	5	0.0490	2.456	0
2	6	7	0.0686	2.335	0
3	7	6	0.0588	2.241	0
4	5	4	0.0392	2.456	0
5	6	8	0.0784	2.335	0
6	9	10	0.0980	2.103	0.035
7	5	6	0.0588	2.456	0
8	7	9	0.0883	2.241	0
9	10	11	0.1078	2.050	0.088
10	4	4	0.0392	2.620	0
11	6	7	0.0686	2.335	0
12	8	8	0.0784	2.166	0
13	6	5	0.0490	2.335	0
14	9	9	0.0882	2.103	0.035
15	9	10	0.0980	2.103	0.035
Total	**102**	**109**	**1.0683**		

$$UCL_{ui} = \bar{u} + 3\sqrt{\frac{\bar{u}}{n_i}},\ i = 1, 2, 3, \ldots, m$$

$$LCL_{ui} = \bar{u} - 3\sqrt{\frac{\bar{u}}{n_i}},\ i = 1, 2, 3, \ldots, m$$

Example 6.8: Develop a u Chart with Varying Sample Size

A u chart is to be constructed for the component characteristics data in Table 6.12. Raw data are given. In-process data are also given. The data have a varying sample size. Calculate the centerline of the u chart, UCL, and LCL for each sample. Utilize the MINITAB software tool to plot a u chart.

Solution:

The centerline is based on simple average:

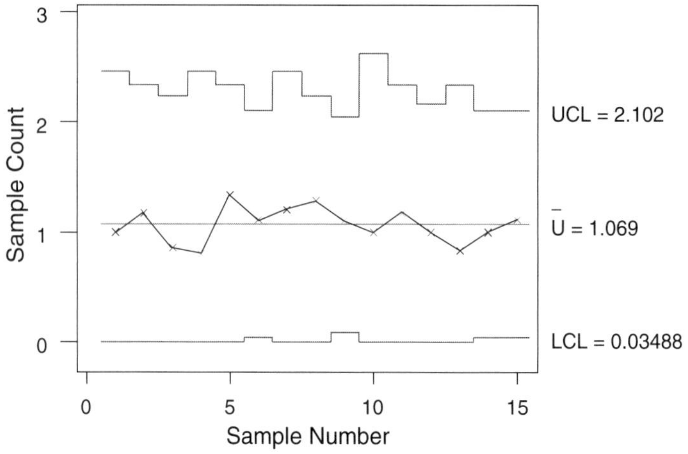

Figure 6.15. u Chart of Characteristics Failure per Unit for Selected Component and Varying Sample Size

$\bar{u} = 109/102 = 1.0686$

The u chart is presented in Figure 6.15.

6.4.6 SPC Summary

General information is useful in analyzing charts:

Trends—When a process is not stabilized and it is gradually and continuously decreasing or increasing, as the process continues, the out-of-control points will be noticed first on one side of the chart and then later on the other side of the chart. Cause factors for trends include seasonal effects, fatigue/stress, tool wearing, etc. If the amount of variability in a process is increasing or decreasing, the variation will be seen in the form of a trend in an R chart. Trend is a time-based change in process variable(s).

False Conclusion—At times control chart data may lead to a false conclusion. If a user has a good understanding of the process, the sampling plan that is used, and the control charts, then this phenomenon can be minimized. A false conclusion can occur in the following conditions:

- Data may need stratification when several different groups are included or if two groups are included in such a way that individually they are unstable, but in a group they are stable.
- The chart is out of control, but the process is stable.

- The chart is in control, but the process is out of control.

Chart Instability—A user is attempting to *control* a process by constantly adjusting parameter settings based on past results. Other causes of instability include:

- Improperly or carelessly setting process parameters
- Automatic control malfunctioning
- Using poor techniques (An R chart may show instability for several reasons, e.g., using poor logic to define subgroups, using nonrandom sampling, having an improperly trained workforce, etc.)
- Shewhart Control Charts—Generally the control limits set on Shewhart charts are ± 3 sigma of the central line. Shewhart control charts are considered to be robust due to the 3-sigma limits.

Control charts show various types of nonrandom patterns, e.g., gradual change, sudden change, staying on one side of the central line for a long time, and some combination of these situations.

A number of other basic and special control charts are available to resolve issues and help control processes. They all depend on similar logic to determine the essential decision points that detect out-of-control conditions.

Process—A process need not have a normally distributed variation for control charts to work. Process variation can be predicted only when process variation is known to be in a state of statistical control.

Exercise 6.4: Using SPC Charts

- Identify an opportunity to apply SPC to an input or in-process variable as well as to an output in your specific project.
- Determine the type of chart that would be most appropriate for the selected variables.
- Identify:
  - Who will be responsible for collecting, charting, and analyzing the data?
  - Does this person have the authority to act in an out-of-control condition?
  - Are any guidelines in place for troubleshooting an out-of-control condition?

6.5 FINAL PROJECT SUMMARY

The structural relationship of the sections discussed in this chapter is presented in Figure 6.1. The activities in Figure 6.1 are control-related activities in the DMAIC process. Self-control, monitor constraints, error proofing, and SPC have been detailed and discussed in previous sections of this chapter. The Six Sigma team is now at a stage when the recommended solution has been implemented and control measures have been installed. The next requirement of the team is to complete the final project steps, which include project documentation, implemented process instructions, process training, maintenance training, replication opportunities, project closure checklist, and identifying opportunities for future projects.

6.5.1 Project Documentation

Project documentation is a key step in a Six Sigma project. Format requirements can vary from business to business, but project documentation is a type of "virtual reality" of the process that was followed to accomplish the Six Sigma improvements. Project documentation is a permanent record of the project as well as a guidance tool for others who will be working on a similar type of project or who plan to continue to work on a recommended project(s) that developed from the completed project. Essential elements of project documentation include:

1. State project goals with constraints. State the project goals with applicable metrics and identifiable constraints:
   - Reduce jet engine (model XXXX) manufacturing cycle time from 18 months to 14 months: 22% manufacturing cycle time reduction by month/year (XX/XXXX).
   - Reduce component and WIP inventory from $XXX to $XXX by month/year (XX/XXXX) to provide $XXX in freed-up capital.
   - Provide the full opportunity cost of $XXX per year by month/year (XX/XXXX).
2. Provide the planned schedule for the project vs. the actual schedule. If the actual schedule is significantly different from the planned schedule, provide an explanation. An explanation will help future teams to develop a more-realistic schedule based on available resources (given constraints).
3. Present the process followed to achieve the project goals. Specifically, identify:
   - Tools used to present the information
   - How issues were evaluated

   - Tools used to develop relationships between independent and dependent variables
   - How alternative solutions were developed and then how the implemented solution was selected.
4. State actual goals achieved.
5. List planned vs. actual achievement of opportunities.
6. State the financial results from the project. Financial results achieved are a most-interesting part of a project. Because the future of a business depends on the bottom line (profitability), business leadership is not only interested in the current profitability, but also very highly interested in future profitability and growth. Six Sigma projects help businesses to improve profitability. Benefits identified at the beginning of the project (during the **D**efine and **M**easure phases) are generally stated as *expected benefits.* As the team progresses and goes through the **A**nalyze and **I**mprove phases and analyzes the alternative solutions, it has an opportunity to better understand the benefits. Once the team recommends a solution to achieve the defined goals, these benefits are considered to be *projected benefits.* When the team implements the recommended solution and collects the savings data, the savings data provide the *actual benefits.* Benefits data may change from the beginning of the project (when they are known as *expected benefits*) throughout the project to the implementation stage of the project (when they are known as *actual benefits*).

Note: The two sources of financial benefits are *cost reduction* with the same revenue and *revenue increase* with or without any cost adjustments. It is easier to measure revenue increase than cost reduction. Cost reduction impacts many resources, e.g., people, equipment, facility, maintenance of the facility and equipment, material, technology, etc. At the beginning of a project, the team analyzes and estimates cost savings and presents them as *expected benefits.* When the recommended solution has been implemented, team collects benefits data in relationship to the impact of the recommended solution on resources. The team then presents this benefits data as actual benefits.

7. Provide "lessons learned" by the project team, e.g., knowledge gained, vital information captured, etc.). Providing lessons learned applies to every employee who was directly or indirectly involved in the project:
   - Knowledge gained
   - Vital information collected

- How to avoid mistakes
- Necessary activities

Documenting information is crucial. Making information available to others in the company is also important.

8. Make recommendations for future projects. Because the team is the best source to recommend future, related projects, the team should document its recommendations soon after implementing the recommended solution.
9. Provide an instruction manual. As a new or modified process is implemented, the team must provide a process instruction manual.

General instructions for all types of documentation include:

- The document must be easily accessible. Users should know where the document is stored.
- The document must be updated as changes take place. Document changes with an effective date.

6.5.2 Implemented Process Instructions

Fundamental rules for developing process instructions include the following:

- Simple, precise, and clear instructions must be given.
- Users and responsible process parties must participate in development of process instructions.
- The text must be limited.
- The instructions must be realistic.

The contents of process instructions should also include, if applicable, the following, with as many examples as possible:

- Purpose and scope
- CTQs (critical to quality characteristics) parameters to be controlled
- Proper procedures and metrics
- Decision criteria and stages
- Preventive actions to avoid (or minimize) losses
- Corrective actions to minimize losses
- Environmental, health, and safety considerations
- Assumptions (The number of assumptions should be as reasonable as possible. The assumptions must be tested.)

- Terms and expressions (Definitions and language used will depend on the users, both professional and/or local.)
- A clear interpretation
- Pictures, flow charts, and tables as appropriate

As a new or modified process is implemented, users of the process must be trained to run as well as maintain the process.

6.5.3 Implemented Process Training

Key elements in process training include:

- The objectives of the training must be clear and precise.
- Training documents must be prepared before training is started. These documents must meet the same requirements identified in Section 6.5.2, *Implemented Process Instructions.*
- Communication between students (trainees) and the instructor (trainer) must be good. Students should also have a good knowledge of the instruction language (reading, writing, understanding, and speaking).
- The instructor should follow the developed training schedule. Training should be consistent with the material provided.
- Student participation in discussions and hands-on practice during training is very important.
- Keep the students-to-instructor ratio as low as possible.
- As the process changes, supplemental training as needed should be provided to users.

6.5.4 Maintenance Training

Two types of maintenance training are preventive and regular service:

Preventive Maintenance Training—A trainer must demonstrate how:

- To utilize resources in process characteristics that are important to customers
- To process maintenance that reduces the chances of system failure
- To replace low-useful-life process components during preventive maintenance
- To identify process components that need improvement
- To maintain and utilize maintenance data

Regular Service Maintenance Training—Critical points about regular service maintenance training include:

- The trainer should demonstrate how to repair and replace components in the process.
- Students should have a good understanding of the process.
- A decision should be made to replace components or to replace a higher-level process unit.
- The trainer should show how to evaluate process elements for repair/replacement.
- Maintenance training should demonstrate how to maintain and utilize repair data.
- Maintenance should demonstrate how to minimize reactive service and develop goals for proactive services.

As the team members develop these documents and provide training to regular users of the process, the team must share its gained knowledge with the other members in the business organization. This will provide replication opportunities in the business (see the next section).

6.5.5 Replication Opportunities

The team should share the information so that other employees in the business will have an opportunity to use the knowledge that team members have acquired:

- To avoid wasting resources in solving the same issue
- To speed up the improvement process in the business
- To rapidly resolve issues and improve customer satisfaction
- To reduce DPMO (the defects per million opportunities) at a faster rate to improve financial benefits

Acquired knowledge can be applied with:

- Direct Replication—By using the same or a similar process for a product or service
- Customization—By using same process for different product or service
- Adaptation—By using the process, but with limited applicability

As the team is engages in the final documentation, training, etc., the team must ensure that a project closure checklist and a future projects list have been completed (see the next two sections).

6.5.6 Project Closure Checklist

Developing a project closure checklist is essential. A checklist can easily identify any leftover activities. Generally, completing a leftover activity is easy for the team to complete as long as the team is still together. Once the team members are no longer a defined team, bringing team members together to complete leftover activities becomes difficult. Guideline items for a project closure checklist include:

- Project documentation is according to business guidelines.
- Project completion is according to defined goals. Project has been declared closed by the project owner.
- The implemented solution has been transferred to regular owners.
- Measurement metrics has been set up to monitor project improvements. Then measurement metrics has documented the plan. Improvement will be remeasured at a future (specified) time.
- Financial benefits have been measured. The benefits have been accepted by all parties, e.g., project owner, project team, financial, program champion, etc. The savings data collection process has been documented.
- Project completion has been identified in the respective databases.

6.5.7 Future Projects

The time to examine the collected data and the processes analyzed to determine the root causes of the issues identified in the project and to identify opportunities for future projects is while the team is still together and memories are still fresh. Questions team members should ask include the following:

- How were key elements in the data identified and verified?
- How did identification of these elements lead to potential causes?
- What was used by the team to make decisions about root causes?
- What was learned and what recommendations were made from:
  - A detailed process map
  - Data collection, analysis, and identification of root causes
  - A project scheduling approach
  - A data analysis approach
  - Root-cause analysis/cause-and-effect analysis
  - Application of qualitative and/or quantitative relationships between independent variables and the dependent variable
  - Financial analysis and data collection

– Project process and procedure

6.6 SUMMARY

In the first five chapters, the first four phases of the DMAIC process (Define, Measure, Analyze, and Improve) have been discussed. Therefore, the process improvement solution has been selected and implemented and projected benefits have been realized. The last phase, Control, of the DMAIC process has been discussed in this sixth and final chapter.

Discussion in this chapter has been based on the premise that retaining gains made from implementation of the improved/modified process, with the help of tools and techniques (e.g., self-control, monitor constraints, error-proofing, and SPC), are important. Guidance has also been given for developing the final project summary report. Key elements of a final project summary report include:

- Project Documentation Instructions
- Implemented Process Instructions
- Implemented Process Training
- Maintenance Training
- Replication Opportunities
- Project Closure Checklist
- Future Projects

The following are elements that should be included in a checklist that team members should review to ensure that the Control phase of the DMAIC process has been completed. The elements of the checklist have been divided into key activities:

Monitoring Plan

- Has the control/monitoring plan been in place for an adequate period of time?
- Will the process owner and regular working team members be able to maintain the gains?
- Have key inputs and outputs been identified to the team members so that they will be able to measure for and detect suboptimal conditions?
- Has adequate training been provided to the owner/team members so that new or emerging customer needs/requirements will be

checked/communicated to orient the process toward meeting new specifications and continually reducing variation?

- Has the team been trained in utilizing control charts?
- Do team members know how to calculate their latest Sigma metrics?
- Does established process performance meet customer requirements?

Documented Procedure

- Has proper documentation been developed to successfully support the improved operation?
- Have team members been trained and educated about the documented procedures?
- If applicable, have team members been given information about any revised work instructions?
- Are developed procedures clear and easy for operators to follow?

Response Plan

- Is a response plan in place so that operators to realize when the input, the process, or the output measures indicate an "out-of-control" condition?
- Has a list of critical parameters been developed for operators to watch?
- Have suggested corrective/restorative actions been listed on the response plan for the known causes to problems that might surface?
- Has a troubleshooting guide been developed should one be needed?

Project Closure/Transfer of Ownership

- Has process responsibility been transferred to the real owner? Specifically, has it been transferred in the database?
- Has day-to-day process monitoring and continual improvement responsibility been transferred to the process owner?
- Does the process owner understand how to calculate future Sigma metrics and the process capabilities?
- Has any recommended frequency of auditing been provided to the process owner?
- Have any future projects been recommended in a related process?

- Have quality tools been recommended to control process improvements?

Project Benefits Linked to the Business

- Has the project closure report recommended other areas of the business that might benefit from the project team's improvements, knowledge, and lessons learned?
- Has the business been recognizing the best practices and lessons learned so that improvement can be leveraged across the business?
- Has the business been recognizing that other systems, operations, processes, and infrastructures need updates, additions, changes, or deletions to facilitate knowledge transfer and improvements, e.g., activities such as hiring practices, training, employee compensation including incentives/rewards, metrics, etc.

Now the team can celebrate their successes and congratulate each other for all their hard work!!!

REFERENCES

1. Kumar, D.2003. *Lean Manufacturing Systems.* Unpublished.
2. Wheeler, D. J. 1995. *Advanced Topics in Statistical Process Control: The Power of Shewhart Charts.* Knoxville, TN: SPC Press.
3. Wheeler, D. J. and D. S. Chambers. 1992. *Understanding Statistical Process Control, Second Edition.* Knoxville, TN: SPC Press.
4. Nater, J., W. Wasserman, and M. Kutner. 1990. *Applied Linear Statistical Models: Regression, Analysis of Variance, and Experimental Designs, Third Edition.* Chicago: Richard D. Irwin.

* * * *

APPENDICES

Appendix A1. Business Strategic Planning
Appendix A2. Manufacturing Strategy and the Supply Chain
Appendix A3. Production Systems and Support Services
Appendix A4. Glossary
Appendix A5. Selected Tables

APPENDIX A1 — BUSINESS STRATEGIC PLANNING

The rate of return in any business is critical for availability of capital. Investors will not tolerate returns below the returns of long-term government securities (adjusted upward by the risk of capital loss). Essential structural features of each industry determine the strength of competitive forces in that industry and, hence, overall industry profitability. The goal of a competitive strategy for a business unit in any industry is to find a position in the industry in which the company can best defend itself against competitive forces or can influence them in its favor. Business management understands the collective strength of competitive forces, and the results of competition are apparent. Studying and analyzing underlying sources of competitive forces are essential. Knowledge of the underlying sources of competitive pressure will highlight critical strengths and weaknesses of a company. Serious analysis of a company's position in its industry clarifies areas in which:

- Strategic changes can yield the greatest payoff
- Significant opportunities exist
- Greatest threats exist

Competitive Forces

Five competitive forces are presented in Figure A1.1. A brief discussion will be presented for:

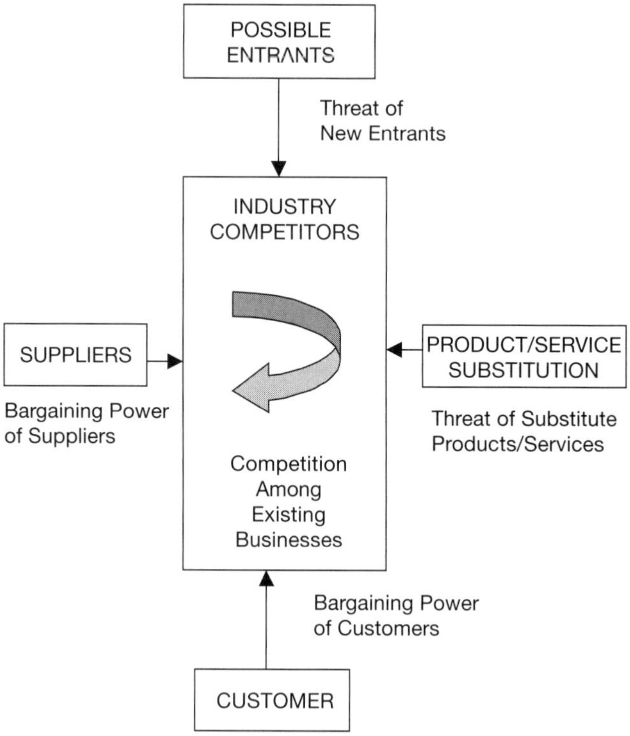

Figure A1.1. Strategic Competitive Forces

- Threat of new entrants
- Threat of substitute products/services/solutions
- Bargaining power of customers
- Bargaining power of suppliers
- Competition among existing businesses

Analyzing and understanding these forces can result in:

- Intensified competition
- Business profitability
- Strategy formulation
- Consideration of areas for diversification

Force 1. Threat of New Entrants—New entrants to an industry bring:

- New capacity
- Desire to gain market share
- Price competition (which generally leads to lower prices that in turn mean consideration of a lower profit margin)

The degree of threat of entry into an industry depends on existing barriers to entry, along with reactions from existing competitors that can be expected by the entrant. If barriers are high and/or a newcomer can expect sharp retaliation from tough competitors, the threat of entry is low. Several elements reduce incentives for new entrants:

- Risk of Capital Investment—Initial capital investment is required in key business activities, such as product development and production, marketing and sales, research and development, service network, etc.
- Industry Maturity—Because growth potential is generally quite limited, a new entrant will avoid entering a maturing industry.
- Government Policy—A government agency can limit or even force a "closed entry" situation in an industry with controls such as licensing requirements or by limiting access to raw materials, e.g., land for coal mining, mountains on which skiing areas can be built, etc.
- Regulation—The size of some industries is limited by regulation, e.g., liquor retailing, railroads, trucking, etc.
- Profit Margin—Generally, new entrants assign low priority to a low-profit-margin business.
- Initial Costs—Initial costs may include the cost to customers of switching to another service or product.
- Product Differentiation—Generally established businesses have:
    - Brand identification
    - Customer loyalty from past and present products and services
    - Customer satisfaction

Force 2. Threat of Substitute Products/Services/Solutions—Most businesses in any industry compete by producing substitute products. This limits potential returns in the industry due to lower prices. Elasticity of product demand is also impacted. Substitute products that receive the most attention are those that:

- Are subject to having a promising improvement in their price performance compared with the industry's existing product
- Are produced by industries earning high profits

Force 3. Bargaining Power of Customers—In a competitive market, a customer negotiates lower prices, with on-time delivery, for a quality product and satisfying services. This creates significant competition among businesses at the expense of industry profitability. The buying power of wholesalers and retailers is determined by the same rules, but retailers get an additional advantage. Retailers can gain significant bargaining power over manufacturers if they can influence the purchasing decisions of consumers, e.g., as is often true in audio and video components, personal computer components, sporting goods, etc. Wholesalers can gain similar bargaining power if they can influence the purchasing decisions of retailers or other firms to which they sell products.

Force 4. Bargaining Power of Suppliers—If there is a limited supply of material (i.e., demand for material is greater than the supply of material), suppliers can exert bargaining pressure over participants in an industry by threatening to raise prices or lower the quality of existing product and/or services. Supplier groups can be powerful in certain conditions, e.g., if an industry:

- Is dominated by a few companies and consumers are widely distributed
- Does not produce a substitutable product
- Is not an important customer of a supplier group(s)
- Is a recognized supplier—A workforce must also be recognized as a supplier. Highly skilled employees and/or a tightly unionized workforce can bargain away a significant fraction of potential profits in any industry.

Force 5. Competition among Existing Businesses—Competition forces businesses to "jockey" their position within an industry, impacting several elements:

- Price competition
- The advertising battle
- Product modification and/or introduction of new products
- Increased customer service
- Extended warranties

Some form of competition among businesses in any industry is good for consumers as well as for the industry. Yet, price competition can sometimes make an industry highly unstable, likely leaving the entire industry worse off from a standpoint of profitability. Price cuts are quickly and easily matched by rivals, and once matched, price cuts lower revenues for all businesses unless the price elasticity of demand in the industry is high.

Advertising battles, on the other hand, may well expand demand or enhance the level of product differentiation in the industry to the benefit of all businesses. Intense competition is a result of several factors:

- Numerous or Equally Balanced Competitors—When businesses are numerous in any industry, some businesses may think that they can make “moves” without being noticed.
- Slow-Growth Industries—Some businesses want to gain market share in a slow-growth industry, which in turn creates intense competition.
- High Fixed or Storage Costs—When excess capacity is available, businesses are forced to produce more and sell more, which often leads to rapidly escalating price cutting, e.g., as in the aluminum and paper industries.
- Lack of Differentiation—Similar services or switching costs may spark competition, e.g., low-cost services.
- High Strategic Stakes—Competition in any industry becomes even more intense if a number of businesses have high stakes in achieving success, e.g., Sony or Philips might perceive a strong need to establish a solid position in the U.S. market to build global prestige or technological credibility.
- High Exit Barriers—Exit barriers are economic, strategic, and emotional factors that keep companies competing in an industry even if they are earning low revenues or losing money. Major barriers to exiting an industry include:
  - Specialized assets
  - High fixed costs of exit
  - Emotional barriers
  - Government and social restrictions

Strategies
As businesses cope with the five competitive forces, three potentially successful generic strategic approaches can result in some businesses outperforming other businesses in a respective industry:

- Overall cost leadership
- Differentiation
- Focus

Sometimes a business can successfully pursue more than one approach as its main target, although this is rarely possible. Effectively implementing any of the generic strategies generally requires strong commitment and supportive organizational arrangements. Organizational commitment and support are often diluted by having more than one primary target.

Strategy 1. Overall Cost Leadership—Lowest-cost-producer leadership requires implementation of at least:

- Efficient-scale facilities
- Vigorous leadership of cost reduction from experience and from tight cost and overhead control
- Minimizing marginal customer accounts
- Cost minimization in areas, e.g., research and development, service, sales, advertising, etc.

A low-cost-producer position in any business generally yields above-average returns in the industry despite the presence of strong competitive forces. A low-cost position:

- Defends a business against buyers—Buyers can exert pressure, driving prices down to the level of the next most-efficient competitor.
- Provides a defense against powerful suppliers by providing more flexibility to cope with input cost increases
- Provides entry barriers in terms of economies of scale or cost advantages
- Usually places a business in a favorable position as well as utilizes a product substitute that is relative to its competitors in the industry

A cost leadership strategy can sometimes revolutionize an industry in which the historical bases of competition have been to use other methods or in which competitors are not prepared perceptually or economically to take the necessary steps for cost minimization, e.g., low-cost Southwest Airlines in competition with other airlines such as American, Delta, etc.

Strategy 2. Providing Differentiation—Offering products or services that are perceived industry-wide as unique is a viable strategy for earning above-average returns in an industry because a defensible position, different from cost leadership, is created for coping with the five competitive forces. Differentiation approaches include:

- Design or brand image
- Technology
- Features
- Customer service
- A dealer network

Strategy 3. Focus—Focusing on a particular customer group, a segment of the product line, or a geographic market is similar to differentiation and can take many forms. Low-cost and differentiation strategies are aimed at achieving objectives industry-wide, but the focus of a strategy is built around serving a particular target very well. Each functional policy is developed with this goal in mind. A business achieving focus can potentially earn above-average returns in its industry. Focus indicates that a business either has a low-cost position compared to its strategic target, high differentiation, or both.

Risks

Each strategy has risks:

- Risks of Generic Strategies—Two risks are linked to generic strategies:
  - Failing to attain or sustain a strategy
  - A strategic advantage that is not strong enough to compensate for losses due to industry evolution
- Risks of Overall Cost Leadership—Cost leadership imposes severe burdens on a business to maintain its position, e.g., reinvesting in upgraded machines (systems), ruthlessly scraping obsolete assets, controlling product line proliferation, and being alert to technological improvements.
- Risk of Differentiation—Risks involved with differentiation include:
  - The cost differential between low-cost competitors and the differentiated business may become too great for differentiation to maintain brand loyalty. Therefore, customers sacrifice some of the features, services, or the image of the differentiated business for larger cost savings.
  - As customers become more sophisticated, they require differentiating factors less.
  - Often, as an industry matures, imitation narrows perceived differentiation.
- Risk of Focus—Focus includes another set of risks:
  - The cost differential between broad-range competitors and a focused business widens to eliminate the cost advantages from serving a narrow target or they offset the differentiation achieved from focusing.
  - Differences between a strategic target and the market as a whole narrow for desired products or services.
  - Competitors find submarkets within the strategic target and “out focus” a focused business.

Detailed Strategic Planning

An introductory analysis of business strategy has been described, but a more-detailed study of strategic business planning would include three steps:

Step 1. Along with introductory analysis, add:

- Analyzing competitors, customers, and suppliers
- Understanding the techniques of reading market signals
- Analyzing theoretic concepts for making and responding to competitive moves
- Developing an approach to mapping strategic groups in the industry and explaining differences in their performance
- Defining a framework for predicting industry evolution

Step 2. Utilize the introductory framework:

- Develop a competitive strategy for the environment in a particular type of industry.
- Identify possibilities for differentiation. Differentiating environments is crucial in determining the strategic context in which a business competes, the strategic alternatives available, and common strategic errors.

Step 3. Identify strategic areas by:

- Examining and categorizing the business:
  - Fragmented industries
  - Emerging industries
  - Industries in transition to industry maturity
  - Declining industries
  - Global industries
- Systematically examining the important types of strategic decisions that confront businesses competing in a single industry
- Utilizing other essential activities, e.g., vertical integration, capacity expansion, and entry into a new business.
- Determining if corporate strategies for marketing, manufacturing, and distribution are a "fit"—Strategies must fit together to meet customer needs at minimum cost. Possible alternatives include:
  - Concentrating on marketing, with total manufacturing and distribution being subcontracted to outside suppliers

– Concentrating on manufacturing activities, with sales and advertising being contracted out

ADDITIONAL READING

1. Kumar, D. 2003. *Lean Manufacturing Systems*. Unpublished.

APPENDIX A2 — MANUFACTURING STRATEGY AND THE SUPPLY CHAIN

Manufacturing strategy and the supply chain are interdependent topics, therefore an overview is required to describe these topics.

Manufacturing Strategy[1]

If strategic planning activities have not been properly performed, knowing if a business is moving in the right direction (or not) will be difficult. A strategic business plan provides a view of the business (with direction) and provides a road map showing the direction the business should take to achieve its goals.

The desired marketplace position of a business to satisfy its customers is stated in a general way in a strategic plan. A strategic plan should also include targets for market share, sales, quality, on-time delivery, inventory level, profitability, etc. A strategic plan leads to a strategic manufacturing plan. A strategic manufacturing plan identifies products to be produced, production technology that will be used to produce the products selected, and manufacturing policies that will be followed for purchasing, manufacturing, and distribution.

Certain essential elements impact any manufacturing strategy:

- Location of manufacturing facilities
- Product distribution network

- Inventory policies that are matched to selected geographical markets and the required speed of delivery
- Policies that are related to the employment level of a knowledgeable workforce, with employee training and benefits
- Core competencies
- Vertical integration
- Supporting decisions
  - Make vs. buy
  - Make-to-stock vs. make-to-order
  - Selection of technology and equipment

The Supply Chain

Natural raw material goes through a series of processes to produce an ultimate customer product. One or more manufacturers might participate in the process. The planning and execution of these processes comprise the logistics function. The logistics function illustrates the entire supply chain from raw materials to delivered product. Key elements of an effective logistics function include:

- The functional capability of all potential suppliers and their geographical locations
- Manufacturing facilities at a business
- Customer markets
- Transportation sources that connect supplier, manufacturer, and customer

The most competitive option is selected from these resources with respect to the product, the cost of the product, quality, on-time availability to customers, and after-delivery service to customers. The logistics function creates a network known as a logistics network. Information management in a logistics network is critical. Twenty-first century logistics or global logistics describes a modern global market.[2]

Global Logistics—The peacetime economy after World War II slowly moved toward globalization, but accelerated at a fast pace at the beginning of the twenty-first century. Businesses were creating global production and distribution networks to take advantage of international opportunities.

In the current global economy, businesses often design, manufacture, and distribute products through a global network to provide the best customer service at a competitive price. Businesses are making a profit margin even with the international challenges of diverse cultures, languages, people, governmental regulations, and measurement systems because conditions are positive for international business, e.g., instantaneous information exchange, improved transportation, etc.

Often, a significant number of products reflect multinational business ventures. Mixing of components in finished products has also become commonplace, e.g., the automobile industry and its utilization of this concept. Participating businesses also benefit by sharing technology and the market.

Other essential elements in supply chain management include:

- Product design and customization to the local market
- Supplier selection, certification, and long-term contracts
- Distribution of finished components and products
- Locating and distributing inventory

Coordinating production schedule information across the supply chain is important. Without proper communication and planning coordination, variation at the final-customer end of the supply chain can accelerate upstream in a chaotic manner. According to Askin and Goldberg,[2] this phenomenon is referred as the "bullwhip effect."

Manufacturing strategy has a critical role in any company's decision to select a supply chain process. Therefore, a strategic plan must consider facilities, processes, people, and products in developing a purchasing, manufacturing, distribution, and service plan.

REFERENCES

1. Kumar, D. 2003. *Lean Manufacturing Systems.* Unpublished.
2. Askin, R.G. and J.B. Goldberg. 2002. *Design and Analysis of Lean Production System.* New York: John Wiley.

APPENDIX A3 — PRODUCTION SYSTEMS AND SUPPORT SERVICES

Production Planning and Support Services Decisions

Production planning and support services decisions are typically made in a hierarchical manner[1] as shown in Figure A3.1. The first column in the figure shows the actual flow of material from raw stage through delivered product/solution. Twenty-first century suppliers deliver solutions to customers. A solution could be a combination of hardware, software, and professional services.

The last column in Figure A3.1 shows associated support functions and design activities that must be available before the start of production and support services activities for customers. The middle column shows the sequence of operational decisions for production planning, scheduling, and control. These decisions are listed in the hierarchical order in which they usually are made.

The level of professional services depends on customer requirements. Professional services may be required before system delivery, during system delivery, and/or during the system's useful life. Demand forecasts define the opportunity to make profits and have gainful employment by providing satisfaction to customers.

The Decision Process

The decision process[2] is hierarchical in a production system. Figure A3.2 summarizes the manufacturing system in an IPO (<u>I</u>nput-<u>P</u>rocess-<u>O</u>utput) format.

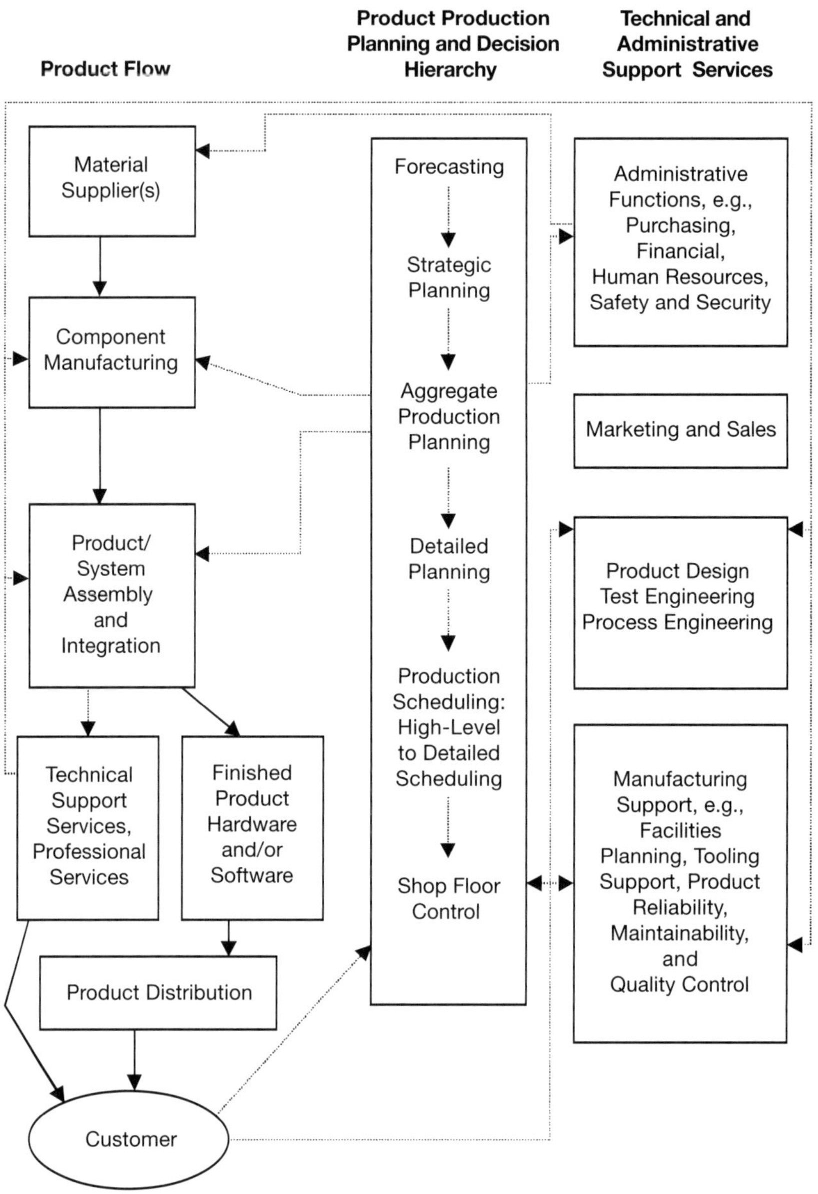

Figure A3.1. Production Planning and Support Services Information Flow Chart

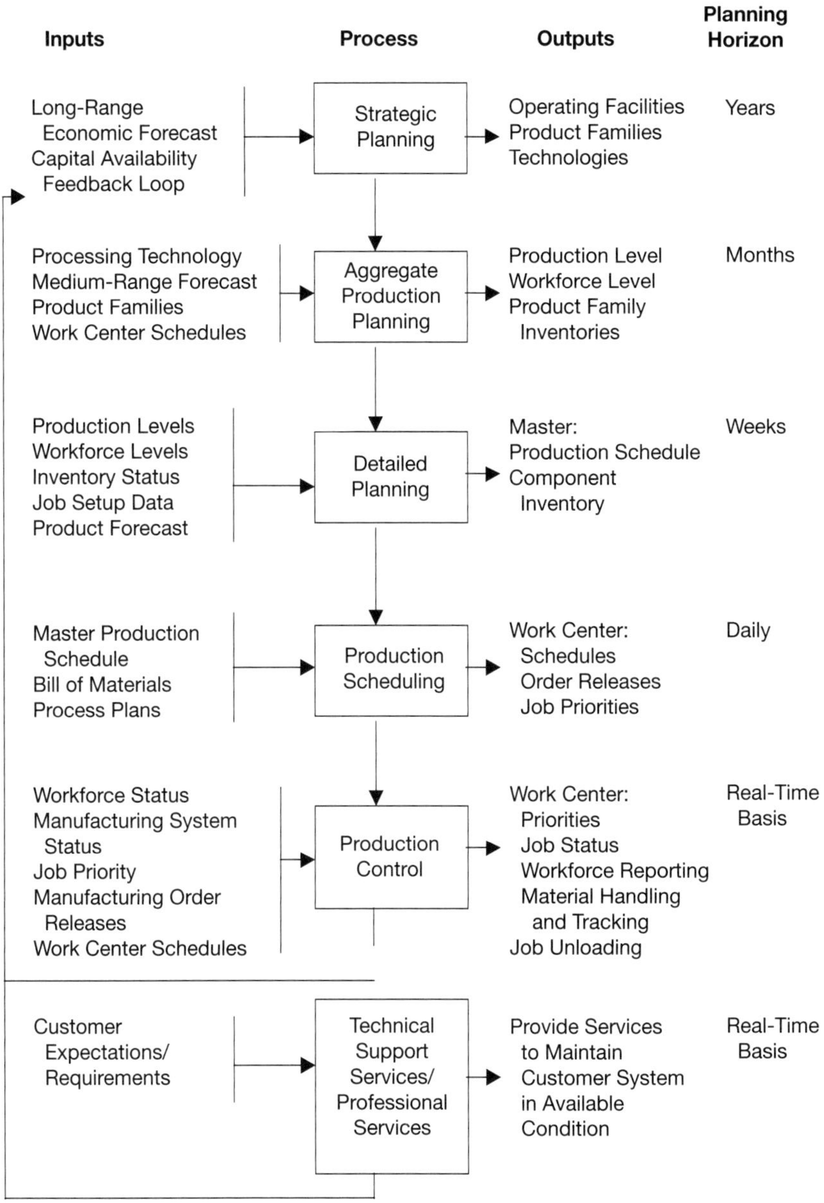

Figure A3.2. Inputs, Processes, and Outputs in a Manufacturing System

Decisions are made at several levels in all businesses. These decisions are generally time-based and, therefore, highly dependent on the type of business:

- Strategic Level—Long-term decisions are at the strategic level and are normally for a 1- to 5-year time frame, but the time frame can be longer in certain industries. Making a capital investment is an example of a strategic-level decision, e.g., an investment in facilities, equipment, tools, etc.
- Tactical Level—A decision at the tactical level is a shorter-term decision (e.g., monthly, quarterly, etc.) to implement strategic-level decisions, e.g., aggregate production planning in a manufacturing area. A typical manufacturing aggregate plan states the levels of major product "families" that are to be produced monthly over the next 12 months or so. Examples of other tactical level manufacturing decisions include:
  - Change in workforce level
  - Scheduling overtime
  - Built-in inventory
- Operational Level—Decisions at the operational level are made on a daily or weekly level, e.g., detailed scheduling at a component and assembly level to meet a customer's requirements. Most customer service decisions fall in this category, especially after product (system) delivery. For customers, on-time service delivery is as critical as delivery of the product.

A hierarchical organizational structure supports production decisions. The size of the organization depends on the type of product (system). A short-life product has a "flatter" production organizational structure than a long-life product. In a complex system, making group decisions for all decisions in a plant/production facility, and also making them in real time, is almost impossible due to the complexity of the entire system.

REFERENCES

1. Kumar, D. 2003. *Lean Manufacturing Systems*. Unpublished.
2. Askin, R.G. and J.B. Goldberg. 2002. *Design and Analysis of Lean Production System*. New York: John Wiley.

APPENDIX A4 — GLOSSARY

A

Accuracy.
The degree to which a measurement system is accurate will generally be the difference between an observed average measurement and the associated known standard value.

Alternate Hypothesis.
The second hypothesis is known as the alternate hypothesis. It is symbolized by H_1.

B

Balanced Design.
A balanced experimental design is a design in which each level for any one factor is repeated the same number of times for all possible combination levels of the other factors, e.g., a factorial design of two factors (A and B) and two levels (–1, 1) will have four runs.

Binomial Distribution.
This distribution is used when a possibility of an occurrence of one of the two possible outcomes exists in every trial (e.g., accept or reject; success or failure) and the probability for each trial remains constant. This distribution is also known as Bernoulli's distribution.

Black Belt (BB) Certified.
A Black Belt-certified person should have sufficient knowledge and technical training to achieve project goals. Black Belt training includes problem solving and improvement skills, quantifying project savings, project management skills, project reporting skills, and training in the statistical tools

required to measure, analyze, improve, and control a project.

Box Plot.
Box plots are similar to histograms. They provide a graphic summary of the variation in a given set of data with "whiskers" and "outliers." A Box Plot groups data points into four main categories known as quartiles. A Box Plot is an excellent tool for comparing samples of data.

C

Capability.
The ability of a process to produce a product/service within defined specification limits is known as capability.

Census.
If all data on a population are collected, census is another descriptive term that can be used.

Chi-square Distribution (χ^2 Distribution).
A χ^2 distribution is specific type of sampling distribution that is known as chi-square or χ^2.

Coefficient of Correlation ($\sqrt{r^2} = r$).
The square root of the sample coefficient of determination is a common alternative index of the degree of association between two quantitative variables.

Coefficient of Determination (r^2).
How well the estimated regression line fits the sample data, or the amount of variation explained by the regression equation, is measured by the coefficient of determination (r^2).

Common Cause.
A common cause is due to inherent interaction among input resources. It is normally expected, random, and predictable.

Confidence Interval.
A confidence interval is an interval that has a designated chance of including the universal value.

Confidence Limits.
The end points of a confidence interval are the confidence limits.

Consumer's Risk (Type II Error or β).
Accepting a hypothesis when it is not true, i.e., a type II error has been made (e.g., accepting bad parts as good), is known as consumer's risk. β is the risk of not finding a difference when there actually is one. See also Producer's Risk.

Control Charts.
Control charts are graphical devices that highlight the average performance of a data series and the dispersion around the average. Control charts are an important tool in statistical process control.

Critical to Quality Characteristics (CTQs).
Key measurable characteristics of product/process/service performance standards that must be met to satisfy an external (ultimate) customer are know as CTQs. From the customer's

point of view, to be a satisfied customer, CTQs are the "vital few" measurable characteristics of a product or a process in which performance standards must be met.

Customer.
Customer defines a product and/or service requirement that is delivered by a manufacturer and/or supplier. Consumer may also be defined as an individual or organization that receives the processed output.

D

Defect.
A defect is anything that prevents a business from serving its customers as they prefer to be served.

Dependent Variable.
The value of the dependent variable is assumed to be unknown and is symbolized by Y. This variable is often called the response variable.

Design of Experiment (DOE).
DOE is an acronym that identifies how factors (independent variables, Xs), individually and in combination, affect a process and its output (dependent variables, Ys). DOE develops a mathematical relationship and determines the best configuration or combination of independent variables, Xs.

DFSS .
DFSS is an acronym for design for Six Sigma. See DMADV methodology.

DMADV Methodology (Duh-may-dove).
DMADV is an acronym for a five-phase process—Define, Measure, Analyze, Design, and Verify. DMADV is a scientific closed-loop process that is systematic and relies on the use of statistics. It applies to a product or process that is not in existence at a business and needs to be developed.

DMAIC Methodology (Duh-may-ik).
DMAIC is another acronym for a five-phase process—Define, Measure, Analyze, Improve, and Control. DMAIC is a scientific closed-loop process that is systematic and relies on the use of statistics. It is a popular Six Sigma process. Existing products or processes are optimized using the DMAIC process.

DPMO.
DPMO is an acronym for defects per million opportunities. See PPM.

E

Effectiveness of Measures.
Effectiveness of measures indicates meeting and exceeding customer needs and requirements, e.g., in areas such as service response time, percent product defective, and product functionality.

Efficiency of Measures.
Meeting and exceeding customer requirements based on the amount of the resources allocated is known as efficiency of measures, e.g., product rework time, product cost, and activity time.

EPMO.
The acronym EMPO, or the errors per million opportunities, is a metric for measuring and comparing the performance of distinct administrative, service, or transactional processes. EPMO quantifies the total number of errors or mistakes produced by a process per million iterations of the process.

Experiment, in Six Sigma.
In a Six Sigma context, an experiment is a planned inquiry, to obtain new facts or to confirm or deny the results of previous experiments, in which the inquiry is made to aid a team in a decision-making process.

Exponential Distribution.
Exponential distribution represents activity performance time. This distribution is closely related to the Poisson distribution, e.g., if customer arrival at the bank has a Poisson distribution, customer service time at the bank would have an exponential distribution.

F

Factor.
A factor is an input in an experiment. It could be a controlled or uncontrolled variable whose impact on a response is being studied in an experiment. The factor could be qualitative, e.g., different operators, machine types, etc., or it could be quantitative, e.g., distance in feet or miles, time in minutes, etc.

Factorial $k1 \times k2 \times k3$ ...
This is a basic description of a factorial experiment design. Each k represents a factor. The value of k is the number of levels of interest for that factor, e.g, a $3 \times 2 \times 2$ design indicates that there are three input variables (factors). One input has three levels and the other two have two levels each.

FMEA.
FMEA is an acronym for failure mode and effects analysis.

FMECA.
FMECA is an acronym for failure, mode, effects, and criticality analysis.

Flow Chart.
A flow chart is a pictorial representation of a process where all the steps of the process are presented. A flow chart is also a planning and analysis tool. It is a graphic of the steps in a work process. A flow chart is also a formalized graphic representation of a work or process, a programming logic sequence, or a similar formalized procedure.

G

Gamma Distribution.
The gamma distribution takes different shapes as the value of the shape parameter (r) changes. When r = 1, a gamma distribution reduces to an exponential distribution.

Green Belt (GB) Certified.
A Green Belt-certified person should be trained to support/participate in a Champion's Six Sigma implementation

program. A GB should also be able to lead a small Six Sigma project. A GB training program provides a thorough understanding of Six Sigma and the Six Sigma focus on eliminating defects through fundamental process knowledge. GB-certified employees are also trained to integrate the principles of business, statistics, and engineering to achieve tangible benefits.

H

Histogram.
A histogram is a bar diagram representing a frequency distribution.

Hypothesis.
A hypothesis is an intial proposition (for the time being) that is recognized as possibly being true.

Hypothesis Testing.
Hypothesis testing is a systematic approach for assessing an initial belief (a hypothesis) about reality. It confronts the belief with evidence and then decides, in light of this evidence, if the initial belief/hypothesis can be maintained as "reasonable" or if it must be discarded as "untenable."

I

Independent Variable.
The value of a variable assumed to be known is symbolized by X and known as the independent variable.

Input.
Resources (equipment, facility, material, people, technology, and utilities) and the data that is required to execute a process (operation) are known as input.

L

Level(s).
The input values of a factor being studied in an experiment are known as levels. Levels should be set far enough apart so that effects on the dependent variable Y can be detected. Levels are generally referred to as "–1" and "1." A level is also known as a treatment.

LCL.
LCL is an acronym for lower control limit. The LCL is equal to $(\mu - n\sigma)$ for population and (Xbar – ns) for sample.

LSL.
LSL is an acronym for lower specification limit.

M

Master Black Belt (MBB, also Master).
MBBs are generally program-site technical experts in Six Sigma methodology. MBBs are responsible for providing technical guidance to team leaders and members. Most of the time, MBBs are dedicated full time to support a program. They are to be an expert resource for their teams, e.g., for coaching, statistical analysis, and Just-In-Time training. Masters, along with team leaders, determine the team charter, goals, and team members. They also formalize studies and projects. A Master can support up to ten projects.

Method of Least Squares.
Fitting the data to a line in a scatter diagram is known as the method of least squares. The line is developed so that the sum of the squares of the vertical deviations between the line and the individual data plots is minimized.

MINITAB®.
MINITAB® is a statistical software package with high-quality, exportable graphics. Input data can be transported directly from an Excel™ spreadsheet. Recognizing the difference between text data and numeric data is important when using MINITAB.

N

NID(0, σ^2).
For hypothesis testing, model errors are assumed to be normally and independently distributed random variables with a mean of zero and a variance of σ^2 [abbreviated as NID(0, σ^2)]. The variance σ^2 is assumed constant for all levels of the factor.

Nominal Group Technique.
A structured process which identifies and ranks the major problems or issues that need addressing is known as a nominal group technique.

Non-Value-Added Activity.
Activity that a customer is not interested in and for which a customer is not willing to pay is known as non-value-added activity. Manufacturers/suppliers need non-value-added activity to support their businesses.

Normal Data (Common Language Communication).
A frequency distribution of normal data appears to cluster around an average (mean) and trails off symmetrically in both directions from the mean. A graph of the frequency distribution of normal data forms the shape of a bell (known as a bell curve). In statistical terms, this type of distribution is known as a normal distribution or a Gaussian distribution. A standard normal distribution has a mean of zero and a standard deviation of 1.

Null Hypothesis.
The first hypothesis in a set is known as a null hypothesis. It is symbolized by H_0.

O

One-Sided Hypothesis.
An alternate hypothesis that holds for deviations from the null hypothesis in *one direction only* is known as a one-sided hypothesis.

Outlier.
Any data point (usually considered anomalous), which is well beyond expectations, is known as an outlier. In a Box Plot, outliers are displayed as asterisks (*) beyond the "whiskers." See also Box Plot.

Output.
Output is a tangible product or service that is the result of a process to meet customer demand.

P

Pareto Chart.
A bar graph of counted data is known as a Pareto chart. The frequency of each category is displayed on the Y-axis (vertical axis). Category type is displayed on the X-axis. Frequency data are arranged in descending order.

Poisson Distribution.
The Poisson distribution estimates the occurrence of a number of events that are of the same type during a defined period.

PPM.
PPM is an acronym for parts per million or the number of defects in a population of a sample of one million (1,000,000). See DPMO.

Process.
A process is one or more operations that is performed over the input(s) and that change(s) the input into an output to meet a customer's demand.

Process Boundary.
The limits of a particular process are known as the process boundary (usually identified by the inputs and outputs which are outside the process boundary).

Process Capability Index (C_pk).
C_pk measures the ability of a process to create a product within specification limits.

Process Potential Index (C_p).
C_p measures the potential capability of a process. C_p is defined as the ratio of the allowable spread over the actual spread.

Producer's Risk (Type I Error or α).
To reject a hypothesis when it is actually true is known as producer's risk, e.g., rejecting good parts as being bad parts. α is the risk of finding a difference when there actually is a difference. See also Consumer's Risk.

R

Randomness.
Data should be collected in no predetermined order. Therefore, each element will have an equal probability to be selected for measurement.

Reengineering.
Reengineering is a process in which unnecessary tasks are eliminated, tasks can be combined or reordered, and information can be shared among the entire workforce involved in a process, etc.

Regression Analysis.
A statistical method, with a key focus on establishing an equation that allows the unknown value of one variable to be estimated from the known value of one or more other variables, is known as regression analysis.

Regression Equation.
A prediction equation, which can be linear or curvilinear, allows the unknown value of one variable to be estimated from the known value of one or more other variables.

Regression Line.
In regression analysis, a line that summarizes the relationship between an independent variable, X, and a dependent variable, Y, while also minimizing the errors made when the equation of that line is developed to estimate Y from X, is known as the regression line.

Repeatability.
If data being collected (measured) are repeatable, this condition is known as repeatability.

Repetition.
Running more than one experiment consecutively, and using the same treatment combinations, is known as repetition.

Replication.
Using the same experimental setup, with no change in the treatment levels, more than once, to collect more than one data point is known as replication. Replicating an experiment would allow a user to estimate the residual or the experimental error.

Reproducibility.
If all data collectors are observing the same activity and measuring the time for an activity with the same equipment, they should all reach essentially the same outcome.

Response Variable. See Dependent Variable.

Root Cause.
The lowest-level basic cause of a variance is known as the root cause.

S

Sampling.
Sampling is a portion or subset of the total data collection process.

Sigma.
Sigma is a symbol for the standard deviation of a process mean on either side of the specification limit.

Significance Level.
All sample results, which are possible when a null hypothesis is true, are known as the significance level. It is the (arbitrary) maximum proportion that is considered sufficiently unusual to reject a null hypothesis.

Simple Correlation Analysis.
A key focus of this statistical method is establishment of an index that provides, in a single number, an instant measure of the strength of association between two variables. Depending on the value of this measure (0 to 1), one can tell how closely together two variables move and, therefore, how confidently one variable can be estimated with the help of the other.

Simple Regression Analysis.
When a single variable is used to estimate the value of an unknown variable, the method is known as simple regression analysis.

SIPOC (Sy-pock).
SIPOC is an acronym for a process of steps in high level-business mapping, where S = supplier, I = input from supplier, P = business performed process, O = process output, and C = customer (internal and external). Supplier(s) provide input(s). A business performs one or more operations on the input(s) to produce an output to meet a customer's demand.

Six Sigma, the Statistical Term.
In pure statistical terms, Six Sigma is 0.002 defect per million parts, or 2 defects per billion parts, or a yield 99.9999998%.

Six Sigma, the Motorola Terminology.
In Motorola terminology, Six Sigma is a process, a metric, a statistic, a value, a vision, or a philosophy, depending on the context being discussed. It is a process that is focused on excellence. Six Sigma reduces the variance in any parameter that a customer deems critical to quality. It is a defect rate of not more than 3.4 parts per million, which allows a ± 1.5 sigma (long-term) shift from the statistical value (3.4 PPM is only ± 4.5 σ on the statistical scale).

Special Cause.
An especially large influence by one of the input resources is known as a special cause. A special cause is generally unpredictable or abnormal.

Stakeholders.
Stakeholders sponsor a project. A project team periodically reports project status to stakeholders. Stakeholders impact a process or a process impacts them.

Standard Deviation (SD).
The square root of the average of the squared deviations from the mean is known as the standard deviation. Standard deviation is designated by the symbol σ for population and by the symbol s for sample. Standard deviation is also a commonly used measure of the general variability of the data from the mean.

Statistic.
A function of sample observations that is used to estimate a universe parameter is known as a statistic.

Statistical Hypothesis.
A statistical hypothesis is a statement about the probability distribution of a random variable, e.g., interest may be in determining the mean tensile strength of a particular type of steel, i.e., specifically, the interest is in deciding whether or not the mean tensile strength is 15,000 psi.

Statistical Process Control (SPC).
An SPC is a problem-solving tool that may be applied to any process. Several SPC tools are available. SPC is also a desire by all individuals in a business/product/process group for continuous improvement in quality through the systematic reduction of variability.

Stratification.
Stratification is the process of separating data into categories (or groups) based on data variation.

Student's Distribution. See t Distribution.
The t distribution is also known as Student's distribution.

Supplier.
A supplier is source that provides input to a business process.

T

t Distribution. See Student's Distribution.
A t distribution is particular type of sample distribution. It is also known as Student's distribution.

Total Sum of Squares (TSS).
TSS is the sum of the squares of the deviations of individual items from the means of all the data.

Treatment Combination.
Identifying the experiment runs, using a set of specific levels for each input variable, is known as treatment combination. A full experiment uses all treatment combinations for all factors, e.g., a 3 × 2 × 2 factorial experimental design will have 12 possible treatment combinations in the experiment.

Two-Sided Hypothesis.
An alternate hypothesis that holds (is true) for deviations from the null hypothesis in both directions is known as a two-sided hypothesis.

Type I Error.
See Producer's Risk or α.

Type II Error.
See Consumer's Risk or β.

U

Unbalanced Design.
A designed experiment that is not meeting the criteria of a balanced design is known as unbalanced design. An unbalanced design is also a design in which each experimental level for any one factor is not repeated the same number of times for all possible levels of the other factors.

UCL.
UCL is an acronym for the upper control limit. UCL is equal to $(\mu + n\sigma)$ for population and $(\overline{X} + ns)$ for sample.

USL.
USL is an acronym for the upper specification limit.

V

Value-Added Activity.
An activity for which a customer is willing to pay and to support is known as value-added activity.

Variance.
The square of the standard deviation is known as variance.

W

Waste.
An activity that does not support either a customer or a manufacturer

/supplier and for which no one is willing to pay is known as waste.

Weibull Distribution.
This distribution provides an excellent approximation of the probability law of many random variables. An important area of the Weibull distribution application is as a model for the time-to-failure in electrical and mechanical products and systems.

Z

Z Value.
Any value away from the mean is measured in terms of standard deviation. Z is a unit of measure that is equivalent to the number of standard deviations.

APPENDIX A5 — SELECTED TABLES

Table A5.1. t-Distribution

1 − α	1	2	3	4	5	6	7	8	9	10
0.5	0.00	0.00	0.00	0.00	0.00	0.00	0.00	0.00	0.00	0.00
0.6	0.33	0.29	0.28	0.27	0.27	0.27	0.27	0.26	0.26	0.26
0.7	0.73	0.62	0.58	0.57	0.56	0.55	0.55	0.55	0.54	0.54
0.8	1.38	1.05	0.98	0.94	0.92	0.91	0.90	0.89	0.88	0.88
0.9	3.08	1.89	1.64	1.53	1.48	1.44	1.42	1.40	1.38	1.37
0.95	6.31	2.92	2.35	2.13	2.02	1.94	1.90	1.86	1.83	1.81
0.975	12.7	4.30	3.18	2.78	2.57	2.45	2.37	2.31	2.26	2.23
0.99	31.8	6.97	4.54	3.75	3.37	3.14	3.00	2.90	2.82	2.76
0.995	63.7	9.93	5.84	4.60	4.03	3.71	3.50	3.36	3.25	3.17
0.999	318.3	22.3	10.2	7.17	5.89	5.21	4.79	4.50	4.30	4.14

1 − α	11	12	13	14	15	16	17	18	19	20
0.5	0.00	0.00	0.00	0.00	0.00	0.00	0.00	0.00	0.00	0.00
0.6	0.26	0.26	0.26	0.26	0.26	0.26	0.26	0.26	0.26	0.26
0.7	0.54	0.54	0.54	0.54	0.54	0.54	0.53	0.53	0.53	0.53
0.8	0.88	0.87	0.87	0.87	0.87	0.86	0.86	0.86	0.86	0.86
0.9	1.36	1.36	1.35	1.35	1.34	1.34	1.33	1.33	1.33	1.33
0.95	1.80	1.78	1.77	1.76	1.75	1.75	1.74	1.73	1.73	1.73
0.975	2.20	2.18	2.16	2.15	2.13	2.12	2.11	2.10	2.09	2.09
0.99	2.72	2.68	2.65	2.62	2.60	2.58	2.57	2.55	2.54	2.53
0.995	3.11	3.06	3.01	2.98	2.95	2.92	2.90	2.88	2.86	2.85
0.999	4.03	3.93	3.85	3.79	3.73	3.69	3.65	3.61	3.58	3.55

1 − α	22	24	26	28	30	40	50	100	200	∞
0.5	0.00	0.00	0.00	0.00	0.00	0.00	0.00	0.00	0.00	0.00
0.6	0.26	0.26	0.26	0.26	0.26	0.26	0.26	0.25	0.25	0.25
0.7	0.53	0.53	0.53	0.53	0.53	0.53	0.53	0.53	0.53	0.52
0.8	0.86	0.86	0.86	0.86	0.85	0.85	0.85	0.85	0.84	0.84
0.9	1.32	1.32	1.32	1.31	1.31	1.30	1.30	1.29	1.29	1.28
0.95	1.72	1.71	1.71	1.70	1.70	1.68	1.68	1.66	1.65	1.65
0.975	2.07	2.06	2.06	2.05	2.04	2.02	2.01	1.98	1.97	1.96
0.99	2.51	2.49	2.48	2.47	2.46	2.42	2.40	2.37	2.35	2.33
0.995	2.82	2.80	2.78	2.76	2.75	2.70	2.68	2.63	2.60	2.58
0.999	3.51	3.47	3.44	3.41	3.39	3.31	3.26	3.17	3.13	3.09

ν = Number of degrees of freedom

Note: P (Student's t with ν degrees of freedom $\leq$ table value) = $1 - \alpha$.

Source: Kreyszig, E. 1967. *Advanced Engineering Mathematics, Second Editon*. New York: John Wiley. Copyright © 1967. Printed with permission of John Wiley and Sons, Inc. and Erwin Kreyszig.

Table A5.2. Chi-Square Distribution with ν Degrees of Freedom

1 – α	1	2	3	4	5	6	7	8	9	10
0.005	0.00	0.01	0.07	0.21	0.41	0.68	0.99	1.34	1.73	2.16
0.01	0.00	0.02	0.11	0.03	0.55	0.87	1.24	1.65	2.09	2.56
0.025	0.00	0.05	0.22	0.48	0.83	1.24	1.69	2.18	2.70	3.25
0.05	0.00	0.10	0.35	0.71	1.15	1.64	2.17	2.73	3.33	3.94
0.95	3.84	5.99	7.81	9.49	11.07	12.59	14.07	15.51	16.92	18.31
0.975	5.02	7.38	9.35	11.14	12.83	14.45	16.01	17.53	19.02	20.48
0.99	6.63	9.21	11.34	13.28	15.09	16.81	18.48	20.09	21.67	23.21
0.995	7.88	10.60	12.84	14.86	16.75	18.55	20.28	21.96	23.59	25.19
1 – α	**11**	**12**	**13**	**14**	**15**	**16**	**17**	**18**	**19**	**20**
0.005	2.60	3.07	3.57	4.07	4.60	5.14	5.70	6.26	6.84	7.43
0.01	3.05	3.57	4.11	4.66	5.23	5.81	6.41	7.01	7.63	8.26
0.025	3.82	4.40	5.01	5.63	6.26	6.91	7.56	8.23	8.91	9.59
0.05	4.57	5.23	5.89	6.57	7.26	7.96	8.67	9.39	10.12	10.85
0.95	19.68	21.03	22.36	23.68	25.00	26.30	27.59	28.87	30.14	31.41
0.975	21.92	23.34	24.74	26.12	27.49	28.85	30.19	31.53	32.85	34.17
0.99	24.73	26.22	27.69	29.14	30.58	32.00	33.41	34.81	36.19	37.57
0.995	26.76	28.30	29.82	31.32	32.80	34.27	35.72	37.16	38.58	40.00
1 – α	**21**	**22**	**23**	**24**	**25**	**26**	**27**	**28**	**29**	**30**
0.005	8.0	8.6	9.3	9.9	10.5	11.2	11.8	12.5	13.1	13.8
0.01	8.9	9.5	10.2	10.9	11.5	12.2	12.9	13.6	14.3	15.0
0.025	10.3	11.0	11.7	12.4	13.1	13.8	14.6	15.3	16.0	16.8
0.05	11.6	12.3	13.1	13.8	14.6	15.4	16.2	16.9	17.7	18.5
0.95	32.7	33.9	35.2	36.4	37.7	38.9	40.1	41.3	42.6	43.8
0.975	35.5	36.8	38.1	39.4	40.6	41.9	43.2	44.5	45.7	47.0
0.99	38.9	40.3	41.6	43.0	44.3	45.6	47.0	48.3	49.6	50.9
0.995	41.4	42.8	44.2	45.6	46.9	48.3	49.6	51.0	52.3	53.7
1 – α	**40**	**50**	**60**	**70**	**80**	**90**	**100**		**>100 (approx.)[a]**	
0.005	20.7	28.0	35.5	43.3	51.2	59.2	67.3		$1/2\,(h - 2.58)^2$	
0.01	22.2	29.7	37.5	45.4	53.5	61.8	70.1		$1/2\,(h - 2.33)^2$	
0.025	24.4	32.4	40.5	48.8	57.2	65.6	74.2		$1/2\,(h - 1.96)^2$	
0.05	26.5	34.8	43.2	51.7	60.4	69.1	77.9		$1/2\,(h - 1.64)^2$	
0.95	55.8	67.5	79.1	90.5	101.9	113.1	124.3		$1/2\,(h + 1.64)^2$	
0.975	59.3	71.4	83.3	95.0	106.6	118.1	129.6		$1/2\,(h + 1.96)^2$	
0.99	63.7	76.2	88.4	100.4	112.3	124.1	135.8		$1/2\,(h + 2.33)^2$	
0.995	66.8	79.5	92.0	104.2	116.3	128.3	140.2		$1/2\,(h + 2.58)^2$	

[a]In the last column, $h = \sqrt{(2\nu - 1)}$, where ν is the number of degrees of freedom.

ν = Number of degrees of freedom.

Note: P (chi-square with ν degrees of freedom ≤ table value) = 1 – α.

Source: Kreyszig, E. 1967. *Advanced Engineering Mathematics, Second Editon*. New York: John Wiley. Copyright © 1967. Printed with permission of John Wiley and Sons, Inc. and Erwin Kreyszig.

Table A5.3. F-Distribution with (ν_1, ν_2) Degrees of Freedom[a]

Denominator Degrees of Freedom, ν_2	Numerator Degrees of Freedom, ν_1									
	1	2	3	4	5	6	7	8	9	10
1	161	200	216	225	230	234	237	239	241	242
2	18.5	19.0	19.2	19.2	19.3	19.3	19.4	19.4	19.4	19.4
3	10.1	9.55	9.28	9.12	9.01	8.94	8.89	8.85	8.81	8.79
4	7.71	6.94	6.59	6.39	6.26	6.16	6.09	6.04	6.00	5.96
5	6.61	5.79	5.41	5.19	5.05	4.95	4.88	4.82	4.77	4.74
6	5.99	5.14	4.76	4.53	4.39	4.28	4.21	4.15	4.10	4.06
7	5.59	4.74	4.35	4.12	3.97	3.87	3.79	3.73	3.68	3.64
8	5.32	4.46	4.07	3.84	3.69	3.58	3.50	3.44	3.39	3.35
9	5.12	4.26	3.86	3.63	3.48	3.37	3.29	3.23	3.18	3.14
10	4.96	4.10	3.71	3.48	3.33	3.22	3.14	3.07	3.02	2.98
11	4.84	3.98	3.59	3.36	3.20	3.09	3.01	2.95	2.90	2.85
12	4.75	3.89	3.49	3.26	3.11	3.00	2.91	2.85	2.80	2.75
13	4.67	3.81	3.41	3.18	3.03	2.92	2.83	2.77	2.71	2.67
14	4.60	3.74	3.34	3.11	2.96	2.85	2.76	2.70	2.65	2.60
15	4.54	3.68	3.29	3.06	2.90	2.79	2.71	2.64	2.59	2.54
16	4.49	3.63	3.24	3.01	2.85	2.74	2.66	2.59	2.54	2.49
17	4.45	3.59	3.20	2.96	2.81	2.70	2.61	2.55	2.49	2.45
18	4.41	3.55	3.16	2.93	2.77	2.66	2.58	2.51	2.46	2.41
19	4.38	3.52	3.13	2.90	2.74	2.63	2.54	2.48	2.42	2.38
20	4.35	3.49	3.10	2.87	2.71	2.60	2.51	2.45	2.39	2.35
22	4.30	3.44	3.05	2.82	2.66	2.55	2.46	2.40	2.34	2.30
24	4.26	3.40	3.01	2.78	2.62	2.51	2.42	2.36	2.30	2.25
26	4.23	3.37	2.98	2.74	2.59	2.47	2.39	2.32	2.27	2.22
28	4.20	3.34	2.95	2.71	2.56	2.45	2.36	2.29	2.24	2.19
30	4.17	3.32	2.92	2.69	2.53	2.42	2.33	2.27	2.21	2.16
32	4.15	3.30	2.90	2.67	2.51	2.40	2.31	2.24	2.19	2.14
34	4.13	3.28	2.88	2.65	2.49	2.38	2.29	2.23	2.17	2.12
36	4.11	3.26	2.87	2.63	2.48	2.36	2.28	2.21	2.15	2.11
38	4.10	3.24	2.85	2.62	2.46	2.35	2.26	2.19	2.14	2.09
40	4.08	3.23	2.84	2.61	2.45	2.34	2.25	2.18	2.12	2.08

[a]Critical values for the F-distribution for $\alpha = 0.05$.

Source: Kreyszig, E. 1967. *Advanced Engineering Mathematics, Second Editon*. New York: John Wiley. Copyright © 1967. Printed with permission of John Wiley and Sons, Inc. and Erwin Kreyszig.

Table A5.3. F-Distribution with (ν_1, ν_2) Degrees of Freedom[b] (Continued)

Denominator Degrees of Freedom, ν_2	Numerator Degrees of Freedom, ν_1									
	1	2	3	4	5	6	7	8	9	10
1	4052	4999	5403	5625	5764	5859	5928	5982	6022	6056
2	98.5	99.0	99.2	99.3	99.3	99.3	99.4	99.4	99.4	99.4
3	34.1	30.8	29.5	28.7	28.2	27.9	27.7	27.5	27.3	27.2
4	21.2	18.0	16.7	16.0	15.5	15.2	15.0	14.8	14.7	14.5
5	16.3	13.3	12.1	11.4	11.0	10.7	10.5	10.3	10.2	10.1
6	13.7	10.9	9.78	9.15	8.75	8.47	8.26	8.10	7.98	7.87
7	12.2	9.55	8.45	7.85	7.46	7.19	6.99	6.84	6.72	6.62
8	11.3	8.65	7.59	7.01	6.63	6.37	6.18	6.03	5.91	5.81
9	10.6	8.02	6.99	6.42	6.06	5.80	5.61	5.47	5.35	5.26
10	10.0	7.56	6.55	5.99	5.64	5.39	5.20	5.06	4.94	4.85
11	9.65	7.21	6.22	5.67	5.32	5.07	4.89	4.74	4.63	4.54
12	9.33	6.93	5.95	5.41	5.06	4.82	4.64	4.50	4.39	4.30
13	9.07	6.70	5.74	5.21	4.86	4.62	4.44	4.30	4.19	4.10
14	8.86	6.51	5.56	5.04	4.70	4.46	4.28	4.14	4.03	3.94
15	8.68	8.36	5.42	4.89	4.56	4.32	4.14	4.00	3.89	3.80
16	8.53	6.23	5.29	4.77	4.44	4.20	4.03	3.89	3.78	3.69
17	8.40	6.11	5.18	4.67	4.34	4.10	3.93	3.79	3.68	3.59
18	8.29	6.01	5.09	4.58	4.25	4.01	3.84	3.71	3.60	3.51
19	8.18	5.93	5.01	4.50	4.17	3.94	3.77	3.63	3.52	3.43
20	8.10	5.85	4.94	4.43	4.10	3.87	3.70	3.56	3.46	3.37
22	7.95	5.72	4.82	4.31	3.99	3.76	3.59	3.45	3.35	3.26
24	7.82	5.61	4.72	4.22	3.90	3.67	3.50	3.36	3.26	3.17
26	7.72	5.53	4.64	4.14	3.82	3.59	3.42	3.29	3.18	3.09
28	7.64	5.45	4.57	4.07	3.75	3.53	3.36	3.23	3.12	3.03
30	7.56	5.39	4.51	4.02	3.70	3.47	3.30	3.17	3.07	2.98
32	7.50	5.34	4.46	3.97	3.65	3.43	3.26	3.13	3.02	2.93
34	7.44	5.29	4.42	3.93	3.61	3.39	3.22	3.09	2.98	2.89
36	7.40	5.25	4.38	3.89	3.57	3.35	3.18	3.05	2.95	2.86
38	7.35	5.21	4.34	3.86	3.54	3.32	3.15	3.02	2.92	2.83
40	7.31	5.18	4.31	3.83	3.51	3.29	33.12	2.99	2.89	2.80

[b]Critical values for the F-distribution for $\alpha = 0.01$.

INDEX

C

G

H

Q